# THE
# NATIVE AMERICANS

His spirit finds its way
into the spirit world,
lifted on the wind above
the grandeur and beauty
of the earth.

—YELLOW WOLF (Kiowa), 1920

# THE NATIVE

## AN ILLUSTRA

Introduction by
ALVIN M. JOSEPHY, JR.

Text by
DAVID HURST THOMAS

JAY MILLER

RICHARD WHITE

PETER NABOKOV

PHILIP J. DELORIA

Edited by
BETTY BALLANTINE

IAN BALLANTINE

# AMERICANS
## TED HISTORY

Published by World Publications Group, Inc.
455 Somerset Avenue
North Dighton, MA 02764

"I Have Bowed Before the Sun" copyright © 1992 Anna Lee Walters, from *Talking Indian: Reflections of Survival and Writing*
Reprinted by permission of Firebrand Books, Ithaca, New York.

ISBN 1-57215-303-2

Produced in association with Welcome Enterprises, Inc.
164 East 95th Street, New York, NY 10128

Printed and bound in China by Leefung-Asco Printers Trading Limited

EDITORIAL:
*Editorial Directors*: Betty Ballantine and
Ian Ballantine
*Executive Editor*: George Young
*Special Editor*: Newton Koltz
*Chief Consultant*: Alvin M. Josephy, Jr.
*Special Consultant*: Patricia Limerick
*Editorial, Development and Research*:
Walton Rawls, Larry Larson,
Ellen Mendlow, Shannon Rothenberger
*Copyediting*: Elaine Luthy Brennan,
Robin James

DESIGN:
*Art Director*: Michael J. Walsh
*Design*: Nai Chang, Hiro Clark
*Illustration Art Direction*: Elaine Streithof
*Map Illustration*: Oliver Williams
*Map Typography*: Gregory Wakabayashi
*Map Editorial and Research*: Jonathan Glick

ART & PHOTO RESEARCH:
*Picture Research Editor*: Marty Moore
*Picture Coordinator*: Courtney Kealy
*Picture Research Assistants*:
Robin Luehrman, J.Stoll

PRODUCTION:
*Director*: Nancy Robins
*Production Assistant*: Caroline Reaves

PAGE 1: *For Dear Life* by Jeffrey Chapman (Ojibwa), ca. 1989; PAGES 2–3: *Paling of Winter* by Dan V. Lomahaftewa (Hopi-Choctaw), 1992; PAGES 4–5: *And They Moved Without Him* by Blackbear Bosin (Kiowa-Comanche), ca. 1956; PAGES 6–7: *They Dance Victorious* by Mike Larsen (Chickasaw), 1992; PAGE 8, CLOCKWISE FROM TOP LEFT: Wah-wa-ah-Ton; Nez Perce child; Comisita, Apache (ca. 1907); unknown; Two Crow girls; Sitting Bull, Hunkpapa Lakota; Eskimo woman; Iron Bull, Crow chief; Seminole man; Alchesoy, White Mountain Apache chief (ca. 1910); Chola Cactus, Pima (1902); unknown; unknown; PAGE 9, CLOCKWISE FROM TOP LEFT: Amelia Chaves and Loreta Blacktooth, Pala; unknown; Mohawk woman; Haida woman (1882); unknown; unknown; Quanah Parker, Comanche; unknown child; Joseph Oklahombi, Choctaw; unknown; Comanche man; Osh-Tisch, Crow; Louise Laruse, Spokane; PAGES 10–11: An encampment of Bloods, Piegans, and Sarsis, Alberta, Canada.

# CONTENTS

OPPOSITE: Two Piegan tipis (1910).

# INTRODUCTION

THE YEAR WAS 1849. The place, the California Trail where it crossed the vast sagebrush and alkali desert of Nevada. To the hordes of fortune hunters hurrying from the East to the newly opened California gold mines, no part of their route seemed more dangerous than this inhospitable stretch. Not only were there few sources of water, but the desolate land was full of "treacherous savages"—bands of horseless Northern Paiute, Bannock, and Western Shoshone Indians. The whites compared them unfavorably with the bold, mounted, buffalo-hunting tribes of the Plains and referred to them contemptuously as "Diggers" because they dug with sticks for roots, a main component of the diet that had sustained them in their harsh Great Basin homeland for ten thousand years.

In the travelers' diaries, journals, and letters—which served for generations afterwards as the prime source of what white men knew about these Indians—the writers described them as "wretched, degraded, and despicable," "the meanest Indians in existence," who hid from sight during the day but came out from among the desert vegetation after dark to sneak into the emigrants' camps along the trail and steal their food and livestock. At night the fearful, travel-worn whites had to mount guard, listening intently for every rustle and sound in the desert. When they heard a suspicious noise, they shot in the direction of its source, and at dawn they often found a dead Indian lying nearby. Sometimes it was the body of a young child, a woman, or a gnarled elder, and the travelers' stories circulated this information as proof that all "Diggers" were skulking thieves, no matter what their age or sex.

The Indians' side of what was going on was quite different. It never got into the history books, although in later years survivors, including the very articulate Sarah Winnemucca, who in 1849 had been a five-year-old Paiute child living along the Oregon Trail with her family, recalled poignant and terrible memories that cast a different light on those shots in the night.

What the whites had believed were "skulking" thieves and murderers in the darkness were in fact hungry and terrified Indian families trying to get safely across a road that the white men had unwittingly cut directly through territory where for centuries the Indians had lived, gathered food, and held their ceremonies. The bisecting road had crippled the Indians' freedom of movement across their lands, for they lived in mortal dread of the stream of trigger-happy white travelers who shot at them as if they were rabbits.

Attempting to get past them, from one part of their territory to another, to reach relatives or a desperately needed wild food source, Indian fathers and mothers hid anxiously with their children behind clumps of sage or other desert brush during the day, then at night directed the young ones to scamper silently across the road past the white men's camps and hide on the other side until all the elders, one by one, also got across.

If the whites had been careless with their livestock, some of the bolder young Indians, who naturally blamed the intruders for overrunning and destroying their food-gathering grounds and polluting their waterholes, saw no wrong in helping

*Prairie Fire* by Blackbear Bosin (Kiowa-Comanche), ca. 1953.
"We all have adopted a responsibility to our people and to the art world, in depicting as accurately as possible the ways, the customs, attitudes and dogmas of our forefathers." —BLACKBEAR BOSIN

*Koshares of Taos*
by Pablita Velarde
(Santa Clara), ca. 1947.

themselves to one or two of the emigrants' cows—as the Indians perceived it, an acceptable act of reciprocity. These, in short, were what the travelers cursed as "the meanest Indians in existence"—men, women, and children, trying to survive, but whom the whites occasionally heard in the night and killed.

In the history of native American nations, the California Trail story is not unique. Ever since Europeans first arrived in the Western Hemisphere in 1492, their relations with Indians have been marked—even until today—by the stain of countless similar episodes in which groundless fears, prejudices, and misunderstandings have led to tragedy.

Through the years, individuals and groups with noble aims and the best intentions have existed on each side, trying to create trust and harmony. But they have never been numerous enough, powerful enough, or realistic enough to overcome a historically pervasive and long-enduring gap in mutual understanding, the beginnings of which date back to Columbus's initial arrival in what the Europeans perceived as·the "barbaric, virgin wilderness" of a "New World." To the Indians, of course, this "New World" was a very ancient one of many millions of persons and a myriad sophisticated and thriving cultures and civilizations.

To a large extent, the fundamental problem stemmed (and continues to stem) from the non-Indians' Eurocentrism, an ingrained conviction on the part of those who first came to the Americas from Europe, as well as by their American descendants, that their cultures, values, religions, lifeways, abilities, and achievements were more advanced and of a higher order than those of the Indians. It followed, therefore, that they deemed the Indians to be inferior peoples—uncivilized Stone Age savages, perhaps even subhuman—and their cultures irrelevant or barbaric and dangerous to civilized mankind.

More importantly, through the centuries, the belief in their own superiority justified, to the white invaders, the enslavement of Indians, the seizure of their lands and resources, the destruction of their societies, the cultivation of anti-Indian prejudice, and the patronization that still treats Indians as inferiors and denies them self-determination, sovereignty, and respect for their spiritual life.

In truth, in 1492 two totally different but bustling worlds of rich, complex societies and advanced cultures collided, each with its own distinctive heritage and view of the universe. The Europeans, we need hardly be reminded, were heirs to the legacies of early Near Eastern cultures and the civilizations of Egypt, Greece, and Rome; to the Judeo-Christian ethical and religious teachings; to the political and intellectual life of the many competing states, nations, and empires of eastern and western Europe; and to the economic institutions of feudalism and expanding capitalism. All of this heritage was alien and unknown to the Indians, whose own long and awesome inheritance was foreign to, and unshared by, the whites. Some of it had been formed in Asia and was thousands of years old; the rest was the product of a pre-Columbian procession of remarkable cultures and civilizations with diverse social and spiritual systems created by the Indians during a thousand generations of living in the different American environments. In the Indians' eyes, when they met the whites, they did so at least as their equals.

It was a point of view generally ignored by the aggressive invaders from Europe, who were well supplied with firearms, fierce warhorses and attack dogs, steel swords, and virulent European diseases that unexpectedly but helpfully struck down whole tribes. The arrant racism introduced by the Spaniards against the Indians in the Caribbean and the southern lands of North America was adopted in various forms by other European powers and spread throughout the continent, everywhere maiming and poisoning whatever chance there might have been for harmonious coexistence and mutual respect and understanding between the Europeans and the indigenous peoples.

*Corn Dancers*
by Peter H. Shelton, Jr. (Hopi).

Among the whites, there was scarcely the blinking of an eye over the devastating impact of the Europeans on an Indian world that had been millennia in the making. During the first centuries of contact, pandemics of smallpox, measles, and other sicknesses against which the Indians had no immunity, plus the Europeans' acquisitive, crusading zeal and their use of superior military power, were disastrous for the indigenous populations and cultures. Native populations were massacred; Indian cities and towns destroyed and abandoned to the elements; religious structures defiled and looted; political and spiritual leaders slain; confederacies, chiefdoms, and other societies ripped apart; and disoriented, leaderless survivors enslaved or forced to flee and move in with other groups—or revert, as many of them did, to more primitive levels of existence, hunting or foraging again for wild foods in the wake of the collapse of their world.

It has been estimated by some demographers that by the seventeenth century, more than fifty million natives of North and South America had perished as a result of war, disease, enslavement, and the careless or deliberate brutality of Europeans—history's greatest holocaust by far.

As the pre-Columbian world disappeared, the fires of Eurocentrism burned on, now attempting to erase the history, cultures, and achievements of that world from memory. In Yucatán, the Spaniards burned or destroyed almost every Mayan book in their efforts to convert those Indians to Christianity. In the flames, posterity lost, until recently, the ability to read Maya glyphs that would reveal the true history and meanings of the Mayas' radiant pre-Columbian civilization.

In New England, after the Puritans of Massachusetts Bay had come to view the powerful Pequot Indians as "children of Satan," they tried with fire and sword

*Waiting Dancers* (detail)
by Arthur Amiotte
(Oglala Lakota), 1978.

to blot out every sign that these Indians had ever existed. Making holy war on them in 1637, they massacred Pequots by the hundreds, parceling out the relatively few survivors among other tribes with the vain hope that even the name Pequot would vanish. Across both continents, only a small number of Europeans thought it worthwhile to pass on to future generations records of the "curious" societies they were destroying.

As new nations like the United States succeeded the colonial powers, there was little change in the white man's belief that the Indians were inferior peoples who were destined either to rise above their Indianness to the level of the whites, or else to vanish. Throughout most of the nineteenth century, while the gap in communication and understanding grew steadily deeper, on one frontier after another whites dispossessed Indians, seeking to eliminate them by "removal," or by forced conversion to white lifeways, or by death. Andrew Jackson likened Indians to wolves, and General Philip Sheridan quipped that the only good Indian was a dead one. Most non-Indian Americans agreed with both men.

In some places, like the eastern United States, from which Indians had at last been driven out, or where they were no longer numerous enough to constitute a threat to the new non-Indian society, there was an ironic consequence of the conquerors' Eurocentric failure to understand and appreciate the Indians. In those areas, some non-Indians, now secure, began to look back on Indians with nostalgia and romanticism, viewing them as "noble savages." Benevolent as these romanticizers might have been, however, few of them knew very much about Indians, and what they did know was mostly distorted, or outright false, still laced with the conviction that Indians were indeed, "savage and backward" and—regrettably—had to go.

Although racism took less violent forms toward the end of the nineteenth century after the final crushing of the Indians' power of resistance, it was still far from dead. Patronization, condescension, policies of forced assimilation—the determined attempt to stamp out Indianness—continued on through the first part of the twentieth century. And all were manifestations of the white Americans' deep-rooted prejudice, sense of superiority, and belief that little in the Indians' world was worth saving, or even worth knowing about.

During this dreadful period, the U.S. Indian population sank to an all-time low of some 250,000 people, and morale among native Americans hit bottom as well. Now truly vanishing Americans, living and dying on reservations as little more than prisoners, Indians were out of sight and out of mind to most non-Indians. Denied freedom of religion, the right to govern themselves and manage their own affairs, and having their Indianness literally beaten out of them by all manner of prohibitions and punishments, they experienced minimal contact with whites. The latter did not miss them; if they thought about Indians at all, their thoughts were dominated and colored by inherited feelings of superiority and new stereotypical images of contemptible "drunken Indians," "lazy Indians," and "Indians who don't pay taxes like the rest of us."

Despite the greatly accelerated assimilation and acculturation among Indians and the rapid and fundamental changes in Indian–white relations in the United States during the last part of the twentieth century (described by Philip Deloria in Part Five of this book), anti-Indian hostility, prejudice, condescension, and

*Death and the New Life*
by W. Richard West (Cheyenne).

discrimination that result from Eurocentrism are still apparent among large numbers of non-Indians.

Daily, these feelings continue to take many forms and to undermine Indian struggles for equal opportunity and recognition. An able, experienced, and widely respected Indian running for attorney general of Idaho a full one hundred years after Wounded Knee was told by white friends "We think you're the best candidate running and would do a wonderful job, but we just couldn't vote to put the legal affairs of our state in the hands of an Indian." While appreciating the honesty of this statement, if not its sentiments, the Indian continued to run for office—and won. But in a major city, the trustees of a famous natural history museum that proudly contains numerous Indian exhibits shrink from accepting Indians on their board, in part because "Indians are like children who would not know how to run the affairs of this museum." The board has remained all white.

No wonder that today, after five centuries of contact and interrelated history, it can honestly be said that to most non-Indian Americans, Indians are familiar strangers—the first Americans, indeed, but ironically the least known of all members of the American population. Eurocentrism did its job: behind the legends and beyond the myths, few non-Indians yet know the reality.

At the same time, it has long been clear to many persons that the whites' false and stereotypical thinking has done great harm, not only to the Indians, but also to those who conquered and dispossessed them. From the Indians' point of view, the harm lies not only in the irretrievable loss of so many of their people, but also in the continued ignorance and misunderstanding of non-Indian Americans that too often deny Indians support in opposing injustice and achieving their rightful place in American society. The whites, meanwhile, by denying the value of Indian histories and cultures, have turned their backs on thousands

*Noble Indian*
by Fritz Scholder (Luiseño), 1973.

of years of Indian learning and experience with the American land, and on the enormous richness and diversity of Indian spiritual and creative life.

From the vast lore of Indian mythology and story that inspires present-day Indian painters, authors, musicians, poets, dramatists, dancers, jewelers, film-makers, sculptors, and other creative artists, to the practicality of centuries-old Indian knowledge in managing fisheries and forests and even deserts, the Indian universe is full of lessons for the modern-day world. Not to recognize this enormous resource is both foolish and terribly wasteful. Indeed, not to understand the reality of Indian history is not to understand ourselves as Americans. Nor can anyone claim to know American history without a full and undistorted appreciation of Indian history.

All of this, and more, are underlying themes of this book, a comprehensive history of the native peoples of North America spanning twenty thousand years, from the earliest known presence of their ancestors in the Western Hemisphere until today. The five authors, all expert and recognized scholars on the subjects with which they deal, unfold the full Indian story accurately and accessibly, and—most importantly—from the Indian perspective. The object of the book is simple: to help bridge, if not end, the communications gap of misunderstandings and false images that have so plagued Indian–white relations.

That this book could be undertaken with that end in view is a testament to extraordinary recent advances in technology and to interdisciplinary cooperation. Archaeologists, anthropologists, geneticists, physicists, ethnohistorians, geologists, microbiologists, botanists, zoologists, linguistic scholars, and other scientists in many different disciplines, often working together and using new methods and technologies, from computers to space-age satellite images, have taken great leaps in uncovering and interpreting the past. At the same time, Indians have played a large role by asserting themselves more strongly than ever before in interpreting to the rest of the world their own heritage and cultures and in relating their own histories. As partners of non-Indian scholars, modern-day native American writers, artists, scientists, teachers, tradition-keepers, and tribal cultural leaders have often joined to illuminate Indian perspectives of the past, making known and understandable much that whites, on their own, had not grasped, and on the whole providing a far greater measure of objectivity and truth to the telling of the Indians' story.

All of these developments are reflected in the various parts of this book, both in the text and in the illustrations. To most readers, there will be new information and many new perspectives and fascinating surprises. Even scholars will discover much that is fresh and interesting, including material and points of view that have not been published before in works for the general reader, but are still being studied and debated among specialists and in professional journals.

In David Hurst Thomas's Part One, for instance, readers will find not only the revolutionary reassessments of the Classic Maya civilization that resulted when the code of their glyphs was broken in the late 1960s and aerial and other technologies revealed their massive reclamation works and fortifications, but also the dramatic discovery of the independent invention of nonmaize agriculture by precontact Indians in the Northeastern Woodlands; vivid new insights into the Hopewell and Mississippian mound-building societies; and the turquoise-based

*Making Wild Rice*
by Patrick DesJarlait
(Chippewa), 1946.

economy and road systems of the Chacoans in the pre-Columbian Southwest.

Most significantly, perhaps, the book brings native Americans to life—who they are and were, how they live and lived, their motives and struggles, their humanity and individuality. In Part Two, for example, Jay Miller takes us inside the world of the Indians as their pre-Columbian universe falls apart under the onslaughts of the Europeans and the white man's new and terrible diseases. Continuing the narrative into the eighteenth century, Richard White's Part Three relates how the native Americans tried (but ultimately failed) to put their world together again, and how, as new tribes, institutions, and values arose to replace all that had been lost, whites, in time, came to think these had always existed. The final defeat and harsh treatment of the Indians as the new Americans overran the last of the native Americans' lands in the nineteenth century are the subject of Peter Nabokov's Part Four. Part Five contains Philip Deloria's fresh, perceptive account of the Indians' slow and tortured twentieth-century revival, marked by struggles for justice and the right to regain the sovereignty and self-determination they had once possessed.

Finally, in demolishing stereotypes and presenting Indian points of view, the book underscores the lesson of the California Chumash Indian quoted by David Hurst Thomas. "There is," Kote Kotah said, "no 'better' or 'worse,' only different. That difference has to be respected whether it's skin color, way of life, or ideas."

—ALVIN M. JOSEPHY, JR.

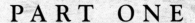

# PART ONE

# THE
# WORLD
# AS
# IT WAS

*When we were created we were
given our ground to live on and from this
time these were our rights. This is all true.
We were put here by the Creator—
I was not brought from a foreign country
and did not come here.
I was put here by the Creator.*

CHIEF WENINOCK, YAKIMA, 1915

**Anasazi ruins at Mesa Verde, Colorado.**

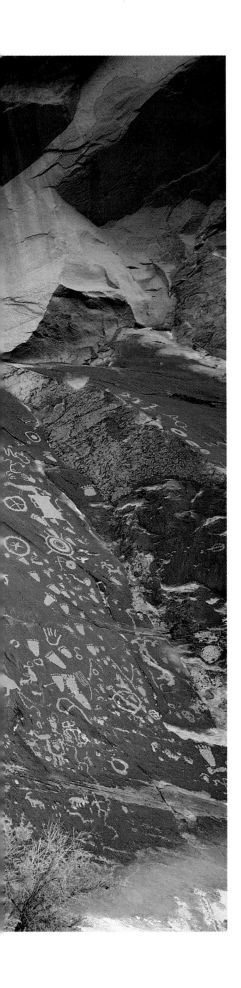

# CHAPTER ONE

# THE LONG SPAN OF TIME

*RAINBOW MYTH*
BY DAN V. LOMAHAFTEWA (HOPI-CHOCTAW), 1992

FOR A THOUSAND GENERATIONS, the American continents have been home to Indian people. From forager to farmer, tribe to nation, the native American civilizations waxed and waned. They developed sophisticated forms of art, elaborate political and social structures, intricate intellectual patterns, mathematics, handicrafts, agriculture, writing, complex religious and belief systems, imaginative architecture—indeed a whole panoply of human endeavor that rivaled the cultures developing in the Middle East, Europe, and China. These early native American achievements still astonish the world of today.

Where did these people originate? How were their civilizations formed?

Oddly, the most consequential, if least dramatic event in American history occurred when that first human footprint appeared on the northern continent. Nobody knows for sure when this happened, or exactly where. Nobody knows for sure what these first Americans—often called Paleo-Indians—wore, spoke, or thought. We do not know when they left their ancient homelands, what conditions they experienced along the way, or even why people first came to America.

But whenever and however, come they did. Without doubt, the first Americans arrived as fully developed, modern human beings. They were most definitely not "primordial" or "primitive," not stooped and shambling, had no heavily ridged brows. They walked upright and looked much the way American Indians look today. They brought with them an Ice Age patrimony, including many basic human skills: fire making, flintknapping, and effective ways to feed,

---

The petroglyphs inscribed by Indians on this huge boulder known as Newspaper Rock and located in Utah date from approximately A.D. 900 to the eighteenth century.

*I am an American Indian, and I believe that I can therefore speak to the question of America before Columbus with a certain advantage of ancestral experience, a cultural continuity that reaches far back in time. My forebears have been in North America for many thousands of years. In my blood I have a real sense of that occupation. It is worth something to me, as indeed that long, unbroken tenure is worth something to every native American.*

*When man set foot on the continent of north America he was surely an endangered species. His resources were few, as we think of them from our vantage point in the twentieth century. He was almost wholly at the mercy of the elements, and the world he inhabited was hard and unforgiving. The simple accomplishment of survival must have demanded all of his strength. But he had certain indispensable resources. He knew how to hunt. He possessed tools and weapons, however crude. He could make fire. He probably had dogs and travois, perhaps sleds. He had some sense of society, of community, of cooperation. And, alone among the creatures of the earth, he could think and speak. He had a human sense of morality, an irresistible craving for order, beauty, appropriate behavior. He was intensely spiritual.*

—N. SCOTT MOMADAY (Kiowa)
from *America in 1492*

OPPOSITE:
*People of the Early Tundra*
by Greg Harlin. A pit house, utilizing mammoth tusks and bones as a framework. These snug homes were large and built to house several families.

shelter, and clothe themselves. As early immigrants, they lived in close-knit kin groups, enjoyed social interactions, and shared beliefs about magic and the supernatural. They spoke a fully human language. As they dispersed throughout the Western Hemisphere, they lived in diverse and sometimes unstable environments. But they continued to feed their families and to safeguard their new homeland. Over the generations, the first American ancestors confronted and solved colossal challenges.

In time, they would speak more than two thousand languages. Although some of this linguistic diversity was brought in by later migrations, most of these languages evolved here in America, as successive waves of people drifted down the river valleys and across the plains. Later surges of American Indian explorers followed, and the population slowly increased and expanded. Some groups became isolated. Over the generations, distinctive languages and cultures evolved, each adapted to its individual environment.

From their arrival a thousand generations ago to the time of Columbus—a scant twenty-five generations ago—native Americans domesticated dozens of kinds of plant foods. They charted their farming cycles through complicated cosmologies involving solar calendars, astronomical observatories, prayerful rites, and celebrations. Indian people learned to use wild plants for healing, strengthening, and restoring health. Native American architecture matched anything Columbus had seen in his travels.

The native people of America modified their traditions and ideas to suit changing conditions. They crafted efficient, down-to-earth solutions to the unforeseeable. Their struggle for survival—the countless individual agreements and compromises, solutions and inventions—gave rise to the thousands of American Indian traditions and beliefs that so amazed the European explorers.

This is the story of America's first thousand generations: of how, over a period of fifteen to twenty thousand years, the vast diversity of Indian peoples developed in their own world. And of why they are still here.

## Drifting Continents, Migrating People

The origins of American Indian life reach back into the very beginnings of humanity, and even before. At a point remote in time, all the lands of this earth were fused in a single supercontinent, today known as Pangaea. The Pacific Ocean covered half the globe. Then, more than 200 million years ago, Pangaea fractured into two huge landmasses, Laurasia to the north and Gondwanaland to the south. More time passed, and new oceans surged between the further splitting terrestrial fragments, which began to look like today's water-locked continents. These large stable areas, the plates, moved at a constant velocity, sometimes colliding, sometimes spreading away from one another. Along the western American rim, the plate margin corresponds to the modern continental boundaries. Elsewhere—from the Alps through the Himalayas, in the Rockies, and throughout America's Basin and Range Province—the plate boundaries created mountain chains that straddle continents.

For millions upon millions of years, life diverged and differentiated on the separating continental masses. Three million years ago, the "southern ape"

# THE SO-CALLED BERING STRAIT THEORY

*The Bering Strait theory is tenaciously held by white scholars against the varied migration traditions of the natives and is an example of the triumph of doctrine over facts. Excavating ancient fireplaces and campsites may be exciting, but there are no well-worn paths which clearly show migratory patterns from Asia to North America, and if there were such paths, there would be no indication anywhere which way the footprints were heading. We can be certain of only one thing: the Bering Strait theory is preferred by whites and consequently becomes accepted as scientific fact. If the universities were controlled by the Indians, we would have an entirely different explanation of the peopling of the New World and it would be just as respectable for the scholarly establishment to support it. The theory does illustrate a constant theme . . . a good many scientific and/or scholarly beliefs about Indians originated as religious doctrines. As religion lost its influence as an opinion maker, the idea was picked up by some secular scholars, transformed into scientific theory, and published as orthodox science.*

—VINE DELORIA, JR.
(Standing Rock Sioux)
From *America in 1492*

(*Australopithecus*) emerged on the African plain. The best known fossils of this genus, from northern Ethiopia, were named Lucy by her excavators. Through the recurring processes of adaptation, evolution, and survival, Lucy's relatives eventually developed into an implement-using, large-brained hominid now named *Homo habilis* (Latin for "handy person"—literally a toolmaker). By 1.5 million years ago, the first incontestably human form appeared, classified by paleontologists as *Homo erectus*. As these Middle Pleistocene ("Ice Age") populations grew, Africa could no longer contain them. A million years or so ago, *Homo erectus* began to migrate slowly northward, first crossing the connecting lands of the Middle East, fanning out across Europe and across Asia. Now our human ancestors could demonstrate their phenomenal adaptability to environments as diverse as tropical rain forests, temperate regions, and even near-arctic surroundings.

*Homo erectus* populations remained fairly stable until perhaps 150,000 to 200,000 years ago, when the more evolved Neanderthals (*Homo sapiens neanderthalensis*) appeared. Unlike today's cartoon cavemen, real Neanderthals walked upright, as agile as modern people.

What happened next is uncertain. It may be that Neanderthals evolved directly into modern humans—in Asia, in Europe, and also back in Africa. Or maybe modern humans evolved only in Africa. If so, then all living human beings might stem from a single first mother ("Eve"), who lived about 200,000 years ago in South Africa. This "Out of Africa" theory holds that 100,000 or so years ago, these first human beings undertook a second colossal migration into Europe and Asia, superseding the vestigial *Homo erectus* communities. Either way, it was not long before the migrating branches of humanity found themselves at opposite ends of the earth.

Completely modern people (*Homo sapiens sapiens*)—often called "Cro-Magnon" after a key archaeological site in France—first appeared about forty thousand years ago. With great skill, they fashioned new, more specialized tools of stone, bone, and antler. They crafted sexually suggestive female figurines, evidence of increasingly entrenched ritual and ceremonial systems that spanned continents. Little by little, their skin color lightened, enabling them to absorb more vitamin D in the areas of limited solar radiation of the northerly latitudes. These painters of caves were the ancestors of Leif Eriksson, Christopher

Columbus, and the millions of other Europeans who would eventually cruise westward to an unfamiliar American landscape.

Equally intelligent and adaptive populations spread eastward across Eurasia. Remarkably, by forty thousand years ago, they had navigated their way to Australia. Sea levels back then were considerably lower than today, and many modern islands (including Australia and New Guinea) were connected. But vast stretches of open sea still isolated Australia from the Southeast Asian mainland. To undertake this incredible voyage the first Australians built seaworthy boats to navigate across the open, uncharted waters—well beyond the comforting sight of land.

Far to the north, mammoth-hunting pioneers slowly moved eastward across the unforgiving Siberian tundras. Archaeologists digging in Siberia commonly find tiny needles made of perforated bone, silent proof of ancient people's skill in sewing leather clothing. To impale their quarry at greater distances—a survival necessity in an open, treeless landscape—these hunters fashioned often richly decorated antler spear-throwers. So remarkable was this invention that it spread around the world. Today, we call the spear-thrower by its Aztec name, the *atlatl*.

These people of the tundra used everything at their disposal to survive. Even discarded mammoth bones were important, burnt as fuel and used as supports to prop up the roofs of their impressive pit houses. Huge mammoth tusks were erected into a riblike framework beneath the arched roofs, and made draft-proof with hides. These massive houses, and the great number of firepits inside, tell us

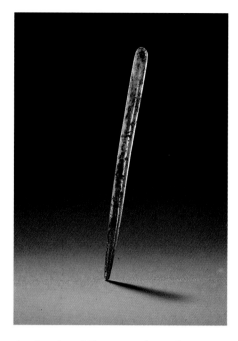

An Ice Age (Pleistocene) needle with a drilled eyehole, made from a bone splinter, and used to sew hides into clothing suited to the colder climate.

LEFT:
*Pre-Columbian Indian with Atlatl* by James Bama. The atlatl is a two-to-three-foot-long piece of wood with a bone or stone-headed spear resting on it and held in place by a carved base and the hunter's hand. The device was designed to provide increased leverage, accuracy, and power. To throw the spear, the hunter hurled it overhand, similar to throwing a javelin. Use of the atlatl required great skill and is now almost a lost art.

© Bama 74

OPPOSITE:
*Creation Story of the Northwest Coast* by Valjean McCarty Hessing (Choctaw), 1986.

that several families must have lived in each pit house, with perhaps as many as fifty people to a community.

Some people stayed in Africa. Through time, their skin slowly darkened as a genetic sunscreen. So it was, independently, that the people and the continents of the earth drifted apart. Only in America would these diverse strains of humanity reunite. European windjammers carrying African captives eventually arrived by sea to encounter other descendants of Eve.

But the indigenous people of America had taken a very different journey en route to their new homeland.

## The First Americans: Who, and When?

Native American origins are not a mystery to most Indian people. American Indian culture embodies a cornucopia of oral tradition to explain where they came from. These so-called *origin myths* address the most profound of human questions. Who are we? Why are we here? What is the purpose of life and death? What is our place in the world, in time, and in space?

These are not questions that occur to primitive minds, nor do such ideas really address fact or reality. They deal with central issues of value and meaning. Myth is so powerful not only because it embodies cultural attitudes, but because origin myths shape such cultural attitudes toward fact and reality.

In contrast to the realities inherent in myth, today's scientific explanation of American Indian origins dates back to a remarkably prescient Jesuit missionary, José de Acosta, who first suggested that American Indians shared a Siberian homeland. In 1589, Acosta wrote that small groups of hunters, driven from their Asiatic homeland by starvation or warfare, might have followed now-extinct beasts across Asia into America millennia before the Spaniards arrived in the Caribbean. To support his theory, he noted that such a journey would require "only short stretches of navigations"—an extraordinary premise, given that Europeans would not "discover" the Bering Strait for another 136 years.

Contemporary science supports Acosta's theory, more or less. There certainly remains no reasonable doubt that the first Americans came from Asia into America sometime during the last Ice Age. For one thing, fossil bones from archaic human ancestors—such as Neanderthals—are entirely absent from the Americas, suggesting that it was anatomically modern humans who first populated America. Archaeologists working in Asia have found that humans did not arrive in Siberia until perhaps thirty-five thousand years ago. This means that the first humans must have arrived in America sometime after that.

Climatic conditions favored a migration through Siberia about this time. Twenty thousand years ago, Pleistocene ice covered one-third of the earth, three times the area covered today. During this last glacial maximum, nearly all of Canada was buried beneath massive continental ice sheets, draping across the present Great Lakes into the eastern United States. In places, these ice masses were two miles thick. Monumental Pleistocene glaciers locked up so much water that the world's oceans dropped markedly, exposing a massive unglaciated tract known as the Bering Land Bridge. It connected Siberia to modern Alaska.

Three independent lines of evidence support an Asian homeland for America's Indians. Geneticists have analyzed the DNA in human mitochondria—tiny energy-producing bodies found in each cell. Comparing genetic similarities and differences across widely separated contemporary American Indian groups, they found that these people share a common genetic ancestor, going back perhaps 15,000 to 30,000 years. Some microbiologists even believe that more than 95 percent of all native Americans are descended from a single pioneering founder population—perhaps a few families that crossed the Bering Strait together in the late Ice Age. Similar genetic evidence suggests that the Eskimo-Aleut and Na-Dene people—today confined mostly to the northern rim of America—may derive from later migrations out of Asia, perhaps 7,500 years ago.

Christy Turner, a physical anthropologist from Arizona State University, tells a similar story based on his extensive studies of variability in human teeth. Focusing on the crown and root areas, Turner discovered that modern and precontact American Indian teeth most closely resemble those of northern Asians. Turner, too, postulates an initial late Ice Age migration out of northeast Asia, followed by two later migrations.

The most controversial evidence comes from linguist Joseph Greenberg of Stanford University, who has recently reanalyzed data from every known American Indian language—a gargantuan task. He agrees that native Americans migrated in three major waves, the Eskimo-Aleut and Na-Dene populations of the northland arriving in relatively recent times. And like the mitochrondrial DNA assessment, his linguistic reconstruction suggests that the first wave must have arrived about 12,000 years ago. These ancestral American Indians then spread throughout most of North, Central, and South America. According to Greenberg, virtually all of the indigenous languages spoken throughout the Americas derived from this single ancestral language.

Considerable controversy surrounds Greenberg's broad-brush linguistic reconstructions, and skeptics also question the relevance of the dental and genetic testimony in tracing the first Americans. Nevertheless, both biology and language point to an Asian home, a possibility strongly confirmed by today's archaeological evidence.

Ice Age glaciation also displaced the belts of natural vegetation southward, and many cold-adapted animals followed the plants. During the Pleistocene, reindeer, wolverines, and lemmings all lived in places that today are too warm for them. The range of musk-ox, now found only in the Arctic, extended into Mexico. The skull of a ten-thousand-year-old walrus, no doubt an inhabitant of frigid waters, has been uncovered on the Virginia coast.

Then the glaciers began to recede. Although scientists still debate the causes of these dramatic shifts, it seems likely that the earth's tilt and orbit about the sun must have changed, increasing the amount of sunlight reaching the poles. As summers warmed up, glacial meltwater poured back into the oceans and sea levels rose again, eventually submerging the exposed continental shelf. By twelve thousand years ago, contracting continental ice sheets exposed an ice-free corridor that stretched from the Yukon to Montana. The first Americans may have walked through this passageway onto the Great Plains.

## Clovis: The First Americans

The first identifiable American Indian people are called *Clovis*, after an archaeological site in New Mexico. Our picture of these Clovis people derives mainly from archaeology, especially from mammoth kill sites dating from about 9500 B.C. to 9000 B.C. Without known cultural antecedents, these sites contain thousands of artifacts—the distinctive "Clovis" fluted spear points, scraping and cutting tools of stone, and some well-made tools of bone and ivory. Most Clovis sites are near water—springs, streams, rivers, lakeshores, and ponds. Only a few campsites have been found—pretty small affairs, probably not occupied very long.

But the Clovis people were not stones and bones. They were human beings, the first Americans. While we cannot project ourselves back in time and will never encounter a Clovis person firsthand, we can learn from other, more recent hunting groups about the past. Eskimo caribou hunters and the postcontact bison hunters of the Great Plains have taught us well about these early peoples. Clovis men and women faced extinction every day. They lived close to the land, and America in the late Ice Age was a tough and unmerciful place. One critical mistake, and a hunter could suffer serious injury. If he died, his family was immediately at risk. Clovis hunters competed one-on-one for food with fierce predators and scavengers. Once acquired, stored food was carefully guarded.

Life in earliest America centered on the family. Although capable of great self-sufficiency, Clovis people lived in small informal bands, consisting of perhaps four to ten nuclear families. Political leadership, such as it was, fell to the dominant male, who derived his authority from well-advertised exploits as hunter and provider. Each band hailed from a traditional territory, where men hunted everything but mates. To marry within the band was as reprehensible as incest, so Clovis bands got together from throughout their broad territories in times of plenty. The elders gambled and exchanged food and gossip. The young people played their own games with skill and flair. They compared adventures and they fell in love. When a Clovis man was ready to marry, he brought his bride to his home, where she was expected to stay.

In this way, men remained on the land most familiar to them. As boys grew up, they discovered the nature and needs of their homeland—how to stalk, where to hide, how the wind worked, how animals behaved when startled. They accepted that mammoths and long-horned bison willingly made themselves available to humans, but only in exchange for a measure of deference. Disrespect was an affront that not only sabotaged the hunt, but also threatened the success of other hunters. Religious specialists were sometimes required to ensure appropriate etiquette toward the supernatural.

Clovis ritual vanished long ago, but perhaps vestiges lingered on among the Naskapi Indians of Labrador. Maybe, like the Naskapi, Clovis medicine men addressed the animal spirit by entranced drumming and singing. Perhaps before the kill—facing down a mammoth standing fourteen feet tall at the shoulder—the Clovis hunter would call his prey by ritual and kinship name. He might have apologized for what was to come, explaining his needs and those of his family. Perhaps the hunter asked the animal not to be angry, and offered assurance that its body would be treated with respect. The carcass was butchered in a special way, with some parts placed on display or disposed of ritually. It was important that the animal's life force return home, regenerate its flesh, and come back another time.

Hunting skill, in all its forms and complexities, was passed along across the generations. This is why men wanted to stay put, insisting that the wife must leave her family and immediate homeland. The way the Clovis men saw it, their familiarity with the land spelled the difference between life and death. Women could dig up roots and pick berries anywhere—or so the men said.

*The Mammoth Hunt by Narda Lebo.*

*He who obeys the requirements is given caribou, and he who disobeys is not given caribou. If he wastes much caribou he cannot be given them, because he wastes too much of his food—the good things. And now, as much as I have spoken, you will know forever how it is. For so now it is as I have said. I, indeed, am Caribou Man. So I am called.*

—*Ati'k'wape'o, The Story of Caribou Man* (Naskapi)

# THE GREAT AMERICAN DIE-OFF

The first Americans witnessed one of the world's most dramatic episodes of extinction. Before their eyes, Clovis hunters saw native American animal species die out in droves. The large herbivores were the hardest hit—twenty-foot-long ground sloths, giant beaver the size of modern bears, horses, camels, mammoths, mastodon, and musk-oxen. As the ecological noose tightened, the carnivores soon followed—the saber-toothed cat (with its eight-inch canines), the American cheetah and lion, and the dire wolf. Perhaps most impressive was the short-faced bear, twice the size of today's grizzly. In North America alone, three dozen genera of mammals disappeared.

Some paleontologists claim that ancestral American Indians hunted these animals to extinction. It is barely possible that, because the large herbivores had never before confronted a two-legged predator, these beasts lacked the necessary defenses and the Clovis hunters took merciless advantage. But this suggests that the Clovis people, as they blitzed their way southward, carelessly left in their wake the bleaching bones of hundreds, even thousands of animals rapidly passing into extinction.

Most modern scientists discount the overkill hypothesis. They emphasize instead the degree to which the Clovis people were themselves at risk during a period of rapid global warming. As the climate changed, sea levels rose, growing seasons became longer, and snowfall and annual precipitation decreased significantly.

Many smaller mammals could adapt to these shifting conditions by modifying their ranges. But the larger ones—the mammoths, mastodons, camels, and horses—placed greater demands on their environments. They could not cope with the transformed surroundings and they were pushed beyond the brink to extinction.

Maybe human hunters did play a role in wiping out certain animal populations. But most scientists now believe that these animals fell victim to a rapidly changing climate. Clovis people adapted. The extinct megafauna did not.

OPPOSITE:

An assortment of stone implements excavated from early archaeological sites in North America. Each is made of a flake removed from a larger stone core with an antler hammer or a stream cobble. The flake blank was progressively fashioned by carefully removing smaller flakes from the margins. Only a highly skilled flintknapper could have achieved the final form evident in these artifacts, all of which were made prior to 5000 B.C.

Some of this division of labor seems biologically determined. In a small-scale, non-food-producing society like Clovis, subsistence activities might have been allocated by gender and age. For physiological reasons, adult women are mostly responsible for nourishing and socializing infants and small children. These physical constraints led foraging women to do things that did not interfere with child care and that could be performed near home. Yet even in male-dominated Clovis society, women provided critically important everyday sustenance by cooking and collecting stationary resources such as plants and firewood. Women probably also took care of the meat after the hunt. Many times, their daily caloric contributions must have spelled the difference between survival and catastrophe.

Other biological factors must have charged adult men with the primary responsibility for safeguarding the home. The Clovis lifestyle centered on the male hunter. Those stalwarts felling six-ton mammoths must have been richly rewarded in ritual and folklore, in tribute and station. But in truth, it was the primary male–female symbiotic bond that enabled Clovis society to survive.

Another survival secret was their absolute dedication to reciprocity. Regardless of who killed an animal, or who harvested a plant, everyone was entitled to a share. Even the most esteemed hunter failed sometimes, and this prudent practice of sharing shielded all from short-term setbacks. Great honor was accorded both to those who provided best and to those who shared most willingly. Food hoarding was a public and criminal transgression.

Through the centuries, the Clovis people continued to adapt, to expand their range, and to exploit the dwindling resources of the open grassland. Then, about eleven thousand years ago, the Clovis lifeway itself ended. But as a people, the first Americans survived and continued to adapt. Many of today's American Indians are descended, in one way or another, from these Clovis pioneers.

## PRE-CLOVIS AMERICANS

The Clovis people left the earliest well-documented archaeological remains in America. This relatively conservative judgment remains reasonable because, despite decades of concerted research, no undisputed evidence of a pre-Clovis presence has been uncovered anywhere in the Western Hemisphere.

Although still controversial, archaeological evidence is nevertheless emerging from a number of sites suggesting that people arrived well before the well-documented Clovis complex. Many modern archaeologists have begun to acknowledge, if sometimes only privately, that native Americans could have arrived as early as 40,000 years ago. Numerous sites throughout North and South America offer tantalizing suggestions of pre-Clovis occu-

pations, but none provides ironclad proof acceptable to all archaeologists.

Some of the best evidence derives from excavations at Meadowcroft Shelter, a remarkably well-stratified site in southwestern Pennsylvania. Evidence for early human occupation consists of occupation floors containing firepits, some stone tools and by-products, a wooden spearshaft, a piece of plaited basketry, and two human bone fragments. The oldest radiocarbon date is slightly earlier than 19,000 years ago, and the earliest stone artifacts appear to date between 15,000 and 14,000 years ago.

Another leading pre-Clovis candidate is the Monte Verde site in southern Chile. Nearly one dozen house foundations and the fallen pole-frames of residential huts have been exca-

vated, with fragments of skin (perhaps mastodon) still clinging to the poles. The upper layers contain evidence suggesting a human presence about 13,000 years ago. Even more controversial are the deep layers at Monte Verde, which have produced two radiocarbon dates of 33,000 years ago, associated with possible cultural features and several fractured stones.

Despite the evidence from Meadowcroft, Monte Verde, and numerous other sites, there is no unequivocal, indisputable archaeological documentation of a pre-Clovis occupation in the New World. But the debate continues, and until more solid information becomes available, the identity of the first Americans will, in the words of one skeptic, remain "as much psychological as archaeological."

# CHAPTER TWO

# SPREADING OUT ACROSS AMERICA

MAKAH WHALING CANOE MODEL

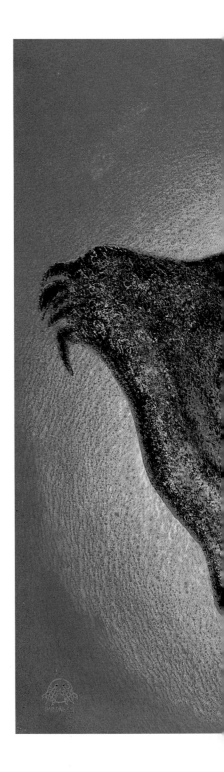

THE PASSING OF CLOVIS was not a dead end; it was a new beginning. The American Indian homeland would ultimately cover one-quarter of the world's habitable surface. Indian people would spread out across the American landmass, exploring the ten thousand miles from the Arctic to Cape Horn. They would learn to prosper in this varied landscape: some would hunt and others would fish, some would harvest wild plants and others would farm. Many would blend multiple survival strategies into a mix appropriate to their unique local homeland.

While always retaining an essential "Indianness," native American culture adjusted and adapted to regional extremes of temperature and climate, to the mountains, the deserts, the woodlands, and the prairies. As time passed, the increasingly varied Indian cultures would presage the extraordinary diversity that was to become America.

## Life in the Changing Desert

As the climate warmed up, the gigantic lakes that had once flooded the western American deserts began drying up. Some Indian people clustered about the shorelines, where they collected bulrush, cattail, and insect larvae, and fished during the rich spawning runs. Others abandoned the disappearing lakes to live in upland mountain valleys. Here they hunted bighorn sheep and collected plant resources in the ever-changing post–Ice Age landscape.

Six thousand years ago, piñon pine rapidly spread northward from the Southwest, blanketing much of the intermountain west. The nutritious piñon

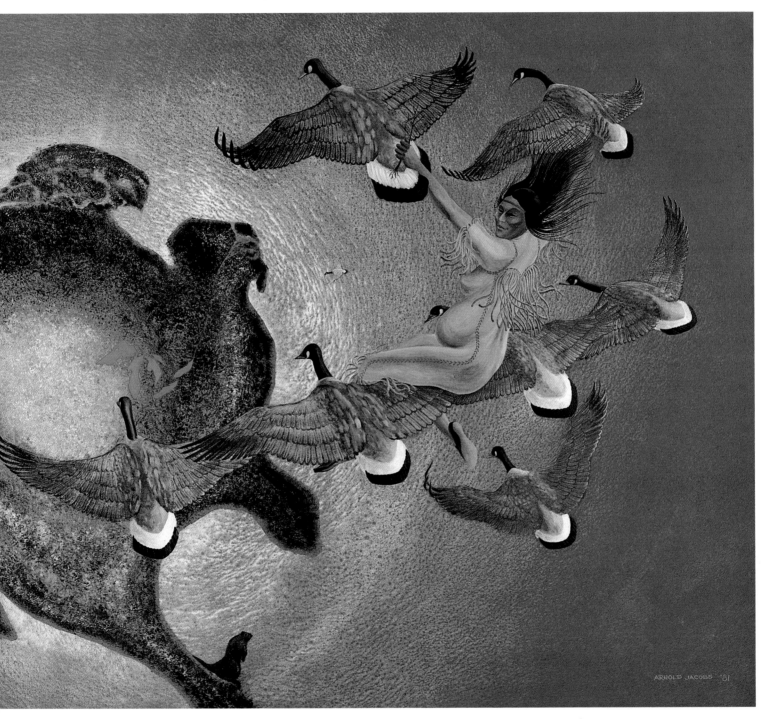

*Skywoman Descending Great Turtle Island* by Arnold Jacobs (Onondaga), 1981.
Among the Iroquois, human life began when Skywoman was pushed out of her domain.
She fell to an island that grew when a muskrat brought mud from under the sea and
placed it on a turtle's shell. Turtle and island grew to make a home for Skywoman, who
shortly gave birth to a daughter—the beginning of the world.

nut, ripening over a brief period in the fall, provides a high-bulk food that can be stored for two or three years. Like the postcontact Paiute and Shoshone people, these ancient uplanders followed a scheduled seasonal round—often moving several times throughout the year—with piñon nuts providing a primary staple whenever and wherever it grew.

When the nuts were ready to gather, perhaps these early foragers would, like their Paiute descendants, greet the first sunrise among the pines in prayer. The first day's harvest was always set aside for the all-night ritual piñon dance that started at sunset. A wise elder, a woman, exorcised any lingering ghosts, then scattered the nuts over the ground, demonstrating her people's thankfulness for the abundance of nature. As dancers slowly revolved around the campfire in shuffling steps, they sang in gratitude.

Countless basic survival skills enabled the people of America's high desert to survive in one of the world's most severe environments. Jackrabbits were driven into long nets, handmade of twisted fiber cordage. They were as long as modern tennis nets. As the meat was roasting, the women cut the rabbit skins into continuous lengths and twirled them into furry strands. One good-sized rabbit might

produce a fur ribbon fifteen feet long. More than one hundred jackrabbits were needed to make a single man's robe.

Archaeologists working at Lovelock Cave in northwestern Nevada in 1924 found a blanket made from the skins of six hundred meadow mice. Imagine snaring all those mice, painstakingly skinning each one, cutting the fur into tiny strips, joining them into two hundred feet of mouse fur rope, then sewing the strips together. Although two thousand years old, this tightly woven blanket is in perfect shape, still capable of warding off the blustery high desert winter.

Lovelock Cave also contained a basket full of ancient duck decoys made from buoyant tule rushes, covered with feathered bird skins. Nobody knows how they were used. They may have been tied to a float, serving as a come-on to water birds. Or maybe the hunters put the decoys on their heads, and then crept stealthily beneath and between the paddling ducks, pulling the birds, one at a time, underwater, to drown.

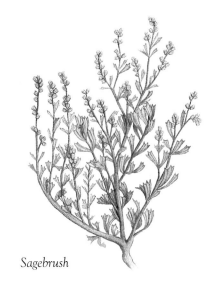

*Sagebrush*

The modern Paiute and Shoshone people are the cultural descendants of these early desert dwellers. Life in these communities, whether earliest American or postcontact, centered on the nuclear family and was characterized by a simple division of labor according to gender.

Men continued to hunt, but the economic burden had shifted to women. Aside from their role as companion and mother, their foraging and gathering made them the principal providers. And as the woman's economic role became more central, her status and sociopolitical power increased. These women of the desert were respected

*Puffball Fungus*

and admired. They became virtuoso weavers, and sometimes took over the shaman's responsibility. A particularly prosperous woman might take several husbands. When women were locally scarce, a man might elect to share a wife rather than go without.

*Rabbitbrush*

No longer did brides always have to move into the husband's home territory. Among desert dwellers, the man commonly moved into his wife's home camp, where the women were familiar with the local resources. Descent was usually reckoned through both male and female lines. Without agriculture, these foraging people persisted for thousands of years in their harsh homeland.

The postcontact Paiute knew the healing properties of many drugs found in nature, employing more than two hundred native plants as medicine. Boiled sagebrush leaves relieved headaches and rheumatism; when brewed into tea, the branches cured influenza. Swellings and sores were dressed with a poultice made of puffball fungus. Rabbitbrush stems and leaves proved to be an effective cough medicine when simmered and taken once or twice a day. Rubbed vigorously into the hair and scalp, boiled willow leaves and twigs cured dandruff.

Other native American people were to discover the natural source of digitalis and salicylic acid, the active ingredient in today's aspirin. Some pharmacologists believe that American Indian people's knowledge of herbal medicines equaled, or

OPPOSITE:
**Gathering piñon nuts (TOP) and trapping rabbits (BOTTOM).**

*Burning Off the Chaparral*
by Greg Harlin. Native Californians
set brushfires deliberately to burn off
the shrubby plants, minimizing the possibility of more catastrophic fires and
encouraging the growth of new sprouts.

maybe even surpassed, modern man's expertise with natural drugs. Tragically, such traditional prescriptions were to prove impotent in curing the virulent European diseases that swept across a later America.

Because of their mobile lifestyle, these desert people did not individually own either the land or its resources. All were entitled to fish, to collect plant foods, and to hunt anywhere they wished. But good manners dictated that visitors request permission to hunt or collect in another's territory. Such permission was always granted. This communal outlook reflects an American Indian philosophy toward cooperation and group identity, an attitude very different from the white man's seemingly unquenchable lust for land and property. An anthropologist once asked a group of Paiutes: "If a man had lost all of his food and was starving, would it be all right for him to take somebody's pinenuts if he found them?" The Paiute people did not know how to answer. This situation had never come up. They simply said a man would be ashamed to be in such impoverished straits.

## California Before Columbus

Farther west, native Californians adapted in still different ways. Unlike their Clovis ancestors—who tended to focus their subsistence efforts on a few select species—these foraging peoples exploited an immense array of environments, with no single food item becoming the crucial staple. Their broad-based lifestyle served them well in the long run. In the chaparral—dense thickets of shrubs—they found plentiful sources of protein-rich seeds, and they hunted deer and smaller mammals. Along the coastline, they exploited a great profusion of fish, shellfish, seals, and even whales that periodically became beached. The mountains hosted deer, bear, and elk, plus the midsummer plant foods. The major rivers yielded huge quantities of spawning salmon, trout, and eel.

Through time, native Californians exploited additional resources and spread into areas that had never before been permanently settled. When the first European explorers arrived, they were astonished by the dense Indian popula-tions, characterized by tremendous cultural and linguistic diversity. The sizable populations puzzled many, since California Indians did not farm.

Native Californians managed their homeland with a discriminating hand. The all-too-common lightning fires were a threat to the indispensable acorn har-vest, and California Indians clearly understood the principles of fire ecology. When the chaparral becomes overly mature, it is ecologically unstable; when a fire finally does erupt, it can be catastrophic. They took preventive action by deliberately setting brushfires to burn off older growth, litter, and seedlings. Periodic controlled torching of the underbrush eliminated the danger of destruc-tive crown fires—which all too often darken today's California summer sky.

Native Californians also understood that burning off chaparral vegetation in the Sierra foothills promoted new growth. Tender new sprouts appeared within a month of a spring burn, providing attractive browse for deer; fall burning was cer-tain to provide springtime fare for the Indian people. Judicious burning also increased the available grazing lands for deer, elk, and antelope, and facilitated the gathering of acorns that ripened after the burning took place.

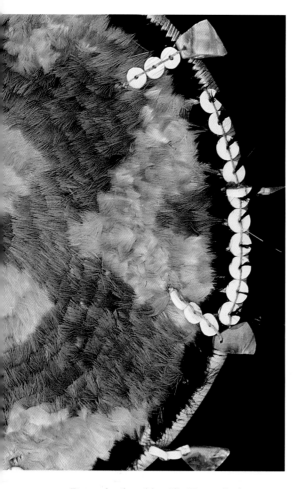

Pomo basket (detail). Pomo Indians were famous for the intricacy and variety of their basket designs. The women were the creators of the highly decorated baskets, such as the one shown here, in which both beads and feathers have been woven into the design.

OPPOSITE:
*Chumash Sacred Pictographs* by Lloyd Townsend. A Chumash shaman derived supernatural power from a guardian spirit that might appear during a dream or a trance. Such powers might be kindly or malevolent; they could control the weather or heal the sick. The semiabstract designs painted on the walls of a sacred cave helped to perpetuate the power of the vision. Some of these designs would be symbolic, representing objects, creatures, or phenomena known to the shaman, and some would certainly be unique to the mind of the artist.

Although pottery was never particularly important here, native Californians made basketry unsurpassed anywhere in the Americas. Sometimes, bright feathers from wild birds and seashells embellished their baskets. The Pomo, living north of San Francisco Bay, crafted baskets that ranged in size from three feet tall to thimble-sized. Unlike some other tribes, the Pomo men wove as well, making relatively simple things like mats and fish traps. But the elegant basketwork was restricted to the women, who used more than thirty kinds of wild plant materials.

Each Pomo basket maker could execute more than a dozen designs, integrated in endless variety. But she never allowed a design to encircle the basket completely; otherwise, she believed, she would go blind. Some women even created virtuoso examples the size of a pinhead, made of stitches so microscopic they defy counting with the naked eye. When Sir Francis Drake landed here in 1578, he marveled at the feathered baskets "so well wrought as to hold water."

Also notable among California Indians were the Chumash people of the picturesque Santa Barbara Channel. The Chumash hunted deer and smaller game for winter meat and hides; and, like most native Californians, the Chumash relied on an abundant acorn harvest. Preparing the acorn was no easy matter because acorns are inedible when gathered; the bitter-tasting tannic acid must first be leached away. A woman would kneel before a sandbanked leaching pit and pour hot water on unrefined acorn meal, which was then cooked in a watertight coiled basket by dropping heated stones inside.

But it was saltwater fishing that defined the distinctive Chumash lifestyle. The great coastal kelp beds provided a rich fishery, home to more than 125 species of fish and numerous sea mammals such as otters, dolphins, whales, and sea lions. Tidal shorelines provided mussels, abalone, oysters, scallops, and clams.

So far from home, the Spanish explorers appreciated good seamanship when they saw it, and they marveled at Chumash fishermen in their twenty-five-foot-long plank canoes, sewn with fiber cordage, and caulked with asphalt. Like dories, these oceangoing canoes were double-ended; a crew of three or four could easily manage this swift and maneuverable craft. The Chumash harpooned sea mammals and fished for swordfish, halibut, and tuna.

Chumash villages sometimes numbered more than a thousand people. In a special ceremonial area set aside for religious functions, they gave thanks to the plants and animals that gave them life. They danced to honor the swordfish, the barracuda, and the bear. The Chumash were linked into an extensive trading network using olivella bead money, mostly produced on the Channel Islands. The most powerful chiefs derived their considerable wealth and authority by brokering exchange between offshore islands and inland areas.

## Coping with Abundance

Farther north lived the people of America's Northwest Coast. This shoreline, extending from Yakutat Bay in Alaska to northern California, is slowly sinking into the Pacific, creating innumerable channels and fiords and thousands of islands, large and small. The warm Japanese Current, flowing southward from Alaska, assures a moderate climate with heavy rainfall.

Through time, a distinctive Northwest Coast culture developed along the Pacific Slope. Archaeological evidence left by the earliest people living there shows little difference between coastal and interior lifeways. An early hunting tradition developed at least ten thousand years ago. Elk, deer, antelope, beavers, rabbits, and rodents were all favored prey. Gradually, the subsistence base broadened to include river mussels and especially salmon.

Northwest Coast people considered salmon to be a race of eternal beings who lived in underwater houses during the winter. In the spring they took on their fish form and swam up the rivers in huge numbers, bestowing themselves upon humans for food. The first salmon caught each year was placed on an altar, facing upstream, and prayers were said. After each villager sampled the roasted flesh, the intact skeleton was returned to the river, and it swam back to the underwater world of the salmon people. One day, this skeleton would return as a whole fish.

Major villages were located at the water's edge on a beach convenient for landing canoes. Smaller, special-purpose encampments also appeared in time, suggesting increasing local differentiation. In the north, houses were nearly square, 25 to 75 feet across, with vertical side planking and a gabled roof; the fire burned on the floor, warming sleeping compartments on the upper levels. The southern houses were long, narrow, and occupied by several families, each with its own fire; one such house was nearly 500 feet long and 75 feet wide. Large wooden houses like these have been constructed here for more than three thousand years, suggesting the development of an extended family organization.

## Visiting a Fourteenth-Century Kwakiutl House

If we could visit a precontact Kwakiutl village, say along the Queen Charlotte Strait, we would first see a row of great cedar-plank houses, each with its own name, heraldic crest, and distinctive identity. Each house has a substantial false-front facade portraying mythical killer whales and thunderbirds, grizzly bears and ravens. One door is a gaping mouth, forewarning that only the worthy can enter without harm. Another doorway recalls symbolically the birth and death cycle. At the far end of the beach stands a cedar house carved to represent *sisiyutl*, the double-headed serpent. Totem poles, hewn with the images of still other mythological animals, reach skyward. On wooden decks extending over the canoe-lined beach, the Kwakiutl people rest, talk, work, and make speeches.

The highest-ranking chief might invite us inside with these words:

*This is the house of my great-great-grandfather Mahwa, who invited you here. This is the house of my great-grandfather Mahwa, who invited you to Sandy Beach. This is the house of my grandfather Mahwa who invited you at Crooked Beach. This is the feasting house of my father who invited you at Tide Beach. Now I have taken the place of my father. I invite you, tribes, that you should come and see my house here.*

Entering the largest house, we confront four massive roof supports, each carved into huge hook-nosed thunderbirds, wings spread and staring ominously downward. In the squared off central area is an earthen floor, a smoldering fireplace at each corner. Here and there are exquisitely carved backrests, each emblazoned with heraldic crests and mythical beasts. They are reserved for noblemen and their families.

Each fireplace warms an elevated sleeping compartment, built like small interior houses to create semiprivate bedroom spaces. The chief's compartment stands in the place of highest honor, toward the rear and in the middle of the house. Those of lesser rank are assigned lateral spaces. Slaves sleep near the fires.

Overhead are wooden racks laden with dried salmon, halibut, and eulachon. Baskets heaped with salmonberries, herring eggs, and smoked mussels are stashed about. Carved wooden boxes stowed near the walls are filled with additional preserved foods and fish oil. Others hold the carved feast dishes. One is a double-headed wolf, each face baring teeth of sharpened bone. Other chests contain fur and button blankets, bighorn sheep spoons, and rattles.

Several more elaborately carved cedar trunks, clearly more important than the others, stand in the chief's special area. Each is covered by a triangular lid, inlaid with dozens of otter teeth. Inside are kept the traditional dance masks. Some commemorate mythological encounters with demons; others reaffirm the family's elevated status and standing in the community. A few masks and puppets

**Kwakiutl Chief Tsawatenok, wearing a wooden headdress carved in the image of a thunderbird (1914).**

## NOT BLIND OPPOSITION TO PROGRESS, BUT OPPOSITION TO BLIND PROGRESS

The Clovis, the Paiute, the Chumash, the Kwakiutl, and a thousand others—these were America's foraging people. Some will tell you that these people were primitive because they did not become farmers, because they did not live in cities.

But this image of so-called "progress" in human history derives from the limited experiences of a privileged class in an affluent society. This "progressive" view of humanity is heavily conditioned by stereotypes of "primitive" and "civilized." While on the one hand there is an infatuation with romantic visions of vanished American Indians, the Western love affair with science and improvement instills contempt for anything primitive or underdeveloped. In the popular mind, at least, to be "primitive" is to be backward, shabby, ailing, and famished. Group poverty is taken to demonstrate a lack of technological polish—a lack of "development."

Western civilization has built its own past, a perception of history based on clichés projected backward. Nineteenth-century scholars wrote of the three major stages of human culture: a progression from "savagery" to "barbarism" and finally to "civilization." Later social historians characterized the technological innovations as somehow "rescuing" human beings from the "pressures" of simpler lifestyles and "permitting" new, more progressive customs to unfold.

This mistaken view simply assumes that people are always out to get a break, to gain an edge. It assumes that people would simply invent agriculture as a natural culmination of human evolution. But do these forms of society that some consider to be "civilized" necessarily bring with them improvements in the health and well-being of its members? Do they really imply "progress" in the sense that we commonly use the term?

The answer is no. This short-sighted view of "progress" ignores the fact that specialization can itself be destabilizing. Farmers often must work much harder than hunters, gatherers, and fishing people. Typical preindustrial farmers spent four to six days a week working the fields. People like the Chumash and the Kwakiutl foragers only needed to work two days to feed their families. Farming people usually require that their children help out in the fields. Children in foraging societies are not part of the labor force.

We have much to learn from non-agricultural foraging people. These are not "noble savages," living in unspoiled harmony with nature, without want, avarice, or possessiveness, untainted by contact with civilization. Hunger was clearly a seasonal problem for many American Indian groups and starvation was not unknown.

But these more generalized economies have demonstrated a degree of long-term cultural stability and survival unknown in today's world. Native people of California achieved the highest aboriginal population density in North America without an agricultural base. The nonagricultural people of the Great Plains, the Northwest Coast, and the Canadian Shield crafted ecologically viable alliances capable of weathering the long-term storm. The Great Basin foragers maintained determined, if flexible, adaptation to the harshest of environments for ten thousand years.

We must revise our notion that so-called civilization will always represent progress in human well-being.

---

are simply intended to entertain, to fill an audience with wonder and delight. Like the houses, each mask has a proper name. They are fed and cared for. These masks cannot be purchased for any price. They must be earned.

Stowed in repose, the masks are heirlooms to be revered, ancient artworks, long possessed. But taken out and properly worn, the masks come alive with a new energy, capable of inflicting both absolute terror and immense pride. For the moment, the dancer becomes somebody else. The finest box contains the grizzly bear dancer's claws, worn by initiates of the Grizzly Bear Society during the Winter Ceremony. The grizzly bear dancer frightens his audience with his potential power, acting as a ceremonial policeman to enforce proper behavior.

Another box conceals an ancient transformation mask. The dancer first appears wearing the mask of an imperious blue and red eagle. Then, by cleverly manipulating the sinew rigging, the dancer suddenly snaps his mask open. The beaks part to the sides and the "chin" lowers, revealing a scowling, hook-nosed human being. As the dancer transforms supernatural animal life into humanity, he also transforms himself into his own ancestors, to share the dreams and visions of those who lived generations ago.

Masks are brought out when it is time to observe long-standing Kwakiutl family traditions: marriage, birth, death, or the transfer of important property. The outsider is bewildered by the number of names and titles being passed from person to person. But to the Kwakiutl, the memory of such events becomes their civil and church registry. Like traditional European societies, the Kwakiutl are deeply concerned with recording descent, status, and property. Myth and ritual are the inscribed pages of their family bible.

Dancers are motivated by supernatural beings whose original contact with the ancestors began the tradition. The dance performance is a reenactment of the ancestors, adventures, or a demonstration of the power given them by super-natural beings.

Elaborate family histories identified Kwakiutl people with a specific *numaym*—a kind of a "house," like the medieval European Houses of York and Lancaster, or the Japanese House of Minamoto. Each *numaym* owned one or more plank houses, charted its own tradition of origin, and owned rights to resources, hereditary titles, and ceremonial prerogative. Each *numaym* had a head chief, ritually defined as descending from the founding ancestor. Lesser chiefs and commoners also lived in the *numaym* house. In exchange for managing the assets, the ranking chief received a share of all fish, game, roots, and berries harvested in his *numaym's* territory.

The position of chief was transmitted from oldest child to oldest child, whether son or daughter (although among the Kwakiutl, it was mostly men who occupied this position). Other positions (or "seats") in a *numaym* were also trans-ferred to the next generation as they became vacated by death. Assuming one's seat in a *numaym* required a potlatch, a proper validating ceremony. When a bride returned to the house of her father, she had to give away property to estab-lish her position as heir, to authorize her son to assume her father's seat and title. Bestowing an ancestral name to a child required yet another potlatch feast.

Potlatches represent an uninterrupted tradition from the remote past to the present. The various grades of potlatches ranged from minor events in a child's life through more significant festivals celebrating the assumption of dance privi-leges. The most important potlatch—called "Doing a Great Thing"—took place when a noble assumed a ritual name and position, exchanged one of the highly valued coppers, married, erected a memorial totem pole, or built a new house.

The Northwest Coast would become the land of the Tlingit and Tsimshian, the Haida and Kwakiutl. Although agriculture was not practiced and ceramics were unknown, Northwest Coast populations developed a lavish lifestyle, an extraordinary ceremonialism integrating property, rank, and personal pride.

Kwakiutl mask.

*And all the while he danced to the high, hectic rattle of the drum, virtu-ally in place, his motion translated into the pure illusion. . . . Sometimes you look at a thing and see only that it is opaque, that it cannot be looked into. And this opacity is its essence, the very truth of the matter. So it was for me with the . . . mask. The man inside was merely motion and he had no face, and his name was the name of the mask itself. Had I lifted . . . [it], there should have been no one and nothing to see.*

—N. SCOTT MOMADAY
(Kiowa), *The Names*

# CHAPTER THREE

# MIDDLE AMERICAN CIVILIZATIONS

MAYA CORN GOD

THE MIDDLE AMERICAN STATES and empires were to develop by extending political domination, usually by conquest, over a vast area, unified by a common centralized political organization but not necessarily sharing a common language or culture.

Civilization in this sense emerged in Middle America about 1500 B.C. or so, when settled agricultural village life became widespread. In this region characterized by extreme environmental diversity, households had previously moved seasonally between different encampments. But an increasing dependence on domesticated crops fostered a more sedentary lifestyle.

The earliest such Mexican civilization can be traced to the Olmec people. Although their culture was once called Middle America's "mother culture," most now recognize this distinction as being a bit theatrical and overstated. But few would dispute the fact that Olmec was a new, seminal force in Middle American politics and military authority.

For reasons still not fully understood, Olmec arose along the Mexican Gulf Coast, amid a loosely organized farming culture that soon evolved into one governed by authoritarian and stratified rule. Like the later Hopewell in the Eastern Woodlands, Olmec was not itself a culture. It was a pan–Middle American religion that embodied symbols, rituals, godly perception, and probably economic exchange, extending its power some fifteen hundred years before the birth of a man who would eventually be deified as the personification of the first pan-European religion, Christianity. The primary Olmec religious icon was the Rain

*The Market of Tenochtitlán: Manufacture of Mosaic and Golden Jewelry Under the Zapotec* by Diego Rivera, 1942.

God, an ogre intermingling both human and jaguar aspects. With eyebrows aflame and downturned snarling mouth this distinctive iconography turns up on both architecture and artifacts. The Olmec Rain God would be handed down and worshiped by later Middle American civilizations.

The so-called Olmec style is also evident on the impressive twenty-ton stone heads found at some sites. Each figure wears a close-fitting cap, functioning much like old-fashioned leather football helmets. Perhaps these were portraits of a specific priest-ruler; or maybe they depict more generalized Olmec deities. In either case, these monuments are manufactured from huge boulders of basalt. The nearest source for this hard volcanic stone lies nearly fifty miles away. Clearly, the massive basalt blocks must have been hauled across the jungle by hand, then floated down the rivers into Tabasco and Vera Cruz.

At sites like La Venta and San Lorenzo, and the newly discovered Olmec site near Acapulco, the Olmec constructed huge mounds. The earthen pyramid at La Venta contains more than a hundred thousand cubic feet of fill. The Olmec may

*The Pre-Columbian Civilizations of Middle America.*
**These cultures included the Olmec (1500–600 B.C.), Zapotec (500 B.C.–A.D. 700), Teotihuacán (150 B.C.–A.D. 750), Mayan (A.D. 300–900), Toltec (A.D. 900–1100), and Aztec (A.D. 1325–1520).**

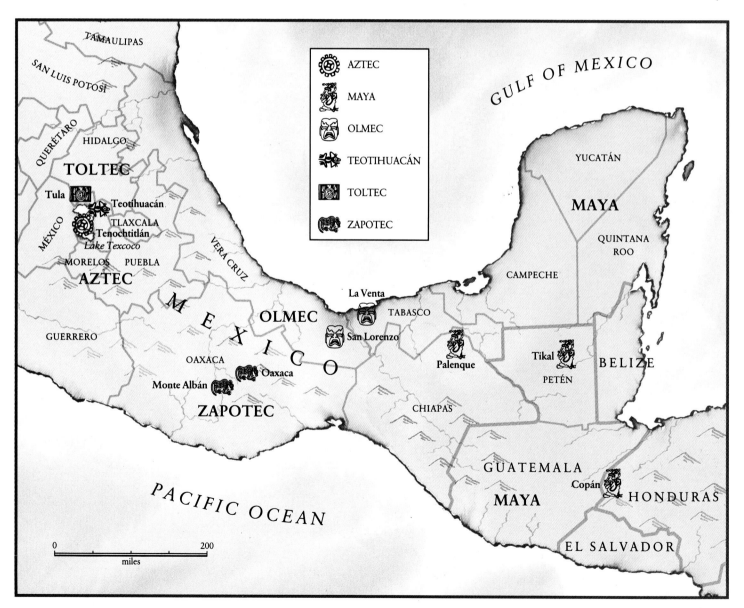

Two outstanding Olmec carvings, both depicting variations on the familiar jaguar-human monster concept that is central to Olmec art and religion.

LEFT:
The famous Kunz axe is made of blue-green jade and named for its former owner.

RIGHT:
This figure, carved of dark green serpentine, exhibits an unusual bulbous forehead and curious hairstyle.

have kept a complex calendar and even developed a numbering system. Their pottery and work with jade is renowned. Their talented artisans also manufactured concave magnetite mirrors, so highly polished that today they still can be used to light a fire.

Why did such advances occur in the Gulf Coast lowlands? Perhaps because the rich environmental potential surrounding the largest rivers could be exploited without the heavy investments of labor necessary in the semiarid highlands. Although abundant in agricultural terms, the Gulf Coast environment was impoverished in other key resources; obsidian for edged tools, magnetite for mirrors, and basalt for the huge stone heads were all transported from elsewhere.

Olmec society was to endure only a few centuries. The Middle American highlands gained control of trade in raw materials, soon transcending the lowland merchants, both economically and politically. Eventually, multiple local social systems developed, each with its own specialized forms of social control, culture, and language. These sedentary communities interacted with each other across their individual frontiers. They exchanged merchandise, and members of elite families generally married their social equals from distant enclaves. Such interactions created a multisocietal system throughout Middle America.

For centuries, the Zapotec people living in the Valley of Oaxaca (Mexico) had been in contact with the Olmecs, and their shared interactions allowed both to prosper. But after the Olmec demise, Oaxaca solidified its position in regional trade and extended its influence beyond the immediate area.

About 500 B.C., an elite group founded the first true city in ancient Mexico, the hilltop stronghold at Monte Albán. Perched atop an artificially flattened mountain, its outskirts overflowed downhill in terrace communities. For the next half-millennium, Monte Albán grew in size and importance, just as Rome was doing during the same period in Europe.

Overview of Tenochtitlán. By A.D. 1400, the Aztecs had developed an extensive civilization that covered central and southern Mexico and the Mexican Gulf Coast. Tenochtitlán, the imperial city of the Aztecs, was the heart of a vast kingdom of city-states that paid tribute to their ruling center—the home of some quarter of a million people. The marketplace alone could accommodate sixty thousand.

Civilizations such as the Olmec, the Zapotec, and the Maya shared many similarities, including their famous calendrical system. In effect the Middle American calendar consisted of two calendars, the 365-day solar year and the 260-day ritual cycle. These two calendars operated in tandem, which meant that the beginning days of the two coincided only every fifty-two years. Native peoples of Middle America believed that these fifty-two-year cycles held great significance, and public ceremonies were carried out at the beginning of each cycle to ensure world renewal.

Some think that the most remarkable of the Middle American civilizations was that at Teotihuacán, the often-visited "pyramids" within an hour's drive northeast of Mexico City. Begun in 150 B.C. and lasting a millennium, Teotihuacán was a carefully planned city, divided into hundreds of neighborhoods, or barrios. Six hundred pyramids, one of them extending two hundred feet overhead, dominate the Teotihuacán skyscape. The downtown portion stretched for two miles along the Avenue of the Dead, fronting lavishly ornamented temples. Teotihuacán contained two thousand interlinked apartment complexes and plazas, workshops, and a huge central marketplace.

The rulers of Teotihuacán controlled the precious, highly valued obsidian source at Cerro de las Navajas. But the city derived most of its leverage and authority from the miles of irrigated fields that supported its huge population, perhaps 125,000 residents during the city's heyday; during festivals, this number probably doubled with visitors.

Decline set in sometime prior to about A.D. 750. Perhaps the fields were overextended. Maybe there was a rebellion. Possibly the costs of foreign trade were too high for the local populace to bear. By A.D. 800, the city's population dropped precipitously as many Teotihuacános moved eastward and southward. The city was eventually abandoned.

New empires would arise. North of Mexico City were the Toltecs, their capital city of Tula protected by fifteen-foot-tall statues of warriors armed with feather-decorated spear-throwers. Tula arose in a time of fragmentation, conflict, and turmoil. Although not as impressive a city as Teotihuacán, Tula became the homeland to the powerful Toltec armies of soldiers and merchants who intensified their control throughout ancient Mexico and into Central America. But late in the twelfth century, Tula was burned and the population scattered.

*And they named the hearts of the captives "precious eagle-cactus fruit." They lifted them up to the sun, the turquoise prince, the soaring eagle. They offered it to him, they nourished him with it.*

*This was called "the sending upward of the eagle man"; because he who died in war went into the presence of [the sun]; he went before and rested in the presence of the sun. That is, he did not go to the land of the dead.*

*Thus the captive's valor would not in vain perish; thus he took from the captive his renown.*

—*Florentine Codex*
*Book II: The Ceremonies*
*(Aztec), ca. 1550*

The succeeding Aztecs were destined to be the last of the great pre-European civilizations to spring up in Middle America. Their ancestors, the Mexicas, had migrated into the Valley of Mexico in the late twelfth century and by 1325 had founded what would become the legendary Aztec capital, Tenochtitlán. Built in the most unlikely spot imaginable, the dismal swamps of Lake Texcoco, the capital was connected to the mainland by three causeways that converged near its main temple. Over the years, a massive reclamation project around the capital created a fabulously productive system of raised field agriculture; remnants of these remarkably fertile fields, the *chinampas*, can still be seen in the "floating gardens" of Lake Xochimilco. When Hernán Cortés arrived in 1519, the size of Tenochtitlán exceeded that of every European city except London. More than sixty thousand merchants and customers crammed its marketplace alone.

As the feared Aztec troops spread throughout Middle America in the fifteenth century, they forged an empire that supplied them with abundant tribute and trade goods as well as thousands of captives for human sacrifice to their war god, Huitzilopochtli. In one year alone, Aztec priests sacrificed more than twenty thousand victims to this voracious deity.

In the Aztec empire and across Middle America, society was stratified into two classes of people, the elite or ruling nobility and the various commoners. The ruling elite controlled the major social institutions including religion, civil government, warfare, and sometimes even basic production and distribution. Most art and public architecture was sponsored by the elite, and writing (both in books and on stone monuments) was largely their province. Elite groups, in effect, had more in common with elite groups from distant regions than they did with their own commoners, and long-distance interactions provided a key element to legitimize power for the wealthy.

The social world of the commoner was more localized. Most commoners were farmers, living in nuclear family households, although near the cities, craft specialists, traders, and warriors were to be found. Their shared belief system legitimized the social dichotomies between nobility and commoner. This ideology was the glue that bonded Middle American civilization together.

Perhaps these principles are best seen in the most famous of all the Middle American civilizations, the Classic Maya.

## The Classic Maya

Although the earliest Mayas were contemporaries of the Olmec peoples, by A.D. 300 they had developed a remarkably distinctive, advanced culture that continued to flourish until around A.D. 900. The ruins of this Classic Maya civilization have long attracted explorers, adventurers, tourists, and archaeologists. One renowned Maya site, Tikal, remains so enigmatic and otherworldly that film producer George Lucas featured the 150-foot-tall temples of the Tikal acropolis in his epic *Star Wars* saga. Explaining why and how such a progressive and creative civilization could materialize in the jungles of Middle America has occupied generations of scholars. And although the traditional view of the Maya may have changed, their core origins remain a puzzle.

Traditional explanations of Classic Maya society go like this. Over the six-century interval from A.D. 300 to 900, the Maya people pulled off a cultural masterpiece, contributing numerous breakthroughs, but in a strangely "nonurban" setting. Most of the Maya population probably lived the lives of simple rural peasants, visiting breathtaking sites like Tikal, Copán, and Palenque only for the occasional market and religious festivals. During the rest of the year, these ceremonial centers were nearly empty, except for the priests, rulers, and their acolytes who lived and worked there. This traditional view held that the peasants supplied the ruling class with food and contributed their labor to erect the monumental architecture; in return, the priesthood ministered to the gods to ensure community well-being.

The Classic Maya were meticulous astronomers, charting their observations and calculations in screen folds (painted "books" made of lime-covered bark paper). Maya scribes also wrote calendrical, astronomic, and other religious inscriptions on polychrome ceramic vessels, objects of stone and bone, and outdoor monuments. Although such notation was recognized technically as "writing," it was thought to record simply the passage of time. And because the Maya did not write down historical events or record economic transactions, Western scholars considered Maya writing to be inferior to the ancient scripts developed in classic Old World civilizations, such as Sumerian cuneiform, Egyptian hieroglyphics, proto-Elamite, and many others.

Mayan ceramic figure. This refined and elegant figure, from the coast of Campeche, Mexico, was made during the late Classic period. It depicts a man dressed in elaborate clothing and headdress, probably a dignitary dressed for a ceremonial occasion.

The Classic Maya peasantry was thought to have practiced a kind of slash-and-burn farming, like the modern Maya living in Mexico and Guatemala. After the forests and jungle were arduously cleared with stone tools, the dead trees and undergrowth were left to dry, then torched so as to return the nutrients to the soil. Fields could be planted for two successive years, then the natural vegetation was allowed to take over for a decade or so. The Classic Maya could not live in cities, the traditional argument went, because such shifting agricultural patterns were highly land-intensive.

Above all, the Classic Maya were perceived as a peaceful people—the so-called Greeks of the New World. Archaeologists thought that the isolated and independent ceremonial centers coexisted for half a millennium in harmony with one another. "Nothing in excess," wrote one Mayan archaeologist. "Live and let live," nodded another.

Then, between about A.D. 800 and 900, the ceremonial centers of the southern lowlands slipped into decline. Within a century, Classic Maya civilization self-destructed. Archaeologists have speculated about the reasons behind the collapse. Some ecologically oriented scholars felt that slash-and-burn agriculture deforested the land (creating savanna grassland from the native rain forest), exhausted the soil, and eroded away the topsoil. Others thought that natural catastrophes had undermined the Classic Maya. Still others argued that the peasants revolted after centuries of tyranny to throw off the burdensome yoke of oppression. Or maybe disease or human invaders had wiped out the Maya. But whatever the reason, it was clear to all that when the Classic Maya collapsed, civilization was erased from the southern lowlands.

The Classic Maya have traditionally been viewed as somehow unique, different in kind from all other Middle American civilizations—indeed different from

Only three pre-conquest Maya codices (ancient manuscripts of pictures and writing) survived destruction by the Spanish. Above is a page from the *Dresden Codex,* so known as it is preserved in the city of Dresden, Germany. Written like a picture album, and made by gluing together pieces of paper into a single long strip that is folded accordian-style, the *Dresden Codex* is particularly valuable for its lunar tabulations recorded in vertical hieroglyphs; the codices also address astronomy, chronology, disease, hunting, and agricultural ceremonies and deities.

civilizations anywhere else in the world. Their primeval rain forest environment, according to this view, somehow fostered a peaceful, harmonious nonurban lifestyle characterized by incomparable intellectual and aesthetic proficiency.

## The New, Unfinished Mayan Synthesis

A new assessment of Maya civilization has emerged in recent years. The major breakthrough began in the late 1960s, when experts in phonetic analysis and iconography (known as epigraphers) broke the code and deciphered previously incomprehensible Mayan texts. Maya writing employed about eight hundred known hieroglyphs—roughly the same number used by ancient Egyptians—and nearly two-thirds of these glyphs have now been deciphered. Combined with innovative archaeology, this has revolutionized our understanding of the Maya world. Today we know that the Classic Maya had developed a sophisticated writing system, merging whole word and phonetic symbols to spell out words in the spoken language—just as our own alphabet does.

Maya glyphs can no longer be dismissed as esoteric, astronomical musings. Now that specialists can read Mayan texts, they realize that these record a wealth of historical information, particularly genealogical information about the hereditary noble class, including birthdays, inaugurations, marriages, and deaths of rulers and their close family members. Some Mayan texts read like propaganda, boasting of major victories in battle and recording the names of enemy captives, some of whom were slated for sacrifice.

We also now realize that the Maya writing system was not unique in Middle America; the Zapotec, Mixtec, and Aztec also developed their own writing systems. But the Maya system was the most elaborate, and also the longest-lived (having begun in earnest about A.D. 1 and lasted into the sixteenth century). The epigraphers have demonstrated the Maya were indeed writing their own history—not an "objective" history in the Western sense, but a culturally nuanced account of consequential historical events as the Maya perceived them.

Archaeology came up with some surprises of its own. In the 1980s, joined by physicists, geologists, biologists, botanists, and zoologists, archaeologists boasted a rich arsenal of weapons for attacking problems of the ancient Maya: new ways of dating artifacts, new techniques for extracting ecological data, and new methods for finding previously invisible sites.

For one thing, archaeologists started looking beyond the eye-catching elite centers to see what the everyday Maya were like. Entire archaeological sites were cleared and mapped—including more than forty acres at Tikal, which had long been buried beneath the oppressive Petén jungle. Millions of potsherds were recovered and analyzed, previously undiscovered carved monuments were unearthed, and dozens of rural house sites were excavated.

These results from Tikal and elsewhere amazed a generation of Mayan archaeologists. They calculated that more than ten thousand people lived in downtown Tikal during Classic Maya times—and another forty thousand could be found living in the nearby suburbs. In other words, Tikal was not a vacant ceremonial center at all—it was a full-blown city!

The notion of Tikal-as-city raised a conundrum. We know from modern studies that slash-and-burn agriculture could have supported only a third of the Classic Maya population at Tikal. So what did all these people eat?

The answer came from above—literally. As archaeologists embraced increasingly high-tech methods, the by-products of aerial photography, satellite imaging, and side-looking airborne radar created another surprise. The Maya cities did not exist in isolation; they were surrounded by sophisticated and massive agricultural earthworks. Virtually invisible on the ground, these networks of canals and raised fields were not produced by casual slash-and-burn technology.

The Classic Maya had launched massive public works projects to reclaim the low-lying swampland. Not only did they dig canals to bring nutrient-rich waters into dry areas, but they piled up the muck from canal bottoms to create raised beds of incredibly rich soil, capable of producing multiple crops year after year. And because the fields were now above the floodplain, the maize crops were no longer flooded out during the rainy season.

This labor-intensive reclamation campaign created a totally new—and long forgotten—method of intensive agriculture, fully capable of feeding the masses of people known to have lived in Classic Maya cities.

About this time, the sitewide survey at Tikal revealed a strange and disturbing series of long, narrow ditches and ridges. When completely mapped, these features turned out to be an intricate five-mile-long series of moats and parapets. In other words, Tikal had been fortified against attack—an odd precaution for a basically pacific people. Could the Classic Maya have been more warlike than previously thought?

Once archaeologists started looking for it, the evidence of warfare turned up. Fortifications at Becán stood nearly twenty feet high, surrounded by a ditch of the same depth. Newly deciphered Maya hieroglyphics—confirmed by data from the ceramics—showed unequivocal evidence of one Maya city after another being conquered by Mayan adversaries. Rulers were violently murdered, captives taken and tortured.

The older storyline of the gentle Maya is clearly mistaken. As regional population increased, conflicts over land, resources, and people intensified; disputes over market rights heated up, with territoriality and warfare jarring the Maya world throughout the Classic period. The conventional view of isolated Maya ceremonial centers also misjudged the significance and sweep of economic ties between the city-states. As the more prosperous peasants flocked into town from the countryside, the dichotomy between rich and poor intensified: the wealthy upper class lived in urban palaces, with only the poorest peasants left in the hinterlands. Access to sacred areas was restricted to the affluent, and the elite became increasingly distanced from the middle and lower classes.

Like many societies in today's world, the Classic Maya suffered from deforestation, burgeoning population pressure, agricultural breakdown, and polarization between rich and poor. Gone is the idealized image of the Maya as lowland pacifists. Today, we realize that the Classic Maya were part of the overall fabric of civilized native society that developed in large parts of Middle America.

*When the sun appeared on the horizon and its light fell on the mountain, the outcry and shouts of war broke forth, banners were unfurled, and the big flutes, drums, and conch shells resounded. . . . Immediately was the encounter. Truly the contest was terrible. . . . Then the warriors performed their acts of magic. Quickly the Quichés were defeated; they ceased to fight and were dispersed, annihilated and dead. . . . Thus our fathers and grandfathers recount, oh my sons! This is what they did, the Kings Oxlahuh Tzii and Cablahuh Tihax together with Voo Ymox and Dokel Batzin. And in no other way was Iximchée made great.*

—*Memorial de Tecpan-Atitlan*
(Maya)

# CHAPTER FOUR

# NATIVE FARMING INGENUITY

*KOSHARES ENTERING THE WORLD*
BY FERNANDO PADILLA, JR. (SAN FELIPE PUEBLO), 1991

IMAGINE TRADITIONAL ITALIAN CUISINE without the tomato. And what would Irish cooking be without the potato? Could African people survive without their gardens of corn? The truth is that each of these life-giving staples—tomatoes, potatoes, and corn—came from America, developed by the hand of the American Indian. In fact, *60 percent of the food eaten all over the world today* derives from plants that were originally domesticated by native Americans. In itself this is remarkable, but the extended global implications are immeasurable.

However, neither the crops nor the farming lifeway evolved overnight. Both are derivatives of long-term native American resourcefulness. For millennia, nonagricultural Indians had been interacting with, and to some extent manipulating, wild plants to their own advantage—without actually domesticating them.

In addition to their ecologically based use of fire, some precontact Californian foragers planted prickly-pear hedges around their villages, both for protection and for the seasonal fruits. Farther south, the Cahuilla, another California Indian group, carefully pruned thorny mesquite trees to make their harvest of edible pods easier. The Owens Valley Paiute irrigated large stands of Indian ricegrass and other wild plant resources, even though most of their diet came from purely wild foods. Although the acorn, mesquite, and Indian ricegrass were never domesticated in California, enduring plant-people interactions such as these set the stage for the development of complex agricultural systems elsewhere in the Americas.

---

**Hopi women grinding corn (ca. 1907).**

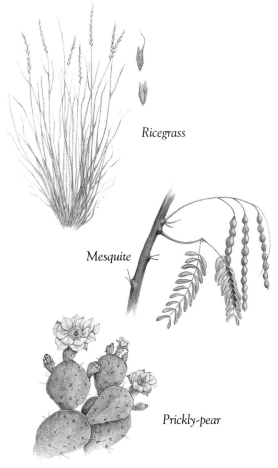

Ricegrass

Mesquite

Prickly-pear

Acorn

Incidental plant domestication began when people took over the task of dispersing and protecting key wild plant resources. The very process of harvesting wild plants can inadvertently trigger key genetic modifications in these plants. Century after century, the choices made by foragers—for example, favoring larger seeds over smaller ones—can have significant genetic consequences, eventually selecting for certain more "desirable" genetic traits—such as larger seeds—"preadapting" these species for full-blown domestication. This relationship both promoted and preserved a "conservative" ecological liaison between plant communities and human beings. The size of Indian populations supported by such plant communities remained controlled; in return, the rate of change in the incidental domesticate was slow. More specialized kinds of domestication took place as plant–people interactions elaborated and intensified. As people became more responsible for the dispersal of various plant species, a new brand of ecological succession evolved, with plants important as human food becoming increasingly common in areas where people lived.

## The Corn Mothers Come to the American Southwest

Even today, Pueblo people know where their corn came from. The Corn Mothers—Blue Corn Woman and White Corn Maiden—brought it with them when they climbed through the kiva roof onto the earth's surface. At birth, every infant receives an ear of corn made into a fetish, a reminder that the Corn Mothers gave life to all humans, plants, and animals. The Acoma call their fetish *latiku* because it contains the heart and breath of the Corn Mothers. Pueblo people keep their corn fetish for life, because when crops fail, its perfect seeds hold the promise of a new crop cycle.

What the Pueblos understand through tradition and allegory, the archaeologist approaches through excavation and radiocarbon dating. Corn (maize) became the staff of life throughout precontact America, from Argentina to southern Canada, from sea level to the towering Andes. Over a seven-thousand-year period, Indian people domesticated hundreds of kinds of maize, beginning in the semiarid highlands of Mexico with a common wild grass called *teosinte*. Thumbnail-sized wild teosinte cobs evolved over the millennia, becoming larger and larger, until they became the formidable corn ears sold in modern markets.

Full-blown agricultural lifestyles did not develop overnight in the American Southwest. For a thousand years, maize and other cultivated plants were seamlessly integrated into the hunter-gatherer economy, without wide-ranging changes in the environment or sociocultural context of the people involved. Aspects of this pattern survived into the contact period among the Pueblo, O'Odham, and Western Apache people. In some years, they ate little or no domesticated food; in other years, they relied almost exclusively on farm products. When Hopi crops failed—as they did from time to time—Pueblo communities broke up into smaller family foraging groups capable of living off naturally available foodstuffs. These people of the contact period are hardly relics or living fossils; their balanced approach has much to teach us about change and survival.

# Western Apache Farming: A Life in Balance

Archaeologists sometimes look to the postcontact Western Apache to experience something of the early Southwest farming lifestyle. The Western Apache of east-central Arizona live where some of the earliest cultivated plants in the American Southwest were first grown, and their way of life has lessons to teach.

The Western Apache believed in balance. Men hunted large game, but they did not eat so much meat that they drove game from their territory. They farmed, but not so much that they depended on crops alone to sustain them throughout the year. They gathered wild plant foods and trapped small game, but not enough to keep men from their big game hunts.

Western Apache people moved around. Their winter camps were in the south. Then in spring they moved higher up into the mountains, to plant, to hunt, and to collect wild things such as piñon nuts, acorns, and juniper berries. They harvested in late August to October, then moved back to their winter homes. Farming was always a backup, a buffer.

The farms were small. As the elders put it, "Apache never grow a big patch of corn, just a little patch . . . not too many pumpkins, just five or six is all . . . just enough for family." The Apache were not like Anglo farmers; they were not driven by the land hunger.

A family might own six small farms, but they would plant only two or three a year. After harvest, it was necessary for the land to rest for a year. They did not use animal manure in the fields, because they believed that contact with animal excrement causes sickness.

Apache people watched the sun to learn when to plant the corn. When the "Standing Moon" arrived, and they felt the gentle "time to plant wind"—sometime in March—they began to think about planting. The animals and plants also told them the time of year. When the grasses turned green and the mesquite yellow with flowers, and when spring birds came below the Salt River, they knew it was time to return to the planting grounds.

Farm work was women's work and there was nothing degrading or menial about it. Men helped out, but women took a more serious view of farming than men. Apache men said, "In the old days the woman was the head of it; the man he don't much care; the man, he's apt to make the mistake; women have always been the better farmers."

Women always knew how to keep up with the agricultural rituals, and they liked to do all the planting themselves. Usually, they chose a particularly "lucky" woman to drop the seeds into the holes. As she planted, she would say, "Grow fast, don't bother it worms, make a good crop." They also asked their mythical "corn people" to help out. Unlucky women—those who had been bitten by a snake or struck by lightning—were not allowed to plant. Neither were pregnant women. Most women prayed while irrigating the land.

When worms threatened the maize, Apache women collected them in a jar of water and let them rot. Then in a special ritual, they sprinkled them over a field, to keep other worms away.

They did not do that with crickets. These were the "music of the crop," and no one ever intentionally injured them. If Apaches accidentally stepped on a

**The Corn Maiden**
**by Harry Sakyesva (Hopi), 1945.**

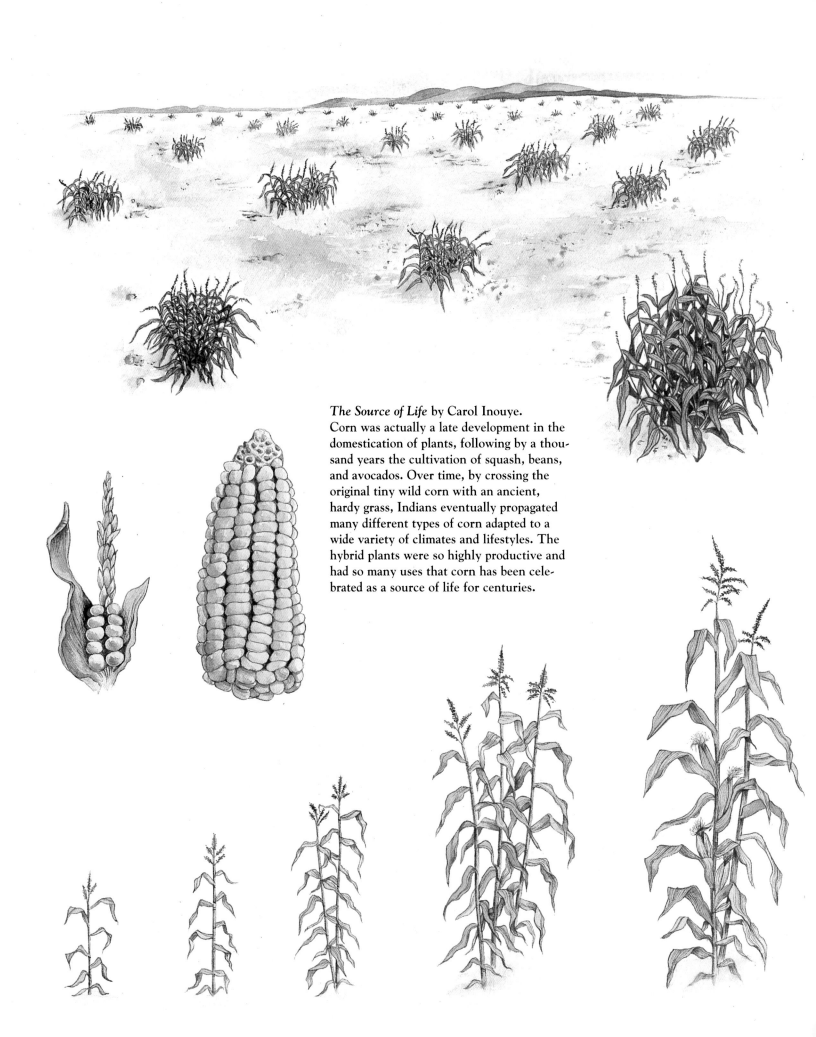

*The Source of Life* by Carol Inouye.
Corn was actually a late development in the domestication of plants, following by a thousand years the cultivation of squash, beans, and avocados. Over time, by crossing the original tiny wild corn with an ancient, hardy grass, Indians eventually propagated many different types of corn adapted to a wide variety of climates and lifestyles. The hybrid plants were so highly productive and had so many uses that corn has been celebrated as a source of life for centuries.

cricket, they quickly asked its forgiveness. During cold weather, they gathered up the friendly insects and put them in the brush, where it was warmer. In the autumn, the crickets called in a sound like the Apache words, "It's time to harvest, it's time to harvest." So they did.

Apache mythology harks back to a time when all creatures and objects could speak and move and show human traits. Later, everything went on its own and became different from the human. To Apache eyes, the natural world was alive and aware of problems. Objects of nature did not ordinarily speak or assume human form. But if the need was extreme, the trees, plants, animals, and insects might take pity and provide warning or advice.

A plant with smaller ones of the same kind around was called "a mother and her children." A dead tree was called "an old lady with gray hair." Some plants were "brother," others were "sister." Accidentally killing a spider could lead to retaliation from other spiders. When Apaches accidentally stepped on a spider, they said "So-and-so killed you." During their later wars with the United States, whenever such a mishap occurred, Apache soldiers said "Washington did it."

## Full-blown Southwestern Farming

Beginning about three thousand years ago, casual agriculture was well established in the Mogollon highlands of the American Southwest. By then these farming people had become increasingly dependent upon agriculture for a significant proportion of their diet. About A.D. 200–700, southwestern ecology had changed forever—for both farmers and nonagriculturalists.

Committing to serious maize agriculture in an arid region requires strong incentives. The adoption of agriculture was hardly an inevitable process, and the archaeological record documents a two-thousand-year history of cycles of population expansion and contraction, growing population densities within limited areas that subsequently dispersed across the landscape. Sometimes such expansions succeeded, and stable farming societies lasted for centuries. Elsewhere, the experiment failed, and the land was temporarily abandoned.

But once agriculture took firm hold in the Southwest, elusive reliance on hunting and gathering was no longer a viable option. High-risk farming, by people showing ingenuity and remarkable technological skill, survived for millennia. This endurance is both an important lesson in itself and also a preamble to the achievements that were to follow.

Ceramics and agricultural crops arrived at different times from the Mexican southland. Together, they would greatly enhance an already rich Indian heritage in the Southwest. Archaeologists conventionally divide the late pre-contact period of the Southwest into three major cultures—the Mogollon, the Hohokam, and the Anasazi—each occupying a distinctive ecological niche within the mosaic of southwestern environments.

The Mogollon were highlanders, farming the forests and upland meadows along the Arizona–New Mexico border. They are best known as makers of the legendary Mimbres pottery. Painted with long brushes of yucca fibers, the intricate motifs range from complex geometric designs to stylized human forms, birds,

*Long ago when all the animals talked like people, Turkey overheard a boy begging his sister for food. "What does your little brother want?" he asked the girl. "He's hungry, but we have nothing to eat," she said.*

*When Turkey heard this, he shook himself all over. Many kinds of fruits and wild food dropped out of his body, and the brother and sister ate these up. Turkey shook himself again, and a variety of corn that is very large dropped out of his feathers. He shook himself a third time, and yellow corn dropped out. And when he shook himself for the fourth time, white corn dropped out.*

*Bear came over, and Turkey told him, "I'm helping to feed my sister and my brother, over there." Bear said, "You can shake only four times to make food come out of you, but I have every kind of food on me, from my feet to my head."*

*—White Mountain Apache Legend*

bats, bighorn sheep, rabbits, and insects. The earliest Mimbres pottery, dating from about A.D. 750 to 1000, is painted in the classic black-on-white tradition. Later pots, made between A.D. 1050 and 1200 employ polychrome designs, particularly blacks and reds. Mimbres pottery commonly accompanied the dead, and these pots were often "killed" with neat holes punched through the bottom, symbolically releasing the spirits of the painted figures.

The earlier Mogollon people lived in villages of randomly spaced pit houses. Through time, they shifted to above-ground apartmentlike structures. The Mogollon culture began a decline about 1100, reaching total eclipse by 1250.

In the scorching Sonoran desert to the west lived the Hohokam people. Archaeologists have been taught that these people migrated directly from Mexico about 300 B.C. But now, most think that the Hohokans developed from a local, nonagricultural base, about A.D. 200.

Either way, the Hohokam were accomplished desert-dwelling farmers who constructed hundreds of miles of irrigation canals throughout central Arizona. The modern city of Phoenix employs a canal system virtually superimposed on the early Hohokam plan for diverting water from the Salt River, a mute and unintentional tribute to the native American engineers who came before.

By about 1450, classic Hohokam culture had declined, perhaps due to drought or increased salinity of the soil. Many believe that the modern O'Odham (Pima and Papago) descended from the Hohokam pioneers.

Northward, in the high desert of the Colorado Plateau, was the homeland of the Anasazi, whose name derived from a Mexican word meaning "enemy ancestors." Although proto-Anasazi people lived in pit houses, between A.D. 700 and 1000 the Anasazi began constructing their distinctive multiroom apartment complexes that were to give their descendants, the Pueblo Indians, their name.

About A.D. 900, the Anasazi people of northwestern New Mexico generated a sustained burst of cultural energy. Today, this experience is best known as the Chaco Phenomenon.

*Painting Pottery* by Narda Lebo. The design motifs are precontact Mimbres.

OPPOSITE:
**Mimbres pot with a hole in the bottom to symbolically release the spirits of the painted figures. The Mimbres potters, a branch of the Mogollon people, used the ribbon or coil method in making their bowls, that is, rolling a long, thin strip of clay, coiling and braiding it layer on layer to the desired shape, then smoothing and burnishing it. When the pot was dried, coated, and reburnished, it was ready for painting with the highly developed and individual designs of the artist. Despite the simplicity of their materials and tools, the Mimbres potters achieved extraordinary degrees of delicacy and sophistication in their art.**

## The Chaco Phenomenon

Lieutenant James H. Simpson, surveyor for the U.S. Army, could not believe his eyes when he came upon the Chaco Canyon ruins in 1848. Nothing had prepared him for what he saw: hundreds of contiguous rooms of beautifully shaped and coursed stonework, three or four stories high, forming huge sweeping arcs. Within its thirty-odd square miles, the canyon contains more than 2,400 archaeological sites. Nine full-blown towns (the "Great Houses"), each containing hundreds of rooms, had grown up along a nine-mile stretch of Chaco Canyon.

Chaco Canyon was once home to a vanished civilization that intrigued and puzzled the European mind. Lieutenant Simpson believed that the ancestors of the Pueblo Indians could not possibly have constructed these massive towns. Dismissing Pueblo building techniques as too crude, Simpson called up the ancient Toltec tribes of Mexico as the architects of Pueblo Bonito and the other Great Houses. Over the years, others nominated additional candidates, including the Aztecs and even the Romans.

The sun, especially in the Southwest, was a significant factor in the lives of native people. All objects in the sky— the moon, the stars, the sun—were sacred. By careful observation and very precise, sophisticated measurement, celestial movements were used to mark the best times for planting and harvesting, to judge when to expect rainfall or major migrations of animals, or to set the dates for many important events. The sky gods, in a very real sense, managed the daily lives of the people.

The Anasazi constructed an ingenious seasonal "clock" in Chaco Canyon, based on sunrays striking particular points on a spiral. Similar spiral motifs appear incised on rocks in many places throughout the Southwest. The one pictured here is located near Tuba City, Arizona.

*The whole Southwest was a House Made of Dawn. It was made of pollen and of rain. The land was old and everlasting. There were many colors on the hills and on the plain, and there was a dark wilderness on the mountains beyond. The land was tilled and strong and it was beautiful all around.*

—Southwest Indian Song

Secret religious rites were commonly carried out in underground *kivas*. The Anasazi kiva probably developed out of the ancient residential pit house, which was eventually replaced with above-ground *pueblo* surface dwellings. Kivas are still in use by Pueblo Indians of New Mexico and Arizona.

OPPOSITE:

*The Roads to Chaco Canyon.*
Chaco Canyon (DETAIL), ten miles long, was the center of the Colorado Plateau civilization of the Anasazi. Four hundred miles of roads connected some seventy-five settlements, of which eight were located in the canyon. Each pueblo within the canyon was built with connecting walls of mortared sandstone, plastered with wet clay, and supported by beams carried from as far away as twenty-five miles.

The Chaco outliers, connected by the road system, used "Chaco core veneer" masonry: the load-bearing core consisted of flat stones set in mortar. The wall core was then covered on both sides with a veneer of coarse ashlar, often alternating bands of thick and thin stones, creating various striking patterns that emerged through the final adobe plastering or matting.

Modern generations no longer look south of the Mexican border to understand Chaco Canyon. Archaeologists now recognize that the people of Chaco Canyon belong to the home-grown Anasazi culture. Still, even after a century of mapping, collecting, photographing, and excavating in remote Chaco Canyon, archaeologists debate the many unanswered riddles.

*What did all those people eat?* Archaeologists now estimate that perhaps five thousand Anasazi people lived in Chaco in A.D. 1100. But, curiously, the canyon and its environs contain only enough arable land to feed two thousand.

*Where did they bury their dead?* Despite this huge precontact population and a century of intensive archaeological exploration, very few human burials have been found at Chaco. Perhaps they disposed of their dead in some other way, possibly conveying them to an undiscovered area a good distance from the canyon, where they might have been exposed.

*Why are the Chaco ruins so rich?* For decades, archaeologists have found exotic turquoise, as well as copper bells and colorful parrots from Mexico, and seashells from the Pacific. We can see that, on the average, Chaco families used up maybe 17 ceramic vessels every year. But at one Chaco pueblo, Pueblo Alto, a single trash heap contained 150,000 broken pots. Could it be that some families destroyed 125 pots each year? Why so many pots? Where did all that pottery come from?

*Why did the Chaco people build arrow-straight roads running hundreds of miles into the surrounding desert?* Archaeologists poring over satellite-produced infrared photographs have recently discovered an elaborate road system covering more than a hundred thousand square miles. Why are the roads are so wide, so straight? What were they were used for?

This is the Chaco Phenomenon: large planned towns next to haphazard villages; extensive roadways built by people who relied on neither wheeled vehicles nor draft animals; a people affluent enough to import luxury items by the thou-

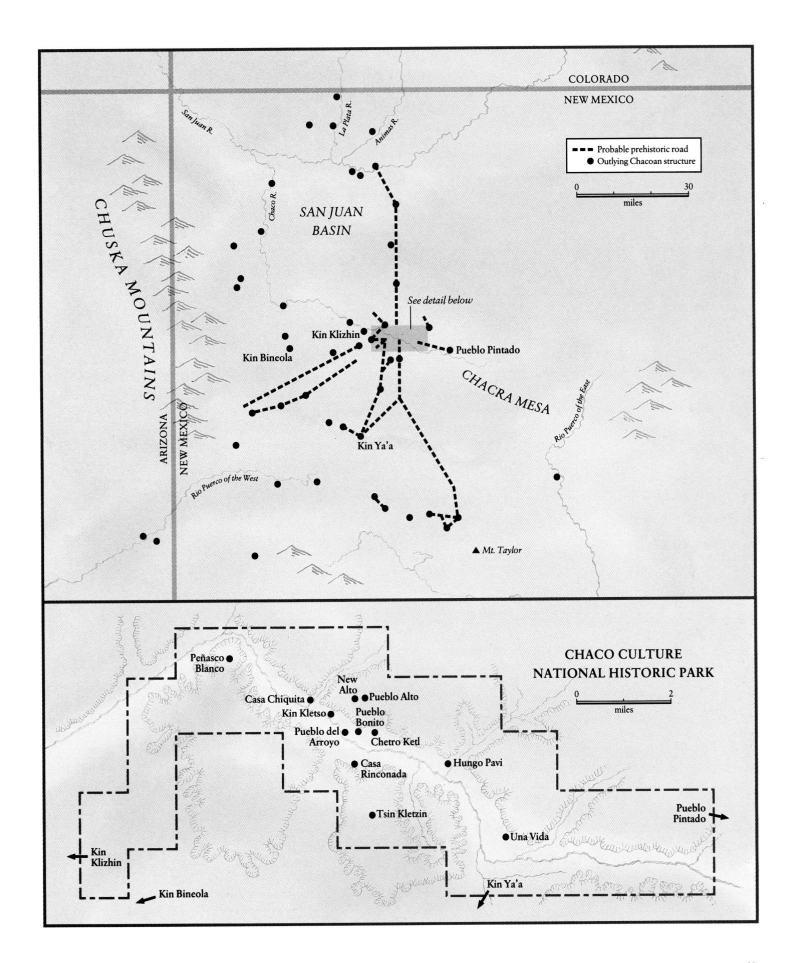

COLORADO

NEW MEXICO

San Juan R.

La Plata R.

Animas R.

Chaco R.

SAN JUAN
BASIN

Probable prehistoric road
Outlying Chacoan structure

0                    30
miles

C
H
U
S
K
A

M
O
U
N
T
A
I
N
S

See detail below

Kin Klizhin

Kin Bineola

Pueblo Pintado

CHACRA MESA

Rio Puerco of the East

ARIZONA

NEW MEXICO

Kin Ya'a

Rio Puerco of the West

▲ Mt. Taylor

CHACO CULTURE
NATIONAL HISTORIC PARK

Peñasco
Blanco

New
Alto

0                    2
miles

Casa Chiquita

Pueblo Alto

Kin Kletso

Pueblo
Bonito

Pueblo del
Arroyo

Chetro Ketl

Casa
Rinconada

Hungo Pavi

Pueblo
Pintado

Tsin Kletzin

Una Vida

Kin
Klizhin

Kin Ya'a

Kin Bineola

sands, who simply packed up and moved elsewhere about A.D. 1150.

Chaco Canyon was a very unusual place. Maybe it was exclusively a ceremonial and commercial center where only a ritual hierarchy lived. A thousand years ago, the Chacoan people defined themselves as somehow special. The key to spiritual and economic good fortune, they said, was turquoise. In the turquoise-based Chacoan economy, the future belonged to those who acquired raw turquoise ore and could process it into finished jewelry and other ritual necessities.

Towns that could control and manipulate the turquoise trade were soon able to amass capital. Chaco people started banking their prosperity, storing up resources, and carefully redistributing them to other places under their domain. Before long, Chaco became the place to be. A ritual hierarchy took over. Social distinctions began to separate the people living in Great Houses from the commoners who lived in scattered villages.

By the early eleventh century, the cult of turquoise had spread across a huge regional network. Over time, key Chacoan towns tightened their grip on the primary turquoise source at Cerrillos (near present-day Santa Fe). Distinctive black-on-white pottery and trendy architectural styles joined turquoise as symbols of Chaco's economic and spiritual dominance over the Pueblo world.

Throughout this first century, perhaps two thousand people made Chaco Canyon their home on a permanent year-round basis. But a room-by-room analysis shows that the Chacoan towns could have readily housed three times that number. Curious.

During this golden age, the human population of Chaco Canyon seems to have fluctuated dramatically. Floods of relatives showed up in Chaco Canyon during the so-called pilgrimage fairs, when Chacoan people from the hinterlands would periodically visit the canyon to trade for turquoise, which had become increasingly important in their ritual and ceremonial lives.

So long as Chaco controlled the turquoise trade, its people were protected against localized agricultural failures. Turquoise was a liquid asset. In good years, you brought extra food on the pilgrimage, and maybe reaped a rich harvest of turquoise, macaws, or copper bells. But if your local community was drought-stricken, and you came to the pilgrimage festival hungry, you could trade off some of your working capital, exchanging turquoise wealth for more immediate needs, like food for your clan.

These formalized trade fairs were scheduled well in advance. Both production and distribution of goods were carefully timed to anticipate the next festival. Although people came from throughout the land, primed to trade their goods and services, they were all identified as Chacoan people. The festivals reinforced this common bond with rituals of belonging. As time passed, more pilgrims showed up at the fairs, as spiritual and economic ties bound them more tightly into the Chacoan sphere.

Maybe these pilgrimage fairs explain the extensive number of pots destroyed at Pueblo Alto atop the rim of Chaco Canyon. Maybe these were dishes brought in by nonresidents, who destroyed their pottery after feasting.

How did all these people get to Chaco Canyon? By the newly discovered

ABOVE AND OPPOSITE:
**Examples of early native American turquoise art.**

roadways, of course. The entire Chacoan system was physically integrated by an infrastructure of roads that spread across three states. Aerial photographs reveal more than four hundred miles of ancient roadways radiating out from Chaco Canyon, appearing as narrow, dark lines running through the surrounding landscape. Sometimes not visible at ground level, the roads are merely shallow, concave depressions only a couple of inches deep, twenty-five to thirty-five feet wide, littered with potsherds. They often turn with sudden, angular, dogleg jogs and are occasionally edged by low rock berms.

The longest and best-defined roads, probably constructed between A.D. 1075 and 1140, extend more than fifty miles. In places the Chacoans constructed causeways, and elsewhere they cut stairways into sheer cliffs. The generally straight bearings suggest that all these arteries were laid out, "engineered," prior to construction, although nobody understands how this was done.

Perhaps the well-built Chaco roads operated like a lowercase version of the amazing Inka road system that spanned the twelve thousand miles from Ecuador to Chile. Like the Inka roads, the Chacoan roads could have served for communication as well as transport. Several related mesa-top signal stations have been found near Chaco that provided for line-of-sight communication—presumably by smoke, fire, or reflected light.

In both cases, the roads tied far-flung regions together, moving the goods and people required to build and maintain extensive public works. The Inka roads were manned with messenger-runners, who waited at frequent intervals to carry important messages from the capital to the hinterlands. Officials and bureaucrats could move along the public roads to inspect, to coordinate, and to supervise. Roads became narrower as they passed through valuable agricultural lands and over steep slopes, but they widened out in the flats. There, the roads were much wider than necessary for the traffic they carried.

At least in the Inka case, the road system assumed a symbolic importance far beyond that of today's highways. The roads themselves became symbols of authority, linear banners proclaiming affinity and cooperation, signifying participation in a system whose importance exceeded the mere sum of its parts.

As communication became easier and the trade fairs prospered, the Chaco elite began to regulate the outlying participants. Red tape intensified, but the benefits of a broadly shared religious base outbalanced the bureaucratic burden. Increasingly, the roads defined one's place in the world. Cooperation has always been a major fact of Pueblo life. As the people of Taos pueblo say, "We are in one nest." Everyone united by these vital arteries became part of a larger whole, linked by a common religion and economy that provided for all within its sweep.

Many of the rituals of Chaco religion took place in the sunlit pueblo plazas like those at Pueblo Bonito. Others were played out below ground, in the cylindrical kivas that still penetrate the pueblo buildings. The kiva is an earthly representation of the original, primordial homeland, built in darkness underwater. Into this, the ultimate cave, Chaco people descended by ladder through the smokehole. Set into the ground was the round, shallow, navel-like *sipapu*, symbolic of

The sun-baked ruins of a mission church, pueblo adobes, and a kiva located in the Pecos National Monument, New Mexico.

Kivas originated as pit houses dug into the earth for added shelter and safe storage. Their circular shape eventually took on sacred meaning: the emergence of life from earth.

The word *kiva* means "world below," and the ladder that men climbed to reach the roof opening was symbolic of life emerging from the Earth Mother.

the place where the Corn Mothers emerged from the earth, assuring spiritual access to still another world deep below.

Kivas reflect the Pueblo belief that people emerged from a previous world into this one, and this process was symbolically reenacted as the Chacoans came from the kiva into full view of the plaza. Ritual derived its power from its degree of secrecy. Gradually, from initial induction into Pueblo secret societies to the growing obligations of later adult life, the mysteries of belief were revealed.

Kivas are an omnipresent part of the contemporary Puebloan world. But the Great Kivas of the Chaco towns and their outliers were special. Each Chacoan town had a Great Kiva, and several others are found up and down the canyon. The Great Kiva at Chetro Ketl, just down the road from Pueblo Bonito, is more than fifty feet in diameter. Its great curving walls held special niches, each filled with strings of stone and shell beads, then sealed with masonry. There is the encircling bench, the central raised square firebox, the paired rectangular masonry "vaults," and the stair entryway. Massive sandstone disks supported equally huge roof-support timbers, carried, by hand from mountains forty miles away.

Although the smaller kivas served the local clans, the Great Kivas involved larger social units—perhaps half an entire pueblo. And the largest of these may have nurtured the town as a whole. Centrally placed for all to see, the greatest of the Great Kivas dominated all directions. So built, the Great Kivas required that ritual extend beyond the human scale to the natural world beyond.

## PASSIVE SOLAR ENGINEERING AT PUEBLO BONITO

The major terminus of the Chacoan roads was Pueblo Bonito (Beautiful Town), once reaching five stories into the sky. It could house a thousand people. America would not witness a larger apartment building until the Industrial Revolution of the nineteenth century.

But Pueblo Bonito is far more than a trade and ceremonial center. It is a deliberately designed temple to honor the sun. An impressive assemblage of ceremonial painted wooden artifacts has been recovered from Pueblo Bonito, recalling a rich theatrical and artistic tradition. Similar headdresses, bird-shaped puppets, and costume elements still function today in modern Pueblo ceremony.

Pueblo Bonito is a huge amphitheater, its stage surrounded by curving rows of seats too big for people. It is a theater scaled for gods. The huge curving apartment house was stepped in terraces, surrounded by a high wall defining the north, east, and west boundaries. These terraces descend toward the center into two main courts, separated by buildings and wall arrangements. Here, the rhythmic seasonal and daily changes in lighting emphasized Bonito's distinctive architectural form.

The principles of passive solar heating, of considerable interest today, were obviously familiar to the architects of Pueblo Bonito. They fine-tuned the basics of classic pueblo design to provide additional comfort. In summer, the sun beats down mostly on horizontal surfaces, which store little of the incoming solar energy. But in the winter, the sunlight strikes vertical surfaces, which retain and store heat, radiating it into the interior spaces during cold winter days. Pueblo Bonito collected solar heat, from first light to the end of each winter day.

Terraces started warming only a few minutes after the sun broke over the eastern horizon. The center of the pueblo was warmed toward midday, and the eastward part heated up late in the afternoon.

Shadows shift daily from east to west. But north–south shadowing of Pueblo Bonito varies by season. Each courtyard is segmented into spotlighted areas, where rituals took place at different locations in the courtyards, depending upon time of day and year. Morning dances took place in the glaring light of the western part of each court; evening performances were staged eastward. Summer celebrations took place in the southern portions of the court, while winter observances shifted north to gain exposure from the sun. Similar rituals occur today on the terraces and in the courtyards of modern pueblos.

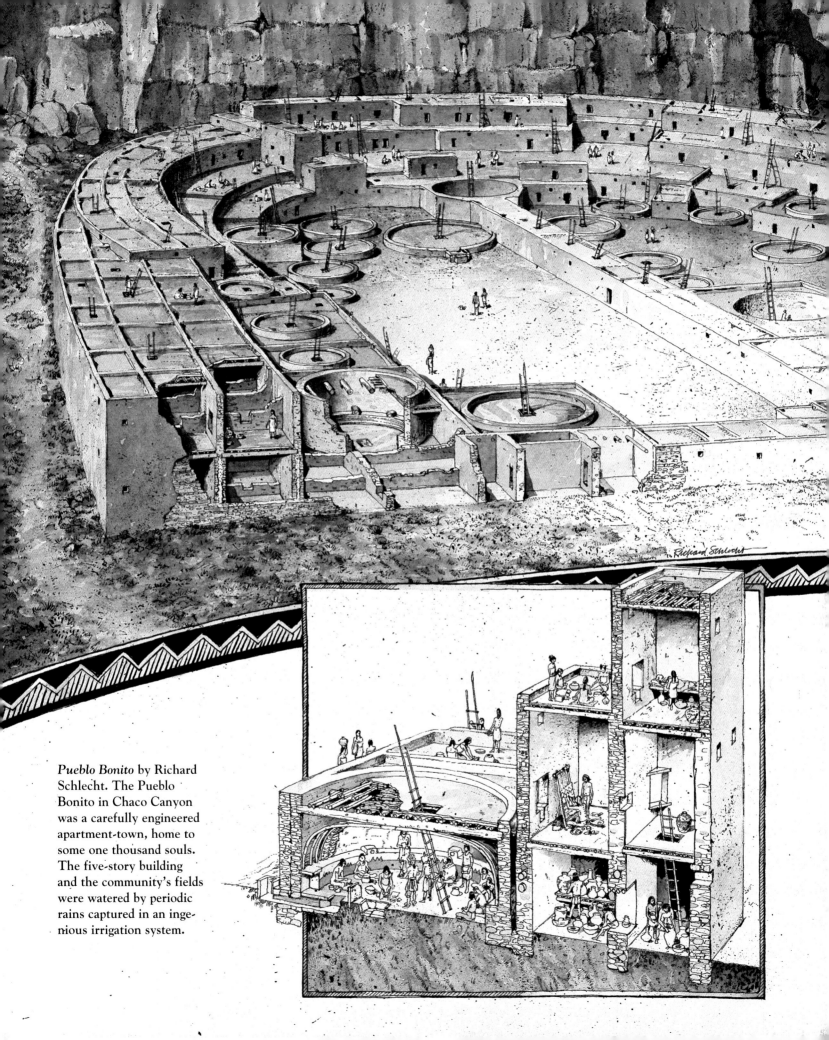

*Pueblo Bonito* by Richard Schlecht. The Pueblo Bonito in Chaco Canyon was a carefully engineered apartment-town, home to some one thousand souls. The five-story building and the community's fields were watered by periodic rains captured in an ingenious irrigation system.

The Hyde Expedition, conducted during the late 1890s, was the first of several scientific excavations in Pueblo Bonito and Chaco Canyon.

The shadowy figures of the Chaco Anasazi populated the sweeping landscape they created for centuries. They developed one of the most progressive and prosperous social systems in precontact North America, perhaps more socially stratified and more hierarchically organized than that of their modern Pueblo descendants. Through their ritual and economic networks, dozens of formerly autonomous communities pooled their strengths, reducing the possibility that any one of them would suffer natural or economic disaster in their precarious high-risk environment.

Then came the end. Beginning about A.D. 1130, a series of severe droughts afflicted the Chacoan landscape. For the next fifty years, the life-giving summer rains stayed away. As the Chaco world dried up, people naturally intensified their efforts to extract yet more from the earth and sky. Water was channeled into

Chaco Canyon from greater distances, and the Great Kiva ceremonies began to spill out into a larger external space. Rooftop ritual called out to still greater distances. Increasing numbers of the community were drawn into the web of concern about the destruction of their known world. As our own modern globe warms up, we are responding in very similar ways.

The Chacoan lifestyle was threatened. Who could eat turquoise? Fewer and fewer people trekked the sacred roads to Chaco. Why should they? What did they have to trade? The bottom dropped out of the turquoise market as everyone tried to pawn turquoise bangles for maize and beans. More and more, Chaco Canyon became a poor place to venerate. By the early twelfth century, the ritual center of gravity had shifted northward, toward the San Juan River.

Real estate boomed in the Chacoan suburbs, particularly in places with better local climates. But choice property was scarce in the twelfth century, and good lots commanded premium prices. There was tremendous competition for prime land, and Pueblo people started fortifying and protecting their villages.

During the Chacoan heyday, northwestern New Mexico had become supersaturated with Pueblo people. The combination of favorable climate, sought-after commodities, and religious piety drew families and clans from far away. When the climate went sour and the Chacoan system collapsed, some may have returned to their ancient homelands—hoping that their blood ties were strong enough for them to be allowed to return.

But if you held no prime property, and you had no distant relatives to take you in, maybe you gave up full-time farming to take up the more mobile, more flexible lifestyle of hunting and gathering wild plant foods.

The Chaco system worked wonderfully for 150 years, as long as summer rainfall was good throughout the region. But when the five-decade drought struck—and nobody showed up at Chaco with surplus food—the system disintegrated.

Ritual pilgrimages might have continued for a while, but Chaco was no longer viable. Lacking summer rainfall, Pueblo Bonito and the other towns began to fade away. New construction ceased, and people quit the canyon entirely by the middle of the twelfth century.

But the Chaco people did not die out. There was no violence or mass suicide. The Chaco towns were evacuated in orderly fashion. Most of the useful material goods were taken along. Chaco people simply reorganized, shifting their social and religious priorities to meet the challenges of survival in their new world order.

Modern Pueblo people know that the Anasazi left Chaco because the serpent deity, the one in charge of rain and fertility, mysteriously left them. Helpless without their god, the people followed the snake's trail until they reached a river where they built houses once again. Four centuries later, the incursions of the Spanish explorers were observed by fifty thousand Pueblo people living in more than a hundred towns along the margins of the San Juan Basin and the Rio Grande drainage, descendants of these same people.

**A typical assortment of vessels unearthed by the hundreds from Pueblo Bonito in the late 1890s.**

# CHAPTER FIVE

# LIFE OF THE PLAINS AND WOODLANDS

COPPER FALCON
FROM A MISSISSIPPIAN BURIAL MOUND

PICK UP ANY TRADITIONAL TEXTBOOK on "Western civilization," and it will tell you that agriculture originated independently in three places: wheat farming in the Fertile Crescent of the Near East, rice cultivation in Southeast Asia, and domestication of maize in highland Mexico. It would be remarkable, indeed, if farming had been invented independently at three different times, in three different places.

However, the textbooks have it wrong. Archaeologists have just discovered a *fourth* localized center of plant domestication, entirely separate from the others. It is in northeastern America. Although early explorers recorded extensive maize agriculture throughout the Eastern Woodlands, full-blown maize agriculture developed there only five centuries before the Europeans themselves arrived.

The agricultural roots of native American society run much deeper. We now understand that over the past four thousand years, the transition from foraging to farming along the rivers of the Eastern Woodlands involved three key steps. First came the domestication of native North American seed plants about 2000 B.C. Then, between 250 B.C. and A.D. 100, food production economies emerged based on these local crops. Finally, maize was introduced, and, between about A.D. 800 and 1100, the role of maize changed from minor use to major crop.

This still-unfolding story is yet another example of native American ingenuity and enterprise. Here is how their unique way of life came to be.

---

OPPOSITE:
*Hopewell Harvest* by Merlin Little Thunder (Southern Cheyenne), 1993.

## Evolving Economy, Evolving Society

*Sunflower*

The Eastern Woodlands—millions of acres of primeval forests cut by countless coursing "river roads"—hosted native American people speaking at least sixty-eight distinct languages. From the Micmac of Maine to the Calusa of south Florida, the Woodlands were home to people for at least ten thousand years and perhaps much longer.

The first Americans living in the Eastern Woodlands made stone tools similar to those used by Great Plains people, but eastern Paleo-Indians were not big-game hunters. Sticking close to the major river valleys, they systematically moved from one part of their home range to another, taking advantage of the seasonal availability of grasses, fruits, nuts, fish, and game. Their broad-spectrum adaptation spread out the risk and buffered people against the failure of any particular plant or animal species. This generalized ecological adaptation was to gain them a head start toward the more intensive gathering economies evident in later periods. As their population increased, Eastern Woodland people became more efficient, intensifying their economic exchanges with others, and improving their ability to store food for the future. They learned to protect themselves against year-to-year fluctuations in resources.

The earliest true pottery in North America appears about 2500 B.C. in coastal and riverine Georgia, unassociated with any archaeologically visible trace of agriculture. In this simple pottery tradition, organic fibers were added to the clay to keep vessels from cracking when fired. Some of the round bowls were adorned with drag-and-jab decoration.

Inevitably, some people harvested and produced more food than their neighbors. Others excelled at trade and barter. With time, only a few very important people seemed to have access to the more valued, "exotic" items. In response to growing competition over scarce resources, the older, more egalitarian social structures became more rigid and controlled. Grave goods reflected this increased disparity in social status.

*Sumpweed*

Look what happened at Poverty Point, the spectacular archaeological site in northeastern Louisiana. Sometime after about 1300 B.C., native people began constructing a large bird-shaped earthwork, about seventy-five feet high. Not far away were massive geometrical earthworks of six concentric ridges—probably used as dwelling sites—with an outer perimeter extending two-thirds of a mile. Millions of cubic feet of earth were required to build these earthen features.

The people of Poverty Point participated in far-flung exchange networks, trading for native copper and a wide range of stone resources. They did not make pottery, so most of their cooking took place in baskets. Usually, it was a simple matter for native Americans to boil water in a basket: Californians simply heated up some stones and dropped them in. But Poverty Point was built on alluvial soil, which lacked the stones commonly used for boiling and for baking. Poverty Point people cleverly solved this problem by using "artificial stones": These were actually ingeniously crafted and decorated clay balls.

Poverty Point remains an enigma. Despite the massive earthworks, which suggest the existence of a major ceremonial area, its material culture does not differ greatly from that at other contemporary sites. Some evidence suggests that Poverty Point groups might have cultivated small garden plots of bottle gourd and squash, both for use as containers and for their edible seeds. Whatever the dietary basis, the Poverty Point center was eventually abandoned, and nearly a thousand years passed before North America again saw such elaborate ceremonial spaces.

## Part-time Woodland Farmers

Poverty Point is compelling because it foreshadowed the creativity soon evident elsewhere in the East. Earlier, by about 4000 B.C., the climate had changed, and many river valley environments in the region became richer. Shoals and lakes developed, and the abundance of wild seed plants, shellfish, fish, and animals such as deer and raccoon encouraged people to settle down in permanent river valley settlements. Men hunted, women collected wild plants; shellfish, so abundant in the shallow waters, were available to all.

*Squash*

Over the years, these permanent settlements—a few families or more— became laboratories for experimenting with plant domestication. For thousands of years, women had collected the wild plants of the river valleys and uplands. While fathers passed on the secrets of stalking white-tailed deer, mothers and daughters learned about the complex mosaic of available wild food plants.

For countless generations they had studied the life cycles and habits of the nut trees and seed plants so important to them; now, in the rich soils of their permanent settlements, the women had begun the great experiments that would produce domesticated plants. Perhaps they tried many plants, but in the end, it was weeds from the floodplains that worked. Sunflower and its distant cousins, marsh elder, goosefoot, and a wild gourd—ancestor of the summer squashes— became success stories. These aggressive, weedy plants, colonizers of the areas swept clean by spring floodwaters, all produced highly nutritious seeds, and were important wild foods. They thrived on the rich soils of human settlements, providing experimental plots for early attempts to increase yield and dependability. These seed crops, deliberately planted for at least four thousand years, began providing a dependable, managed food supply that could be stored for late winter use and even into early spring.

## Hopewell Lifeways

Then came the so-called Hopewell period, named after a huge Ohio mound excavated in the nineteenth century. From about 200 B.C. to A.D. 500, people of

## AMERICA'S FIRST FARMER

Geneticists tell us that plants grow best in disturbed soil such as the pits, mounds, and middens surrounding Indian campsites; these became home to the weedy species, which turned into America's earliest cultivated and domesticated foods.

But who was the first actually to disturb the soil and introduce seeds into it? Who was America's first geneticist? America's first farmer?

Many will be surprised to learn that—accidentally or deliberately—it was the hand of woman that first domesticated the plants of the Eastern Woodlands. Throughout native America, it was always the woman who retained the botanical information. She knew exactly what plants to feed her family. She knew what plants made the best clothing and dyes, and when to harvest materials for making cordage and weaving textiles. She knew which leaves, bark, roots, stems, and berries could cure disease.

And through the centuries to come, it would be the woman who would plant the seeds, tend the garden, harvest the bounty, and prepare the meal. Because she enjoyed a corner on botanical knowledge, she was the one to harness the potential of domesticated plants. For the next hundred generations, she would support thousands of people every year.

Why did she do it? Did she realize the significance of her contributions to those who would follow? Was she curious, or simply anxious to experiment in order to meet the immediate needs of family and kin? Or was there some religious significance attached to providing bounty from the earth? We may never know the whole answer.

But we do know that she was America's first farmer, at least in the eastern sector of the continent.

the Eastern Woodlands continued to build impressive earthworks and bury their dead in conical mortuary mounds. Neither a particular culture nor a political power, Hopewell became the first North American pan-Indian religion, stretching from Mississippi to Minnesota, from Missouri to West Virginia. For the first time, people sharing neither language nor culture were drawn together by a set of beliefs and symbols. For centuries, Hopewell reigned as the dominant force across eastern North America.

Because both burial mounds and plant domestication had occurred earlier in Mexico, archaeologists long believed that mound building and agriculture must have arrived in the Southeast as a package from elsewhere. And, for years, most archaeologists talked of Hopewell economics strictly in terms of growing maize. But archaeology has now gone high-tech, and we have learned that the Hopewell produced a great diversity of locally cultivated and domesticated foods long before Mother Corn arrived, about A.D. 100 or so. There is no direct evidence that any group ever moved from Mexico into the Southeast. Maize and beans arrived in the East at different times, apparently from the Southwest. Direct introduction from Mexico of either item is unlikely.

These new insights are important because they demonstrate that imported Mexican corn neither precipitated the development of Hopewellian society nor a rapid shift toward agriculture in eastern North America. For centuries, maize was only a minor, almost invisible addition to already well-established food-producing economies. The extraordinary Hopewellian accomplishments in agricultural, religious, and belief systems resulted from homegrown ingenuity and inventiveness, reflecting indigenous human experience spanning millennia.

But how, precisely, did such a remarkable agricultural system evolve? Utilization of particular plant crops was extremely localized, depending on the area's ecological circumstances. In some places, foragers relying very little on cultivated plants also persisted. But generally the broad mid-latitude riverine zone—stretching from the Appalachian wall west to the prairie margin—became a homeland to these early food-producing societies cultivating several high-yield, highly nutritious local crops.

These native people grew not only squash, marsh elder, sunflower, and goosefoot, but also erect knotweed, little barley, and maygrass. Modern experiments demonstrate the previously unappreciated economic potential of these indigenous eastern North American crop plants, whose harvest yields compare to those of the various European wheats cultivated during the nineteenth century.

From such modest beginnings, people and plants came to interact so intensively that some human groups began reoccupying selected sites simply because the domesticated and cultivated plants grew better there. By 200 B.C. horticultural experimentation had reached a critical threshold of productivity and flexibility. From about A.D. 1 to 200, Hopewellian habitation sites remained small, generally one- to three-household settlements dispersed along stream and river valley corridors. In segments of some protein-rich floodplain lakes and marshes—such as the lower Illinois River—small household settlements formed loose spatial concentrations that can appropriately be termed "villages," even though they lack any suggestion of an overall community plan.

The broad-spectrum and flexible pre-maize economies of these household

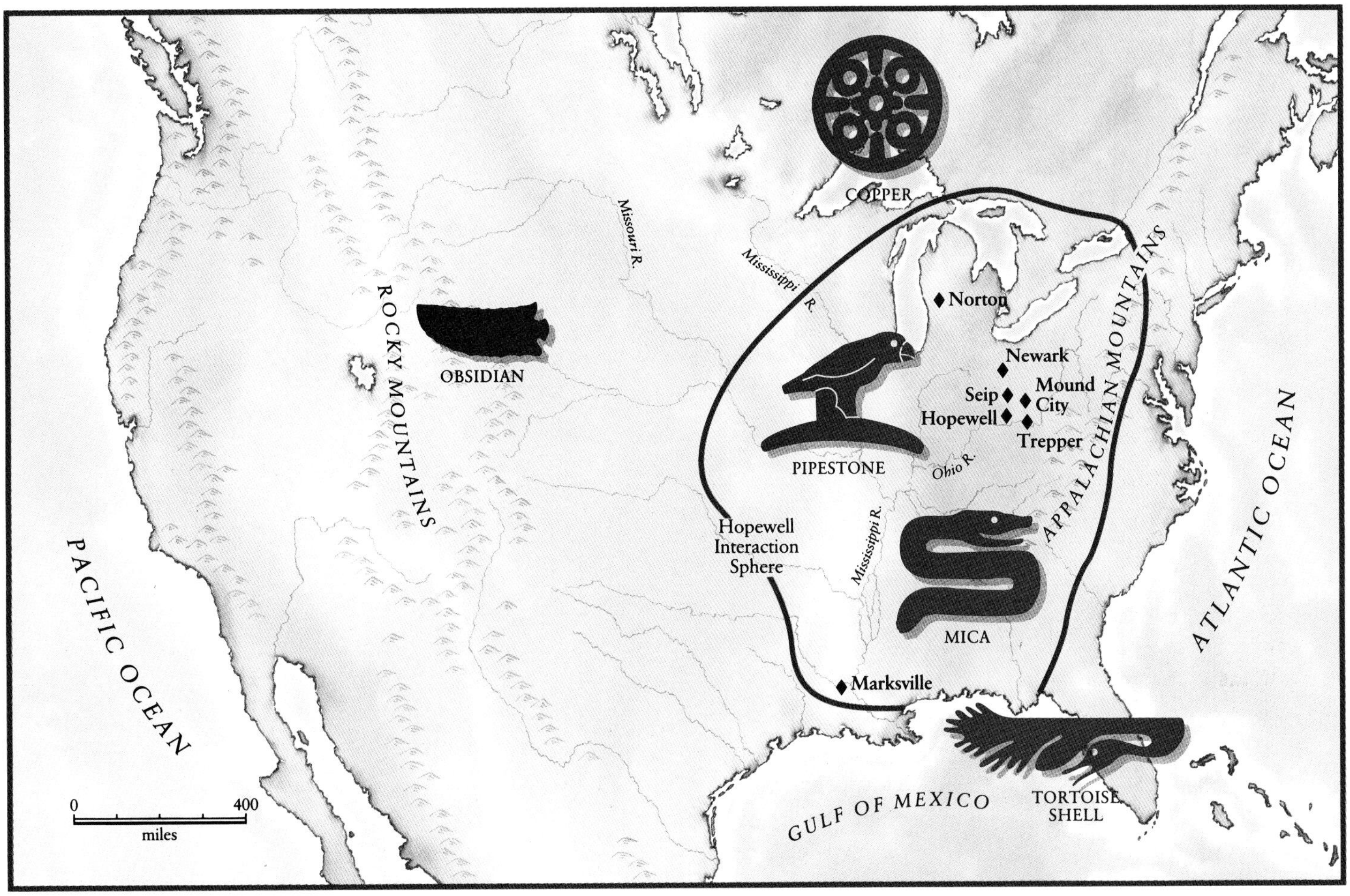
COPPER
OBSIDIAN
ROCKY MOUNTAINS
Missouri R.
Mississippi R.
Norton
Newark
Seip
Mound City
Hopewell
Trepper
PIPESTONE
Ohio R.
Hopewell Interaction Sphere
Mississippi R.
APPALACHIAN MOUNTAINS
MICA
Marksville
PACIFIC OCEAN
ATLANTIC OCEAN
GULF OF MEXICO
TORTOISE SHELL
0
400
miles

units also demonstrate the degree to which production of storable food harvests was simply overlaid on an already successful foraging pattern. The domesticates simply provided a hedge against potential food shortages. There was, in short, no wholesale replacement of the earlier hunting and gathering ecology.

Nevertheless, as Hopewellian societies began to increase the boundaries of their river valley fields, their horizons expanded dramatically in other ways. Across the Eastern Woodlands, small farming settlements became focused on centrally located ceremonial sites, where various rites of social integration took place. Today, the only visible clue to the location of such special areas are the low earthen domes that were built up over the graves of revered persons.

Although we know about such sites largely because of the mortuary activities they housed, they were not just places of death. These centers were also the scenes of lavish Hopewellian feasts and other celebrations that brought together families scattered across the countryside. Along the rivers of northern Mississippi and northern Alabama, people built and maintained flat-topped earthen mounds that elevated the ceremonial above the everyday world; these mounds foreshadowed the later and much larger Mississippian pyramids. Elsewhere, earthen embankments, often of great size and planned with remarkable engineering skill, surrounded such ceremonial areas, setting them apart. In south-central Ohio, elaborate earthen banks extended for hundreds of yards, forming octagons, circles, and squares, both defining and protecting these sacred sites.

***The Hopewell Sphere of Interaction.*** **For nearly five hundred years, the Hopewell people dominated the Midwest from their Ohio homeland. The so-called Hopewell interaction sphere provided these skilled artisans with raw materials gathered from half the continent, including copper from the Great Lakes, tortoise shell from the Gulf of Mexico, and mica from North Carolina for making elaborate ornaments; pipestone from Ohio for fashioning pipes and other objects; and obsidian quarried in Yellowstone and knapped to create points and blades for both everyday and ritual uses.**

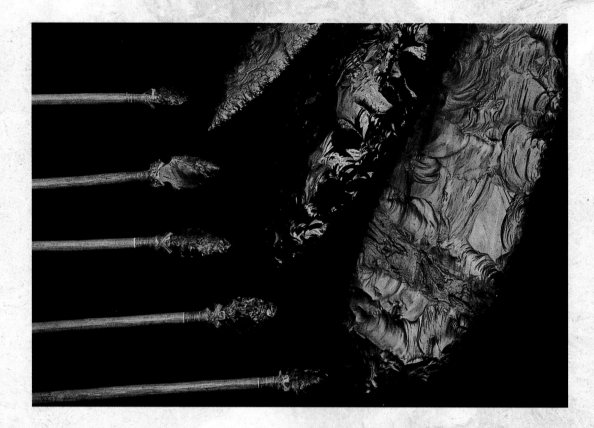

Mining a source deep in Yellowstone, the Hopewell people exchanged volcanic glass–obsidian–far eastward. Why so much effort for some bits of black glass?

To understand the value placed on volcanic glass by the first Americans, many archaeologists have tried their hands at flintknapping–chipping hand-held stone with a hammer or another stone to create flint weapons and tools. In his fifty years of flintknapping, the Master, Don Crabtree, has slashed himself in about every conceivable way: across his fingers, through the palm, through a fingernail—one flake zipped right through his shoe. One day, while surveying the carnage, he noted that, whereas he still had epic scars from jagged-edged flint flakes, the wounds caused by obsidian had healed quickly and were almost invisible. He wondered about that.

Then he saw a friend slice himself while handling some obsidian artifacts Crabtree had just made. The gash bled profusely, and a physician was summoned. But by the time the doctor arrived, some twenty minutes later, the wound had already begun to heal.

A curious soul, Crabtree decided to use an electron microscope to compare some of his obsidian flakes with the sharpest razor blades. His observations included the following: "The *platinum plus* razor blade is the sharpest thing man has ever developed, far sharper than the old surgeon's scalpel. But this razor [blade] had a rounded edge at about 750 diameters. Still the obsidian blade is far sharper even at 10,000 diameters. That *platinum plus* may be like an aerial view of west Kansas, you know—pretty nearly flat. But the obsidian blade can be magnified so many thousand times more and still have been sharp. It fractures right to the last molecule of the matter." What

he seems to be saying is that the obsidian edge is so thin that it virtually slips between the cells of skin and flesh.

Subsequently, obsidian was used experimentally (and with great success) in modern surgery. Obsidian blades are as sharp as the newest diamond scalpels, which, in turn, are one hundred to three hundred times sharper than steel blades. Experiments showed that the size of the steel cut was not only much larger than the glass cut but also very irregular. Moreover, the steel blade caused considerable tissue translocation, drawing "hamburgerized" tissue into the incision area.

Such medical research cannot proceed without the hands-on assistance of flintknapping archaeologists, for somebody must still be skilled enough to create the blades in the first place. Perhaps there is yet a place for such ancient Indian skills.

The ritual focus points not only witnessed the gathering of dispersed Hopewellian families, they also provided public meeting grounds for representatives of distant Hopewellian societies. Each such community must certainly have been self-sustaining, each possibly having its own language and divergent worldview. Yet these disparate societies, separated by many weeks of travel time, were linked into complex webs of communication and exchange. Evidence of this connection of people and materials takes the form of exquisite works of art, usually quite small, formed out of often exotic materials carried over great distances. Volcanic glass from Yellowstone was carried to Ohio. Silver from Ontario was transported to Mississippi. Copper from the Great Lakes, mica from North Carolina, shells and sharks' teeth from the Gulf, meteoric iron from Kansas—all these, and more, were transformed into beautiful objects, then exchanged across the East.

Hopewellian people cared deeply about their ancestors, and such objects of wonder in most cases accompanied the departed ancestors to the afterworld. Their presence in such large quantities and in such a diversity of sites argues that the Hopewell, if not the first, was certainly among the earliest of large-scale trade networks established in precontact North America.

## Enigmatic Effigy Mounds

Gradually, the attitudes toward the ancestors began to change. Although the Hopewell world view still flourished, people stopped trading for long-distance riches to deposit in graves. They decided to save their precious copper and obsidian to fashion into tools for the living. No longer crafting decorations for the dead, they venerated their ancestors with awesome monuments. Huge earthen likenesses of oversized bears, birds, and serpents began to appear across the northeastern landscape.

At the ancient mounds near McGregor, Iowa, on high ground bypassed by the Ice Age glaciers, ancient Americans built two hundred massive mounds. Some are geometric cones and ridges. But the most impressive are the huge birds and the Marching Bears. Today, twenty-seven such effigy mounds survive along the Iowa–Wisconsin state border.

Why were they built? Why here? What do they mean?

We have no answer, but there are some clues.

Native Americans have always lived close to the heavens, paying attention to what was overhead and intertwining their lives with the perpetual cycles of sun, moon, planets, and stars. They observed eclipses and the conjunctions of planets, devised calendars for festivals, and established dates for planting. All this was vital knowledge.

Today's astronomers capture this wisdom in books and scientific journals. Ancient Americans did the same thing in their folk stories, myths, elaborate rituals and festivals, symbolic architecture, dance, and costume. The Anasazi have left us their sacred spaces, the organized rocks of architecture, and markings on canyon walls as records of their astronomy. In the Eastern Woodlands, we have the effigy mounds.

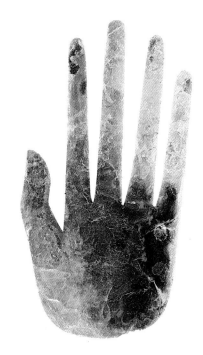

The Hopewell Hand. Carved of mica and discovered at the Hopewell Indian Mounds in Ohio. Hopewell people were also fine metalworkers in copper, and, occasionally, in silver and gold. Their gravesites have yielded exquisite carvings of stone, wood, and bone, along with fine pottery. The most elaborate earthwork, located in present-day Newark, Ohio, occupied several square miles and included avenues, plazas, burial mounds, and a two-and-a-half mile corridor stretching to the Licking River.

OVERLEAF:
*Building the Serpent Mound* by Greg Harlin. For the Hopi, the Great Horned Serpent had udders, "conforming to the legend that all the blood and water from the Earth came from the breast of the Great Serpent."

The Lightning Snake also rules terrestrial waters—vital to people in a dry landscape. In late summer, many Pueblos dance with live rattlesnakes, which are then released into the desert to carry the prayers of those in need of water.

And the snake can punish, particularly when sexual misconduct is involved.

## THE VENERABLE SERPENT OF OHIO

The most mystifying of all the mounds may be the strange serpent mound constructed two hundred generations ago near Chillicothe, Ohio. The people first marked the outline of a monstrous snake nearly one-quarter of a mile long with small stones and lumps of clay. Then they dug up tons of yellow clay, piled it into burden baskets, and buried their markers.

The result is a flawlessly modeled serpent, wriggling northward, mouth agape, trying to swallow a massive egg. Although ancestors were buried nearby, the serpent mound was itself a deliberate religious effigy, not a place of burial.

It is pure art. It still amazes. It still has power. But why was it built? And what does it mean?

The serpent has always been the most mysterious of all the creatures. Alone among the animals, it is swift without feet, fins, or wings. The snake sheds its skin every spring. To many, it symbolizes the annual renewal of life. For many Indian people, the cast-off snakeskin has the power to cure and heal.

The rattlesnake is slow to attack, but venomous in the extreme. It is like lightning: the quick spring and rapid flash, its mortal bite, its zigzag course, the sudden stroke of released intensity.

The modern Cherokee call the rattlesnake *Uktena:*

*a great snake, as large as a tree trunk, with horns on its head, and a bright, blazing crest like a diamond upon its forehead. Its scales glittering like sparks of fire. The blazing diamond is called Ulunsuti [transparent], and he who can win it may become the greatest wonder-worker of the tribe. It is worth a man's life to attempt it, for whoever is seen by the Uktena is so dazed by the bright light that he runs toward the snake instead of trying to escape.*

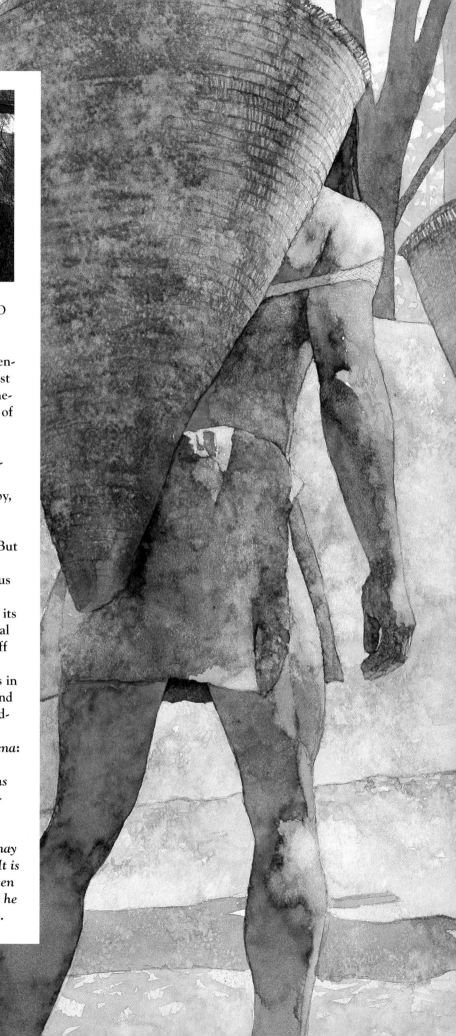

OPPOSITE:
*Kiowa Story* by Mike Larsen (Chickasaw), 1993. The boy struggles to release his spirit while his physical self transforms into the bear. The metamorphosis is almost complete.

The seven sisters have been cast into the night sky and, through the brightness of their fear, have become the Big Dipper.

Some believe that the huge effigies were built to face skyward. Many of them are impossible to recognize at ground level. One bird effigy has a wingspan of six hundred feet. Could it be that they were constructed to reflect the perceived size of heavenly constellations?

Gazing into today's polluted sky, it is sometimes difficult to imagine the power of the heavens observed by Indian eyes over the generations. Some Pueblo people watched the rising and setting sun to calibrate their ritual calendars. The Rio Grande Tewa feared that an eclipse of the sun signaled displeasure from the Sun Father; they worried that he had retired to his house in the underworld.

Some of the light forms of the night's vault, most of them in fact, seem simply cast about the sky at random, without pattern. Navajo and Pueblo traditions tell us that they were scattered about by Coyote, the great trickster who played his pranks and made his mischief across the expanse of western America.

But other stars and planets are clearly locked in relationship to one another. They move together, methodically from east to west. They provide the world with a convenient and reliable time device. The Pawnee watched for the appearance of the Swimming Ducks, paired stars that told them to start their spring Thunder Ritual. The Pomo used the position of the Big Dipper to schedule their fishing expeditions. The Klamath people of California watched the changing position of Orion to determine the time in winter.

The Milky Way is a monumental collection of stars. To the naked eye, it appears to be a hazy ribbon cutting across the celestial sphere. To some, it looks like a pathway. The Cherokee believed it was made of flour. To many Californian groups and to the Pawnee, it was the path of the dead. The Pomo saw in the Milky Way the massive foot of a bear that had once walked across this part of the sky. The Fox Indians saw a bear in the four stars outlining the bowl of what we call the Big Dipper.

The Kiowa tell a story about Tsoai, the boy who turned into a bear:

*Eight children were there at play, seven sisters and their brother. Suddenly the boy was struck dumb; he trembled and began to run upon his hands and feet. His fingers became claws, and his body was covered with fur. Directly there was a bear where the boy had been. The sisters were terrified; they ran, and the bear came after them. They came up to the stump of a tree, and the tree spoke to them. It bade them climb upon it, and as they did so it began to rise into the air. The bear came to kill them, but they were beyond its reach. It reared against the trunk and scored the bark all around with its claws. The seven sisters were borne into the sky, and they became the stars of the Big Dipper.*

In the Marching Bears group of Iowa, thirteen individual effigy mounds were built along an arc. They are nearly symmetrically spaced around an east–west line. Is it significant that on early spring evenings the Big Dipper is located precisely over the top of this arc? Does it matter that during late summer you can see the Big Dipper exactly over the bottom position of the effigies? Could it be that the earthen Marching Bears represent the march of the Big Dipper around Polaris—the North Star? Some astronomers think so.

The truth is that life in precontact America was neither idyllic nor brutish. Indians—like all people—had their share of strife and rivalry. And American Indian society—like all societies—developed cultural means for mitigating conflict. Most of the time, these buffering mechanisms were ritualized, nonviolent, and successful.

But on occasion there was violence. At Crow Creek village located on the Missouri River in present-day South Dakota, archaeologists uncovered indisputable evidence of pre-Columbian, red-on-red violence, one of the largest, most archaeologically visible massacres in the world. In A.D. 1325, increasing population density and environmental deterioration culminated in a massacre of five hundred Arikara men, women, and children—probably 60 percent of the village inhabitants. The attackers overwhelmed and burned the partially palisaded village. They mutilated the dead, apparently carrying away hands and feet as trophies. Remains of young women and older males are surprisingly underrepresented. The victims were left exposed for some time, then interred in a mass grave, where they were discovered and excavated by crews from the University of South Dakota in 1978.

The Crow Creek massacre appears to have been an exception to the common form of Plains warfare, which usually involved small ambushes and ritualized battles in which few were killed. When the osteological analysis was completed, all bones were returned to the Crow Creek Sioux reservation for reburial. There they rest today.

## Life on the Great Plains

The Great North American Plains—a flat land of cold winters and hot summers, of sparse and unpredictable precipitation—cover three-quarters of a million square miles. Paleo-Indian people hunted mammoths and other extinct Ice Age game throughout the Plains. At the end of the Pleistocene, the primeval northern conifer forest was gradually replaced by deciduous forests; then, between 8000 and 6000 B.C. these forests were in turn replaced by a postglacial vegetation cover of perennial grasses. Trees occur today only in stream valleys, scarp lands, and hilly localities.

Early Europeans exploring the Great Plains were overwhelmed by the prodigious numbers of "wild cows," the bison that roamed across an endless "sea of grass." Present-day estimates of the herds of that time hover around the fifty million mark. This vast resource gave the postcontact Plains Indian horsemen their characteristic—to many, romantic—lifestyle. This image fostered the false assumption that the only food animal available in numbers on the Great Plains was the bison. Moreover, it was assumed—because such intimidating, intractable, and mobile prey could be hunted only on horseback, and Indians did not ride horses until some escaped from the Spanish—that Indians could not possibly have lived on the Plains in pre-Columbian times.

Actually, bison-hunting and corn-growing Indians prospered on the Plains for hundreds of generations before the arrival of the horse. Foraging Plains people once followed a natural cycle, hunting game of all kinds, gathering seeds, tubers, nuts, and berries. This foraging lifeway survived for millennia on the Great Plains, spawning a number of locally distinctive traditions.

Then, sometime between 250 B.C. and A.D. 1000, the people of the Great

Plains learned to plant maize, fashion earthenware ceramics, and erect mounds to honor their dead. The ruins that resulted from this settled village life are scattered from Oklahoma and Texas to North Dakota.

These Plains villages shared a number of characteristics. All groups were significantly dependent on maize and other cultivated plants. They worked the rich, alluvial soils of the Missouri and its tributaries with hoes made of bison scapulae. In the east, native plant foods and fauna (including bison) formed a major portion of the diet. Bison became even more important in the central and western Plains, a drought-prone area in which agriculture was hazardous. The shifting eastward of the boundary between long- and shortgrass prairie allowed the bison herds to expand.

Many of these eastern Plains villages were fortified with dry moats and stockades, protecting several hundred nearly year-round residents. Numerous underground storage pits were safeguarded inside. Western Plains groups bartered with the Pueblo peoples of the Southwest, adopting some of their practices.

## Hunting Buffalo Afoot

The first horse on this earth evolved forty million years ago on American soil. And although it became extinct in its own homeland at the end of the Pleistocene, horses survived in Eurasia, having traveled westward toward Siberia along the Bering Land Bridge. Christopher Columbus completed the horse's transglobal circuit when he reintroduced horses to America on his second voyage in 1493.

*Pte Ta Tiyopa* by Greg Beecham, 1991. "The various entrances to the hills were very rough and rugged, but there was one very beautiful and easy pass through which both buffalo and Lakota entered the hills. Every fall thousands of buffalo went through this pass to spend the winter in the hills.

"*Pte ta tiyopa*, or Gate of the Buffalo, it was called by the Lakota."
—LUTHER STANDING BEAR (Oglala Sioux)

*1492: When the Valleys Were Full*
by John Dawson, 1992.

*Buffalo Pis'kun*
by Will Williams, 1992.

Long before the horse returned to the Plains, native American hunters invented highly successful ways of procuring adequate supplies of bison meat. Although sometimes they hunted buffalo individually, they learned the hard way that driving a stone-tipped arrow or spear through the tough buffalo hide was no easy task. Many arrows were lost before one struck home. So the Plains Indians developed ways to take large numbers of buffalo without the dangers and uncertainties of individual stalking. The Crow tell a story about that first buffalo drive:

*Once when Old Man Coyote saw some buffalo, he wanted to eat them and tried to think of a scheme to do this.*

*He approached the buffalo and said to them: "You buffalo are the most awkward of all animals—your heads are heavy, your hairy legs are chopped off short and your bellies stick out like a big pot." The buffalo said to him, "We were made this way."*

*Old Man Coyote said to them: "I'll tell you what let's do—we will run a race"—and all went to the level place with a steep cut bank at one end. Old Man Coyote said to himself, "I will go and put my robe over the edge of the bank," and turning to the buffalo, he said "Just as we get to the place where my robe is we will all shut our eyes and see how far we can go with our eyes closed."*

*The race was started, and just before getting to the robe, all of the buffalo shut their eyes and jumped over the steep cut bank and were killed; and Old Man Coyote feasted off the dead buffalo.*

Since that time, men of the Great Plains have always looked to the buffalo for their life and livelihood.

The Blackfeet built what they called the *pis'kun* (or deep-blood-kettle), a huge corral of rocks, logs, or brush, constructed at the foot of a steep cliff. From the top of the bluff, directly over the *pis'kun* they laid out two lines of rock piles and brush, extending far out along the prairie, forming a huge V-shaped drive.

Several prehunt rituals were necessary to ensure that buffalo would come close enough to be easily taken by hunters, for this was a serious venture controlled by the supernatural. Every Plains tribe had specific songs, charms, dances, ritualistic offerings, and prayers for calling in the buffalo. Among the Blackfeet, certain buffalo songs could be sung only during times of near-starvation.

To ensure that buffalo were not startled and sent into flight prematurely, Plains people prohibited buffalo hunting by individuals while communal hunt preparations were underway. Camp police patrolled for individual hunters, and offenders were flogged or beaten. Their property was sometimes confiscated.

On the night before the buffalo drive, a medicine man would slowly unwrap his pipe, and pray to the Sun for success. The next morning, the man assigned to call in the buffalo arose very early. He told his wives that they must not leave the lodge, or even look outside, until he returned. They should burn sweet grass and pray to the Sun for his success and safety. Without eating or drinking, he joined the others and went up on the prairie. The medicine man put on his robe and headdress made of a buffalo head, and began to approach the herd. When he was near enough, he moved about until some of the buffalo noticed him. As they watched, he slowly shuffled toward the drive lane. If his prayers were granted, the buffalo followed. He increased his pace. Quicker and quicker they went. Then, when the buffalo were fairly within the chute, people rose up from behind their rock piles, shouting and waving their robes as the buffalo passed by. This startled the bison bringing up the rear, and they jostled those in front of them. Before long, the whole herd was stampeding headlong toward the precipice, the rock piles directing them to a single point above the *pis'kun* enclosure.

As they reached the cliff's edge, most buffalo plunged blindly downward, into the *pis'kun*. The fall killed many outright; others were disabled by broken legs and backs. Because the barricades prevented escape, the Blackfeet could easily dispatch the living with arrows.

Archaeological evidence found throughout the Plains shows that similar buffalo drives had taken place for millennia.

*"Take this Horned Hat to wear when you perform the ceremony I have given you, and you will control the buffalo and all other animals. Put the cap on you as you go from here and the Earth will bless you." Made from the skin of a buffalo cow's head, the horns attached, Issiwun—the Sacred Hat—thus came to the Suhtaio.*

—The Story of Issiwun
(Northern Cheyenne)

A Mandan Indian uses a bleached buffalo skull as part of a ritual to ensure success in the hunt (ca. 1908).

*The Birth of the Ikce Wicasa* by Colleen Cutschall (Lakota), 1990.
The emergence of the *Ikce Wicasa*, the common people. Glowing in the dark underworld, man (on the right) and woman (on the left) make their way across and upward
to their awakening in the surface light. The central figure is *Tokahe*, the first man to
emerge, holding the "hoop of the nations" and the flowering stick.

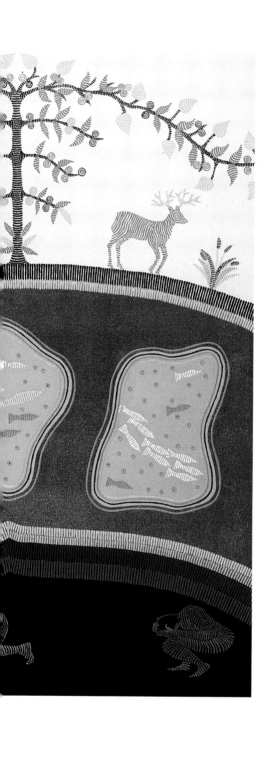

# CHAPTER SIX

# INDIAN CONFEDERACIES

INCISED SHELL GORGET
FOUND IN SPIRO, OKLAHOMA

THE ANCESTORS OF THE IROQUOIS were a successful corn-growing people
called Owasco, who lived along the valleys, mountains, and flatlands of upper
New York State between A.D. 100 and 1300. These Iroquois ancestors erected
huge houses, longer than a modern football field and covered with slabs of elm
bark. The longhouse was to become a lasting symbol of the Iroquois social order.

The Iroquois determined their kin relations through the female line. In each
longhouse, under a single roof, lived the women and their children. They all
belonged to a single matrilineal clan, presided over by a "mother," the oldest
woman. Over the door of the longhouse were depictions of the clan's original
ancestor. The Iroquois clans were named after the first ancestor: the Eagle clan,
the Heron clan, the Wolf clan, the Beaver clan.

Iroquois men left home upon marriage to live in the longhouse of their wives.
Except for their weapons, clothing, and personal possessions that the men
brought with them, everything in Iroquois society, including the longhouse itself,
belonged to women. Even if a husband might be shabby, his wife was expected to
be well-dressed and respectable. Should a male kinsman be killed in war, a
woman was entitled to demand an enemy captive in compensation. She was free
to torture or kill him as she pleased. The clan mothers appointed and dismissed
all councillor-chiefs.

Women controlled Iroquois society for solid, practical reasons. As hunters
and traders, men traveled extensively. An ambitious military campaign meant
that war parties might be gone for days or months. Although a handful of
younger men were left behind to defend the longhouses, most aspects of community life, from nursing to child care, from planting to harvesting, were the
Iroquois woman's responsibility. Women of the Seneca tribe brought in more
than a million bushels of corn a year, plus tons of beans, squash, and sunflower

OPPOSITE:
*Creation Story of the Seneca* by Valjean McCarty Hessing (Choctaw), 1986.

seeds. What they did not prepare immediately, they stored for the future in underground granaries. These matrilineal clans were to become the building blocks of a brand new political institution.

## Founding the Confederation

The remarkable Confederation of the Iroquois was founded sometime before the arrival of the European intruder. According to Iroquois tradition, there was once a time when all the tribes in the region were locked in bloody and endless warfare. Deganawidah, a holy man said to be born of a virgin mother, was the first to express horror and outrage at the senseless violence. He had a vision in which he saw the Five Nations drawn together, unified. The Iroquois, Deganawidah argued, must cease arguing with one another. They must unite under the sheltering branches of a symbolic Tree of Great Peace. They must live in harmony and justice by forming a government of law.

A noble Mohawk named Hiawatha was so moved by Deganawidah's words that he began spreading the message himself, traveling from one tribe to another, traversing the area that is today New York State. Finally, all agreed with Hiawatha's diplomatic mission. A great council for all the chiefs of the five Iroquois tribes was called. The laws of the confederacy, the customs that were to be maintained, were stated and agreed to. Each of the Five Nations clasped the hands of the sister tribes, "so firmly that a falling tree should not sever them."

Thus the Confederacy of the Iroquois was born. At the first council, it was decided that the Onondagas would be the "fire keepers," and from that time on all the great councils of the league would be held at Onondaga, the most centrally located of the five Iroquois tribes. As the first among equals, the Onondagas were to call in the other tribes each year to discuss their differences, and maintain the Great Peace.

The Onondagas also became the "wampum keepers." By Iroquois custom, all important statements were to be accompanied by a gift, ensuring that the statement was important and true. Eventually, wampum came to be regarded as the appropriate and customary gift. White wampum was most often made from the central column of the whelk shell. The only source of the more valuable purple wampum was the hard-shell quahog clam. Treaties between Iroquois and other Indian or European nations were customarily accompanied by an exchange of wampum—a symbol of the sincerity of each party.

Surrounded by their Algonquian-speaking enemies, the Iroquois people lived in a huge rectangle, extending from the Hudson River to Lake Erie. Calling themselves the People of the Longhouse, the Iroquois divided their homeland into five north–south strips, each area watered by its own lake or river, each governed by its own tribal council. The site of each governing council was symbolized by a ceremonial fire; the parallel plumes of smoke were likened to a gigantic longhouse. Human-scaled longhouses had long dominated Iroquois village life. These new symbolic geographic longhouses, each more than two hundred miles long, were to rule the political landscape of upper New York State for centuries.

An embossed copper sheet depicts a Mississippian man wearing the "Forked Eye" motif, a probable representation of the symbolic association with the duck hawk or peregrine falcon, which were both known for their keen vision and skill as hunters.

## From Mississippian Nobility to the Five Civilized Nations

Indian confederacies of the southland, including the so-called Five Civilized Tribes, are deeply rooted in the Mississippian past. Archaeologists use this term, *Mississippian*, to describe the hundreds of late precontact societies that thrived throughout the Tennessee, Cumberland, Mississippi, and other river valleys of the Eastern Woodlands. The Mississippian period began about A.D. 750 and lasted forty generations, until Hernando de Soto and his army slogged ashore in Tampa Bay in late May 1539.

De Soto left the Southeast depopulated, decentralized, and demoralized. Mississippian people became refugees in their own land. Facing alien invaders and slavers, survivors tried to confederate. In Georgia and Alabama, a confederation of many refugee groups came to be dominated by the Creeks (as the English called them). Other descendants of the mound-building Mississippians became the Chickasaws, the Seminoles, and the Choctaws. Still other refugees, the Cherokees, came to occupy the hill and mountain country of western North Carolina and eastern Tennessee. Survivors, they were to become the largest tribe in the Southeast, with some twenty thousand people living in sixty towns. Today, many of their descendants still live in the southern United States.

But during their heyday, the Mississippian leaders presided over great ceremonial centers such as Etowah (Georgia) and Spiro (Oklahoma), Moundville (Alabama), and Cahokia (Illinois). This aristocracy was sanctioned and revered by the thousands upon thousands of farming people who lived in palisaded villages and farmsteads across the Eastern Woodlands. Although much of eastern America did not participate in the full Mississippian pattern, people here were also dependent upon agriculture and pushed maize growing northward to the shores of Lake Superior, the middle Ottawa River valley, and the Maritimes.

## Mississippian Agriculture

The centuries between A.D. 800 and 1100 saw a dramatic development in American farming. The Mississippian people looked beyond the traditional cultivation of native plant crops to focus on a single, nonindigenous species—maize. Corn would come to dominate both their fields and their lives.

This shift to a maize-centered food source across eastern North America was associated with the emergence of more complex social and political structures. Maize would support the evolving Oneota people of the Great Lakes, the Iroquoian confederacy of the Northeast, and the Fort Ancient polities along the middle Ohio River valley, as well as the diverse array of Mississippian chiefdoms that emerged along the river valleys of the Southeast and Midwest. It would be maize that later fostered the Creek and Choctaw to the south, the Mandan and the Pawnee people of the Plains.

Maize had dominated the southwestern agricultural complex from the time of its initial introduction via Mexico. But in the East, more than six centuries elapsed from the initial introduction of maize as a minor vegetable until it became a major crop. Why?

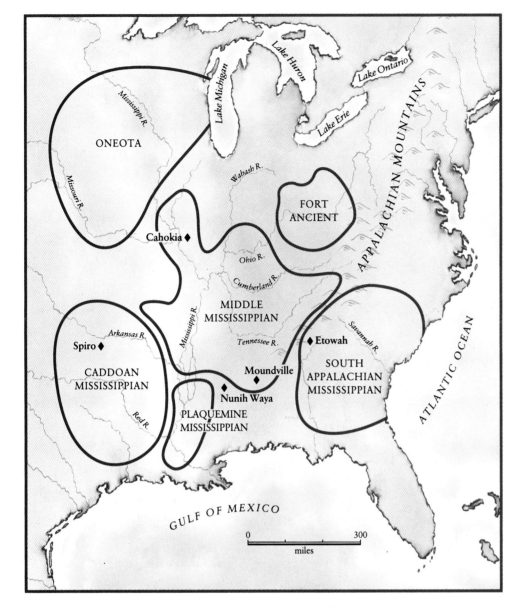

*The Mississippian Culture Complex.*
The culture of the Mississippian mound builders covered an extensive area in the southeast of the continent, as far west as present-day Oklahoma and north to Wisconsin.

Although most of Mississippian culture was not in direct contact with the oceans, extensive trade routes provided the mound towns along the continent's main waterways with exotic items from coastal areas. These objects, particularly shells and freshwater pearls, were used for decoration and in paying tribute to the dead.

This lag can be explained in part by genetic modifications in the plant itself. About A.D. 1000, a new variety of corn was developed in the East, one that was frost resistant and specifically adapted to short growing seasons. This new breed of corn quickly spread to the northern latitude people in eastern North America. By the time of European contact, corn dominated native American agriculture across the Northeast, the Ohio Valley, and the Great Lakes.

Farther south, however, the limited role of corn before A.D. 1000 is a deeper puzzle. It may be that maize came to the East as a controlled substance, used only in certain ritual or commemorative situations. Maybe it became available to the general populace only after A.D. 800. Or it might be that maize was initially harvested and consumed only in its green state (not dried and stored as surplus). Whereas maize has a much higher harvest productivity than the local Hopewellian crops like marsh elder and goosefoot, maize farming entails a considerable up-front investment in land clearing and field maintenance. Maybe the cost-benefit economics of maize agriculture only became attractive after A.D. 800

*October 1540: The Cacique was at home, in a piazza. Before his dwelling, on a high place, was spread a mat for him, upon which two cushions were placed, one above another, to which he went and sat down, his men placing themselves around, some way removed, so that an open circle was formed about him, the Indians of the highest rank being nearest to his person. One of them shaded him from the sun with a circular umbrella, spread wide, the size of a target, with a small stem, and having deerskin extended over cross-sticks quartered with red and white, which at a distance make it look of taffeta, the colors were so very perfect. It formed the standard of the Chief, which he carried into battle. His appearance was full of dignity: He was tall of person, muscular, lean, and symmetrical. He was the suzerain of many territories, and of a numerous people, being equally feared by his vassals and the neighboring nations.*

— Recorded by a Portugese knight (name unknown) in his journal, upon encountering native royalty at Tascaluza (central Alabama).

(possibly because increasing human population size put pressure on existing wild and cultivated resources). Whatever the reason, in the three centuries following A.D. 800, American Indian agriculture rapidly expanded in a new direction.

Mississippian agriculture differed greatly from European farming, because native Americans did not domesticate draft animals. They farmed without oxen and mules. Their fields, usually along the fertile river valleys or abandoned levee meanders, were tilled by hand and by hoe. They settled the best farmland, and also where water and land routes provided communication with both neighboring and distant settlements. The major population centers clustered inland, away from the coast.

## Emerging Mississippian Aristocracies

The emergence of maize-based food production in the Eastern Woodlands was a watershed event in American history. However, the Mississippian character was forged not by agribusiness, but through a radical change in the social fabric. As people became more agricultural, they came to rely more heavily on centralized authority and economic redistribution. At the same time, as economic and social controls became more concentrated, larger agricultural surpluses were needed to support the infrastructure. Mississippian society entered a positive feedback cycle. Change required more change.

The Mississippian people responded to this challenge. They reorganized their settlements into ranked hierarchies, reflecting in their spatial arrangement the increasing social distance between nobles and commoners. Sporting clothing and jewelry befitting their elevated status, the new nobility—maybe 5 percent of the total population—literally towered over everybody and everything. Atop huge, flat-topped mounds, eastern native American aristocrats presided over the ceremonies and rituals that codified the Mississippian lifeway. Townspeople supported their royalty, setting them apart from commoners both socially and politically. Although Mississippian communities remained largely autonomous, their extensive economic and kin ties created far-flung alliances, which, in turn, created rivalries. But (unlike European forms of conquest) when rivalry broke out into open conflict, Mississippian warlords exacted tribute and allegiance, allowing the vanquished to remain on their land.

Mississippian life played out in long-term political cycles. Regional communities—involving thousands of people—accepted the rule and leadership of a particularly effective chief. But upon his or her death, they fragmented once again into constituent townships. Competition for power and prestige often became intense. As political and social ranking proliferated, the Mississippian mindset was increasingly reinforced by ceremony and sacrament. These beliefs expressed ancestral obligations, celebrated successful harvests, hunts, and warfare, and reinforced esteem for social leaders through elaborate mortuary ritual.

So evolved the Southern Cult, also called the Southeastern Ceremonial Complex, a distribution network of artifacts, including ceramics modeled on animal and human forms, that extended over much of the East during Mississippian times. The striking similarities in theme, motif, and medium transcend simple trade networks, however, and indicate shared elements of belief and worldview. This was a higher degree of social interaction at work. Many of the Southern Cult motifs—crosses, hand and eye, sun symbols, serpent, woodpecker, falcon, raccoon, and others—can still be seen in the belief systems of postcontact native Americans of the Southeast, and in their folktales, myths, and religion.

The distribution of Southern Cult objects extended beyond the limits of any single Mississippian society, spreading from Mississippi to Minnesota, from the Plains to the Atlantic coast. In addition to small, "expensive" items, and quantities of a product indigenous to a particular area, exchange may have involved critical technological and subsistence resources such as hoes and salt.

## Mississippian Demise and Survival

Although some of the great Mississippian centers were already in decline by the time de Soto tramped through the American Southeast, their ultimate collapse can be directly related to European incursions into their territory.

Disease and disorder overtook the surviving Mississippian towns. As American Indian population plummeted, most Mississippian societies imploded. The complex political and social ties that had defined the Mississippian lifeway unraveled as epidemics diminished population numbers. People no longer constructed public works such as mounds and palisades. They no longer supported their royalty. They no longer hosted elaborate mortuary rituals for their ancestors.

Although the Mississippian elite system would disappear at European contact, many of the Mississippian beliefs live on among southeastern Indian people. Vestiges of their belief systems survive in the *puskita* (or Green Corn ceremony), the most important postcontact ritual of the tribes in the Southeast. Toward the end of each summer's corn harvest, the Busk (as it was also called) was held to celebrate and give thanks. It was a time for renewing life. Men repaired the

Mississippian people used shell for many purposes, including jewelry. A large conch shell, like the one above from Spiro, Oklahoma, offered a surface that could be incised, perhaps with sacred Southern Cult images, and used in daily life as a drinking cup.

### HEALTH AND DIET IN MISSISSIPPIAN SOCIETY

Some new evidence has suggested that increased reliance on domesticated plants was a mixed blessing for the Mississippian people. At the Dickson Mounds in Illinois, for instance, the health, nutrition, and longevity of Mississippian people declined significantly from earlier times. There were higher rates of malnutrition and infectious pathology (probably due to crowding), singularly high rates of trauma (suggesting increased interpersonal violence), high rates of porotic hyperostosis (suggestive of anemia), greater incidence of dental disease, a generally elevated level of biological stress, and generally lower life expectancy. Other evidence suggests that the percentage of individuals displaying signs of infection in Mississippian populations may have doubled in the transition from hunting and gathering to intensive maize agriculture.

Things were apparently better in some sectors than others. The Mississippian communities at Moundville and Etowah were generally healthy and long-lived, but there was a substantial difference between classes. Although the high-status male adults—those buried in mounds—had a relatively high average age at death, those in surrounding village cemeteries (presumably a lower-status area) had a much lower average age at death. Contemporary hunter-gatherers from an outlying satellite near Etowah were taller, more robust, and had lower rates of infection and arthritis than their farming neighbors.

*Mythical Corn Ceremony*
by Ignacio Moquino (Zia Pueblo), 1938.

communal buildings. Old feuds and animosities were patched up. Women extinguished their hearth fires, cleansed their houses, and broke their cooking pots. All male–female contact was forbidden.

A handful of specially designated village chiefs—medicine men, tribal elders, and celebrated young warriors—gathered in the town square to fast and to purify themselves. Tribal elders occupied their own places of distinction, opposite the honored warriors, whose faces and torsos had been painted red. The high priest began the most critical part of the Green Corn ritual, ceremonially lighting the new sacred fire. To the sound of drumbeats and incantations, selected elders circled the flame. All wore white, the symbolic color of the Busk.

The Green Corn dance completed, coals from the ceremonial fire rekindled the home fires. Village women prepared a sumptuous feast of celebration and thanksgiving. It remained only for the villagers to file to the nearby stream for a

Some scholars, like archaeologist and ethnohistorian Henry F. Dobyns, take the position that the pre-Columbian Americas once had a huge population—112 million people—that was virtually wiped out by Old World disease. Dobyns argues that several pandemics, hemisphere-wide epidemics, spread out from an initial point of contact with traders and explorers to engulf both continents, rapidly killing millions, often before the actual arrival of the first European colonist in the area. In North America alone, according to Dobyns, the numbers dropped from 18 million in 1492 to as low as 350,000 by 1900.

To arrive at this conclusion, Dobyns employed the methods of historical demography, using archaeological records to isolate the most reliable population numbers from the available documentation, then projecting these estimates back to the earliest contact period, a time for which there are no (or very few) records. For South America, he began with firm population estimates from two periods—one close to the Spanish conquest, and one later—then computed a "depopulation ratio" to estimate the degree of population decline from the first smallpox epidemic (in 1519) to the population a century later. This ratio—calculated to be 20:1—can then be applied to the rest of the hemisphere.

While some would agree such estimates may work for the Andes and Central America, areas of relatively reliable census figures, the picture is muddied considerably in North America, where early eyewitness accounts are rare and faulty. North America was the perimeter of the Spanish world, and by the time the earliest Spanish colonists arrived, entire cultures may already have been wiped out by disease brought by the early explorers.

On the other hand, some scholars believe that epidemics were neither so widespread nor so frequent as Dobyns believes. Some argue that only 2 million American Indians lived in pre-Columbian North America (as opposed to Dobyns's 18 million).

Those choosing the lower figures either believe that disease was a less significant factor in changes made during the contact period, or presume that it postdates documentary sources. Others, like Dobyns, argue that most historical documents postdate epidemics and that native populations were already drastically reduced and cultural systems profoundly changed by the time Europeans actually recorded their observations.

Part of the debate turns on how one views the historical documents themselves. Whereas some believe that the best evidence comes from eyewitness accounts, others argue that sixteenth-century narratives should be viewed with extreme skepticism. How are these original documents decoded, and how does one assess the bias? Many believe that the truth about American Indian population must be derived from archaeological records, which are free of the biases inherent in the historical documents.

communal bath, purifying themselves for the new year to come and completing a sacrament handed down from ancient Mississippian times.

The Black Drink, another element of Southern Cult ceremonialism, survived as well. Formerly drunk from shell cups embellished with Southern Cult motifs, the black drink was made from roasted leaves of the cassina shrub, boiled into a frothy, caffeine-rich brew. Drunk with great ceremony, the black drink conferred spiritual purification upon all who participated. The minds of village leaders were cleared for debate, the bodies of warriors cleansed and strengthened for battle.

Mississippian survivals can also be seen in the symbolism of the mound itself. While Indians of the contact period no longer constructed pyramids, the beliefs underlying the practice persevered in southeastern Indian language, folklore, and ritual. Linguistic and traditional beliefs of the Muskogee, the Chickasaw, the Choctaw, and the Cherokee demonstrate a coherent picture of the continued symbolic significance of these Mississippian sacred places. The ancient earthen mounds, often called *earth islands*, symbolized a oneness with the land. They became concrete manifestations of unbroken ritual traditions of fertility and purification, as carried on in the Green Corn ceremonialism of the displaced southeastern tribes.

In one Muskogee legend, warriors encounter and subsequently kill their enemies in a rival town. The survivors, mourning for their dead kinsmen, begin to build earthen mounds in which to bury their dead. These symbolic mounds provide supernatural support and sanctuary, creating a sanctified place for ritual purification. Another tradition describes a legendary attack by Cherokees upon the Muskogee, whose warriors were said to have hidden inside a ceremonial mound. The Muskogee surprise their attackers by "pouring up from the bowels of the earth" to defeat the invading Cherokees. Both cases show clear-cut continuities linking ancient Mississippian people with historic southeastern tribes.

The huge platform mound at Nunih Waya (in modern Winston County, Mississippi) is considered by the Choctaw to be the Great Mother in their creation tale. Legend holds that while wandering in search of a homeland, the Choctaw people carried with them the bones of their deceased elders. Finally, reaching the correct place, the ancestors' bones were piled high on the ground and covered with cypress bark to create the great mound at Nunih Waya. Thereafter the mound surface was planted with trees, and to symbolize the renewal and purification of their world, the Choctaws held their Green Corn dances here. They would sing:

*Behold the wonderful work of our hands: and let us be glad. Look upon the great mound; its top is above the trees, and its black shadow lies on the ground, a bowshot. It is surmounted by the golden emblem of the sun; its glitter dazzles the eyes of the multitude. It inhumes the bones of fathers and relatives; they died on our sojourn in the wilderness. They died in a far off wild country. They rest at Nunih Waya. Our journey lasted many winters; it ends at Nunih Waya.*

## The First Thousand Generations

The story told in Part One spans a thousand generations, a time of native American enterprise, innovation, and originality. These first Americans had much to learn and plenty to cope with. They invented and they mastered. These were the original discoverers, explorers, settlers, and colonizers of America. Many of their victories seem today almost elemental, so basic to survival that we can easily overlook them. (Sometimes, we wrongly ascribe these achievements to the so-called civilized Europeans who were to follow.) This is a story of rising numbers and increasing power. It is a rich experience, a record that can stand against that of any other part of the world.

But the American Indian story is not a simple upward spiral, a fifteen-thousand-year-old bootstrap operation that elevated primitive Paleo-Indians into formidable "civilized" alliances.

Too often in America's classrooms, we are sold a past interpreted as a mechanistic progression of allegedly uplifting revolutions. We are told that "progress" always makes the world a better place to live. We convince ourselves that through cultural inventiveness and reform, our ancestors gradually whittled away at the problems and dangers that once faced all humankind. We are told to assume that, thanks to the contributions of a few clever men and women, the

OPPOSITE:
*Creation Legend* by Tom Two-Arrows (Onondaga), 1946. The Iroquois creation story tells how white water birds met Skywoman as she descended onto a water-turtle—the Earth. The Iroquois say that when the Earth cracks, the turtle is stretching.

human workload must have lightened through time, nutrition become better, and diseases fewer. We are lulled into believing that the human condition has progressed along an irregular, but always upward trend.

The world has always been more complex than that. In native America as elsewhere, "progress" has sometimes cost more than most would like to admit. Farming has not always freed people from hardship in making a living; in fact, many ancient farmers worked longer hours than their foraging cousins. Sometimes, foragers live healthier and longer lives than farmers.

Agriculture is neither a necessary stage of cultural achievement nor an emblem of human progress. Neither are the other so-called signposts of human development: larger human populations, intensified subsistence, more complex social relations, ever larger economic and political networks.

Kote Kotah, a Chumash man, grasped the dilemma of human change and evolution:

> There is no "better" or "worse," only different. That difference has to be respected whether it's skin color, way of life, or ideas. The Chumash have a story about this. It begins with a worm who is eaten by a bird. The bird is eaten by a cat whose self-satisfaction is disrupted by a mean-looking dog. After devouring the cat, the dog is killed by a grizzly bear who congratulates himself for being the strongest of all. About that time comes a man who kills the bear and climbs a mountain to proclaim his ultimate superiority. He ran so hard up the mountain that he died at the top. Before long the worm crawled out of his body.

We must appreciate the variety and diversity in native North America. This has not been an odyssey from primitive to civilized. The first thousand generations are a chronicle of adapting, problem-solving, and, above all else, surviving.

But nothing in this rich and varied experience could have prepared the first Americans for the onslaught of men and microbes that awaited them at the dawn of the sixteenth century.

—DAVID HURST THOMAS

*Creation Story of the Comanche* by Valjean McCarty Hessing (Choctaw), 1986.
One day the Great Spirit collected swirls of dust from the four directions in order to create the Comanche people. These people formed from the earth had the strength of mighty storms. Unfortunately, a shape-shifting demon was also created and began to torment the people. The Great Spirit cast the demon into a bottomless pit. To seek revenge the demon took refuge in the fangs and stingers of poisonous creatures and continues to harm people every chance it gets.

# PART TWO

# BLENDING WORLDS

*A long time ago my father told me what*
*his father had told him, that there was once a Lakota*
*holy man, called Drinks Water, who dreamed what was*
*to be. . . . He dreamed that the four-leggeds were going*
*back to the Earth, and that a strange race would weave*
*a web all around the Lakotas. He said, "You shall live*
*in square gray houses, in a barren land. . . ."*
*Sometimes dreams are wiser than waking.*

BLACK ELK, OGLALA SIOUX, ca. 1932

Indians greeting French explorers
during the sixteenth century.

# CHAPTER SEVEN

# THE RICHNESS OF A VAST CONTINENT

KAROK DANCE WANDS WITH WOODPECKER HEADS

THE RICH DIVERSITY THAT HAD DEVELOPED over millennia among the native peoples of North America still flourished in the very early 1500s. Although all these peoples were careful nurturers of the land, some lived largely by their own skilled farming while others relied primarily on the bountiful wild resources of their territories. The difference was not absolute, but rather a reflection of the kinds of terrain occupied: farmers gathered some foods from the wild, and hunter-gatherers, to some extent, controlled their food sources.

In addition to these two broadly distributed lifestyles, other peoples had accommodated themselves to various terrains in specialized ways. In the high mesas of the arid Southwest, the Anasazi, ancestors of the Pueblos, had developed the cliff houses that allowed a large number of people to live in a small area above the fields intensively farmed to feed them. In regions of greater natural abundance, however, such as native California and the North Pacific Coast, people who lived off the wild bounty provided by the sea and a kind climate had also developed elaborately layered societies. Because the populations were large, and available living sites in these rugged terrains were scarce, people were concentrated in much larger numbers. This created an intensification of religious ritual and strikingly sophisticated arts.

In the south and along the fertile river systems from the Mississippi to the Atlantic coast were many settled communities, separated from one another by space and language but holding in common their ability to farm. They raised corn, beans, squash, sunflowers, and a host of other plants long domesticated in

*Temple Mound Town of the Mississippi Valley* by Lloyd Townsend.

## THE HUNTER-GATHERERS

Because of their dispersed populations, hunter-gatherer families organized into *kindreds*. These kindreds traced bonds through both father and mother to a broad network of other people, not necessarily blood relatives, but definitely "kin." The kindreds were usually organized in the simplest, most practical way; social distinctions were limited to factors such as age, gender, skill, and access to the spirits.

The vast networks of kin allowed everyone to travel and visit widely. And this further enabled them to survive in sometimes severely fluctuating conditions, particularly during times of famine or scarcity in their own homegrounds. While every kindred had a home base, member families ranged among a series of fixed locations or camps near seasonally available resources. The kindreds, in turn, grouped into bands, each occupying recognized territorial areas.

Hunter-gatherers thus enjoyed all the freedom of a loosely knit society while relying on the support, in times of need, of close family ties.

OPPOSITE:

*Passing into Womanhood* by Howard Terpning, 1989. A coming-of-age ceremony celebrating the importance of becoming a woman in Cheyenne society. It was a Cheyenne custom to go through a ritual of purification and education. The young girl would be assisted by a close relative, her grandmother perhaps, and other female members of her family.

North America, and supplemented this well-controlled food supply with game from abundant woods and fish from lake, river, and ocean.

Farther west and north, along rivers or near other sources of water, were a variety of peoples who relied more on wild bounty, following an annual round of age-old campsites—fishing the salmon runs, hunting the mammals of sea and forest, and harvesting seasonal plants, shoots, seeds, nuts, fruit, and roots. The best of the wild seed would be scattered to give a good yield the following year, while regular spring burning of underbrush in the towering forests ensured enrichment of the soil and opened areas for deer to browse freely on new-fed growth. The hunter-gatherers lived a varied, rich, migratory life, covering large territorial areas, but always identifying with a home village.

All these diversified lifestyles depended on close, careful, and reverential relationships with the environments that supported them. Everywhere, people recognized that life lived off life, and they respected the innate gift of renewal that the death of any animal or plant made to the living. Each lifestyle—sedentary farmer, nomadic hunter-gatherer, and everything in between—had different social and religious expressions, but all were based in the life-giving source of the natural world.

## The Power of Female Kinship

Farm communities, with their larger populations living in more settled abodes, required more complex social and political organization than did the mobile peoples. In the context of reverence for nature, this had one very particular result. While all peoples acknowledged bonds of kinship with all expressions of life (believing that humans were only one of many forms of persons such as rocks, trees, plants, animals, fish, water, birds, stars, and earth), farmers tended to recognize a single kinship bond, to the virtual exclusion of every other, for tracing family descent. Most frequently, they traced the family tree through the mother since women, themselves the bearers of life, obviously had a special bond with the land and its life-giving properties—and hence with all other forms of life.

So the towns throughout the south and east, including the great Indian culture that later would come to be known as the Mississippi Mound civilization—or simply as Mississippian—traced their ancestry primarily through their women, creating patterns of descent that were matrilineal. Generations of mothers and daughters formed increasingly larger social units that they recognized as lineages. Matrilineages were composed of mothers and their children, with positions of authority passing from brothers of women to the senior matron's sons—that is, from maternal uncles to nephews. It was a distinct advantage for a man to be brother to a powerful matriarch, as they were clearly blood kin.

The predominant political structures among farming communities as far distanced as the Mississippian and Pueblo cultures were chiefdoms headed by leaders of hereditary descent. Each community was led by a member of a matrilineal elite, and he—or sometimes she—served as a pivot for an extensive network of religious and trade relationships. The leader was responsible for the transmission to the community, and to the region, of both practical necessities

## THE LINE OF POWER

Matrilineages were further linked into a clan by a mystical bond traced through women to a common ancestor who was supernatural in origin. The clan might be named for that source, which could be flint (since rocks were sacred persons), corn, deer, oak, star, or any of various bodies or things that connected humans, spirits, and species together in a common unity. The linking of clans into clan-clusters reflected natural connections in the sacred world of the sources—thus owl was linked to eagle, fish to river, and field to mountain.

These nonblood kin ties provided the means for cooperation that went beyond the clan. Then, if a lineage, or even a clan, were to become extinct, its rituals and leadership functions could be reallocated to a related clan. These lines of connection were among the strengths that helped to hold Indian peoples together, creating new unities in the face of the devastation brought by the Europeans.

Extending beyond the clan-cluster to the universe itself there were even more powerful linkages within the matrilineal societies. Because Indians saw opposites—sky and earth, land and water, right and left, or any other likely contrast—as parts of a whole, they formed a double set of connections that represented the two sides of the universe.

Along the southern tier of the country, the sophisticated Indian farmers of the Mississippi waterways identified with Red and White, symbolic of War and Peace. Along the upper Mississippi and Missouri rivers, various Siouian peoples were Earth and Sky. And all the way over to the Southwest, the Pueblos were Summer and Winter, also Squash and Turquoise.

such as food supplies, and supernatural power, the two life-sustaining requirements being intimately linked.

Religion pervaded all of life and provided a sense of context. Everything in the world had its spiritual component and every action had to be accompanied by proper ritual. It was not enough to accept a new plant or artifact; one had to know the exact ritual that applied to its special characteristics in order to be able to use it effectively. The entire farming complex of corn, beans, and squash was originally transmitted north from Mexico as a ritual rather than an economic system. By accepting the rituals of planting, tending, and harvesting, natives throughout the southern and eastern regions eventually developed domesticated crops and thus became farmers. The ritually established connections of crops to the larger cosmos of seasonal cycles changed their way of life, but it was a religious rather than an agricultural development.

Because all life was connected and functioned in terms of well-ordered patterns of respect and mutual aid, the hereditary leaders of chiefdoms played special roles. In the Mississippi Valley they were literally and figuratively distanced from everyone else by elaborate accounts of their descent from stars, the sun, the sky, or other illustrious supernatural ancestors. These rulers were "elevated" above everyone else; accordingly they lived in homes atop constructed earthen mounds and were carried in litters resting on the shoulders of bearers so as to be freed as much as possible from the touch of the ground. By being suspended, these leaders were equivalent to lightning rods, attracting and dispersing the power they acquired from cosmic and human forces.

This elevation of the chiefs—their superiority—was rarely resented or even envied. On the contrary, the chiefs were valued and honored. For the high chief not only attracted information, goods, and food to his or her own town, but shared these with a wider region of people. Generosity was not only the primary virtue, it was the primary engine of the native economy. By having one family elevated above the rest, more benefits could be attracted to more people.

## River Families, Trade, and Diversity

Peoples who lived along a particular river usually shared the same language, culture, and traditions. Those communities in the same watershed frequently recognized a common ancestry. Portages and easy terrain linked river systems to form networks of common understanding and exchange. Indeed, rivers themselves were thought to be people—often women—who received offerings and prayers to assure safe passage. Women, because of their domestic roles as wives and mothers, were peacekeepers and mediators. They were binders and joiners, just as rivers and trails were.

The whole country was linked by a vast network of trade. Itinerant merchants traveled into remote villages; and trading centers were located on the margins of ecological and cultural regions. Especially important markets, for

OPPOSITE: *The Gathering of the Clans* by Arnold Jacobs (Onondaga), 1992.
A symbolic painting depicting beings that were the inspirational founders of the clans.

THE RICHNESS OF A VAST CONTINENT · 117

## HOME ENTERTAINMENT

The allies of a chief, whether linked through economics or ritual, made regular visits to exchange gifts and reach consensus on important matters. These delegations were often large, including heirs who needed to gain experience, former town members returning to visit kin, and others curious about the wider world.

But sometimes visitors came to entertain or teach rather than to conduct business. During the winter, when people were shut in by the weather, cripples or handicapped individuals traveled around as entertainers, advisors, or trainers. If they were too crippled or feeble to walk, young apprentices carried them from town to town for the chance to memorize the stories they told, the games they led, or the crafts they taught and produced. Everyone enjoyed these visits, because everyone benefited from them. Such special regard for the handicapped was related to the all-pervasive regard for differences and was a distinguishing characteristic of native Americans. The belief still holds that the curtailing of some ability, whether physical or mental, was more than compensated for by some special gift at storytelling, herbal cures, toolmaking, oratory, or putting people at ease.

Slow Bull, an Oglala Sioux medicine man (ca. 1910).

instance, were located near the northern edge of crop farming, among the Hurons of modern Ontario, or the Mandans of North Dakota, where corn, beans, and squash were exchanged for meat and furs hunted farther north.

These people and goods contributed to a continent-wide mosaic in which, because of mutual respect, every piece was unique, yet each simultaneously meshed with the whole. Throughout the Americas, men and women reveled in

The organizations that we now call tribes were mostly created in the aftermath of European disease and disruptions. Before "tribes," various parts of ancient America were peopled by loosely knit groups whose common identity was created and maintained during the celebration of defining rituals. These periodic celebrations, in which a whole community might join, were intended to renew the world and the connectedness of all living things by enacting the community's Origin Saga. Thus farmers celebrated harvest festivals like the Green Corn rite of the Southeast or, in the Southwest, the Solstice rites of the Pueblos. Hunter-gatherers held ritual celebrations to welcome the arrival of fish runs, the harvest of acorns, or the shift from plant foods to hunting in the fall.

Ritual definition of identity served to unite people into congregations that often included communities from several watersheds. Over the millennia, the differences between separated communities gradually increased.

Yet, while every waterway had its own dialect and way of living, these blended with similar traditions throughout the watershed. And so, at least during times of ritual celebration, differences of housing, foods, kinship, and language could be celebrated in shared acts of communion.

Along the greater rivers, however, the long distances eventually created cultural boundaries that gradually separated one tradition from another, and, in the long term, fostered suspicion, if not hostilities. Even so, diversity was valued for its own sake, because it added to the richness of the mosaic of life.

the nuances of variety. They took delight in difference: a traveler from a far region, an exotic shell, a distinctive feature of the landscape, a cultural tradition handed down from the past, or whatever was unusual, odd, or special—all such things were treated with interest and respect.

## The World of the Spirits

Shamans, native physicians and ritualists, were frequent travelers on the roads and waterways of the country. They traveled widely to learn new techniques and improve established ones; and they maintained extensive ties with many communities over a broad region, mostly through other shamans. Yet, since shamans had direct ties to the spirits and powers of the universe, a visit by one of them had fearsome aspects.

Shamans were relied on to assure the success of the hunt by visiting a cave to meet the spirit in charge of the local animal population. Together, they worked out a redistribution of lives within their region: so many human souls were exchanged for the spirits of animals killed in the hunt. Since souls were immortal and thus available for later exchanges, these reapportionments balanced out over time, as long as the mortal remains of the animals were treated with respect by humans. Thus game that gave up its life willingly was welcomed into the home of the hunter, and what little of the body was not used had to be disposed of ritually by burning, submersion, or placement in a shrine.

Not surprisingly, a shaman was more likely to offer the lives of people from neighboring villages than from his or her own. Therefore, when shamans were around, people had to be very circumspect. Yet a powerful shaman could help as well as harm, and might provide the only hope during a fatal disease. And so, unless they had lost a number of patients, were in failing health themselves, or gave other evidence of weakness or malevolent intent, shamans were always welcome. At least, it was infinitely safer to give that impression.

A Tlingit shaman mask
with mother-of-pearl inlay.

## An Astonishment of Languages

After a century of research, and going all the way back to origins, scholars have concluded that there were about three waves of migration into the Americas, each with its own parent language. Later, these split into over twenty major stocks, each giving rise to as many varieties of speech as Indo-European or Chinese. Some stocks were dispersed over huge areas, others were regional, and a few, known as isolates, not traceable to any other language, were spoken in only one location. The base stocks split into some two thousand separate languages that were being spoken in North America at the time of European contact.

OPPOSITE:
*The Major Native American Language Stocks.*

*Chinigchinich then proceeded to make a new people from clay, and they became the Indians of today. He placed these people in groups all over the country and gave them what they needed to survive. He gave them their languages and their customs and all was good.*

—Origin Tale of the Gabrielinos

# Language and Cultural Variations

Throughout much of the country's heartland, Mississippians spoke languages of several stocks, such as Muskogean and Tunican in the south, Siouian along the Missouri, and Caddoan along the southwestern tributaries. Among the matrilineal farmers of the Northeast, Algonquian was the base language stock, interspersed with clusters of Iroquoian speakers. The latter included the Five Nations of New York (later to become the Six Nations), the Hurons north of the St. Lawrence, and the Cherokee of the Carolinas. Algonquians south of the St. Lawrence were farmers, those to the north and west were hunters, and those living along the Great Lakes fished, hunted, and gathered wild rice.

In later centuries, some of these Algonquians were displaced, leaving Minnesota for the northern Plains, where they relinquished their town living and clans for a life of tending bison herds, eventually to become the Cheyenne, Blackfeet, and Arapaho. The southern Plains was home to Caddoan speakers, who formed several powerful chiefdoms, at least until the proliferation of the horse in the late 1600s heightened the appeal of bison hunting and camp life. By the 1700s, the invasive pressures of Europeans were pushing native peoples of many different languages onto the Plains.

In the Southwest, the Pueblos, despite their strongly related culture, belonged to four different language stocks. Native California, however, was the area of greatest linguistic and cultural diversity, with its many mountains and valleys encouraging isolated development.

To the north, the Pacific Coast was so rich in natural resources that populations were large, but concentrated in relatively few towns. Many distinct language stocks and dialect groups occupied this region. Of these, Na-Dene was spread across the largest area and represented one of the last great migrations out of Asia to the Americas some five thousand years ago. Na-Dene was the source for the many Athapaskan languages, some of which found their way into the Southwest, where they became ancestors to modern Navajo and Apache. Other Athapaskan speakers settled along the present California–Oregon border, and still others made their homes near the Kiowa on the southern Plains.

These Athapaskan groups retained their languages, yet they each adopted aspects of the local culture and made it their own. The Apaches continued their old pattern of a mixed economy that included some farming, harvesting of wild foods, and raiding.

However, in the late 1600s, the Navajos diverged from their old ways by adopting sheep herding. They also assumed many features from the Pueblo culture, such as clans, sand painting, and weaving, but they modified each in their own distinctive ways. In adapting Pueblo rituals, the Navajo changed the emphasis from the town solidarity, so important to Pueblo communities, to the cosmic harmony that was central to their own lives. And while Pueblo men were the weavers for their communities, it was Navajo women who wove blankets and rugs in theirs.

The harsh, far northern coasts of the continent remained the homeland of Eskimo-Aleut stock, the languages spoken from Siberia to Greenland. All these northern peoples lived as big game hunters, taking caribou and marine mammals.

Because life in their frozen lands discouraged visitors, aside from occasional hostilities with Athapaskans or Algonquians along their southern border, Eskimos kept largely to themselves.

## The Diversity of Leadership

Outbreaks of aggression were a consequence of regional and cultural differences throughout the continent, and these tended to be dealt with everywhere in similar ways. In most towns, leadership was divided between a chief and a war captain, and most clans also had peace and war leaders. Most of the time, old and respected men led the community by example, persuading rather than commanding, and gaining a reputation for faultless generosity. During attack, battles, or threatening times, however, a kind of martial law was instituted and the captain took over authority.

This was a mature man chosen for his leadership and fighting abilities, a man whom the warriors of the group would be willing to follow, for he, too, led by example rather than command. But once hostilities were over, the war captain

*The Storyteller* by Howard Terpning, 1988. The oral tradition was a highly respected skill in most Indian cultures, going all the way from uproarious appreciation for the ability to tell a good story to the deep respect accorded the men and women who preserved a tribe's history in the epics that were told and retold, both for entertainment and edification.

He was a man who was kind to everybody. He was very peaceful. He was qualified to keep the Sacred Hat because the law that concerns the Keepers says that a man who is Keeper must be honest, peaceful and kindly to everyone.

—FRANK WATERS
   Sweet Medicine Chief of the
   Northern Cheyenne describing
   Coal Bear, ca. 1958.

*We Pray for Abundance*
by K. Henderson, 1992.

relinquished his position to the chief and his council of elders, who would negotiate a peace. Though captains tended to be powerful men with forceful personalities, their functions were carefully curtailed and subordinated to the richly diverse ordering of life so characteristic of the Americans.

European invasions upset this balance, however, and the constant state of war, or impending attack, gave captains an opening to entrench and expand their authority. In many cases, this development was forced on them by circumstance—and all too often theirs turned out to be a last-ditch effort.

Though native peoples did not always and everywhere survive the encounters with Europeans, those who did accomplished survival by relying on the adaptive strengths they had evolved over millennia, combining these with creative innovations suited to living with the invaders. One of the strongest advantages of the native outlook was the tolerance it engendered. Rather than viewing the cosmos as a great hierarchical chain of command, where God sat at the apex and demons swarmed at the base, and where the higher orders oppressed the lower ones, natives believed in a weblike globe composed of concentric and radiating lines of energy.

Intersections of these rings and rays were points of power occupied by spirits, sacred places, and leaders of importance. Each node of intersection served as a smaller or greater center for a more focused pattern or organization of life-forms. Even through recent centuries, the most enduring of these centers included the heart of every person, the hearth of each house, and the sun in the sky, linked together by a sense of focus and community. In all cases, the pattern of these centers was the template for integrating all facets of the universe and providing meaning to the activities of a community.

Jacques Le Moyne, artist for the expedition of René de Laudonniere, recorded this early instance of cultural crossover in Florida in 1564. Timucua Indians, led by their chief, Athore, display harvest bounty and weapons at the foot of a column erected by members of an earlier French colony.

# CHAPTER EIGHT

# CONFRONTATION IN THE "NEW" WORLD

THE ARRIVAL OF EUROPEANS IN THE AMERICAS brought to the native peoples change of a kind that went far beyond their capacity to understand, or even imagine—unprecedented change, terrible change, havoc, and death. South of the lands later to be known as the United States, powerful empires fell. And millions died from the scourge of epidemic diseases unleashed, however unintentionally, by the first conquerors, the Spaniards.

After their success in plundering Mexico and Peru, Spanish conquistadors turned their eyes northward, sending expeditions to explore the coasts of the land they called La Florida—the land of flowers—searching for gold and other wealth. For, at least initially, extracting wealth—easy wealth—was their prime aim in the new lands they had encountered. Anything of value they laid their eyes on, they snatched, looted, and pillaged.

When the coasts of Florida did not provide the kind of portable riches they expected, the Spanish advance guard turned inland. Experience in Mexico and Peru had taught them that wealth was accumulated in the great capital cities of the interior. Soon, marching deep into Florida, they had ravaged and pillaged their way through the populous and prosperous farmlands and the urban centers of the Mississippian chiefdoms—peoples whose descendants would be known as Creeks, Cherokees, Caddos, Choctaws, and Chickasaws.

In the wake of the Spanish invasion, the lofty chiefdoms of the south and east collapsed. The old order could not cope with the onslaught. Finding themselves largely leaderless, and therefore severed from their most powerful access to the gods, at a loss to account for the thousands of friends and families dead from

*Discovery of the Mississippi by De Soto in 1541* by William H. Powell, 1853.
A romanticized image, featuring a nude Indian woman. De Soto's Mississippian
travels were in temple mound country with large villages of plastered houses, home
to a sophisticated and stratified culture with a finely dressed aristocracy supported
by a farming community.

strange and disfiguring diseases, the survivors suffered a profound crisis, both of shock from immediate, multiple loss, and of faith. Their world destroyed, they would need time and radical change before some semblance of their traditional community life could be rebuilt.

## De Soto

The 1539–43 expedition of Hernando de Soto provided a fascinating glimpse of the last great Indian chiefdoms. Though de Soto's chroniclers generally portray the native inhabitants as hardly more than savage obstacles to the business of looting and destroying, at least one, Garcilaso de la Vega, describes the natives and their leaders with enough character to judge them in their own terms, as patriots acting in opposition to a brutal invasion.

Several minor expeditions had ventured inland before de Soto's much larger and better-financed expedition. The first of these forays was launched in 1521 by Ponce de León with 80 men; Lucas Vázquez de Ayllón came in 1526 with 220; and Pánfilo de Narváez in 1528 with a force of 400. As each party bullied and blundered its way into the unknown land, the native populations, at first welcoming, learned to mistrust, and resisted by force when all else failed. And so each of these early expeditions fell apart through a combination of arrogance, ignorance, and attrition in battle. Narváez was so incompetent that only a handful of those with him survived. However, his treasurer, Alvar Núñez Cabeza de Vaca, became justly famous for his own chronicle of eight years of harsh survival spent wandering alone among tribes of the Gulf Coast.

De Soto himself left no personal record, but Garcilaso de la Vega's chronicle, *The Florida of the Inca*, is a masterpiece of Spanish literature. This remarkable document, published in Lisbon in 1605, sixty-three years after de Soto's death, is based primarily on the author's interviews with a veteran of the de Soto expedition. Though Garcilaso's source is somewhat suspect, the account is surprisingly unbiased, offering a largely sympathetic portrayal of the native people. The reason for this probably lies in Garcilaso himself, who was a man of two worlds—the son of an Inka princess and a Spanish conqueror of Peru.

Hernando de Soto had been a dashing young captain during the time of the Peruvian conquest. And later, he gambled his share of the spoils gained there on the chance that Florida would yield even greater riches. He requested and received this region as a personal possession from the king of Spain, but only for the duration of his own life. If riches were found, the terms of the charter were subject to revision by the king. But Spain was far away, and the arrangement was satisfactory to de Soto.

And so, in late May of 1539, de Soto's self-financed expedition, comprising nine ships, their crews, a large number of horses, mules, pigs, and war dogs, together with well over five hundred Europeans (including a pair of women and a few priests), landed on the west coast of Florida, near present-day Tampa Bay.

The previous Spanish expeditions—especially the disastrous, brutal Narváez debacle—had already given the Spaniards a bad reputation in that neighborhood. So their initial reception was for the most part cool.

Detail from a De Bry engraving after drawings by Jodocus Winghe. This engraving, depicting Taino Indians burdened with precious objects for the Spanish, first appeared in *Narratio Regionem, A Brief Telling of the Destruction of the Indians* by Bishop Bartoleme de la Casas of the Order of Santo Domingo, 1552.

But de Soto now and again had lucky moments. A few Spanish survivors had actually remained among the natives, which says a great deal for the forbearance of the locals. De Soto was particularly fortunate to land near the home of Juan Ortiz, a young survivor of Narváez's incompetence, who became probably the most important member of the new expedition, after de Soto himself. For he became de Soto's translator, offering a window through the language barriers between the conquistador and the great variety of peoples he encountered across most of the Southeast.

Ortiz had not had an easy time of it in his new home. During his first year and a half there, he was a prisoner in the household of Hirrihigua, a local chief, who had suffered greatly from Narváez, even after he went so far in accommodating him as to convert to Catholicism. When Narváez continued to bluster about and bully everyone in sight, Hirrihigua stood up to him. In retaliation, Narváez tortured Hirrihigua, and fed his mother to the pack of huge war dogs that accompanied every Spanish expedition. After that, Hirrihigua had little inclination to befriend Spaniards. And his young prisoner Ortiz survived the chief's rages only with the help of the women of the household, who eventually helped Ortiz escape to the home of Mucozo, a neighboring, and rival, chief.

Despite Ortiz's gifts as a translator, communication was hard. Because the expedition encountered several language families and every town spoke its own dialect, translation was a complicated process. At every encounter, there was a line of translators, with a local speaker standing at one end and Ortiz at the other. Predictably, misunderstandings were frequent, both by accident and intention. The Spanish wanted to locate gold, gems, and other portable wealth. Natives wanted to protect their homes, and, if possible, to use these foreigners for their own purposes; or to lure the Spanish off toward other communities.

The existing rivalries among local chiefs provided de Soto with his second stroke of good luck. And he continued to benefit from such rivalries as he led his horde of plunderers north. Even though earlier expeditions had taught native people not to expect friendly dealings with the Spanish, the Southeast had always been a complex political system of allies and potential enemies. Though every native community that met de Soto was all too aware of the terror he was prepared to unleash, each community also had its own particular aims: though a Hirrihigua was hostile, a Mucozo turned out to be friendly.

As the expedition proceeded, other important men here and there volunteered to join de Soto, hoping to benefit from the alliance. Such men used their involvement with the invaders to enhance their authority with their own people—provided that the Spaniards did not turn on them first. Under Spanish protection, some chiefs were able to attack and sometimes destroy their rivals within the regional system, and even to loot their temples. Indian allies often proved helpful to de Soto. During the first winter at Tallahassee, for instance, archers showed de Soto's men the penetrating power of native bows and arrows, which easily pierced European chain mail armor. And with native help, the amazed Spaniards managed to produce quilted cotton tunics (similar to a kind of body protection used by the Aztecs) that stopped most arrows and spears.

This Theodore De Bry engraving of 1590 depicts Indians forced to carry the baggage and supplies of the Spanish invaders. The de Soto expedition carried equipment for the taking of slaves.

As de Soto's Europeans wandered, though they carried some provisions of their own, they expected native communities to feed them. Friendly groups did this willingly up to a point, but hostile towns had to be plundered. In every community, soldiers took women as cooks and concubines. And slaves were captured to act as bearers and servants. Indeed, de Soto had planned this before he left Spain; for he carried with him iron collars and chains, the better to form slave baggage trains. Indians who refused to cooperate were put to the sword, burned alive, or thrown to the hounds. The more fortunate might only lose a hand or a foot to a Spanish blade. Again and again, after initial native attempts at cordiality were followed by long, crippling stays hardly different from a military occupation, the Indians turned on the Spanish and tried to drive them away, usually with great loss of life.

As de Soto's force left one community for another, hostages were taken along to guarantee safe conduct. Most went in cowering fear of the fierce war hounds and the extraordinary horses. Guides were especially abused to assure good conduct, even though such treatment often had the opposite effect.

Although de Soto was more inclined to use brute force, he did, nevertheless, learn, possibly with Ortiz's advice, some forms of persuasion. For instance, now and again, he would enter a new community needing food, guides, or bearers, and would order his interpreters to announce that "he was a son of the sun and came from where it dwelt." He would then hold a mirror before him and claim that no man could hide his thoughts from him, for the face that appeared in the mirror told him whatever anyone else was planning or thinking.

Shortly after the expedition began its march inland from Tampa Bay, a native leader in central Florida called Acuera (after his town and territory, a common practice), who already had suffered from Spanish savagery, tried to stop the

*Very high, powerful, and good master. The things that seldom happen bring astonishment. Think, then, what must be the effect, on me and mine, of the sight of you and your people, whom we have at no time seen, astride the fierce brutes, your horses, entering with such speed and fury into my country, that we have no tidings of your coming—things altogether new, as to strike awe and terror into our hearts. . . .*

—Creek Chief of Achese, 1540

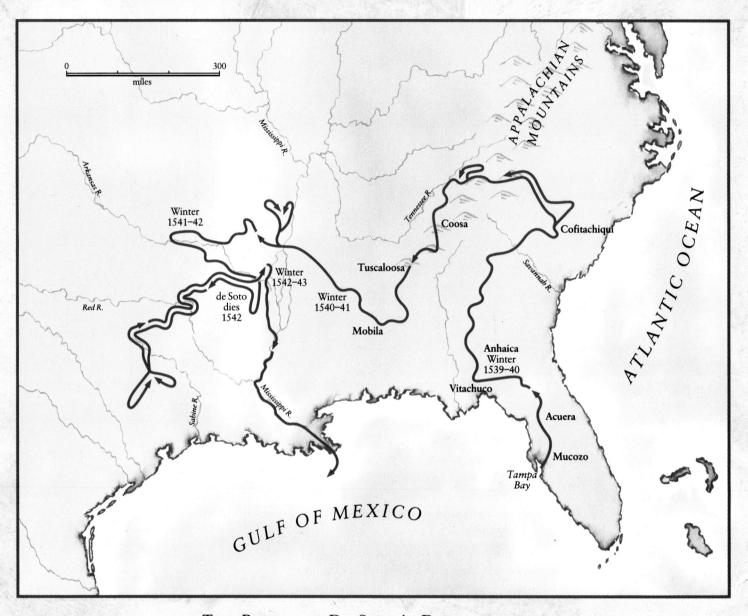

Arkansas R.

Mississippi R.

APPALACHIAN MOUNTAINS

Winter 1541–42

Red R.

Tennessee R.

Coosa

Cofitachiqui

Winter 1542–43

de Soto dies 1542

Tuscaloosa

Winter 1540–41

Savannah R.

ATLANTIC OCEAN

Mobila

Mississippi R.

Anhaica Winter 1539–40

Sabine R.

Vitachuco

Acuera

Mucozo

Tampa Bay

GULF OF MEXICO

## THE ROUTE OF DE SOTO'S DEPREDATIONS

Though de Soto's exact route is not known, its overall scope is fairly clear: over a period of four years, his force traversed much of the present-day southeastern United States. The invaders began by plundering north through the lands of the Tocobagans, and then west through the Florida panhandle. During the winter of 1539–40, de Soto occupied Anhaica, a town at the site of today's Tallahassee, in the country of the Apalachees, an important Mississippian chiefdom.

The Apalachees had abandoned Anhaica at the approach of de Soto's force, but that did not stop them from harassing de Soto's camp throughout the winter, and twice setting fire to it. In March, the Spaniards started northeast through Georgia and South Carolina, then turned west through Mississippi, where, in 1540–41, they spent a cold second winter.

In the spring of 1541, they marched north, and then west, crossing the Mississippi to Arkansas, where they wandered more than a year, wintering south of today's Little Rock. Next, they moved back to the Mississippi, where, in fact, de Soto

would die. After his death the remnants of the expedition meandered southwest through Arkansas, and parts of Louisiana and eastern Texas, before retracing their route back to the Mississippi River for the winter of 1542–43. There they built transports, and fought their way south to New Spain (Mexico). By then, close to three-quarters of the expedition of several hundred had perished. This high degree of attrition was due, in large part, to various native efforts to discourage the Spaniards.

intruders and turn them back the way they had come. He devised grisly messages for the Spaniards by way of announcing his displeasure at their presence: as long as the invaders remained in his territory, Acuera's warriors were ordered to continue bringing him the heads of Spaniards. During the three weeks the expedition tarried, fourteen heads were brought to Acuera. And even after the Spanish soldiers came upon the headless corpses of their comrades and gave them Christian burial, Acuera's warriors would dig up the graves, dismember the bodies, and hang the parts from trees. Undaunted, de Soto pressed on.

Later in 1539, in north Florida, de Soto arrived at the town of Vitachuco, where he met three brothers who, in some ways, shared the leadership. While the younger two proved to be conciliatory, perhaps hoping to gain authority at their elder's expense, the third brother, whose name was Vitachuco, was openly hostile, and made no secret of it.

As the paramount leader, he was the person most deeply and supernaturally bonded with the land; when the Spaniards approached, he invoked his supernatural ties and promised his people that natural disasters would destroy the intruders. If the invaders persisted, he vowed that fissures would open in the earth to swallow them, hills would clash together to crush them, winds would hurl trees at them, and birds would drop poison on them. When the Spanish came nearer, Vitachuco sent more threats to de Soto: he would capture his army, bake half of it, and boil the rest. Clearly he did not intend to respond to the Spanish overtures of friendship.

When no other course seemed open, Vitachuco rallied his people with promises of spiritual protection (as did many native prophets in later centuries and different places) and attempted to drive the Spanish out. Vitachuco failed in this endeavor, and in fleeing from the Spaniards many of his warriors were lost.

Yet when Vitachuco himself was taken prisoner, de Soto still tried to win his allegiance—doubtless because his brothers remained friendly and the Spaniards did not wish to lose their loyalty, and possibly because de Soto himself could not help but admire a man with such grit and fire. And so the native chief was accorded the respect of his position and "quality," for he was definitely among the elite in native terms.

Vitachuco never had any intention of cooperating: he bore the humiliation of feigned submission only until he could make an attempt at killing de Soto, knowing such an attempt surely meant his own death.

One night after dinner, while still seated, Vitachuco launched into a kind of trancelike dance. Summoning powers from the spirit of a mighty bird, he stiffened his spine and rocked forward and back. Then he clenched his fists, stretched his arms, and bent them back, with each fist resting on a shoulder—forming wings. After that, he flapped his elbows so swiftly and vigorously that his joints cracked. Riveted, the other diners gaped at him.

Suddenly, Vitachuco rose to his full height, grasped de Soto's neck with one hand and bludgeoned his face with the other. As de Soto sagged, Vitachuco continued to beat at him until the stunned officers recovered sufficiently to run him through with their swords. He was killed immediately. De Soto recovered, but remained unconscious for a good half hour, bleeding profusely from the eyes, nose, mouth, gums, and lips.

Detail from the title page of *Narratio Regionem, A Brief Telling of the Destruction of the Indians*, 1552.

*Your emperor may be a great prince: I do not doubt it, seeing that he has sent his subjects so far across the waters; and I am willing to treat him as my brother. As for the pope of whom you speak, he must be mad to speak of giving away countries that do not belong to him. As for my faith, I will not change it. Your own god, as you tell me, was put to death by the very men he created. But my god still looks down upon his children.*

—ATAHUALPA
    Inka ruler's response to hearing that Pope Alexander VI had declared Peru to be the possession of Spain, 1533.

## THE RICHES OF COFITACHIQUI

The temple of Cofitachiqui was rectangular, a hundred feet by forty, with benches set along the interior walls. Wooden chests holding the bones of leaders rested on these benches, each placed below a carved portrait statue of the man, woman, or child whose remains were so honored. Smaller boxes and baskets nearby were filled with pearls, and others held finely tanned skins.

Six pairs of standing interior posts were carved to portray giant warriors, each pair holding a different type of weapon. Along the upper walls were two rows of carved men and women. The men held weapons decorated with inlays, pearls, and tinted fringes.

The roof of cane and reeds was decorated, both inside and out, with many shells and long strands of pearls. Interior walls were also made of woven cane. Behind the walls were eight side rooms, each storing a different type of weapon.

During the spring of 1540, at the town of Cofitachiqui in present-day South Carolina, de Soto was welcomed by a younger noblewoman, a relative of the queen who ruled the town. When de Soto made his usual demands, this "Lady of Cofitachiqui" (as the Spanish called her) explained that she would not be able to oblige him: their own food was scarce that year because a great pestilence had recently killed many of their people (most likely either the disease vanguard of de Soto and his men, or lingering pestilence from the prior Spanish intrusions).

Though unable to feed his troops, this woman did her best to placate de Soto by allowing him to loot thousands of freshwater pearls from the local temple. This was the first real booty seized by the expedition, and de Soto triumphantly sent over fifty pounds of Cofitachiqui's pearls to Havana as proof that the region did indeed contain riches.

Since temples were the religious and political centers of towns throughout the Southeast, it is significant that de Soto was even allowed inside to see the treasures there. Indeed, there must have been much to see since each temple served as a repository of tribute and offerings, a cult center for the worship of ancestors, an armory for stockpiled weapons, and the sacred resting place for the bodies and bones of deceased members of noble families.

Unfortunately (though predictably) the Lady of Cofitachiqui's bribe of pearls failed to satisfy de Soto's greed. And so, after pillaging nearby villages, he seized the lady as a hostage and guide and marched onward. Though she managed to escape, the expedition was scarcely inconvenienced.

De Soto's party continued to drive north, then westward into the mountains, where, as experience in Mexico and Peru had taught, they had better hope of finding wealthy civilizations. When hope, once again, failed to triumph, they turned south and proceeded into Coosa, a large and prosperous chiefdom in present-day northeast Alabama and northwest Georgia. From there, de Soto continued south into the territory of Tuscaloosa, where a large allied army, led by the notably tall chief Tuscaloosa, lured the Spanish into a trap at Mobila, near modern day Mobile Bay.

During the pitched battle that ensued in October of 1540, there were many casualties. Thousands of natives were killed, de Soto himself was wounded, and most of the Spanish supplies were lost. Many horses and pigs were also destroyed, along with the vestments of the priests who accompanied the expedition, and the supply of wine and wheat flour used to make wafers for Holy Communion.

Not long after the disastrous encounter with Tuscaloosa, Ortiz, the translator, brought de Soto word that supply ships that might carry him and his men to safety were not far away on the Gulf of Mexico. Characteristically, de Soto decided to press on, so he kept quiet about Ortiz's news lest his men, now beginning to have their doubts about this hostile land making them wealthy, break out in rebellion. He marched north and into the interior, away from the coast with its opportunities for desertion.

For much of the next two years, the expedition wandered through the hills of present-day Arkansas, still searching for gold. Then, during the winter of 1541–42, Ortiz died, and with his death the already shaky expedition began to unravel. And in May of 1542 de Soto himself developed a fever and died.

Luis de Moscoso de Alvarado took over the expedition and led the survivors

The Dutch or Flemish artist who made this 1707 illustration of Indians fighting with the Spanish probably had little firsthand knowledge of the actual event. Many such images found their way into early histories of the "New" World, helping to disseminate distorted ideas of the people who lived there.

west, into the sparsely settled hinterland, where concerted attacks would be less likely. When they reached the land that is now Texas, they saw signs of bison for the first time, which they interpreted as evidence of herding, although they never, in fact, saw an actual bison. Then, finding themselves short of supplies in a desolate region, they backtracked toward the Mississippi River. For part of the way, a young native boy deliberately led them astray. Like a number of other courageous native guides, he was hoping to take the invaders into a trackless wilderness. But after a few days, Moscoso became suspicious and fed the valiant saboteur to the war hounds.

During their retreat inland, according to Garcilaso's chronicle, many suffered terribly from a "lack of salt." The disease that apparently resulted from this condition started with a low fever; then bodies began to turn green and rot. Sufferers eventually died. Though natives had pointed out an herb whose ashes cured the disease, the Spaniards continued to die as they felt it was "beneath their quality" to follow the advice of Indians. It may well be that sixty soldiers perished so that Spanish pride could be upheld.

Back at the Mississippi, the last survivors of de Soto's horde settled into a native town from which the inhabitants had fled. There they built boats that could carry them to New Spain.

After four years of Spanish viciousness and exploitation, the monumental patience of yet another local population had worn out. The large native communities along the Mississippi had had enough, and ten regions confederated to attack the departing Spanish. As the survivors floated down the river in June of 1543, they had to battle warriors in large canoes, each regional fleet painted a different color. Eventually, the remnants of the Moscoso party reached Mexico, where they fought among themselves about the degree of their "success."

# In the Aftermath of Encounter

In their wake, the Spaniards had left more disaster than even they realized. For the onset of diseases that killed the natives by the hundreds—but to which the Europeans were immune—was clear proof to the Indians that they had failed their gods in some way. The continuing deaths and the accompanying native self-blame took a massive toll among the Mississippian chiefdoms, with terrifying speed. By the time Tristán de Luna passed through Florida and Georgia in 1559–61, the full-fledged towns that de Soto had visited had devolved into sparsely occupied villages. When Juan Pardo came through the Carolinas in 1566–68, the towns of de Soto's day housed mere handfuls of refugees.

Again and again, throughout the Americas, as Europeans advanced, they moved into regions already emptied by disease.

With the demise of the Mississippian civilizations, drastic changes were made to create meaningful worlds. The social distance between noble and commoner all but vanished. Previously, the heads of clans had met inside temples set upon high earthen mounds to offer counsel to the chiefs. In the wake of depopulation, a communal labor force became so difficult to muster that palisades and mounds could no longer be built according to ritual requirements. Moreover, the leading families, who had once directed the work and sustained the form of worship, were now gone. These kin had held their literally exalted positions because of a special, age-old bond forged between their ancestors and the resident spirits of that place. With their death and virtual wipeout, this bond with the land was broken, and all spiritual relationships were thrown into disarray.

Religion moved down from the heights and into the town. The plaza or square replaced the mound as a meeting place. The temple with its ranked seats was gone; now men sat according to their clans inside open-fronted buildings constructed along the four sides of the town square. A sacred fire burned in the center, a symbol of the purity and persistence of the town. In large centers with many clans, the four seating areas were built like stepped bleachers, roofed with leafy branches (occasionally the passageways between the bleachers were also roofed). The elders of the clans and the leaders of the town would sit in the front row; above their seats were painted designs representing each clan. The treasures of the town were kept in a small room at the back of the building on the west side where the town chief sat, facing sunrise.

While ceremonies honoring the ancestral elite were abandoned, rites marking the agricultural year grew in importance, for everyone who ate the crop benefited from these ceremonies. Four times during the summer the community gathered to celebrate the maturation of the plantings, with the Green Corn ceremony held just before the harvest and marking the New Year. Everyone gathered to fast, pray, and dance their appreciation of the corn while it was alive and growing in the fields. The last rite was held in the fall when dancers, masked as animals, sanctified the community's economic shift from farming to hunting. Through participation in this ritual series, tribes were able to define their membership and assure continuity.

During the winter, a few towns continued to meet and hold ceremonies inside large domed rotundas, but eventually these too went out of use; the huge

*Creek Baskita Green Corn Dance* by Fred Beaver (Creek), 1953. The Creeks are said to be direct descendants of the Mississippi Mound civilization. During the Green Corn ceremony, now as in the past, a Creek town celebrated its annual renewal over several days. A new fire was kindled at the center of the square ground, fed by logs pointing in the four directions. Men of each clan sat in particular arbors on the north, east, south, and west of the ground. Behind the square was a large rotunda where meetings and ceremonies were held in winter or when secrecy was required.

outlays of labor needed to build and maintain them proved too difficult to organize. The monuments of the Mississippian elite, and the rituals that extolled them, became eclipsed by the summer plaza observances of the ordinary folk.

## Bringing the Remnants Together

In time, survivors from related villages banded together into new alignments, creating communities that were nothing like what had existed before. These new arrangements eventually became the political structures that Europeans later called "tribes." The method for the creation of these tribes took several forms. Survivors from many communities might come together to establish a new town, offering positions of leadership to those best qualified. The result was a more

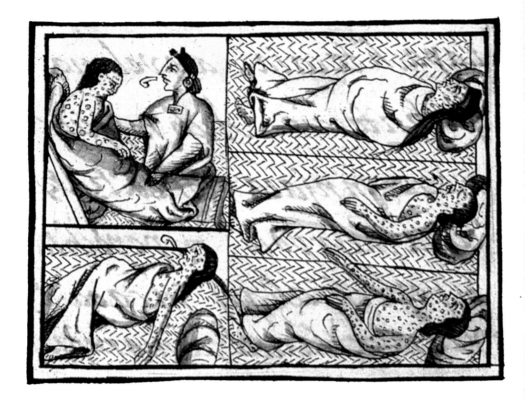

There were many contemporary depictions of the shocking impact of European diseases. Here a sixteenth-century Aztec artist shows the effects of smallpox.

democratic organization of chosen, rather than hereditary, officials. Or, if a large portion of a particular town had come through the epidemics, it might confederate with others to find strength in numbers. In a very few cases, chiefdoms—political units under a paramount or high chief—were created under the aegis of the few remaining members of an important family, which would consolidate its position by extensive regional ties based in marriage alliances and trade networks. But the old order was gone.

The historic Cherokee, Creek (Muskogee), Choctaw, and Chickasaw, rising from the ashes of the Southeast, began to live in farming communities that were smaller and more insular than their ancestors' bustling towns. The few survivors of the Apalachee, Timucua, and Calusa would, very much later, be adopted by some of the Creeks, themselves displaced from farther north. These Creek colonists became the Seminoles, who would eventually successfully battle with U.S. forces well into the 1800s, and would be a thorn in the side of the U.S. government for very much longer than that.

## DISEASE

The end result of the European quest for riches, slaves, and land was the reshaping of the native social order. But it was not the direct action of the Europeans themselves that produced this vast change. Rather, it was their inadvertent introduction of virulent diseases. The germs that Europeans carried to the so-called New World visited utter and complete devastation on its indigenous inhabitants. Diseases unknown in the Americas, to which the natives had no immunity, struck whole communities with fierce and heartrending violence.

Except for parasites, occasional malnutrition, and minor germs, the native population of the Americas was remarkably healthy. The people lived an open, uncrowded life, knew a great deal about herbal remedies and medications, and practiced cleanliness in sweat baths. This was sufficient to deal with most common illnesses. But this way of life proved no match for the germs cradled and nurtured in the filth of European cities and ports.

Smallpox, measles, and other common European diseases wiped out entire communities before most of their inhabitants had actually seen a European. Whole regions were depopulated. Only resourceful and flexible communities were able to retain enough of their integrity to survive one of these mysterious microbial attacks. But outlasting a single epidemic was often only the prelude to a series of epidemic onslaughts that attacked an increasingly weakened population. Sexual contact between the races led to the mutation of new forms of diseases like syphilis, which further decimated the native peoples..

# CHAPTER NINE

# THE SOUTHWEST AND COASTAL CALIFORNIA

*PUEBLO SISTERS*
BY ROGER PERKINS (MOHAWK), 1991

DURING THE WANDERINGS of the de Soto survivors into Texas, they came across native travelers with news that many leagues to the west there were men like themselves who had been seen in native communities. No doubt the natives tactfully did not mention the marauding that was taking place.

These reports referred to the invasion of a large mixed force of Spaniards and Mexican Indians led by Francisco de Coronado. In 1541 and 1542, this army penetrated and explored the lands that later became New Mexico, along with territories to the east and west. In the process, Coronado's men did their best to subdue the people they called the Pueblos, after the kind of structures the natives built. However, Spaniards were still trying to subdue the Pueblos a hundred years later—indeed, two hundred years later.

## Early Pueblo Resistance

In the early 1500s, New Mexico, particularly the Rio Grande Valley, was densely settled and intensively farmed. There were dozens of populous towns, made up of terraced, multistoried apartments skillfully built in compact units, a concentrated mode of living that allowed full exploitation of the available water and the limited fertile land along the creek beds. The Pueblos had developed a rich cul-

---

OPPOSITE: **Moon, Morning Star and Evening Star** by Ernest L. Blumenschein, 1922, depicts a composite of rituals expressing thanksgiving for crops and game animals.

Albert
looking
Elk

tural diversity over more than a millennium: at least four very different, mutually unintelligible language stocks were spoken, and many differing cultural traditions had grown among the close-knit adobe dwellers. In addition to these highly individualistic farmers, the region also included neighboring but hostile tribes—ancestors to the Apache, Navajo, Ute, and Comanche.

So much regional variety initially made resistance to the Spanish difficult, for the Pueblos did not traditionally cooperate easily with each other, much less with their often unfriendly, more nomadic neighbors. Coronado, gullible as all the Spanish were to tales of vast wealth waiting to be picked up, believed extravagant reports of a fabulously rich multistoried city near today's Arizona–New Mexico border. The place, called Cibola, did actually exist—after its own fashion. It was a town of Zuñi pueblos. Coronado and several hundred Spaniards, accompanied by their native Mexican servants, marched north to Zuñi. They found neither a city, nor gold, nor a population in any way disposed to welcome them. So they stormed Zuñi, ravaged the town, and having destroyed what was there, continued east to occupy a similar town near today's Albuquerque.

Though the lands along the Rio Grande were populous, farming was intensive because growing conditions were, at best, only slightly better than marginal. Life for the native inhabitants was more or less comfortable, if hard won, but there were never large surpluses. And so Coronado and his hundreds, wherever they marauded, soon exhausted the stored crops of local Pueblos.

ABOVE: **Zuñi Pueblo, New Mexico.**
LEFT: *View of a Pueblo* by **Albert Looking Elk (Taos Pueblo), pre-1941.**

*The Last Supper*
by **Jonathan Warm Day**
(Taos Pueblo), 1991.

Both Coronado and de Soto, in their separate times and places, taxed native hospitality beyond the limit. The same consequence followed in both the Southeast and the Southwest: when native food supplies became dangerously depleted, people rebelled. When local Pueblos tried to protect their own food caches, Coronado punished them by executing several hundred at a time.

The Pueblos tried craft and very nearly succeeded in luring—with spurious tales of gold—a Spanish detachment into the vast, trackless sea of grass that then existed in the Plains. The hope was that the guide, a non-Pueblo (and a true hero) known as the Turk because of his turbanlike head wrapping, would lose the invaders there. In fact, the Turk got them as far away as Kansas, but when the Spanish captain began to suspect him of treachery, he was tortured and executed.

Eventually, all hopes of wealth proved groundless for the murderous Spanish adventurers. Though Coronado was impressed with the large Pueblo population he found, with their sophisticated buildings, woven cotton clothing, and beautiful pottery, he came to realize that the Southwest and the Plains had nothing to offer him. During Christmastime of 1541, after he had been kicked in the head by his horse, he decided it was time for his expedition to retreat. Coronado had to be carried back to Mexico, where he lingered for several years, a sick and broken man, before dying in 1554.

Although diseases introduced by the Coronado expedition took their toll of the Pueblos, at least the Spanish stayed away for forty years, allowing native societies to regroup under the leadership of their powerful priesthoods. Coronado's visit also served to pave the way to greater unity among the Pueblos in resistance to the hated foreigners.

## Spanish Settlers on Pueblo Land

Eventually, Spanish seekers of wealth, blinded to reality by their greed for gold, returned to New Mexico. An expedition led by Francisco Sanchez Chamuscado in 1581 included several missionaries. When the leader gave up and went back south, the missionaries stayed behind. They were swiftly killed by the Indians, as Antonio de Espejo and his force learned two years later. The missionaries seemed to believe that Indian resistance to the divine message the Spaniards brought would wither under the force of their own arrogance. The Pueblos thought otherwise, and executed them—a fate that awaited any number of later missionaries.

Though these privately financed but officially sanctioned explorations failed to find the fabled gold, the dream of riches attracted several unauthorized attempts to found colonies. These parties were turned back by the Spanish authorities, who themselves wanted full control of exploiting the land and any colonists entering it. But even these abortive efforts on the part of private entrepreneurs did bring disease.

Hopi girl (1907). The characteristic hairstyle indicates that she is a maiden of marriageable age.

## Oñate's Colony Among the Tewa

In 1598, all of present-day New Mexico was granted to Juan de Oñate to found a permanent colony at his own expense, as was the common practice of the Spanish. This colony included 400 men (130 of them with families), many native Mexican servants, and 83 oxcarts, accompanied by over 7,000 horses, plus cattle, sheep, and goats. The Pueblos had no hope of opposing such an assemblage.

Nevertheless, Oñate avoided the central Rio Grande, already brutalized by Coronado and his successors, and instead made his headquarters in the upper valley to the north. Forced to accept the inevitable, the native priests of the pueblo called San Juan agreed to yield a neighborhood of the Tewa town to the Spanish. At the urging of the priests, all the Indians moved out of that neighborhood. The Spanish settled in, christening their new home San Gabriel. In occupying the pueblo, the Spanish enlarged the rooms, added windows, and rearranged the entrances, both for defense—a factor they were always aware of—and to suit their own architectural tastes. A small church was also built, and consecrated to San Miguel. Meanwhile, the displacement of the native population concentrated its members even closer together, increasing the authority of the priests, and making their own defensive actions that much easier to organize.

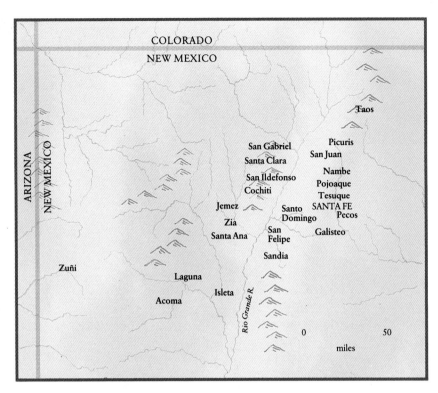

*The Rio Grande Pueblos.*
When Coronado arrived in the Rio Grande Valley in 1540, there were over one hundred pueblos containing rich and distinct cultural traditions.

*Mission San Gabriel* (Los Angeles, California) by Ferdinand Deppe, 1832.

*Cochiti Green Corn Dance with Koshare* by Joe Hilario Herrera (Cochiti), 1947.

BELOW AND FOLLOWING:
**Kachinas are sacred spirits representing many aspects of nature celebrated in dance and song.** *Mosairu Buffalo Kachina* (BELOW) **dances in prayer for the abundance of that life source.**

The Tewa people, then as now, were divided into Summer and Winter moieties. In 1598, these halves were separated by the Rio Grande. The west side, which later became the Spanish San Gabriel, was called Yunge (Mockingbird Place), and it was occupied by the Summer moiety. The east side, called Okeh, was home to the Winter moiety. The entire town was governed by the leaders of each half during its appropriate season, summer or winter, and both halves were integrated by an interlocking hierarchy of priests who combined in their persons both civil authority and religious leadership. Indeed, the two were inseparable.

Each Pueblo town was tightly organized under a series of overlapping priesthoods. Pueblo priests controlled the affairs of each community, conducted elaborate masked rituals dedicated to supernatural beings called *kachinas*, and passed on generations of ecological wisdom that enabled farmers to thrive in an arid environment. The factor that controlled this concentration of power in the priesthood was the division into Summer and Winter moieties. Each half had to perform well for all to benefit, for if either half performed badly, all would suffer. So seeing the world from another point of view, recognizing the needs of others, was built into the Pueblo system of thinking and belief.

The Tewas, like other Pueblo peoples, were profoundly rooted in their land, through the everyday practicalities of their farming economy as well as the spiritual dimensions that pervaded all existence. Every stage of the planting and harvesting of the fields was regulated by the priests and the ritual calendar. The territory surrounding the town was seen as a series of spiritually significant concentric rings that served to direct and focus the life flow into and out of the center of the community. At the margins of the Tewa lands lay a ring of sacred mountains and hills; closer in was a circle of shrines that the Tewa people had constructed; and finally came the town's interior plazas and kivas, where the principal dances and rites were conducted.

When the site of San Juan was developed, over six hundred years ago, these cosmological patterns relating people to the land had already existed for thousands of years, going back to the ancient ancestors of the Pueblos. Though a community might now and again move to a new location nearer fresh fields and timber, that did not end the relationship with the land; rather, the new source of life reaffirmed belief in the renewal of their roots. For the people's bond was with the land itself, not with the homes where they lived, which were viewed merely as shelters from the weather. Indeed, except during cold weather, people mostly lived out of doors. And although, as it always must be, it was a sad wrench to leave their individual homes, the Tewa, eyeing the apparent overabundance of horses, sheep, and cattle in the Spaniards' train, and in keeping with their own naturally generous habit, may well have imagined that there might be advantages to the Spanish occupation.

But the wary hope of the priesthood of possibly coming to terms with the colony was quickly shattered, and the people's lives were almost immediately badly shaken by the Spanish presence. For one of the colony's chief aims was an active program to compel the Pueblos to become Catholics. Ten friars had been assigned to the task, backed by the full force of the military. Any town that resisted this violently arrogant mission was viciously subjugated.

At the same time, soldier-colonists, unable to extract their own food and clothing from the hard land, extorted corn, beans, squash, clothing, and supplies for themselves and their livestock from the increasingly hard-pressed Pueblos— by means of wholesale torture, murder, and rape. Active resistance was immediately and savagely suppressed.

When the people of Acoma, whose adobe houseblocks were built high atop a rock mesa in western New Mexico, attacked a force led by one of Oñate's nephews, killing eleven Spaniards, including the nephew, Oñate's retaliation was swift and brutal. He stormed and burned the entire pueblo, killing in the process some five hundred men and three hundred women and children, then sentenced the survivors to twenty years of labor, and ordered every man among them over twenty-five years old to have a foot cut off.

It is difficult to credit such frank, outright, systematic brutality even at this distance. To the Pueblos, deliberate violence on a massive scale was virtually unthinkable. More and more Pueblos rebelled, and eventually most of Oñate's colonists, beginning to doubt the colony's viability, returned to Mexico. In 1606, Oñate himself was replaced, having been charged with mismanagement.

In 1610, the Spanish capital moved from San Gabriel to a new location called Santa Fe. And new Spanish settlers established haciendas on land grants throughout the Rio Grande region. These grants, in feudal fashion, included resident natives, who were expected to provide food and labor for their *patrón*. Not

*Ahöla,* an important participant in the Powamu ceremony, appeals to the Sun for health, happiness, long life, and good crops.

*Paiyakyamu or Hano Chukuwaiupkia, Hano Clown or Koshare,* is derived from the Kossa spirit of the Tewa, who live on first mesa among the Hopi. Like clowns the world over, he is irreverent and noisy.

*Sowi-ing Kachina,* or *Deer Kachina,* is very powerful and not only appeals to deer but also controls the rain.

*Takus Mana, Yellow Corn Maiden,* depicts the "rasping" of a gourd, part of the accompaniment to the dance.

*Palakwai, Red-tailed Hawk Kachina,* is one of the chief kachinas for the initiation years.

*A-ha Kachina Mana.* The literal meaning of "mana" is "woman." Here it signifies the kachina is female although the actual performer is a man.

surprisingly, these new overlords, if not as frankly brutal as their predecessors, typically abused the unwilling natives by making impossible demands on their time and resources, while the monumental arrogance of forced religious "conversion" continued.

At various times, as the fires of Pueblo hostility smoldered and grew, individual pueblos openly rebelled: Zuñi, in 1632; Taos, in 1639–40; Jemez, in 1644 and again in 1647; and the Tewa villages, in 1650. No doubt there were other outbreaks of violent protest that the Spanish did not mention in their reports—they did not, obviously, want to be replaced for incompetence. And in all of these hostilities, Spaniards lost lives and property, with missionaries being especially vulnerable (perhaps because they were especially hated).

## The Pueblo Revolt

Finally in 1680, exhausted and embittered by decades of Spanish exploitation and religious persecution, the Pueblo Indians united in rebellion. It was largely native priests who managed to organize the Pueblo Revolt that drove the Spanish colonists out of the Pueblo lands and successfully kept them out for twelve years.

Both the 1680 Revolt and the alliance that made it possible were accomplished under the guidance of a native priestly leader of San Juan named Popé. His name, "Ripe Plantings" in English, associated Popé with the Summer moiety, and thus with plants and growth, and with the female, life-giving, nurturing side of existence, which meant that his primary duty was to protect life. It was a duty he would have taken with the utmost seriousness in anything but the most trying times. That such a man, with such a dedication, would feel he must mastermind the attack on the Spanish indicates just how bad times had become.

During the attack, half the colonists were slain, along with most of their livestock. Afterward, such was the disrepute of the Europeans among the Indians that everyone was urged to give up all European goods. And such was the disrepute of the Catholic religion that native priests held rituals to "unbaptize" the converts, to free them of that malign influence.

Though the Pueblos succeeded in keeping the Spanish out of New Mexico only until 1692, when the collapse of their alliance opened the way for the Spanish to reoccupy the region, the Revolt of 1680 was a long-term success, at least for the Pueblo peoples; for never again did the Spanish try to impose their religion or their culture with such brutal ferocity as they had done before the Revolt. They had permanently lost their appetite for total submission from the inhabitants of the pueblos.

## Coastal California

During the seventeenth century, Spanish voyagers like Sebastian Vizcaíno moved up the Pacific coast, charting currents and mapping harbors. Other explorers fol-

OPPOSITE: *The Pueblo Revolt* by Aubrey Sanchez, 1992.

lowed, searching for minerals and converts. Like de Soto's and Coronado's expeditions, these Spanish ventures were authorized by the Spanish viceroy, but conducted at personal expense. This meant that very probably—again, like de Soto and Coronado—they used any means at their disposal to recoup their investment and turn a profit. The local populations suffered to a greater or lesser degree, but whether or not they had suffered from the first arrival of the Spanish, the native peoples of the lands now called California quickly concluded that these visitors were a likely threat, and certainly a sign that major changes were coming. In consequence, they soon developed confederations and realignments for defense that were in many ways similar to those developed by the Pueblos and other groups farther east.

A wide variety of peoples lived in California in those days. Though most of them, encouraged by the rugged terrain, had settled in small, scattered communities along waterways, regional cults and intercultural trade fused these villages into larger networks. However, until the eighteenth century, when Spanish missionaries concentrated them at missions, this dispersed population remained remarkably free from the terrible epidemic scourges that destroyed so many other native populations. But in the densely populated mission centers, diseases were easily transmitted and thousands of natives perished. A number of native tribes were totally, or almost totally, lost.

Among the peoples who only barely survived these mission-borne epidemics were the Chumash, who lived in the neighborhood of today's Santa Barbara. From a population of tens of thousands, only a few hundred survived. Fortunately, a sense of their complex society and sophisticated astrononomical knowledge has been preserved.

The Chumash lived along a zone rich in natural resources, varying from acorns to marine mammals. Then as now, it was regarded as prime real estate. During the middle 1600s, as the increasing number of Spanish visits began to mount to an ever-growing menace, Chumash leaders met to coordinate a response: specifically, to create a political system that would allow them to deal with the Spanish threat as a unified people. Yet, in so doing, they had no thought of producing anything like a new organization; they were drawing upon long-established Chumash practices. The end result of their efforts was a national council modeled after the councils then governing each community: an assembly of twenty leaders representing hereditary elite families, shamans, and the heads of various craft guilds.

The twenty positions of the new Chumash national council were held by a representative from each of the twelve biggest villages and by eight members at large. These people monitored the use of the territory, kept overall track of the various communities (including some apparently minor details like the naming of babies), and gathered necessary information. This national council was placed under the general leadership of a man whose title meant "esteemed." And it proved effective and resilient enough to survive as long as the Chumash lived in dispersed communities—that is, until the rise of the germ-infested missions.

Image of the Virgin Mary painted on a buffalo hide by a native American artist from the southwest around 1675.

*False Face Beggars* by Edson Thomas (Onondaga), 1963.
Known as vision faces, the masks worn by the men holding turtle rattles embody
visions that came in dreams to members of the False Face Society. The man in the
center wears a mask referred to as a "spoon mouth."

# CHAPTER TEN

# THE NORTHEAST

DELAWARE MOCCASIN AND ROACH HEADDRESS

ONCE THE SPANISH had established a firm hold on the southern coasts of America, as well as the interior south, other European nations seeking to develop colonies were forced to explore the possibilities elsewhere. The Atlantic coast was an obvious attraction.

The coastal watersheds of the Northeast were then occupied by diversified Algonquian-speaking communities, while Iroquoians lived along the interior waterways. The Algonquian and Iroquoian peoples had been in contact in these lands for at least a millennium. Although they spoke different languages and engaged in sporadic hostilities, they shared many features of their respective cultures. Both groups were matrilineal, and both were farmers, with women performing the actual life-giving function of putting in and harvesting crops.

The northernmost farmers were the Hurons, living in towns located near present-day Georgian Bay. They thus had direct contact with the migratory bands who roved the Subarctic, periodically bringing furs south for trade. Also in touch with peoples west and south of their own territory, the Hurons were preeminent traders in the Northeast, and their language served as a common means of communication from the Great Lakes to the Atlantic.

The Hurons and the Algonquians also shared certain religious rituals, based on periodic comings together to honor their dead in elaborate ceremonies. The Iroquois, however, were united by a separate and powerful political union.

The whole continent was crisscrossed by a web of trails and routes that constituted a vast trading network. In the Northeast, storable food, raised by the farming communities, would be exchanged for furs, meat, nuts, and other products from the wild, along with more exotic goods like nuggets of iron ore, special flints, mica, shells, and other items that might have traveled several hundred miles through a succession of barters, on the coast-to-coast trade routes.

*The Northeast Longhouse* by Greg Harlin.
These were enormous structures, running 50 to 200 feet long and 25 feet wide. They were kept homey by the fact that many families of the same matrilineage occupied one building. The men built the framework of elmwood and the facings and the roof of elmbark. A man lived with his wife's family.

Smoke from the cookfires that lit the dim interior escaped through staggered holes in the roof. (There were also outdoor fireplaces for use in good weather.) But in heavy rain or winter snow the smokeholes would be partially closed by a series of shutters, and even though the roofs were high, eyes would sting from the smoke, and no doubt the steam from soupkettles and the variety of smells from babies, bear grease, soot, tobacco, and assorted humanity combined to create a rather special atmosphere. At the very least, it was warm and dry.

On each sidewall, widely divided by the central corridors, were raised platforms separated for privacy by skin curtains. Here an entire family could sleep snugly among a variety of furs. Above their heads were deep shelves for storage, and every pole, beam, and rafter carried its load of drying foods—peppers, squash, apples, corn, and herbs of all kinds.

INSET, TOP LEFT:
A firepit for cooking, warmth, light, and socializing.

INSET, TOP RIGHT:
Hollow logs for the pulverizing of dried corn and assorted grains.

INSET, BOTTOM RIGHT:
Shelves holding baskets, pottery, weapons, spare skins, cooking implements, antlers, and corn husk mats.

## Huron Society

Like most natives of the Northeast, the Huron lived in longhouses, skillfully made with saplings bent and tied together at the top, creating a tall framework with curved roof and sides. This framework was then covered with slabs of bark. A central corridor was dotted with firepits, and mat curtains formed cubicles along the sides. Bunks built along the walls did double service as seats and as beds, while storage spaces were located under the bunks, on shelves, and in pits dug into the floor. Many hooks and pegs were available for hanging garments, bags, baskets, and the assorted paraphernalia of family living. Plant foods were hung from the rafters to dry in the heat and smoke that rose from the firepits.

Because the Huron were a matrilineal society, mothers and daughters lived in the same longhouse. Each family occupied a compartment along one side of the central aisle where the cooking fires burned. Everyone snacked from the more or less communal clay pots during the day, but families ate together at mealtimes. The senior woman of each household dished out food and, as a gesture of respect to the protectors of her family, made sure that men ate before women.

The leadership of each of these clan segments rested with a particular household, whose eldest able-bodied woman was the clan matron, the coordinator of the clan's domestic and economic needs. From among her male relatives, she chose two men to lead the clan, a civil chief and a war captain.

Married men lived in the households of their wives. Yet, because a married man's primary relationship was with his own clan (that of his mother and sisters) rather than his wife's (or his wives'), marriages tended to be short-lived. Indeed, when it came to raising a couple's children, it was the brothers of the wives who assumed the role that fathers usually take in other societies, for they and their sisters belonged to the same clan. And so brothers of wives had the responsibility of raising their nieces and nephews to be proper adults, knowledgeable about clan heritage and affairs. However, since men were often away for long periods, trading, raiding, or visiting, the day-to-day rearing of children was usually performed by related women.

The Hurons were divided into eight matrilineal clans, distributed among a confederacy of four tribes. But with the arrival of Europeans and the inevitable disease-borne death toll that followed, two of these tribes, in 1590 and 1610 respectively, joined their reduced numbers for mutual protection against intertribal warfare. Because members had to marry into a clan different from their own, most clans were represented in every village. During ceremonies, clans were grouped into three clan-clusters, known as the Wolves, Turtles, and Deer.

In addition to these kinship-based links, other forms of bonding developed. The various healing or curing fraternities, with strong spiritual significance, and the interclan councils that deliberated over general clan welfare were groupings that required the cooperation of unrelated neighbors and thereby helped to fuse each town into a cohesive community.

With the arrival of the French there was, of course, much change for the Hurons, and, as with the Spanish, whose horses and other goods were prized by the natives, the introduction of European trade goods in the Northeast enhanced many aspects of Huron life. Indeed, all native inhabitants quickly recognized the

Navajo sod or adobe hogan

Plains buffalo hide tipi

Yukon double lean-to

Prairie earthlodge

Seminole stilt chickee

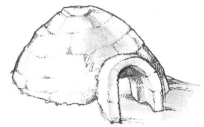

Arctic domed snow house

Great Basin thatched wickiup

Plateau mud pit house

Northwest Coast multifamily plank house

Southeastern wattle and daub hut

Algonquian mat or bark wigwam

Southwest stone or adobe pueblo

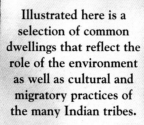

# NATIVE DWELLINGS

Illustrated here is a selection of common dwellings that reflect the role of the environment as well as cultural and migratory practices of the many Indian tribes.

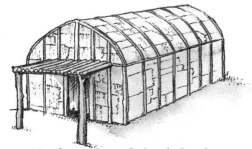

Northeastern multifamily longhouse

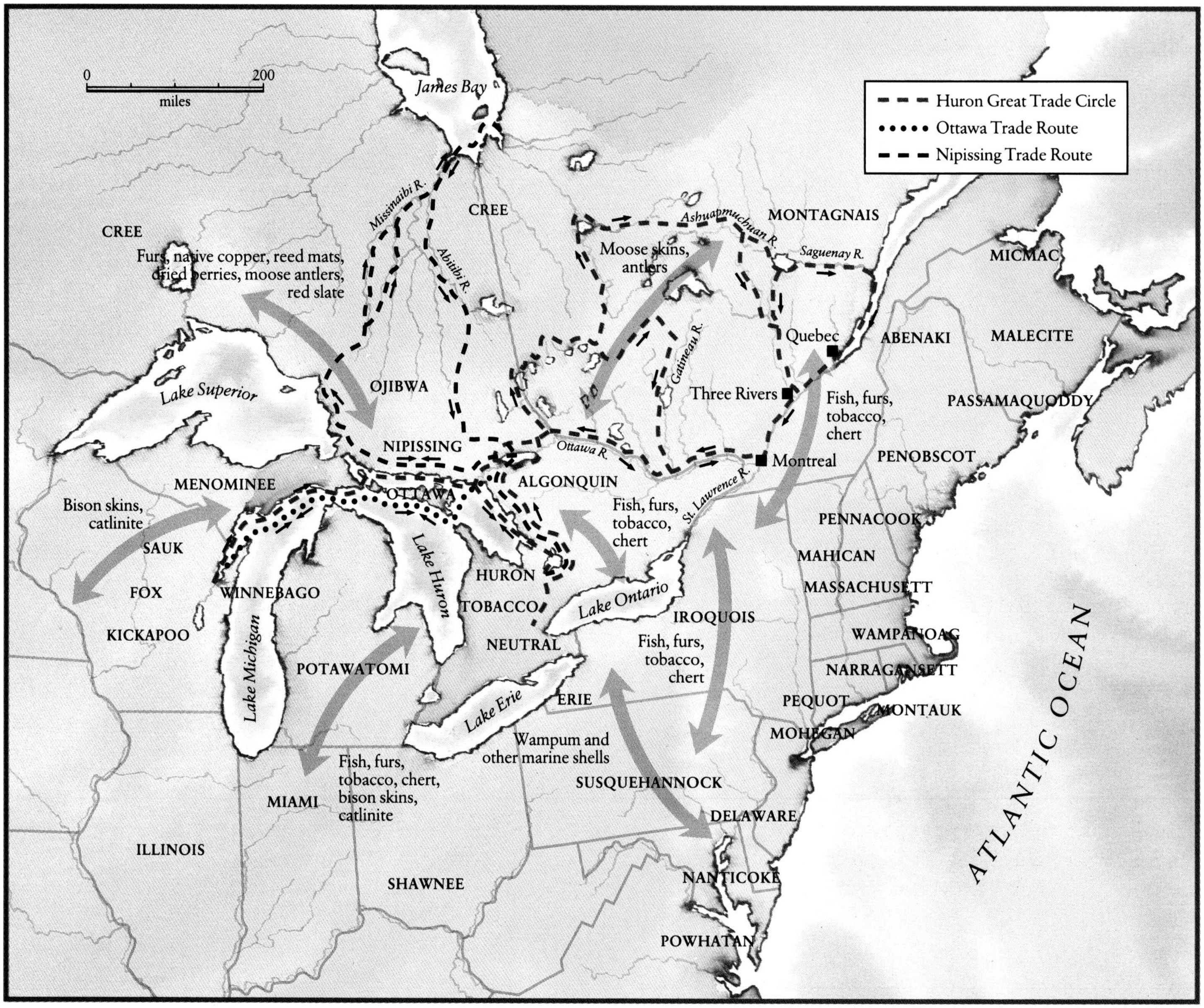

0
200
miles
James Bay
Huron Great Trade Circle
Ottawa Trade Route
Nipissing Trade Route
Missinaibi R.
Abitibi R.
CREE
CREE
MONTAGNAIS
Ashuapmuchuan R.
Saguenay R.
Furs, native copper, reed mats, dried berries, moose antlers, red slate
Moose skins, antlers
MICMAC
Quebec
ABENAKI
MALECITE
Gatineau R.
Lake Superior
OJIBWA
Three Rivers
Fish, furs, tobacco, chert
PASSAMAQUODDY
NIPISSING
Ottawa R.
Montreal
PENOBSCOT
MENOMINEE
ALGONQUIN
Bison skins, catlinite
OTTAWA
St. Lawrence R.
Fish, furs, tobacco, chert
PENNACOOK
SAUK
Lake Huron
MAHICAN
HURON
MASSACHUSETT
FOX
WINNEBAGO
TOBACCO
Lake Ontario
IROQUOIS
KICKAPOO
Lake Michigan
NEUTRAL
Fish, furs, tobacco, chert
WAMPANOAG
POTAWATOMI
NARRAGANSETT
ERIE
PEQUOT
MONTAUK
Lake Erie
MOHEGAN
Wampum and other marine shells
ATLANTIC OCEAN
Fish, furs, tobacco, chert, bison skins, catlinite
MIAMI
SUSQUEHANNOCK
DELAWARE
ILLINOIS
SHAWNEE
NANTICOKE
POWHATAN


***The Northeast Trade Network.***
**A complex system of trade routes linked the northeastern tribes and allowed for the exchange of a wide variety of goods. The Hurons, along with the Nipissings and the Ottawas, played the role of middlemen in an empire that traded agricultural goods from the southern farmers, fishing and hunting bounty from the northern bands, and items such as sea shells (wampum) and bison skins from more distant tribes. The Hurons further extended their influential role with the arrival of the French and the rise of the lucrative fur trade.**

utility of the iron tools that made daily living so much easier. The metal implements were slower to dull than their stone counterparts, and far less liable to break, and the knives and axes were already shaped, fit for immediate use.

But it was the addition of exotic goods such as shiny pieces of jewelry, beads, and bright-colored cloth that particularly delighted the Hurons and made the most notable difference to their lives. For these very quickly became status markers. People who wore them were able to show off their new wealth and demonstrate their close involvement with the trade network (conspicuous consumption affects all peoples now and again, in one way or another). The new trade goods also helped the Huron to make existing ceremonies and rituals more elaborate, especially in the case of the Feast of the Dead. This rite was the most solemn and special ceremony among the Huron—participation in it defined membership in a town and affirmed clanship—and it was deeply connected to the land.

Every decade or so, when its nearby farmlands had become less productive and local firewood scarce, each Huron village relocated. Although fields might ordinarily have a useful life of no more than four to six years, the Hurons were able to plant for as long as a decade or more by adding wood ashes as fertilizer and carefully weeding the crops.

As a last act at the old village, the remains of most of the dead were removed from their graves and placed together in a common pit, or ossuary. Before this final interment, as a last gesture of affection, kinswomen lovingly removed any remaining flesh from the bones. In addition to the bones, many gifts and offerings went into the pit. Because European trade goods were seen as truly "otherworldly," they were especially favored as offerings for the dead. Among the Huron, this rite of unity was known as the Kettle, presumably because the excavated bowl filled with bones was intended to "cook" the spirits of the dead into their final state of release.

The first funeral after the death of each loved one was a time of grief and mourning. Heavy taboos were observed during the funeral, and for some time afterward. During mourning, the closest relatives remained unkempt; and they literally prostrated themselves with grief, lying silently for ten days with their faces pressed to the earth. Mourning continued for an entire year, with mourners maintaining a subdued and aloof demeanor. Such careful regard for the deceased and his or her initial burial ensured the release of the first soul and allowed it entry into the afterworld, there to await the arrival of the second soul.

The Kettle ceremony was therefore anything but sad. It was a joyous celebration, confirming the release of a Huron's second soul, which united with the first soul, making an individual whole again. The Kettle was a great relief to everyone—the long mourning over, the responsibilities of the living to the dead at last discharged, and the dead person's souls joined for the ultimate journey into a pleasant land where everybody lived much as before, but with less hardship. Huron beliefs embraced the living as well. For though the afterworld itself was a land of relative ease, the way there was seen as arduous; and so the souls of the very young and the very old were not strong enough to make the journey. Instead, they stayed at old villages, planting spiritual crops in the depleted fields left to lie fallow, thus renewing the earth in a bond between the dead and the living who would one day return to reoccupy the same earthly places.

## The Iroquois

Across Lake Ontario, south of Huron territory, the Iroquois lived at the headwaters of various streams and rivers in what has become central New York. From meager beginnings in this backwater, these speakers of five different dialects confederated into the League of the Longhouse, or the Iroquois League.

In common with all Indians, the members of the Iroquois League suffered severe population loss from disease, fierce attacks on their towns, devastation of their fields, and internal conflicts. But these Five Nations found a way not only to endure but to preserve their own particular character. They accomplished this primarily by filling their depleted ranks with adopted captives (particularly Hurons), but also by working whenever possible as a confederation, and finally,

## IRON AND BAUBLES

After the waves of epidemics, the next great tremor of consequence that shook the native peoples was the introduction of European manufactured goods.

For thousands of years, trade routes had crisscrossed the Americas. Exotic and prestige goods like galena (iron ore) cubes, crystals, pretty flints, turquoise, shells, and mica moved from coast to coast. The foreign goods first entered the native trade network in rare, and therefore valuable, quantities; but even in small amounts these goods quickly modified power structures and alliances.

Precontact marketplaces were usually at towns located along the border between those people who harvested from nature and those who farmed. The introduction of new sources of exotic goods—from European landfalls, trading posts, and settlements—upset this structure, creating new traders and new routes. Enterprising local families who opened a trade conduit made every effort to maintain it against all rivals. To further complicate matters, these new traders broke into the system at about the same time that more distant communities were being wracked by epidemics. The new trade gave people and communities another economic base from which to develop, just as the old economic bases, and many communities as well, were collapsing.

by allying with the eventual European victor. So while their neighbors were scattered by the foreign invasion, the increasingly powerful Iroquois grew into the most feared and respected native people in the Northeast.

When the Iroquois made their presence most forcefully felt, during the years of the Anglo-French rivalry and conflict in the 1600s and 1700s, the Five Nations asserted their authority over other native peoples with a well-planned campaign of terror. Iroquois war bands attacked and destroyed dozens of towns of their rivals in the fur trade, including the Hurons, Eries, Illinois, and others. And they tortured and killed hundreds of prisoners from these raids. Yet, for all the prisoners they killed, they adopted many hundreds more.

These captives, once they were adopted into a longhouse and clan, became full members of the community. In fact, some of them so identified with their new people that they later joined Iroquois attacks against their former relatives. The ability to accomplish such transferences allowed the Iroquois, in the face of the calamities brought on by the European onslaught, to be hugely successful in maintaining not only their numerical strength but also—and more importantly—their traditions.

In fact, while the ancestry of any modern-day Iroquois might originally derive from any of the nations of the world, the basic cultural and social institutions of the Iroquois heritage have survived and evolved.

## Algonquian Societies

Whether they were hunters or farmers, virtually all other tribes in the Northeast spoke Algonquian languages. Along the coast, among farmers such as the Massachusetts, the Lenape (or Delaware), and the Powhatans of Virginia, the usual political system was the chiefdom. Their towns were linked into regional networks under the care of elite families known as sachems or *sakimas*. Followers gave tribute to these elite families, which was then passed along to the needy, or used in annual ceremonies of thanksgiving, hosted by the sachems in gratitude for the bounty of the fields and lands.

During the spring and fall, everyone (farmers and hunters) left their homes and camped along the coast or in the hills to gather what nature provided. These foods were stored in towns for winter use.

Farther north, above the 160-day growing season required to ripen corn, Algonquians lived in kindred villages, moving to seasonal camps to take advantage of maturing fruits, berries, and nuts. In Maine, Micmacs and Malecites observed a well-ordered sequence of seasonal gatherings that included seal hunting in January; communal hunts for beaver, otter, moose, bear, and caribou during February and March; fishing the spawning runs late in March; gathering herring, sturgeon, salmon, and Canada goose eggs late in April; leisurely cod fishing and shellfish collecting along the coast from May to September, while also harvesting the ripening summer fruits; eel fishing late in September along inland rivers; hunting for fattened beaver and moose in October and November; and, as if by a gift of the gods during a time of normally great need, fishing for spawning tomcod under ice-covered waters in the depths of winter.

THE IROQUOIS LEAGUE

The origins of the Iroquois League, a symbolic longhouse uniting the tribes of central New York, probably date to 1450 when an eclipse was interpreted by the Iroquois as a sign to confederate. While allowing each member tribe to act independently, the League also provided a mechanism for concerted action that could place thousands of warriors in the field, and later served the Indians in their dealing with the Europeans, once they were on the scene.

The original League, also called the Five Nations (not to be confused with the Five Civilized Tribes of the Southeast—a purely European designation), consisted of the Mohawks, Oneidas, Onondagas, Cayugas, and Senecas. In the 1700s, they would be joined by the Tuscarora, to become the Six Nations.

OPPOSITE:
*The Seasonal Harvest*
by Narda Lebo.

*The Moose Chase*
by George de Forest Brush, 1888.

# The French and the Fur Trade

Every oceangoing European country had its own objectives for exploitation of
the Americas. Some came simply to steal portable riches, while others wanted to
establish themselves as landed gentry—courtesy of whatever monarch in the
home country laid claim to a particular piece of New World territory. Some came
to settle and colonize, while others intended only to extract valuable products of
nature for export back to Europe. Some came as refugees from religious persecution (though determined to convert any they encountered to their own views),
while others, representing the religious establishment, came to acquire more souls
to the greater glory of their God. And a very few came to trade, recognized the
Indian as an equal, and entered into the life of the native inhabitants.

The French, after failed attempts at colonies in tropical America—in Brazil
to exploit the brazilwood trade, until the Portuguese drove them out; in Florida
among Mississippian survivors, until the Spanish raided their settlement and
massacred its inhabitants—turned their attention to the northern lands we now
know as Canada. French claims to these territories derived from earlier visits

made by Breton fishermen and more especially from the voyages of Giovanni da Verrazano, an Italian explorer hired by King Francis I to find a western sea passage to China. In 1524 Verrazano identified a body of water—it could have been the Delaware River or Chesapeake Bay—as the passage to the Pacific, but his error went undetected by the French king. The French further bolstered their claims on religious grounds, convinced that they would have success in converting the northern natives to Catholicism.

While the French explorers, like other Europeans, were lured by prospects of finding gold and other precious metals—or even the vaguely rumored direct route to Asia—it turned out to be the unplanned trade in fish and furs that nurtured a French empire.

After initial visits to the coast, the French entered the St. Lawrence River and placed their first settlements along the banks of this great waterway. Through this strategic position they would gain access to the Great Lakes, the Mississippi River, and ultimately to the interior of the whole continent. In the other direction, because it was deep and richly supplied with nutrients from interior drainages, the St. Lawrence nourished the abundant sealife of the Grand Banks off Newfoundland. Soon after Columbus's initial voyages, Basques had come to hunt whales there, and the English, Spanish, and Portuguese had come for cod. Some, like the Bretons from Normandy, may even have arrived before 1492.

The natives did not have much interaction with these early fisherfolk. In those days, fishermen carried their catch away from the fogs of Labrador to the more welcoming coast between Nova Scotia and Maine, where they dried it over low fires. Such land bases became points of brief contact with natives, spreading some trade goods—and of course diseases. Later, during the last decades of the 1600s, a wet cod fishery developed, and this meant even less contact with the locals. For fishermen lived almost entirely aboard the large ships where they dressed the fish and stored them wet between layers of salt. Sailors only came on shore for fresh water, wood, and meat, or to make repairs.

Meanwhile, back on land, economic developments of much greater significance were already making their presence felt—developments that touched every native, and utterly transformed the foundations of their economy and lifestyle. The fur trade began to take hold. This had started in the late 1500s, and by the turn of the century the ancient round of farming-hunting-gathering had taken second place to the more urgent task of trapping for furs. Native men were now employed not only as hunters and trappers but as processors. And the women cleaned and tanned the furs.

Entire families wore beaver pelts to season them for the trade. The best pelts were taken in winter and worn with the fur next to the body for as long as a year and a half. Of course not all pelts were of the same grade, so not all required this special treatment. But the prime pelts were rubbed with animal marrow, and trimmed into rectangular shapes, so that between five and eight could be sewn together to make a cape. When this garment was worn with the fur next to the human skin, the pelts became oiled, pliable, yellow, and downy. The final result was a fine plush of underhair about an inch thick, ideal for making felt. These pelts were then ready for trade. Later, the prime pelts were made into felt hats, the fashion that motivated this whole process.

The Micmac was one of the first native groups to encounter Europeans. The clothes they wore, as illustrated in this portrait of a Micmac mother and son taken in Nova Scotia around 1865, reflect three hundred years of contact with the French.

O, what an ugly man! Is it possible that any woman would look favourably on such a man.

—A Huron upon seeing a bearded Frenchman for the first time, 1632.

An Indian doll made with a porcelain head acquired through trade with the Europeans.

A Huron cigararette case, from the early 1800s, displays beadwork learned from French Jesuits.

One major effect of the trade was the uprooting of native peoples. This was not a deliberate strategy—either by the people themselves or the French—but a necessity. The Ojibwa, in particular, spread from their original homes near today's Sault Sainte Marie, across the Great Lakes and far into the West in pursuit of furs. Some Iroquois did the same. When there were no actual migrations, tribes established new trading links. Ultimately, and much against native wishes, the French themselves pushed into the wilderness to gather in the trade.

By 1610, a flotilla of Huron canoes was arriving in Quebec every spring to deliver furs and to trade (they had to come the long way round, the more direct route being guarded by the hostile Iroquois). Once trading was established, the Hurons began to develop a taste for alcohol—which then became a prime item of trade. French-Canadians quickly taught the Indians how to engage in public and exuberant binges. Although both church and state prohibited the sale of alcohol or its use in the trade, natives were already starting to experience the addiction and disruption that characterized succeeding centuries.

And so in time, the old ways of farming, and of following seasonally fluctuating food sources, were replaced by a steady diet of flour, sugar, and assorted European foods—purchased with beaver and other pelts. While native men spent more and more time hunting for furs rather than meat, native women and children, for their own protection, tended to move closer to the trading posts and missions. With the growing competition among European nations for furs, this separation of men from their families and reliance on manufactured foods and goods only grew more pronounced.

Unlike other Europeans, the French generally showed a warm regard for native peoples. Officials might doubt native loyalty, but the men in the fur trade would not have survived without the kindness of the local inhabitants. Because

they were few in number, the French traders' reliance on locals to feed and shelter them was not the heavy burden on natives that it was farther south with an invading Spanish army. The French interacted with natives in small numbers, and on native turf, and so got along with them much better than did other Europeans. But French and Indian interaction was not without problems. There were benefits for both peoples, but there were also losses, some of them terrible.

As elsewhere throughout the Americas, there were epidemics in New France. Trading, especially, carried germs far and wide, and epidemics killed many Indians before they ever met a Frenchman. Moreover, when the first French arrived, their treatment of the native leaders was often as callous as that of any other European nation. Typically, native leaders would offer cordial welcomes to the newcomers, only to find themselves kidnapped and shipped off to France (for observation, and for language training: there was always a scarcity of interpreters). For their part, natives were never totally without guile in their dealing with the French. In the French-claimed lands the local inhabitants were as adept as those in New Spain at spinning out for Europeans fantastic tales of riches in the hinterland. Leading the bumpkin-French down false trails, for many natives, offered a good laugh.

The consequences for the merry tricksters were sometimes tragic. During one of Jacques Cartier's several explorations along the coast and into the St. Lawrence River, local leaders had great fun at his expense telling him tall tales about a wealthy kingdom called Saguenay. It is possible that they half-believed the stories themselves, or took pride in being splendid raconteurs: or were courteously telling Cartier what they sensed he wanted to hear. In any case, Cartier, taking the tale quite seriously, kidnapped prominent natives to carry this report back to France. There, after they were baptized at major cathedrals and entertained at court, most of them died.

## Samuel de Champlain

The mastermind behind the successful French enterprise in Canada was Samuel de Champlain. Though native peoples themselves liked his strength of will and his loyalty, they found him rigid—when in fact his success was in no small measure due to a flexibility and an enlightened attitude toward native peoples that were remarkable for a European in those days.

Champlain first entered New France in 1603 as an artist, mapmaker, and explorer. Between 1604 and 1607, he explored and mapped the Atlantic coast until turned northward by native hostility in the neighborhood of present-day New York City. He also visited, and mapped, the then densely settled coast of what is now New England (the French called it Norumbega). Champlain was one of the last Europeans to see that prosperous and populous land in its original state. For in 1616–19 (shortly before English colonists arrived in 1620), devastating epidemics virtually wiped out the people there.

Because his professional activities required it, Champlain enjoyed close contacts with natives. He was not reluctant to use experience gained from these contacts to the advantage of the colony. It did not take him long to realize, for

## THE MÉTIS

When the French began settling their colonies, particularly those near the St. Lawrence, they sought to work with and through native communities to develop a trade in furs. Unlike the Spanish lords seeking their own individual domains, Frenchmen, when they were away from the few colonial settlements, lived much as the natives did, the better to survive in the new lands. As a consequence, French settlers developed a much more humane outlook toward native peoples than did other Europeans. They learned to speak native languages, use canoes, and, as much as possible, follow the customs of the country in food, dress, and habits. In time, a separate, blended population of mixed French and native ancestry emerged. These were the *métis*, who, like the *mestizos* of Spanish America, tried to blend Indian and European worlds.

Natives often acted as emissaries for the French, and only when they failed did Frenchmen themselves enter the negotiations. The story of Jean Nicolet is a case in point. In the summer of 1634, Nicolet was handpicked by Champlain to follow up rumors of a great sea in the West. Was this the Pacific? When nothing more was heard of an Odawa (Ottawa) delegation that had been sent ahead of him, Nicolet left the St. Lawrence with a Huron and Odawa trading fleet. Eventually he came upon the Great Lakes, but not the Pacific. He also learned that the Winnebago, who were the preeminent traders in those parts, had eaten the Odawa delegation to scare off the competition.

The Winnebagos spared Nicolet himself, however, for they were much impressed by his flamboyant entrance into Green Bay. Indeed, they first thought he was some kind of thunder spirit. Expecting that this bay was at last the long-sought outlet to the Orient, Nicolet stepped ashore dressed in a Chinese damask robe, wearing a mandarin cap, and firing pistols from each hand.

instance, that Algonquian birchbark canoes had distinct advantages over the clumsy skiffs of the French. So he encouraged their use—an act that not only made eminent practical sense, but also pleased the natives: Champlain did not assume that all European technology was superior. At the same time, he showed surprising tolerance for native religion (a tolerance that he perhaps learned as a young man, a Catholic soldier employed by a Protestant nobleman).

He grew in stature once again in native eyes when, in 1610, he married a Protestant girl who was decades younger than he was (she later converted to her new husband's Catholicism). In native society, only the most prominent of older men could marry younger wives.

Meanwhile, the openness and kindness of native peoples encouraged Champlain to institute cultural exchanges in which French boys were sent to live with native families to learn the language and customs of the region. This sometimes resulted in conflicting loyalties, since the young, impressionable boys readily learned to identify with the freedom and excitement of native life in preference to the strictures of the "civilized" French. Still and all, these exchanges did act as bridges between the two cultures.

More rarely, a native boy was taken to France, but most did not survive the rigors and demands of the very foreign ways that were forced upon them there. Even though handsome reparations of trade goods would be made to the family of the deceased boy, this did not make up for their grief. Consequently, native families did not encourage their young men to attempt the voyage to Paris.

Throughout, Champlain and the French were careful to maintain good relations with their native allies. French colonists were too few and their European rivals too many for them to sustain on their own the settlements and the fur trade—much less the wars that could all too quickly result from a misstep.

In 1608, in order to increase access to the interior, Champlain founded Quebec on the St. Lawrence. Soon the little settlement was being visited by the canoes of canny and experienced Huron traders who sought a link with the larger markets of the French. The Hurons not only achieved their goal but, for a time at least, did it on their own terms: for more than a decade they successfully prevented French entry into the interior, and kept all the trading and transport of furs in their own hands.

Eventually, in 1615, Champlain breached the Huron's barrier by making a reconnaissance into Huron country. During his visit, he joined them on a raid against the Oneida. Though the raid itself turned into a fiasco (Champlain received an arrow wound in the buttocks), the Frenchman's presence was much appreciated by his Huron friends. And so Champlain had succeeded in making a small but serious inroad into the Huron trade monopoly. Meanwhile, because he was their honored guest, Hurons carried the wounded Champlain back to their home village, where he was nursed back to health during the winter of 1615–16.

While justly noted for his loyalty, Champlain did not always blend this quality with wisdom. Sometimes his support for his local allies came at the expense of a more farseeing and prudent course. The most famous instance of this occurred in 1609 along the shores of what became Lake Champlain, when he used his musket to kill two (or perhaps even three) Iroquois chiefs with a single shot. This extraordinary feat lost nothing in the telling, and would prove to be one of the great turning points in native and European relations: these killings increased the already simmering Iroquois antagonism toward the French for their cordial relationship with the Hurons and later turned the Iroquois League toward successive alliances with the Dutch and then the English colonies.

In time, as overtrapping exhausted the supply of beaver near French settlements, natives began to meet more and more French explorers surveying the interior of the continent, both north and south of what would become the Canadian border, searching for other sources of wealth—and of course for the ever-elusive direct route to China.

From their base among eastern Algonquians, the French used their knowledge of these languages to move through the linguistically related Algonquian peoples around the Great Lakes and along the Mississippi. Though reluctant to aid these efforts, natives joined the expeditions as both guides and advisors. And native men who were unable to make the voyage often drew detailed maps with well-marked trails by water and by land.

And so explorers like Jacques Marquette and Louis Joliet, who traveled down the Mississippi River, and René-Robert Cavelier, the sieur de La Salle, who had the monopoly in the Midwest and South, greatly benefited from native help. At native urging, for instance, Marquette carried a feathered pipestem called a calumet. The calumet was universally understood among the towns visited as an emblem of international trade, friendship, and alliance, thus guaranteeing him safe conduct along the Mississippi.

*It is done, we are brothers. The conclusion has been reached, now we are all relatives—Iroquois, Hurons, Algonquins, and French; we are now but one and the same people.*

—JEAN-BAPTISTE ATIRONTA
A Huron captain, at the conclusion of a 1645 peace conference.

Accompanied by Algonquian allies and French musketeers, Samuel de Champlain defeats a group of Mohawk Iroquois. In doing so, he made lifelong enemies of the powerful Iroquois League. This engraving first appeared in Champlain's own account of his explorations, *Les Voyages Sieur de Champlain*, in 1673.

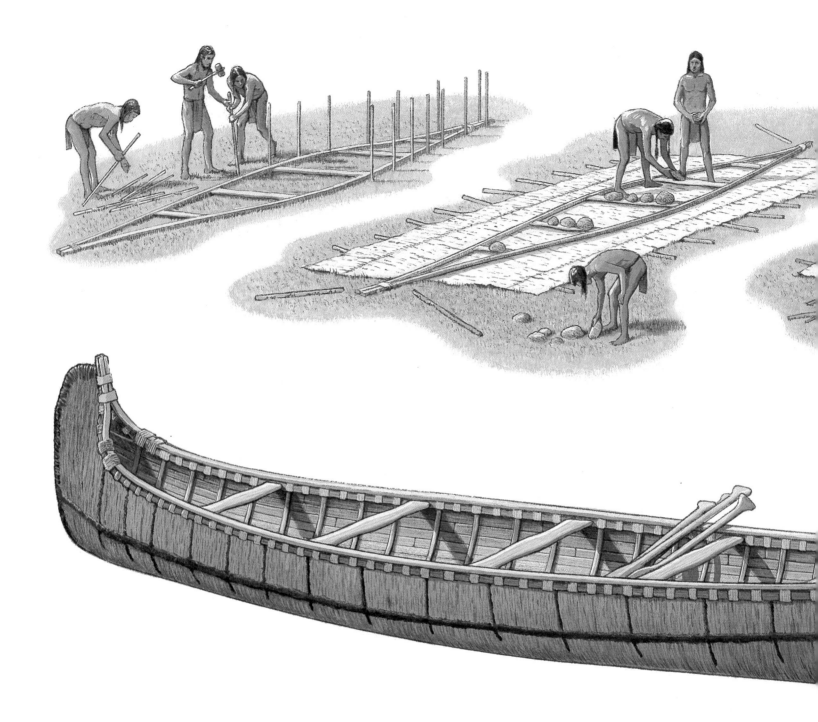

## NATIVE AMERICAN TECHNOLOGY

1. Laying out the gunwales, which make the shape of the canoe. This was done simply by placing two long pieces of white cedar on the ground, binding the ends together with tough roots of black spruce, and forming the shape by forcing the long cedar pieces apart with suitable widths of cedar planks. Stakes were then driven into the ground, outlining and securing the shape.

2. The stakes were pulled up and laid alongside with their ends left in place by the holes outlining the shape. The cedar frame was lifted off and strips of birchbark unrolled to cover the outline. The framework was then very carefully put back in place, and stones left on the crossbars to weight it down.

3. The bark was then fitted to form the sides of the vessel. Longitudinal strips were added. The outer stakes were pounded back into their holes and smaller stakes on the inside of the frame were tied to the outer ones to act as clamps to hold the bark in place.

4. Once raising and securing the bark was complete, the stones were removed and the gunwales raised to the proper height. The women then began the delicate task of fastening bark around the gunwales. By punching holes in the bark with awls and using split ends of spruceroot as binders, they were able to lace the birchbark securely. The spruceroot laces were kept wet for flexibility.

5. Lacing complete, all stakes were removed, the canoe was turned over and the women repaired and patched wherever necessary. They tied the endpoints

of the canoe together with more root
lashings. The canoe was then turned
right side up and the seams and cracks
sealed with hot black spruce gum.

6. Finally, men reinforced the interior
with long strips of white cedar laid in
lengthwise. These were held in place
by shorter pieces of bent wet cedar fitted crosswise and tucked under the
gunwales. The crosswise pieces were
further reinforced by sewing them to
the gunwales with spruce root.

## The Jesuit Mission

At the same time that the growth of the fur trade was making its inroads into native lifeways, the Christian religion, with the Jesuits at the forefront, was making its self-righteous, moral attack on the Indians. Indeed of all the events that transpired to affect the natives of Canada, none was more climactic than the Jesuit mission. Although natives responded genuinely and openly to this religious message, they did so from an innate respect for each person's religious beliefs. Yet they were utterly baffled by the initial insensitivity with which it was conveyed. In time, however, this insensitivity decreased significantly, for the Jesuits were nothing if not flexible men, not to mention superbly educated intellectuals who did their best to learn from their mistakes. At times, in fact, many of them actually looked closely at the people they were trying to convert in order to see them as they really were.

The Jesuits had begun arriving in 1612 after Cardinal Richelieu, as part of the reorganization of the colony in New France (following a brief English occupation), had recruited them to revive a failed Recollect Franciscan mission there.

Intellectuals and scholars, with considerable influence at court, the Jesuits developed and put into effect ambitious plans for their missions: they would go to meet natives in their own communities; they would learn the native languages; and they would tolerate a diversity of native lifestyles. (They would also, as an important secular adjunct to their mission, set out to control the colonial government, with the support of Bishop François de Laval.)

Because Canada was occupied both by native farmers, like the Huron, living on the margins of a safe growing season, and by active hunters, who moved among ancestral camps throughout the year, like the Montagnais, the Jesuits developed two different approaches for dealing with the native inhabitants.

Since migratory congregations were hard to control, the Jesuits tried to settle their putative flock into more permanent communities. They wanted to concentrate them, as they succeeded in doing at Sillery and at "reductions" in Paraguay and Montana. To "reduce," as the Jesuits used the term, meant to bring scattered or mobile communities into a single, permanent, large settlement. An unintended effect of this practice was the literal reduction of these populations by disease. Thus, to achieve religious control, the missionaries were not only undermining the lifestyle of their charges but threatening their very survival as well.

The Jesuits had a somewhat different approach to the more settled Hurons: they went and lived among the natives, doing their best, within their own lights, to make themselves at least acceptable to the people they lived with. They did not always succeed—indeed, especially in the early days, more often than not they failed miserably, not yet having learned the tolerance and flexibility that would gain the respect of the people they were trying to convert. As the missionaries inadvertently committed many offenses against Huron propriety and taste, the Hurons were quite unaware that they were doing the same to the Jesuits.

In time, Jesuit superiors, well versed in the difference between passing customs and eternal truths, were careful to distinguish between those Huron customs that were merely offensive and those that were repugnant to them as Christians. Casting a blind eye on what was merely offensive was encouraged.

A nineteenth-century engraving depicts Jesuit missionaries preaching among the Indians.

*This is well, black Gown, that thou comest to visit us. Take pity on us; thou art a Manitou; we give thee tobacco to smoke. . . . Let the earth give us corn, and the rivers yield us fish; let not disease kill us any more, or famine treat us any longer so harshly.*

—Algonquian elder, upon seeing his first Jesuit, 1670.

This was not always easy. Natives, for example, in a spirit of hospitality and good will, liked to share their favorite foods. But the French, unable to stomach many Huron delicacies, often rejected such offerings—a serious, but perhaps understandable, breach of manners. Among the native delicacies usually avoided by the French was a dish made of small ears of corn fermented for several months in a stagnant pond. Another gourmet item was corn bread made from a dough that women created by chewing kernels in their mouths. The sticky dough was then spat out, collected, kneaded, and baked into loaves. Women, after all, had been chewing hard foods for their babies for centuries, so this was a perfectly acceptable method of preparation, and, indeed, involved going to a great deal of trouble—an obvious gesture of very personal friendliness.

But there were other, less amusing cultural missteps that offended more than just habits and taste. Since kinship was the fundamental basis for all relationships in Huron and other native societies, and since all social relations called for profound respect, one had to be especially careful about the language used in speaking of various kin relationships. For instance, one never used the Huron word for "father" in the presence of a Huron who had lost his or her father; the word itself rekindled the Huron's grief and using it displayed a grievous lack of sensitivity. The Huron language had developed a wide range of substitutes, respectful terms to cover such eventualities. But even with fair working knowledge of Huron, a Jesuit who was unfamiliar with cultural customs would inevitably offend kin sensibilities. The mere mention of "God the Father" could blossom into a terrible breach of decency.

The Hurons were also deeply mystified by the sex lives of the Jesuits. Why don't they bed with women? Hurons asked one another. Of course it was natural for all men who were engaged in serious or sacred duties to stay away from their wives and remain celibate until these duties were finished, but then normal sexual relations were resumed. A life of never-ending celibacy was very hard for the

*The Missionary*
**by Frederic Remington, 1892.**

Huron elders to fathom. They grew suspicious not only of the Jesuits' motives, but even of their basic humanity.

The Jesuits, for their part, saw Huron religious beliefs as a form of primitive paganism, and indeed, because Hurons did not vigorously defend their beliefs, the Jesuits easily convinced themselves that natives did not actually hold firm beliefs. What the priests failed to realize was that direct confrontation, especially in a matter so personal, was itself unthinkable to native peoples. Among the convictions that governed native lives was the simple but strong understanding that everyone was entitled to his or her own cherished beliefs, with the sanction of each individual's personal spirit, provided that such beliefs were not disruptive.

In fact, Huron spiritual beliefs and philosophical ethics were quite profound. Their fundamental belief rested in a supreme female deity, together with other life-giving and life-sustaining gods. They also believed in the duality of the soul, which allowed for two sides to every individual, with unity being the end objective of existence.

As soon as the Jesuits began to realize that Huron spiritual life was in fact more powerful, extensive, and deep-seated than they had imagined, they reacted characteristically. Deciding their converts must be protected from the temptation of reversion, they developed a program to separate "Christian" villages from "pagan" ones. In a very few cases, this plan even worked. In those Huron villages that became Christian, the priest replaced the head of the foremost clan as leader, thus seriously altering the lifestyle of the natives.

In another respect, the Jesuits were not so successful—from their point of view. To illustrate the torments of Hell, the ever-imaginative order often drew vivid analogies to the native torture of captives, not realizing that for most Hurons the threat of Hell carried very different implications. If the avoiding of eternal torment came at the cost of rejecting generations of relatives, most Hurons wanted no part of it, infinitely preferring to stay eternally with their kin. In fact, elders took to portraying Heaven as a grim place filled with stingy Frenchmen and other people who would not share food and comforts the way native friends and kin did freely and generously.

However, conversion for Hurons was not usually a matter of belief, teaching, or doctrine. Most Hurons made the leap for economic reasons, for it was Christian Hurons who proved to be most active in regional politics and had the most to gain from the fur trade. By adopting the trappings of the French faith these "converts" benefited from gifts, guns, and a wider network of trade.

These modest Jesuit inroads among the Hurons began to go sour, however, after epidemics repeatedly struck the Huron villages in the 1630s. During those

terrible times, elders could not help but note that the French were only briefly ill (if they were ill at all) while their own people died in droves. Why are we dying, they asked themselves, and they are not? Could it be the baptism they are offering? Is it a demonic rite that kills our people? Or a healing rite that protects converts? Hurons divided over these issues. But the very question caused them to take an increasingly hard, cold look at the Jesuits.

In particular, chiefs suspected those priests who had evidenced great power of causing the worst of the illness. One Jesuit, for example, who had once awed the faithful by (apparently) bringing rain during a drought, was now suspected of sorcery. In Huron belief, there was no difference between the power to kill and the power to cure. Only the good or bad will of the possessor of such power determined the outcome. A man who could bring rain could just as easily cause death.

Factions developed and threats were made, but epidemics periodically returned. People became desperate, angry; action had to be taken against the powerful, dangerous, frightening Jesuits. And so native peacekeepers executed some of the Jesuits (who are now remembered as martyrs).

Yet, on balance, though they might be mysterious and dangerous, the French were powerful people deserving of respect, and they had brought with them from their "other world" many things that were testimony to their power. Hurons were often most impressed by what the French regarded as ordinary. Cats, for instance. These were animals that actually answered to their own names, and, in a most helpful way, ate the mice that infested the corn stored in the villages. In 1636, chickens were brought from France; and the rooster, to show his special regard for the spirits, prayed to the dawn.

The next year, wheat was planted to provide flour for communion wafers. And that plant proved its power by the vigor with which it took over huge stretches of the country. A chiming clock called "Captain" drew a rapt audience daily (the audience always ended when four bells sounded, for the Jesuits explained that the clock was telling everyone to go home). The Hurons also admired doors, which closed so tightly that they kept out drafts; and the flour mill, which was extremely helpful in the otherwise laborious process of grinding meal—and clearly a much easier method than chewing kernels of corn.

Ultimately, these and other wonders, but most of all simple contact, cost the Huron their nation. Their numbers drastically reduced by disease and the profound changes taking place in their lifestyle, they were unable to resist a massive attack by Iroquois in 1649 that scattered the remaining Huron. Many survivors of this attack died of starvation during the winter. Some sought refuge in Quebec or along Lake Superior. Many more were adopted into the Iroquois tribes, joining

**The Huron Wampum Belt commemorates the 1683 agreement between the Hurons and Jesuit missionaries for the building of the first wooden church on Huron lands.**

other already naturalized relatives. During the first generations of this mixing, Iroquois men actually preferred to marry Huron women, for that meant they would have fewer obligations to the wife's clan.

## The Persistence of Indian Continuity

In spite of the destruction of communities and the conflicts among survivors, kinship and family relations continued to succor the generations, and to provide many Indians with the secure base that allowed them to develop strategies for dealing with the European invasion.

These strategies took three directions: first, *going halfway*, by adapting compromises with the outsiders; second, *going over*, by taking on many of the outsiders' ways, while maintaining an essentially Indian soul (many actually achieved the squaring of that circle); and third, *going against*, by totally, and sometimes violently, rejecting the outsiders.

Three notable seventeenth-century Indian biographies provide in sufficient detail early examples of each of these three very different paths. For Membertou, a chief and sachem of the Micmac, conversion created conflict between his own deeply cherished beliefs as a native and the requirements both of French trade and of his adopted Catholic religion. Toward the end of his very long life, he worked hard to find a balance between the needs of his own people and the demands of Europeans.

For Kateri Tekawitha, of mixed Mohawk and Algonquian descent, going over to the French brought relief from her oppressive Mohawk kin and provided a haven in the Catholic Church, which became for her a sympathetic replacement for the family she lost as a young girl. In the case of Aharihon, an Onondaga leader, he found comfort in his own people—family, clan, town—while preventing any outsiders from threatening that security with devastating cruelty.

## Membertou

Henri Membertou was the first Catholic convert in Canada. On June 24, 1610, a passing Recollect priest baptized Membertou and a good portion of his extensive family at Port Royal, a French fort built in Membertou's territory on an island off the coast of today's Nova Scotia. At that time, Membertou and his band were caring for the buildings at Port Royal during the period from 1608 to 1611 when the French had abandoned the settlement.

With his baptism, Membertou was given the name Henri, after the French king, while twenty close relatives were named for other members of the French royal family. Though he was already a very old man in 1610, a deeply respected chief and sachem, the further cementing of his French alliance—his reason for allowing the pouring of water and ritual words—very greatly increased his power and influence among his own people. As the Micmac leader with most immediate access to French trade, he had the means to advance himself politically. And indeed, the baptism paid off for him; he became a leading chief of the Micmac.

A Micmac flag of 1910 shows Grand Chief Membertou with Jesuit priest Jesse Fléche.

When Jesuits arrived at Port Royal in 1612, they were distressed to find that the newly baptized Micmac knew very little about the teachings of the Church (the Recollects had apparently been more interested in achieving a high body count of baptisms than in offering potential converts religious instruction). The Jesuits were quite scandalized that Membertou continued to act as a shaman and still had several wives (his position of leadership required this; several wives were needed in order to maintain the household of a chief noted for generosity, large quantities of food had to be prepared, and many children had to be raised).

Even though the Jesuit moral pressure that followed could easily have sent a less astute and flexible man into rage, Membertou instead met the Jesuits halfway, for that was always his approach. He began a thorough course of instructions in the Catholic faith. And when that was completed, he agreed—going halfway again—to renounce his position as shaman and all but one wife.

Always a consummate diplomat, Membertou was only too aware of the cost of the strategy he had chosen. He knew that contact with the French was bringing the disruption, disease, and alcoholism that were devastating his people (who, before the French came, he claimed, were as many as the "hairs on my head"). Nevertheless, he believed that he had to accommodate the foreigners.

Once, however, when he refused to go halfway, the Jesuits actually came *more* than halfway to meet him. On his deathbed, they forced a dilemma on Membertou that he would share with all future Indian converts.

After death, according to native belief, entire families were reunited in the afterworld. It was therefore important to be buried with the rest of one's family. But the priests insisted to the dying Membertou that he must be buried in consecrated ground. The old chief, however, would have none of that. He must lie among his deceased relatives; they and all of his ancestors expected him. When he refused to commit himself to Catholicism for all eternity, the priests came close to abandoning him. But after they had had some time to meditate on the

This image, made by Father
Claude Chaucetiere around 1680,
is the oldest known portrait of
Kateri Tekawitha.

situation, and to consult with a translator who knew the people better than they did, the priests came back to administer last rites.

Membertou consented to one final compromise: he would let the Jesuits bury him in the cemetery (presumably he realized that breaking with the Church would harm the welfare and prestige of his people). However, since the Catholic plot lay in his own territory, he did not have to forsake his family's lands, only the comfort of familiar graves. And because he was to lie in consecrated ground, he knew that the alliance between his family and the French would continue.

The alliance not only continued, it blossomed into a commitment to Catholicism that persisted through English dominion and Anglican antagonism. Indeed, today there are special diplomatic relations between the modern Micmac nation and the Vatican.

## Kateri Tekawitha

Born about 1656 to a Christian Algonquian captive and her Mohawk husband, the young girl who later became Kateri Tekawitha was orphaned at an early age. Her mother had been raised as a French Christian by French settlers at Three Rivers, where she lived until 1653, when she was taken captive by Mohawks—a people whose hostility to Christianity was particularly virulent. In 1660, a small-pox epidemic claimed the lives of her family. Kateri was also infected, but she recovered (though with terrible scars) and was taken into the home of her uncle, a leader who was especially hostile to missionaries.

In 1666, a French punitive force from Quebec attacked and burned the Mohawk villages; and in suing for peace, the Mohawks thought it prudent to ask for missionaries. When Jesuits arrived in 1667, the young orphan girl helped feed them, and she went on to listen closely to their sermons and instructions. It is likely that she took so readily to the Jesuits as a way of honoring her dead Christian mother.

She was also a strong-headed and independent young woman, who even at a young age was fighting to escape a community that to her seemed repressive. She fought off all putative marriages planned by her adopted Mohawk family. Since two-thirds of those in her village were captive Christians, she had considerable support for her decision to keep her chastity.

In time, she asked a Jesuit for baptism. The sacrament was performed on Easter Sunday in 1676, and she was named Catherine (in Mohawk, Kateri). Important, well-connected people in the town, her Mohawk family looked at Kateri's conversion as a significant betrayal. Consequently, she was treated quite badly, until she was able to flee to Kahnawake, near Montreal. There, converted friends of her mother prepared her for a religious life. In 1677, she received her first communion and was accepted into the Confraternity of the Holy Family, a society of devout laypeople, which became for her a substitute for the kind of warm and sympathetic family she had lost so long ago.

As she grew more deeply involved in the spiritual practices of the Church, she adopted a regime of meditational exercises and fleshly mortification (self-inflicted pain to build the strength of the spirit was common to both Iroquois and

## MIRACLES

If there was any common ground on which the beliefs of Indians and Christians might meet, it was in the area of miracles. Christians believed wholeheartedly (then and now) in the possibility of miracles—a special benison, or blessing, handed down by God to answer a special need. Indians also looked to their deities for divine signs of approval or kindness—rain after a drought, a cure for a particular illness or injury, an unusual gift of food in hard times.

Both sets of religious representatives, priests and shamans, prayed or performed special rites to remind their respective gods of need. The difference lay in the source of each religion's belief, the Christian relying on church dogma based on generations of scholars making various interpretations of the Bible, and the Indian grounded in a profound connection with the land and all life. Nevertheless, when Christian prayers coincided with the arrival of needed rain, for instance, or when a miraculous healing occurred, Christians and Indians alike were impressed with the power of the white man's God. Such power bore weight in the process of conversion.

Catholics). Later, she planned to form a community of native nuns, and in 1679 she took a personal vow of perpetual chastity. Her devotions and her mortifications notwithstanding, Kateri was by no means dour or self-righteous. She was in fact known for her sense of humor and other humane qualities.

In 1680, at age twenty-four, her labors and mortifications, combined with the long-term damage from smallpox, resulted in her death. Since then, countless native people have prayed for her intercession and received help. As a result, the Roman Catholic Church has beatified her (a step that usually leads to formal sainthood). And the Tekawitha Circle, a very large and active religious movement among native American Catholics today, was named after her.

## Aharihon

Most male captives, unless their captors actually adopted them, did not have Kateri's options. They had no option at all, except a brave death under torture. According to Jesuit history—usually accurate as to detail, if biased in judgment—the Onondaga chief Aharihon was notorious for the torture of captives. He hated outsiders—that is, anyone not of his tribe; he absolutely shunned contact with them, and he used cruelty with deliberation when they fell into his hands. As a result, the name of Aharihon sent chills of terror through the hearts of his enemies, whether native or European. And this was very much his intention: he wanted the enemies of the Iroquois, of whatever stripe, to stay away. In this he was largely successful.

On the face of it, then, at least to Europeans, Aharihon was a sadistic monster. But this was by no means the whole truth. In his own community he was a model of rectitude, according to Iroquois standards. He followed all the rules, although sometimes skirting the edge where torture was concerned.

When Iroquois families adopted prisoners from other tribes, complex factors of situation and personality influenced their decisions. Usually families were looking to find a match for a dead relative and examined captives for similarities of appearance, attitude, age, and gender. When a suitable captive was found, he was indeed adopted as a replacement, having undergone a trial period of fitting into the family, clan, and community before the adoption was accepted as binding. The adoptee then assumed all marriage, clan, priesthood, and like responsibilities of the deceased. But adoption was not always smoothly accomplished.

Aharihon's brother (perhaps his twin) had been killed by the Erie about 1654, and since that time Aharihon had often begun the procedure for adopting a captive. But, with sadistic persistence, he would instead change his mind, condemning the warrior to a death by torture, claiming each time that the captive had proved to be unworthy of his dead brother.

In one gruesome example, he raised a young man's expectations by presenting him with four dogs that would be eaten at the adoption feast. But during the actual celebration, Aharihon rose and denounced the prospective adoptee. And for the rest of the night the youngster was slowly roasted from the feet upward, despite entreaties from other Iroquois to put an end to his suffering. By native standards he did not die well, crying, screaming, and pleading well into the next

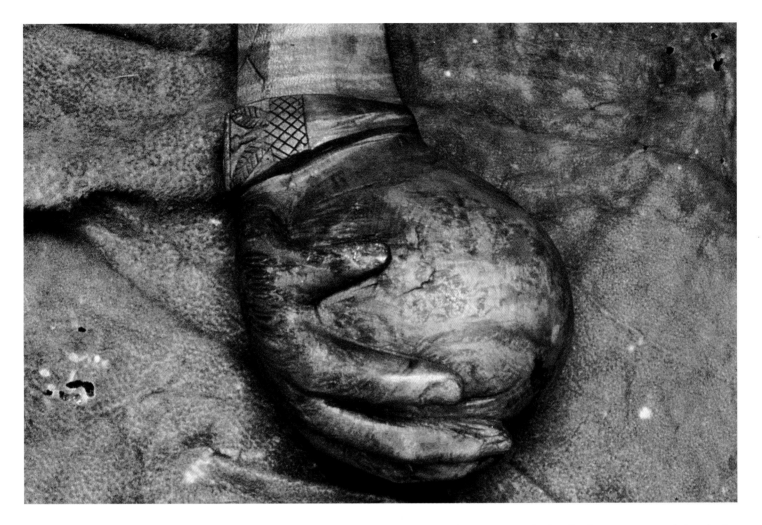

The knob of a Seneca war club, which is carefully carved from a wood burl. The ball is grasped by a hand—a symbol of prowess and dexterity.

day. Prisoners were expected to meet death stoically, singing their personal chants and insulting their captors.

By 1663, Aharihon had personally killed some sixty enemy warriors and subjected another eighty men to death by torture. Was he an evil man? Not in any sense that is meaningful within the context of his time. Yes, he hated outsiders. Yes, he ordered the vengeful death of many. Yet he was more than simply a ruthless executioner. He was a loving husband and father, and a wise leader—indeed, a positive moral force in his community. In a sense, the measures he took provided the community with a kind of cathartic release during a massively threatening period. Though Aharihon was certainly extreme, he lived in extreme times. Within the mores and beliefs of his culture he was always respected by his own people, for such was the range of personal latitude allowed by natives for themselves and their leaders.

# CHAPTER ELEVEN

# THE ENGLISH AND THE ATLANTIC COAST

POCAHONTAS, ca. 1616

WITH THE DEFEAT of the Armada in 1588, England put Spain on the defensive not only in Europe but overseas. The victory gave England an opening to begin its own colonial enterprise in North America. With Spanish Florida in the South and New France firmly in the north, the English chose to dispatch their first colony to the middle Atlantic coast. Because foreign ships had routinely passed by, and some stopped in their bays and estuaries to trade or to take on supplies (and sometimes slaves), the arrival of the English did not take local natives unawares.

## Virginia

In the years immediately before the founding of the royal colony of Jamestown (1607), the Powhatan people, under Chief Powhatan (his name being the same as his people, as was customary), fused the other native peoples of coastal Virginia (all Algonquians, like the Powhatans themselves) into a single chiefdom, led by Chief Powhatan and his family.

Though Powhatan's family was prominent in the region long before the creation of this Powhatan empire, the man who gave the empire its actual start was a native chief who is known historically by the name the Spanish gave him, Don Luis de Valasco. During the 1560s, Don Luis had been captured by the Spanish

*Arrival of Hendrick Hudson in the Bay of New York, September 12, 1609,*
an 1868 chromalithograph after a painting by Frederic A. Chapman.

## A POWHATAN TEMPLE

With one notable exception at the very end of the 1600s, the secluded Powhatan temples were largely ignored by Virginians. The exception occurred when a man named Robert Beverley broke into one of the temples while local natives were away attending a council. He later described what he found: Around its perimeter were standing posts, each carved and painted with a threatening face to warn off unwanted visitors. Inside, the temple was dark, but there was light enough to see shelves holding three bundles. These he ripped open. The first contained bones. (These were the revered remains of former leaders.) In the second were carved and painted weapons. And in the third were the wooden segments of an articulated human figure. (This served as an idol and an oracle.)

Later, Beverley boasted of this sacrilege to one of his native friends, who was visibly shaken. He realized that if the Europeans were now violating native temples, it would not be long before they started to violate native religion. He was right. Within a few decades, native beliefs were replaced by Christianity—at least in public.

OPPOSITE TOP:
This portrait of Pocahontas, first published in *The Indian Tribes of North America* by Thomas L. McKenney and James Hall, was derived from an R. M. Sully copy of a decayed original made during Pocahontas's visit to England in 1616–17.

OPPOSITE BOTTOM:
*The Marriage of Pocahontas* by John McRae, 1855.

on the Virginia coast, then educated in Mexico, Madrid, and Havana. Doubtless believing they had molded him into a proper, Spanish-oriented puppet, the Jesuits, in 1570, brought him back to his Tidewater home to help them found a mission among his people. But he proved to be far from their expectations. Soon after he returned, he took back his position as head of his eminent family and chief of his tribe. And since this included, among other things, taking several wives, the priests were outraged. When they verbally attacked and shamed him—witheringly—in public, Don Luis could not accept the loss of face. Consequently, he led an attack that wiped out the mission.

Though we do not know this for certain, it is probable that Don Luis was Chief Powhatan's father. At any rate, Powhatan and his brothers certainly learned from their elder the lesson that annihilating the opposition is a fairly sure way to get what you want.

Unlike surrounding neighbors who lived in palisaded towns, the Powhatans were so confident of their power that they did not feel they needed such protection. So they scattered over their lands, mostly living in dispersed homesteads along the rivers.

This scattered population depended for its sense of community upon central temples, which were mostly repositories for treasure, idols, and the dried bodies of elite ancestors. Each temple held a sacred fire that symbolized the vitality of the town. These temples were located either among a cluster of randomly placed homes, or, more frequently, in isolated parts of the forest—another sign of Powhatan confidence. The chief temple of the nation was located in the woods of Uttamussak near the mouth of the Pamunkey River.

In 1607, a well-traveled soldier of fortune named John Smith established the Jamestown colony. The site, then a peninsula in the James River, seemed promising; because the natives used it only seasonally the English settlers assumed it was available. Later, when the ground turned to marsh and the settlers realized that the "promised land" they had chosen was truly unsuitable for living, friendly natives suggested that seasonal movements were more healthy than fixed abodes.

By then it was summer, and the marshes surrounding Jamestown were filled with pools and ponds of stagnant water, busily breeding disease, especially around the colony's growing accumulation of garbage. Predictably the natives' advice went unheeded. For several years the colonists held on to their swampy farms with touching persistence. Later, the English families began to move to higher ground on outlying land, and there were fewer deaths from pestilence.

Unlike the French to the north, and the Spanish to the south and west who put a pious face on their hunger for wealth ("We'll find gold for ourselves," they said, "and souls for Jesus"), the English at Jamestown never pretended that their settlement was anything other than a commercial venture. There was not even a single Church of England minister assigned to converting the local peoples. This suited the natives just fine. More attracted to English trade goods than the Anglican religion, the natives, nonetheless, welcomed difference and even produced a few converts, mostly from among those who worked closely with the English. The most famous convert, of course, was Pocahontas, the favorite daughter of Powhatan.

After a very short marriage to a native leader (about whom we know little),

Pocahontas became the wife of John Rolfe, developer of the Virginia tobacco industry. Though sadly brief (she was only twenty-one when she died of smallpox in 1617), the marriage was a diplomatic success that strengthened the alliance between the English and the Powhatans, easing tensions at least for a while. In the long term, the marriage also provided native descendants with special protection, even up to our own time, for many important Virginians claiming descent from the son of Rolfe and Pocahontas have carefully monitored the welfare of their native relatives.

Meanwhile, native leaders and communities were under constant pressure to provide food for the English. Eventually, when the natives could bear no more demands, Powhatan turned the war captaincy over to his brothers. In 1622 and again in 1644 they executed well-planned attacks on the colony, with the intent of driving the English back into Jamestown and out of the nearby settlements called "hundreds," consisting of measured land grants to individuals.

As the Jesuits, the Chesapeakes, and others had learned, the Powhatans were quite capable of ruthlessly annihilating their opponents when that seemed useful. But when they had a chance to exterminate the Jamestown colonists, the Powhatans did not do so. They killed many settlers, certainly, but the aim of these killings was to send the English a moral message.

*Discovery of the Hudson River*
by Alfred Bierstadt, 1874.

*Do you believe me such a fool as not to prefer eating good meat, sleeping quietly with my wives and children, laughing and making merry with you, having copper and hatchets and anything else—as your friend—to flying from you as your enemy, lying cold in the woods, eating acorns and roots, and being so hunted by you meanwhile, that if but a twig break, my men will cry out, "Here comes Captain Smith!" Let us be friends, then. Do not invade us thus with such an armed force. Lay aside these arms.*

—POWHATAN
Chief of the Powhatan
Confederacy, 1609

In the view of the Powhatans, they had not only welcomed these new people into their land, they had helped them out with food and other supplies, when they could. They had treated the newcomers always, and in good faith, according to the proper forms of behavior. But the English only took more, demanded more, acting rudely, sometimes inhumanly, and ultimately insufferably. When the Powhatans had reached the limits of their tolerance, they did their best to send the British a strong but measured message, to tell them they had gone too far, and that they had to stop.

Thus colonists who previously had rudely demanded native food were found dead with bread stuffed in their mouths, a clear statement that they deserved to "choke to death" on their unreasonable appetites. During the 1622 attack, about a third of the colony was killed with their own tools, a message that they were "working everything to death." In other cases, dead colonists were found with their mouths stuffed with dirt, to remind others not to "eat up all the land."

Natives were constantly baffled and frustrated by the colonists' failure to understand their culture, or even to attempt to do so. Consequently, when an English gentleman named George Thorpe made efforts to befriend them, they were initially hopeful.

Thorpe was not a missionary, but he possessed a number of missionary impulses. And he was a decent man, who acted according to his best lights, as he saw them. He wanted to "help" the Indians. And sometimes he succeeded in that aim. He had several mastiffs killed, for instance, after these dogs had terrorized native visitors. And he reached out to the Indians in a number of other kindly ways. But in time it began to dawn on them that Thorpe wanted to convert them; and worse, he wanted to take their children and send them away to a school (this plan would have many sad resonances for Indians of later times). Though this kind man was one of the few people to reach out to the natives, it is not surprising that Thorpe was killed in 1622, and his body mutilated.

But the Powhatan protest killings were unavailing. Eventually, the growing numbers of colonists and the steadily diminishing native population toppled the Powhatan chiefdom. And as the Virginia colony expanded farther, Powhatans were crowded out of their lands.

Later, small reservations were set aside for the exclusive residence and use of the once great Powhatan people. While these Virginia reserves have been even more reduced over the centuries, they remain in native ownership to this day. The Powhatans are not what they once were, and their territory has been forcibly diminished; but they are still very much there, still living on lands where their relatives have lived for many generations.

## New England

There is a legend throughout New England about the first native encounter with Europeans. Forewarned by a dream, a child left his village and climbed up to a high place overlooking the ocean. Once there, he glimpsed a marvelous sight far out on the water. As soon as he saw it, he rushed back to the village to tell of this strange happening. "A huge floating island is approaching the land," he cried. "It

A nineteenth-century rendition of Manhattan Island before the Dutch settled there, showing a stylized depiction of the longhouse structures characteristic of the Northeast.

is covered with tall trees, wrapped with vines, and topped by billowing clouds. Bears wander across its surface. And thunder and lightning call from its depths."

Not long after the child's first sighting, the island came close to shore and stopped. Official greeters went out in a canoe to take stock. Since it was normally from a consensus of the town's holy men and wise men that the community formed its policy on important issues, the first to meet the bears on the floating island were religious leaders and civil officials. If these men determined that the bears were dangerous, then the military would take over.

Even after the greeters actually visited the ship—which, of course, is what it was—they no doubt continued to view it as a magical island. For they had no other frame of reference to apply to this marvel. In time, they became aware that the beings possessed a number of human, albeit hairy, characteristics. But natives also saw a number of qualities that made the creatures seem decidedly inhuman—such as their choices in food and drink. Many were convinced, for instance, that the food the strangers consumed was proof that they were returning ghosts of the dead. Drinking red wine was like drinking blood; eating biscuits was like eating dried flesh; molasses had to be putrifaction; and rice was clearly nothing but maggots.

Furthermore the strangers drank bitter-tasting liquids that produced a great disorientation, something like a vision, but with painful aftereffects. In the initial view of the natives, these visions were not worth the next day's sickness. So for some years, natives avoided strong spirits. In time, also, many Indians, having accepted settlers as neighbors, formed friendships. The early doubts about the colonists' feeding habits disappeared, especially since the settlers themselves adopted several of the Indian dishes, from clambakes to baked beans. Indian words entered the colonists' language—succotash, moccasin, papoose, and many more. For their part, Indians happily adapted European designs to their own intricate beadwork.

So the first intermittent contacts were replaced by short-term settlements, and these in turn, gave way to colonies.

# The Pilgrims

John Eliot preaching to the Pequots. The Indians are shown in native fancy dress, although it seems more likely they would have worn everyday clothing combined with European touches. As with many of these "historic" images, accuracy was not the primary objective.

There were sharp differences among the various kinds of colonists coming from England. In 1620, after Puritan dissenters had severely outworn the patience of their own countrymen, England allowed the "Pilgrims" to settle at Massachusetts Bay. Since these radical dissidents were not viewed favorably by the English government, or by the Church of England, the plan was to establish a buffer zone along the Atlantic that would separate the heretical Puritans from the royal colony of Virginia, which adhered to the state religion. Dutch and Swedish settlements soon occupied parts of this buffer zone. But because the Dutch and the Swedes were fellow Protestants and sometime allies, the English were initially reluctant to drive them off.

The land the British called New England was a rich country where native people had thrived for centuries. Just as elsewhere, its large towns were led by local elite families; and women were the mainstays of the economy. Through their farming of maize, beans, and squash, as well as their gathering of nuts, roots, and berries, women contributed three-quarters of the food supply.

But by 1620, the Pilgrims landed on a widowed coast. Disease had already decimated the huge native population that Champlain had observed only a few years earlier. Thus when the Puritan colonists began to displace the local communities, the native people were too dazed and disorganized by the plagues and their aftermaths to resist.

In the Puritans' view, the huge native population loss was a gift of God—his hand had killed the natives to allow his own chosen people room for their settlements. Blinded by such religious bias, the Puritans did not recognize the humanity of the people who dwelled all about them. And consequently, little was done until the 1640s to relieve native suffering. Even then, colonists were unaware of the vast chasm that separated their perceptions of native life from its realities. For them, native life had no substance, and thus all their "godly" offers to "save" and "improve" the natives would be gratefully welcomed. Natives never agreed.

As a case in point, the Puritans viewed the seasonal movements of native peoples as disorganized, chaotic, and aimless, where in reality they were a meticulously planned series of migrations designed to take advantage of regional bounty. Though the native mixed economy of farming, hunting, fishing, and gathering had taken centuries to perfect, the colonists wanted Indians to abandon all of this ecological resourcefulness and become yeoman farmers living with their families in cramped, unhealthy houses. And they wanted it done overnight.

But the Indians faced even greater dangers from the Puritan colonists than attempts to change their lifeways. By 1637, they began to realize how truly cruel and grasping these newcomers were. Before that year, the Pequots had been a prosperous, populous, and powerful Connecticut chiefdom, owing their wealth mostly to the virtual monopoly they held over the lucrative wampum trade (wampum consisted of cylindrical beads, made from shells found along the coast, that were prized throughout the region). The colonists—following a pattern that would be repeated often in the coming centuries—longingly eyed the Pequots' land and wealth to which they felt perfectly entitled. And they were eager to break the Pequots' power. Using some minor provocation as an excuse, the colonists attacked the Pequots, killing hundreds of Indians when they burned the fort where the natives had taken refuge. This savage and ruthless massacre did not fail to convey the harsh message to other native people in the region. After the Pequot War of 1637, most Indians recognized that the "godly" Puritans were nothing but greedy, violent thieves. In the aftermath of the war, predictably, the colonists took over the Pequots' land, as well as the wampum trade.

Like all wars, this one had a number of unforeseen consequences. When the war broke out, a boy who was visiting from Long Island had the bad luck of finding himself caught in the action. He was taken prisoner, and not long afterward he became the servant of an English family. Since this youth spoke both English and his own Algonquian language, he was sought out by John Eliot, Puritan minister of Roxbury. Eliot was looking for an interpreter who could help him provide instruction to the Massachusetts tribes. Though slightly different, the two dialects were mutually intelligible.

This collaboration soon resulted in one of the more remarkable mission efforts among the Indians, the Massachusetts Praying Towns. It further resulted in a milestone in the history of both American printing and native literacy. In 1633, the first Bible printed in North America was Eliot's translation into the Massachusetts language.

Eliot's efforts were grounded in Puritan beliefs that took a very serious view of conversion. Unlike their fellow countrymen in Virginia, not particularly interested in converting the native peoples, the Calvinist Puritans were an avowedly religious community for whom conversion of others was a divinely sanctioned goal. As a vital component of their "errand in the wilderness," Pilgrims worked to convert their "savage" and "primitive" neighbors. The ability to provide instruction in the natives' own language was obviously helpful in this endeavor.

The Wampanoags of the coast were the first Indians to find themselves the focus of Puritan missionary zeal. And over the years, they would endure the most intense Puritan missionary effort. From the very start of the Plymouth colony, the Indian religion was under assault.

John Eliot was not the first Puritan minister to preach to the native peoples. Before the youth from Long Island helped Eliot preach in Algonquian, Roger Williams was delivering sermons to the natives at Plymouth and Providence. His preaching career in those towns to both Indians and Puritans was short-lived, however, for he had serious doctrinal differences with the other Puritans. Because he advocated such eccentric heresies as religious tolerance and Indian land rights, he was actually banished. He took refuge with Indian friends, eventually founding the colony of Rhode Island.

Some years later, while aboard a ship bound for England, Williams wrote a phrase book for the Narragansett language (published in 1643). This little book was more than just a learning tool, however, for Williams had not lost his dislike for Puritan intolerance. Many of the book's examples cast doubt on the moral superiority of English Christians by drawing sharp comparisons between their intolerance and the generous nature of the natives in their willingness to share and to allow—even enjoy—differences.

Yet there were, even among the Puritans, those whose sense of humanity and decency spoke for itself. For over 163 years and five generations, the Mayhew

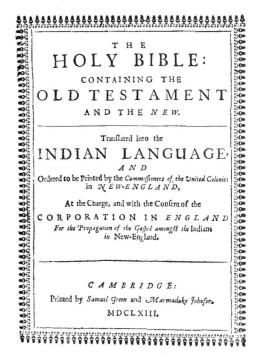

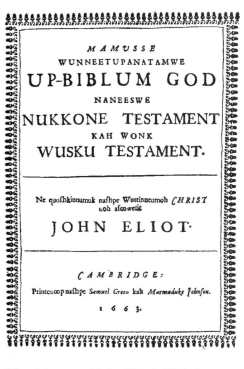

The title page of John Eliot's Bible in English (TOP) and translated into the Massachusetts language (ABOVE).

Wampanoag Chief Metacom, son of Massasoit, was known to his European contemporaries as "King Philip." This lithograph by T. Sinclair appeared in *Events in Indian History,* which was published in 1842.

family maintained a mission on Martha's Vineyard. Theirs was a very different style of missionary effort from Eliot's. While he created a substantial organization, involving a number of well-publicized communities (he was known as the "Apostle to the Indians"), the Mayhews directed their attentions toward individuals, their conversions coming one at a time while they quietly made friends with the Indians. But the legacy of their long efforts had less visible impact.

By the time Eliot started his mission, life had come to seem so hopeless for many natives that even his kind of Christianity began to look like a reasonable medicine against despair. In 1650 he settled converts at Natick. Established on six thousand acres seventeen miles southwest of Boston, the settlement was intended to be a model "Red Puritan" community—a Praying Town.

As time went by, membership in the Natick community became a sign of status among native peoples in the region. Individuals and families were able to achieve prominence, forming a new kind of native elite, and its members went to outlying communities, spreading the Puritan message. When others learned of the relative comfort and prosperity of the Natick Christians, they too wanted to convert. But no native wanted to leave his or her home village. So Praying Towns were founded in other ethnic regions. Soon there were fourteen Praying Towns around the bay, and later another seven in the Nipmuck country of central Massachusetts.

Expansion ended in 1675, however, when war broke out between the colonists and a native alliance led by Metacom, the Wampanoag chief known to the English as "King Philip" (after whom the war was named). The Wampanoag had been under constant pressure from the Plymouth Colony to surrender land and conform to English dictates. The Puritans had even imposed a tax on the tribe. Metacom was joined by the powerful Narragansetts and by most of the lesser tribes nearby. However, Uncas, chief of the Mohegans, joined enthusiastically with the English, seeing the possible destruction of his native American rivals. Meanwhile, the Praying Towns, threatened or suspected by both sides in the hostilities, for their own safety were moved to an island in Boston Harbor and left there to languish.

Metacom's attack was fierce, and at first it seemed he might be successful. Indians were by now making their own muskets in forges hidden in the woods; some even wore English armor. But in fact, although Metacom's forces together might have numbered 20,000, the English colonists had increased to some 50,000. Moreover, 500 armed Mohegans, and even some Naticks, were acting as scouts. The Puritans, as they had done with the Pequots earlier on, engaged in wholesale slaughter of natives—including women and children—whenever the opportunity offered. Their avowed objective, and now a sacred duty, was to rid the world of Indians.

Metacom's strongest field general, a Narragansett sachem, was captured by the English and executed. Then, in the summer of 1676, Metacom's wife and small son were captured and held hostage. In August 1676, Metacom himself was captured and executed, and his family was forced to observe his head displayed on a pole in Plymouth. Later, after much learned debate among church dignitaries as to whether or not the widow and son should also be executed, the gentler view prevailed and they were sold as slaves to the West Indies, along with hundreds of other rebels systematically hunted down and captured after Metacom's death. His defeat effectively ended any concerted resistance in New England.

As for the converts sequestered on that island in Boston Harbor, they were simply abandoned. At war's end, many had died of starvation. It was a hard way to learn that the English would never accept them as equals and were only waiting for a time when they would either die off or move away.

After the war, a few of the Praying Towns were resettled, but constant Mohawk raids whittled them down. Eventually, the towns broke up and people drifted back to the areas where their ancestors had lived for centuries, to try to pick up any living connections that might remain. But only in Mashpee and Gay Head, where land was set aside for reservations, were people able to stay on and maintain any sort of tribal unity.

## RELIGION AND THE LAND

For the native peoples of America, the most prominent themes of the past five hundred years are likely to be, "They took our land" and, "Our religion was changed." For all practical purposes, these two themes, in native eyes, are one; the land and the spiritual life of the people who live on the land are the same. Religion and the land hold the people together. Thus native people feel most acutely and strongly any impact on the land, and any impact on religion.

To America's indigenous peoples the forcing of their ancestors from their lands and the European missionary effort were two sides of the same coin. There is one major difference, however: whereas the theft of the land is seen as an unrelieved catastrophe, some of the changes in native religious life were at least adaptable to older, native ways of belief. Moreover, the new way did produce some positive consequences. By taking the foreign religion, many Indians were able to survive the terrible years that followed the first European contacts. But they were able to do more than just survive. Many were also able to keep their families intact, and even their communities intact. And some were even able to remain on their lands—much diminished though these lands were.

Many, perhaps most of those who survived, believed the Christian message in good faith. At the same time, taking on the new religion gave them status in the "new world" they found themselves in. Christian Indians had access to trade, education, and other benefits that non-Christian Indians could not enjoy. Becoming a Christian did not help any Indian overcome the terrible adversity they all faced. But it was better than most of the alternatives.

In creating a model town at Natick, John Eliot first demonstrated that his converts were good, industrious people. With the help of English carpenters, converts quickly built a footbridge across the Charles River, a meeting house, and houses along three streets. The footbridge was worthy of pride (if Puritans could be allowed such); it spanned an eighty-foot-wide river, its central arch was nine feet high, and it rested on stone abutments on either bank.

The actual townsite, as well as a fishing weir to provide food, was owned by a convert family whose English name was Speene. When Natick was established, the Speene family retained ownership of the weir (for it was the one thing that gave them status). But they were as willing to share the fish they caught as they were to share the townsite.

While work on the construction proceeded, native life was reorganized. Hereditary elite families were replaced by elected representatives. The tribute formerly given to the chief was replaced by tithing to the town. Legal codes were drawn up to punish such unacceptable native behaviors as idleness, seasonal migration, long or unruly hair, polygamy, fornication, wife beating, shamanic curing, protecting the skin with bear grease, killing lice by biting them, and holding elaborate mourning ceremonies.

For all the laboriously demonstrated piety of the Natick community, the Puritans subjected Indians to years of hard scrutiny before receiving them into the religious congregation as fully baptized members. In 1652, native Christians gave testimonials and were thoroughly examined. And they failed. They failed again in 1654. It was not until 1659 that they were finally granted church membership.

That natives were able to live with these demands and strictures is a measure of the deeply personal sense of emptiness and disorientation they had suffered from the losses to disease and the annihilation of their communal way of life. They needed to regroup, to fit in somewhere—perhaps anywhere.

A Theodore De Bry engraving of a palisaded Indian village in the coastal Virginia area. Labeled "Town of Pomeiok," this engraving first appeared in a report published in 1590 entitled *New Found Lands of Virginia.*

# Other Colonies

While the English were building substantial colonial outposts in Massachusetts and Virginia, Swedes were establishing smaller enclaves along the Delaware River, and Dutch colonists were settling along both the Delaware and the Hudson. The Dutch West India Company, founded in 1621, planted colonies near the mouths of both rivers and another colony, Fort Orange (later Albany), near the meeting of the Mohawk and the Hudson rivers. In 1626, the Dutch governor, Peter Minuit, in order to concentrate his forces, improve communications, and tighten his personal control, had these outlying colonies resettled at New Amsterdam (later New York). When the colonists arrived, they brought with them a trade jargon composed of fragments of Unami, one of the dialects spoken by the Lenape (Delaware) people, arranged in more or less European word order. Much of the trade among northeastern Algonquians was conducted in this hybrid language.

Probably the longest lasting and most important accomplishment of the Dutch was the alliance, called the Covenant Chain, that the settlers at Fort Orange (after many blunders and bad starts) formed with Mohawks and other Iroquois. When the English later captured the Dutch colony, the Covenant Chain became an English–Iroquois alliance. The English used this alliance to great advantage in their coming conflicts with the French.

During the winter of 1634–35, the Mohawks allowed Harmen Mayndertsz van den Bogaert to visit their towns—called "castles" because of their palisaded exteriors. His journey took him along well-marked trails through parklike forests, maintained by burning off the undergrowth each year. At regular intervals, he found small cabins that natives used as rest stops (Indians usually built these

A nineteenth-century engraving of the sale of Manhattan Island to Peter Minuit in 1626.

because of some personal vow or vision). When he arrived in Mohawk lands, he was warmly welcomed. The natives showed him various tokens of their faith, and allowed him to attend several curing rites. Van den Bogaert could not help being struck by the peacefulness of the place. At the farthest point, for instance, he met three Oneida women traders bringing fish and tobacco to exchange for Mohawk goods. These women needed no guards nor weapons to protect them.

Life was not nearly so peaceful in areas under Dutch occupation. In 1631, probably in revenge for the abuse of their women, local Delawares wiped out an all-male whale-processing post at Swaanendael. In 1634, by order of the Dutch governor, more than a hundred natives were massacred at Pavonia (modern Jersey City).

Only the short-lived Swedish colony managed to live peacefully with its Indian neighbors. Though there was occasional ill will and disagreement, colonists and Indians never came to blows. In fact, the colony was entirely supported by native hospitality. Most of the colonists were from Finland, which was at that time a Swedish province. The Finns shared with the Indians a mixed economy of hunting, fishing, and farming. They knew how to live in the forest and rely on neighbors. And when natives and Swedes met, they shared their knowledge and experience with each other. So natives learned from the Swedes how to build log cabins and make splint baskets; and in return they taught the Swedes how to grow corn and net fish.

Though the Swedish colony fell to the Dutch in 1655, and the Dutch in turn were defeated by the English in 1664, many of the cultural traits Swedes and natives patiently shared were woven into the fabric of American history.

*Pecos Pueblo Around 1500* by Tom Lovell, 1973.
A harvesttime trade fair, one of the many markets all over the continent that were
served by the extensive trade network. This one, in the Southwest, depicts pueblo
dwellers mixing with a Plains Indian encampment, exchanging foods, cloth, pottery—
their standard trade items—for exotic shells, stone knives, and even a caged eagle.

# CHAPTER TWELVE

# THE PLAINS AND THE NORTHWEST

CROW WAR SHIELD (DETAIL)

ALTHOUGH EUROPEANS did not physically reach the tall grass Plains for more than a century after first contact, profound changes were taking place there in the late 1400s and throughout the 1500s. For centuries before contact, people of the Plains had lived in the river valleys. This long experience had given them a close understanding of the ecology of the region. But a series of decade-long droughts seriously challenged this bond.

As they assessed the new, more difficult and threatening conditions, peoples of the northern Plains began to adopt the round earthlodges characteristic of the central and southern Plains. The inspiration for these round lodges came by way of the Caddoans farther south. As ancestors of the Caddoan people who became Pawnee and Arikara moved north (trading people, they were moving closer to their markets), their building style was copied by Siouians already living along the upper Missouri River. Thus by the mid-1400s, the northern rectangular houses built slightly into the ground were being replaced by tightly clustered, palisaded communities of domed, buried earthlodges. By literally burying their homes in the ground and palisading the community, people achieved a security and preparedness that allowed them to face natural disasters, like droughts, and to survive future difficulties.

Since tribal symbolism throughout the Americas systematically equated the body, the houses, and the cosmos, this housing change had vast ramifications in terms of how the Plains Indians conceptualized the world. Where before, everything—from houses to the earth to the cosmos itself—had been seen as relating to squares, everything was now viewed in relation to the circle. Indeed, by the time explorers reached the Plains, these tribes had an elaborate belief in the sacredness of the circle. When Black Elk, the Lakota (Western Sioux) holy man famous for his great vision of the late 1800s, reported this most forcefully, he was expressing a sentiment already several hundred years old.

As decades passed, the effects of the droughts were combined with rumors of strangers moving inland. Once contact—even minimal contact—was made with early traders and adventurers, disease was carried into the hinterland by Indians traveling along the extensive network of trade routes. Although the widely dispersed Plains Indians were less subject to infection and contagion than the more densely populated peoples of the coasts and major rivers, the epidemics still had terrible impact on them. The devastation caused by disease was made even more severe by the arrival of displaced tribes, who strained the capacity of the land to provide food and other supplies.

On the other hand, wondrous animals had suddenly appeared on the Plains. They were large, strong, and fast, and they patiently bore men on their backs. The animals were called horses. The sacred circle and the horse would revolutionize Plains life within a generation.

That horses thrived on the grasslands is not as amazing as it might seem. For the ancestors of the horse originally evolved on those very grasslands forty million years earlier. Their progeny went west across the Bering Land Bridge to survive in Asia, while the American original became extinct. A few tribes, however, deny this construction of those distant events; they insist that their ancestors used tiny horses before the Spanish reintroduced the modern variety. But no evidence has been found to support this view.

Not surprisingly, the diffusion of the horse followed along the same route as the spread of the earthlodge. As Caddoan communities living along the lower Mississippi had moved north to become the Arikara, they provided a trading link though their Pawnee and Wichita relations to the Caddo proper, who had traded with the Pueblos and other Mississippians long before the Spanish—and Spanish horses—appeared in New Mexico. By the early 1600s, through trade and raids, horses had been added to the exchanges that passed from the southern to the northern Plains tribes. And after the 1680 Pueblo Revolt, many more horses

*Plains People*
by Kevin Warren Smith
(Cherokee), 1991.

**In the Canyon de Chelly National Monument, Arizona, graphic evidence of early encounters with the horse still remains. This pictograph, probably made some time after first contact occurred in the sixteenth century, records a Spanish friar and his entourage traveling on horseback.**

came onto the grasslands and were captured and nurtured by people who by then were familiar with their care.

Though horses were essential to the early explorations, the Spaniards brought only geldings on these journeys (in their view, mares and foals would not survive in this harsh land). Mares and breeding stock were at last brought overland from Mexico to the northern Rio Grande colony around 1600. In time, foals were raised near Santa Fe and traded into the Plains. There they prospered. By then, the people of the Plains already had firsthand knowledge of horses.

No doubt, the sons of allies of the early Spanish explorers were drawn to help out with the tending of the herd, thus learning valuable lessons in the care of these marvelous animals. Inevitably, a few horses would have been stolen from their owners and ridden back to native communities. The stolen animals, though gelded, would be given the best of care, and certainly lived long enough to allow many men throughout the Plains to hear about these new creatures and to glean the rudiments of their care long before horses actually arrived in any numbers.

The rapid adoption of horses among the Plains tribes was also due in part to the fact that these peoples had long since used another not totally dissimilar animal—the dog. As they had already developed techniques for handling dogs, the

*Before the Horse Came*
**by Dan Taulbee (Comanche), 1960.**

*The Return of the Horse.*
The primary routes by which the modern horse was introduced and spread among the native American peoples.

natives found it relatively easy to transfer that experience. Indeed, for many Plains tribes, horses were thought of as a larger, more useful breed of dog.

Among the Lakota, because horses were so wonderful, they became "sacred dogs." Blackfeet and other tribes still refer to the time before horses as their "dog days." And Pawnee and other Caddoans used a large breed of dog to perform many of the functions later taken over by the horse. These dogs dragged crossed posts, forming a travois. Whenever members of a town moved onto the Plains to camp and hunt, the travois was loaded with tents and utensils. When horses replaced dogs these people found that their tents, often called tipis, could be made taller and wider. Thus the horse revolution had many ramifications.

Throughout the Plains during the ensuing centuries, the ownership of horses became the basis for the reorganization of tribes. A family's rank in these newly emerging societies was largely determined by the possession of horses. The status of chief now required wealth in horses, and generous liberality in distributing them. Thus young men marked their success and advancement in terms of their skill in acquiring horses in raids. There were also important roles for specialists, such as breeders, who were responsible for the evolution of special breeds like the Appaloosa, developed by the Nez Perce. For all the harm Europeans caused in the Americas, they are, in the Plains at least, praised for the gift of the horse.

## The Northwest

No one escaped the ravages of first contact. Even before they ever saw a European, natives living in the Northwest suffered from epidemics that moved up the coast or across the Plains and mountains. While there had been intermittent contact with Chinese and Japanese, whose vessels were carried across the North Pacific by the Japanese Current, the consequences of these meetings were no more lasting than those with the Norse on the other side of the continent. About 1750, the Spanish, the English, and the Russians arrived along the Northwest Coast and began a struggle for control in which the English eventually would prove victorious.

Meanwhile, as the elaborate chiefdoms of the Northwest, whose complex societies lived on rich natural harvests of salmon, roots, and berries, were being powerfully stimulated by the maritime fur trade of the Europeans, they were also being devastated by pestilence (some Haida towns lost 90 percent of their people). When elaborate and varied ways of life collapsed, resilient tribes rose

A group of Northwest Coast Indians blends drama and ritual in the celebration of a marriage ceremony.

OVERLEAF:
*Bounty of the Northwest Coast* by Richard Schlecht. Coastal peoples enjoyed the benefits provided by swift-running streams, the ocean, and a benign climate. They clustered in populous communities along the coast as well as extending back into narrow, well-watered valleys, creating sophisticated cultures rich in tradition and highly developed decorative art forms.

This petroglyph of a three-masted vessel located on the West Coast Trail on Vancouver Island in British Columbia was probably carved by a group of Nootka Indians known as the Ditidaht. The petroglyph probably dates from the first fifty years of contact with Europeans (around 1800) but could well have been etched as early as the 1650s, when Juan de Fuca's ship sailed up the Pacific Coast. Many of the other petroglyphs on the same sandstone rock panel relate to traditional histories and include whales and spirit beings, indicating that this was a very important traditional site.

from their remains. Even as epidemics swept through native populations, the new trade goods enabled commoners, who were originally unqualified for tribal office, to host their way into vacant positions among the elite.

In a way, the Northwest peoples were long prepared for the European arrival; their sacred histories had taught them to expect such terrifying persons. Local histories were filled with tales where ancestors encountered dangerous, supernatural beings. After putting them through dreadful trials, the beings gave them great boons—the territories and treasures that were later passed along as the inheritance of royal houses. Of all native American oral literatures, those of the North Pacific Coast pay the most attention to wondrous gifts of technology, preconditioning these tribes toward the acceptance of European goods once these became available to the royal elite.

These royal houses evolved slowly over thousands of years. In early times, communities occupied a series of seasonal camps and winter abodes, managed by elite families. Later, within each town, one house come to outrank the others and its leader became the chief. In this way, the Northwest became a patchwork of petty kingdoms, each led by a chief (usually a man, sometimes a woman), who inherited the hereditary title paramount in that community.

The development of elite families in the Tsimshian nation by observing the trade in exotic goods such as obsidian, amber, jet beads, and shells that were an exclusive privilege of such families. These hereditary leaders rose above the common folk because of their multiple associations with their own priesthoods, other elite houses, and a vast trade network.

As early as 8000 B.C., obsidian was being traded from Mt. Edziza, north of the Stikine River, throughout today's northern British Columbia and the Alaska panhandle. About five thousand years later, long-established trails (today paved as modern highways) were used for moving trade goods throughout the region. After another three thousand years, this trade came to include exotic goods that now belonged to only a few individuals: goods that were kept in some houses, but not others, and placed in some graves, but not others. For example, only elite, wealthy individuals, both men and women, wore labrets—plugs of stone or inlaid wood buttoned into the lower lip. And later, in historic times, only noblewomen among the Tsimshian wore labrets.

The development of trade and rank provoked strong competition among communities, sometimes leading to warfare, as indicated by the armor and weapons that appear in some graves. Indeed, these military activities were themselves aspects of a much larger pattern then occurring on both sides of the Pacific: the use of rod armor (made of wood slats) by the Tsimshian and the ritual use of trophy heads can be traced to the Old Bering Sea complex that occurred on both sides of the Pacific around 1000 B.C., and that in turn had connections with Shang China (1600 B.C.).

As the years passed, the plank houses and towns of the Tsimshian increased in size, and woodworking tools became more complex, suggesting the elaboration of the form-line art style for which the Tsimshian later became famous (they originated the characteristic Northwest Coast style of bold, wavy, and emblematic designs). Social ranks were indicated by differences in house size and by possession of imported goods. Just as in historic times, the town consisted of a row of

The kayak was a skin-covered ocean-going boat, often fitted to an individual hunter. Kayak building was highly developed among the Alaskan Aleuts and the Inuit.

dwellings facing the beach, with the largest houses occupying the center of the row. The chief of a town, in the distant past just as today, lived in the center of his (or her) people.

Meanwhile, raiding and warfare continued. Since Tlingit neighbors to the north were in the path of the transmission of Asian military technology and tactics, the Tlingit used these on the Tsimshian, who in turn used them against the Haida on the Queen Charlotte archipelago to the west and against various Kwakiutlan tribes to the south. The acquiring of slaves was almost surely one of the motivations for these attacks.

By the first century A.D., society had stabilized along the Skeena River (a major waterway of what has become northern British Columbia). Economic territories were claimed by specific royal houses, and the entire region was blended into a system of compatible beliefs and practices. This system continued practically unchanged until the arrival of the Russians, Spaniards, and English in the eighteenth century.

Then, changes came swiftly.

Early on, the Tsimshian began to leave the sites of what had been their winter villages and to move to the trading post at Fort (later Port) Simpson, which was run by the Hudson's Bay Company. Town chiefs appointed heirs to manage

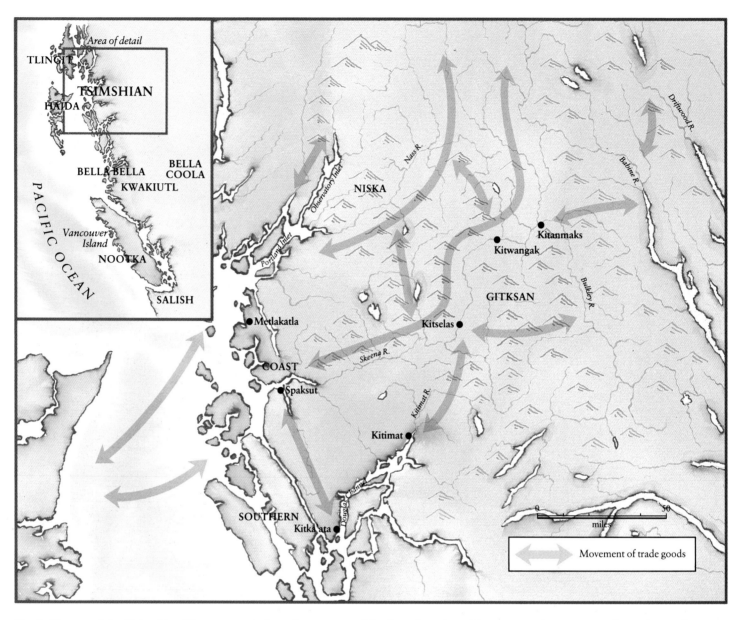

Trade Routes of the Tsimshian Near the End of the Eighteenth Century.

*Trade Routes of the Tsimshian Near the End of the Eighteenth Century.*
**A vast array of products was traded up and down the Nass and Skeena rivers and along the connecting waterways. From the northeastern interior came sheep horns, goat wool, dried berries, obsidian, furs, copper, eulachon (candlefish) grease, jade adze blades, grizzly bear claws, and innumerable other goods. From the Pacific shoreline came items such as marine shells, sea lion teeth and skins, dried fish, killer whale jaws, Haida canoes, shipwreck iron, carvings and carving tools.**

either the new neighborhood or the old town; in the process, they elevated themselves to the role of tribal chiefs, now responsible for several towns. These new ranks were confirmed with the traditional potlatches—lavish generosity at public displays. But these now took on new aspects of rivalry and confrontation, for a new system was needed to sort out the relative rankings of tribes and chiefs. In time, the Tsimshian created a new chiefdom out of this melee, under a high chief named Legex, of the Eagle crest.

There were also changes in religion. For several years after the turn of the nineteenth century, a series of prophets called Bini preached an accommodation between European and traditional beliefs. Though such accommodations may have been possible, the attempts of the Bini collapsed in the 1830s, when a remarkable Victorian lay missionary named William Duncan settled among the Coast Tsimshian, learned the language, and created a cooperative Christian community—something like an Anglican Praying Town—that still exists. Duncan achieved his greatest success after Legex converted. Then Duncan himself became, in all but actual title, the functioning high chief of the Tsimshian. After that, virtually the entire nation became Christian.

Despite ongoing changes—slow during ancient times but rapid during recent centuries—the Tsimshian for several millennia have displayed a marvelous resilience and cultural elegance. For at least five thousand years, even as they have changed and adapted to all manner of influence, the Tsimshian have lived in their own homeland, and they have done that on their own terms.

## Reflections

Two hundred years after Columbus's voyages the Americas were already forever changed—terribly changed. And yet in the face of repeated and devastating catastrophes, the native people proved themselves to be ever resourceful and resilient. The onslaught of Spanish, French, English, Dutch, and Swedish, and other colonies took their toll. Epidemics decimated large regions and wiped out whole villages, but survivors banded together to create new communities, sometimes based on older patterns and sometimes on entirely new ones. In the southern tier of North America, as chiefdoms collapsed, tribes rose to take their place. In the north, communities confederated into loose alliances.

An assortment of tools used by Northwest Coast and Arctic natives, including a carved bone trap stick, which was part of a mechanism for snaring animals; trolling hooks for catching salmon; a whale-shaped box which held harpoon blades, symbolizing the successful spearing of the intended prey; and a spoon made of horn.

An Eskimo from Nome, Alaska, uses a bow drill to carve a walrus tusk (1912). To use the drill, a carver braces one end of the drill shaft against a socket in his mouthpiece, and the other, with the drill bit, against the object he is carving. The carver rapidly draws the bow back and forth so that the strap wrapped around the shaft spins the drill in both directions.

With the loss of traditional lands, new means had to be found to encourage communalism. In particular, tribal identity now became focused primarily in various religious rituals that once had functioned within an annual sequence of celebrations of faith and thanksgiving honoring local spirits. By sharing the same ritual, whether it was the Kettle, the Big House, or the Midwinter rite, communities expressed their solidarity and defined their membership.

Despite the vast changes, disruption, and suffering the native peoples endured, their respect for life in all its forms continued. Tools continued to be decorated to please the spirits resident within them—though trade beads replaced porcupine quills, colored stones, and paints for these designs. Animals continued to be killed with all reverence so that their souls could return to their holy homes where they could, as always, be reborn to serve again.

Carved ivory pendant amulets from a Tlingit shaman's necklace. The circle-and-dot motif seen on some of the amulets was made using a special drill bit that carves both circles and the center dot at the same time.

Later, as animal populations were overhunted and species declined or vanished, natives assumed that some breach of interspecies etiquette—not human greed—was the cause. They believed the animals had not actually died off; rather, the animal spirits had chosen to stay home and out of the forests in order to teach natives and settlers a lesson in faith.

When despair overwhelmed native communities, Christian missionaries used the opportunity to preach a new way of life, a life that promised not only rewards after death but more immediate rewards here on earth. Aided by the clear evidence of these more immediate rewards, and by the occasional "miracle" (that is to say, by events that everyone interpreted as signs of the Christian God's intervention), missionaries achieved notable successes among native peoples. Indeed, since material success was viewed as an outward manifestation of spiritual grace, European technology provided a strong indication that the colonies continued to have a special bond with the divine.

Not as well known as the Christian missionary efforts, but making an equally powerful impact on native peoples, were the efforts of native prophets who tried to interpret the new world in terms of ancient cultural precepts. While many prophets had only a brief prominence, some of their teachings continue to this day among native peoples. Old traditions, renewed by the prophets' messages, continue to give many Indians strength to live in the modern world. Because prophets resanctified them for sustained observance, particular rituals of thanksgiving and respect for nature, such as Corn Harvest and First Foods ceremonies, continue throughout the Americas.

As natives struggled to survive the onslaught of European settlement, their communities were even more severely tested than the people themselves. Some communities failed to adapt to the new conditions and perished; others, more resilient, changed, modified, and lived. In remote areas, some native cultures also lived on. And although finely tuned internal mechanisms that formerly regulated

*All of this [creation] is sacred, and so do not forget. Every dawn as it comes is a holy event, and every day is holy, for the light comes from your Father Wakan-Tanka, and also you must always remember that the two-leggeds and all the other peoples who stand upon this earth are sacred and should be treated as such.*

—WHITE BUFFALO WOMAN
Sioux sacred woman, quoted by
Black Elk (Oglala Sioux), 1947.

relations among people and between people and the land were destroyed, the broad general outlines of their lives—based in traditional ideas, beliefs, and symbols—continued. Towns re-formed around these concepts, and societies regrouped in terms of families, clans, and ancestral localities that had survived the massive genocide. By 1700, while scaled down from their splendid past, these gutted communities found ways to make life worth living, even as they struggled against racism, poverty, and hardship.

Like all humans, native Americans were and are complex beings. Before European contact, the people of this continent were better and more fully integrated into their total environment than the Europeans who came to colonize the Americas. Unlike the rest of the world, with its large-scale wars, devastating religious upheavals, and huge population movements, the Americas were settled over millennia by a slow, steady, and integrative process of "learning from the land." Though their ancestors had traveled across the connected continents of Asia and the Americas, the peoples who became American natives developed on these continents as distinct racial, cultural, and linguistic populations that were uniquely at home here.

Over time, they and the land fused and became one. From this unity came their continuing sense of being and the courage of their moral stands on ecology, the worth of the individual within a community, and the value of all life. From this bond also came their delight in difference and diversity, and their contempt for uniformity. Natives learned that just as the terrain, vegetation, and denizens of an area varied, so too did the human residents.

According to the Indian view, life was filled with variety. Ceremony and seriousness needed to be balanced by joking and fun. Thus, while the earliest Spanish invaders came as military forces, ever at the ready to recognize a chain of command and a belligerent stance, natives thought such constant preparedness was foolish. Why spend your life in lockstep subservience when there were so many more worthwhile things to do? It was well and good to join forces to battle the invader as need be, but there were also families to feed, trails to travel, and sights to see.

When other Europeans arrived, they all attempted to impose their own particular brand of uniformity on the native peoples—employing the might of invading armies, enforced by the ever-spreading Euro-American settlements, and a doctrine of white superiority expounded by teachers, missionaries, and government agents.

Nevertheless, despite the immense negative pressures, despite the incredible inroads into their cultural heritages, native peoples in the first two centuries of contact continued to find strength in their own and others' diversity, and to try to come to terms with the massive changes taking place in their world.

—JAY MILLER

*I know not if the voice of man*
  *can reach to the sky;*
*I know not if the mighty one*
  *will hear as I pray;*
*I know not if the gifts I ask*
  *will all granted be;*
*I know not if the word of old*
  *we truly can hear;*
*I know not what will come to pass*
  *in our future days;*
*I hope that only good will come,*
  *my children, to you.*

—Woman's Song from *The Hako,*
  a ritual drama of the Pawnee.

OPPOSITE:
*Burning of the Cedar*
by Woodrow W. Crumbo (Potawatomi), 1946. Burning cedar is a phase of a peyote ritual. The fragrant fumes clear the minds and hearts of the participants. Officiating in this depiction are a drummer, a singer holding a rattle, and a third person scattering cedar on the fire.

# PART THREE

# EXPANSION AND EXODUS

*Brothers—My people wish for peace;*
*the red men all wish for peace; but where the*
*white people are, there is no peace for them,*
*except it be on the bosom of our mother.*

TECUMSEH, SHAWNEE, ca. 1811

Blackfeet burial platform (1912).

# CHAPTER THIRTEEN

# MAKING THE WORLD WHOLE AGAIN

*CHOCTAW MADONNA*
BY VALJEAN McCARTY HESSING (CHOCTAW), 1986

IN THE EIGHTEENTH CENTURY it seemed as if Indian peoples might make their world whole again. What they attempted was nothing so simple as the preservation of tradition. In more cases than not, they created what would become traditions to their children rather than preserving what had been handed down by their own ancestors. If the Indian peoples of the eighteenth century had been wedded to tradition, then there would have been no horse nomads on the Great Plains, no Navajo sheepherders or silverworkers or weavers. There would, indeed, be no Navajos, nor Lakotas, nor Muskogees, nor numerous other groups who first began to think of themselves as separate and distinct peoples in the eighteenth and early nineteenth centuries.

In a world of disaster, Indian peoples forged opportunities. In the midst of a population collapse that turned villages into piles of rotting corpses, they created new peoples and new tribes and confederacies. In a world where old ideas seemed incapable of explaining so much change, so much misery, and such staggering possibilities, they spawned prophets, rebels, and saviors in a seemingly unending profusion. Since Europeans could not be banished, Indians sought to include them in a common world and pursued new ways and forms to control and contain them. And, for a while, it all seemed possible.

---

OPPOSITE:
**Aged Tutor and Young Students by Harrison Begay (Navajo), ca. 1966.**

## Villages of the Dead

This accommodation and invention took place against enormous odds, and the greatest odds were biological. The ecological invasion that European contact had unleashed continued unabated. Diseases previously unknown to Indians, and to which they had no resistance, ravaged North America. Other diseases, such as syphilis and tuberculosis, which may or may not have been present earlier, spread to new areas.

Diseases destroyed some peoples and decimated others. But these new diseases did more than kill. They polluted the channels of everyday life. Smallpox disfigured those who survived. Rubella harmed the fetuses of pregnant women and marked the children for life. In the wake of epidemics, blind or scarred survivors or mourning relatives could become suicides, taking their lives in what the English trader James Adair called "sullen madness." Venereal diseases turned love and pleasure into pestilence; they also took their toll on the generation to follow. Syphilis caused miscarriages and infected infants at birth. Tuberculosis made what had once been secure if dark longhouses and earthlodges into pesthouses where the tuberculosis bacilli thrived. It made what had been the tasks of daily life—for example, the chewing of fibers to make baskets—into sources of contamination.

From the beginning of the eighteenth century until the mid-nineteenth century, chronicles by Europeans recorded the destruction of peoples. The first wave of diseases often arrived ahead of the Europeans; it seemed a disaster without immediate cause. Later epidemics came directly, spread by contact with the Europeans, and the infected went to their graves knowing the source of the pestilence that killed them.

They died in staggering numbers. In 1698 the French missionary Father St. Cosmé reported that in the villages of the Quapaws of the Mississippi there were now "nothing but graves." In 1738 smallpox struck the Missouri, and where there had been "32 populous villages of Arikara" there were in 1803 but three formed from what the French-Canadian trader Pierre-Antoine Tabeau called the "sad debris" of tribes that had formed the larger Arikara confederation.

In the late 1700s and early 1800s the new epidemics were still sweeping over the Pacific Coast. To the early European explorers, it seemed that they had stumbled on a vast necropolis. When he sailed into Puget Sound in 1792, George Vancouver described deserted villages, the houses in collapse, the buildings and surrounding woods filled with human bones. Theodore Parker wrote similar descriptions on his trip down the Columbia River in 1835. In the 1840s John Sutter and other white travelers in the Sacramento Valley saw collapsed houses filled with skeletons and old village sites littered with skulls and bones.

John Work of the Hudson's Bay Company witnessed the making of such villages of the dead. In August 1833, Work, leading a brigade of Hudson's Bay Company trappers, unwittingly carried malaria among the Indians of the Central Valley. He described the villages of the lower Feather River in California as "populous and swarming with inhabitants. . . ." When he returned during January and February, only five months later, they were "almost deserted & having a desolate appearance." The few "wretched Indians who remain . . . are lying apparently

*Interior of a Mandan Earth Lodge*
by Karl Bodmer, ca. 1834. Bodmer spent five months sketching this lodge at Mih-Tutta-Hang-Kusch in North Dakota.

unable to move." Work passed on to Oregon, and when he arrived, malaria arrived with him. It virtually depopulated the Willamette and lower Columbia. Twenty thousand or more people died in California, untold thousands more in Oregon. They left behind the villages of the dead that Parker later saw.

But what had it been like to live in such villages during the epidemics that transformed them into mausoleums? In 1837 Francis Chardon, in command of the American Fur Company post on the Missouri, witnessed the outbreak of smallpox among the Mandans. On a warm summer day in July a young Mandan died. And with that death, the journal that Chardon kept became one of the most chilling chronicles in American history because he watched so closely and cared so little. He tallied dead Indians; he tallied the rats his men killed in the fort. For him they seemed part of the same equation.

But for the Mandan, Arikara, and Hidatsa who were dying, there could be no detachment. The Mandans blamed the whites for bringing the disease among

*Mató-Tópe, Four Bears, Mandan Chief* by Karl Bodmer, ca. 1834.

*Tombs of Assiniboin Indians on Trees* by Karl Bodmer, ca. 1834. Many Indian cultures used raised platforms on which to place their dead. This foiled scavengers and brought their dead closer to the sky.

---

*Next morning at the dawn of day we attacked the Tents, and with our sharp flat daggers and knives, cut through the tents and entered for the fight; but our war whoop instantly stopt, our eyes were appaled [sic] with terror; there was no one to fight with but the dead and dying, each a mass of corruption.*

—SAUKAMAPEE (Blackfeet) Describing a raid on a Shoshone encampment in the late 1700s.

---

them, and early in the epidemic a young Mandan tried to kill Chardon. The neighboring Arikaras threatened to kill the Mandans if they harmed a white. Chardon offered to arm them. Within a month Chardon was in fear of Arikara threats. A young Arikara, missing his chance to kill Chardon, killed one of his men, and fled to his own brother's grave. There the whites killed him, ripping his body open. That evening his mother came to the fort asking the whites to kill her, too. Thus families disappeared.

By August the Indians were dying so fast Chardon stopped counting. The Mandans and the Arikaras staged "two splendid dances." They did not, they told Chardon, have long to live and would die dancing. Four Bears, a Mandan chief and an old friend of the whites, gave a last speech. The whites, whom, he said, "I always considered as Brothers has turned out to be my Worst enemies." He did not fear death, but it was too much "to die with my face rotten that even the Wolves will shrink in horror at seeing Me." Some Arikaras dreamed of the sun, others of the moon; they made sacrifices to stop the epidemic. The Mandans began to abandon some of the sick and desert their villages. Most of those abandoned died, but one young Mandan recovered, and searched for his father to kill him for having left him to expire alone.

By mid-August, less than six weeks from the introduction of the disease, the suicides began among the Mandans. A man and a wife killed themselves. They did not want to outlive their relatives. A Mandan man killed his sick wife and then himself. A Mandan woman killed her two children and then hanged herself. An Arikara had his father dig a grave for him; he walked to it, laid in it, and died. With his friends dead, he had no wish to live himself. On September 1 two bodies, wrapped in white skins and laid on a raft, passed down the river in front of the fort, a stark symbol of the tragedy of a people. And amidst despair, anger, and desperation, the epidemic dwindled out. The Mandans suffered the worst. By the end, there were, Chardon thought, only forty-one of them left alive; more than eight hundred Mandans alone had died.

Yet pervasive as these new diseases were, they were also selective. They afflicted some people far worse than others. Settled agricultural peoples with their denser populations and ready communications between villages and towns suffered more than nomads. As the Arikaras, Mandans, and Hidatsas of the Missouri River lost population, the neighboring Sioux increased. As the Pueblos declined, their neighbors the Navajos—the Apaches de Nabahu, or "Strangers of the Cultivated Fields"—increased. As small Mississippi groups like the Quapaw dwindled, the Choctaws held their population more successfully.

Navajos and Sioux increased because they were less settled and lived in smaller groups; infection did not spread so rapidly or easily among them. The Choctaws lived away from the major travel—and thus disease—routes. The Choctaws, Navajos, and Sioux, too, maintained themselves by welcoming survivors and refugees from other groups. But in this none were as successful as the Iroquois. In the seventeenth century they had incorporated those they conquered; in the eighteenth century they made Iroquoia the great haven for refugees displaced by wars with Europeans or other tribes. Most eighteenth-century Iroquois were descended from non-Iroquois ancestors.

*Four Bears and the Death of the Mandans* by Mike Larsen (Chickasaw), 1993.

At one time, the Mandans numbered some eight thousand souls. The gift the white explorers brought the Mandan people, as with many other tribes, was disease, notably smallpox.

In the space of one year, the Mandans were reduced to two hundred and fifty individuals. Shortly thereafter, even those few were gone, their culture wiped out.

The artist has chosen to portray this passing in the way the Indians might have done—painting the story on an animal skin. These skins were a year-by-year record of events and were often called a "winter count."

The painting depicts a stylized Mandan village with the customary surrounding fence. Circling the village are all the warriors, their bodies bearing the sign of the fatal disease. Four Bears himself is included in the count. He carries himself proudly, full of power, since he does not fear death.

*Night Chant Ceremonial Hunt*
**by Harrison Begay (Navajo), 1947.
When the Spaniards first arrived riding
the great animals never before seen in
the Americas, some native inhabitants
believed horse and man were joined in
one unearthly beast—perhaps foreshadowing the later skill of Indians in their
handling and control of the horse.**

# Brief Glory: The Horse

The ecological invasion that brought disease and death also brought the means
for a more abundant life. For with Europeans came horses, and sheep, and pigs.
To travel across native North America in the eighteenth or early nineteenth century would mean encountering new possibilities that Indians constructed in their
herds and flocks.

We can start such a journey in the Southeast with the Choctaws. Until about
1750, they raised only a few pigs and some chickens for exchange with the
Europeans. At first they themselves ate neither pork nor chicken, because in the
complicated cosmology of the Choctaws these animals fell between cultural categories. Birds should fly; four-legged animals should eat vegetation. The chickens
were birds that could not fly; the pigs were four-legged animals that were omniv-
orous and they ate filth. Initially, both were thus taboo. But by the late eighteenth century, such taboos weakened and, as game declined, the Choctaws
replaced deer with pigs, cattle, and horses in the forests, and in their diets.

Farther west the Pueblos and Navajos eagerly adopted sheep, goats, and
horses from the Spanish. The Navajos by the mid-nineteenth century found it

hard to imagine a world before sheep, for as Navajo children learned, "Everything comes from the sheep." The sheep were mother and father; the sheep were loved. Maintaining the flocks became the commandment of Navajo life. Most of this happened so quickly, in a century or less, that Choctaws or Navajos who lived at the end of the 1600s would hardly have recognized much of the material life or daily routine of their people in the opening years of the nineteenth century.

But the greatest change came with the horse. By the 1690s some of the Plains tribes of Texas had horses, and the animals had reached the agricultural Caddoan villages of the Red River. From there, through raiding and trading, they spread gradually northward. By the 1730s horses had reached the Missouri River. By the 1770s they were well into Canada at the northern limits of their range. A second route of diffusion ran up the west side of the Rockies. Horses passed from the Navajos to the Utes and then on into Idaho to the Shoshones and Flatheads, who had horses by the beginning of the eighteenth century. From there horses spread east to the Blackfeet and west to the Nez Perce and other peoples of the Columbian Plateau. Finally, more horses came into California with the Spanish in the late 1700s. The Miwoks, Yokuts, and other peoples raided the ranchos and missions, and they adopted horses as a source of food as well as transportation.

On the Great Plains the arrival of the horse in a sea of grass dominated by vast herds of buffalo added the final element in a combination that made mounted nomadism possible. The small bands of nomads using dog travois already on the Plains climbed up onto horses and entered a different world. Other hunters and gatherers, among them the Sioux and Comanches, now also ventured out onto the Plains on horseback. The horse increased the efficiency of the hunt; it increased the ability of the nomads to move their goods. With horses

A Blackfeet woman, with a Dakota cradleboard on her back, leads a horse with travois (1915). The sturdy Indian ponies rendered transport considerably easier than the traditional dog travois, making it easier to carry tipi poles and other cumbersome household goods.

came bigger tipis and larger stores of dried meat. The horse made the nomads better fed and housed, and allowed the sick and the old to travel more easily. The horse became the symbol and center of Plains nomadic life. Indians traded for horses and raided for them. They defined wealth in terms of horses. Horses became a bride price; they became the preferred gift at religious ceremonies. So thoroughly did they take up the horse that the Plains nomads—the Comanches, the Sioux, the Arapahos, and others—all are better understood as nomadic pastoralists traveling with their horse herds than as mere buffalo hunters.

So thoroughly did the horse become a part of their lives that some Plains nomads denied there had ever been a time without horses. But the Piegans, the southernmost group of the Blackfeet confederation, kept alive in cultural memory the arrival of the first horses, or "sky dogs," as many western Plains tribes called them. A Kutenai, an enemy, brought the first horses to a Piegan camp whose headman was named Dog. The Kutenai and his family were starving. For some reason, they had been unable to kill buffalo. The Kutenai brought the horses in a desperate attempt to appease his enemies and get food. On seeing the horses, the Piegans thought they must have come from the heavens or from beneath the earth. Over time, both the horses and Dog prospered. He became,

**On the trail with horses and travois.**

finally, a leading chief named Many Horses. And mounted Blackfeet, Kutenai traditions say, drove them west of the Rockies.

But the horse, like the Europeans, was a visitor not from the sky but from a long-separated biological world. And by their very presence, horses changed the ecology of the regions into which they came. Horses competed for grass with native animals, particularly in the critical riverine habitats. Horses and cattle raided from a Spanish rancho or mission carried with them in their excrement the seeds of European weeds mixed accidentally in the oat and wheat seeds the Spanish had brought. These weeds and European grasses thrived in the Central Valley of California. Cattle and horses trampled and grazed the native grasses much more heavily than native animals had and thus created opportunities for European weeds and grasses that had evolved in tandem with European grazers. Gradually, the whole ecology of the California grasslands changed.

Like Europeans themselves, horses and cattle harbored diseases previously unknown in North America, diseases that could kill native species. And even as the Indians created a new world based on the dynamic mixture of horses, buffalo, and grass, that world, unbeknownst to them, began to unravel.

Before the white hunters ever arrived, it appears that disease and habitat destruction began to seriously cut into bison numbers. The whites would only administer a massive coup de grace.

LEFT:
*In The Days of Plenty*
by Quincy Tahoma (Navajo), 1946.
Mastery of the horse allowed Indians to become even more daring and skillful as hunters.

RIGHT:
*Navajo Woman on Horseback*
by Gerald Nailor (Navajo), 1940.

# CHAPTER FOURTEEN
# OF FURS, BUFFALO, AND TRADE

*THE BEAR DANCE BY GEORGE CATLIN, 1844*

EIGHTEENTH-CENTURY INDIANS sitting on horseback, herding sheep or cattle, cooking in a copper kettle, or mourning relatives dead from smallpox lived in a fundamentally changed world. But it was a world that they still struggled to control. They needed to understand change, to give it meaning, and to direct it. But this could not be done, at least for any length of time, in isolation from whites. As Long Warrior told the Cherokees in 1725, "they have been brought up after another Manner than their forefathers and . . . they must Consider that they could not live without the English." What the best means of living with the English, or the French, or the Spanish consisted of was the great eighteenth-century question for most Indian peoples. This struggle to control their world was religious, it was political, it was sexual, but virtually everywhere it was also economic and tied to the fur trade. Questions of exchange of goods and of trade, not questions of exchange of land and its possession, dominated the attention of most Indian peoples in the eighteenth century.

Paradoxically, our understanding of the historical significance of trade goods can be difficult precisely because so many of these goods survive and are accessible to us. Often the actual goods sit in museum cases and collections. We view the trade beads, the Hudson's Bay blankets, the axes, knives, and guns; they become almost too familiar to us. Many are the functional equivalent of goods we still use. They seem merely less sophisticated versions of our own tools or clothes, and so we jump to a series of conclusions. Indian peoples, we think, used these things for the same purposes we do. Indian peoples, we think, valued them for the same reason we would value them if we found ourselves in their place.

*Trappers on the Big Sandy* by Alfred Jacob Miller.

And on one level, the easy lesson we derive from museums is true enough. Woolen cloth, copper kettles, iron tools, and guns can make life easier. Try cutting down a tree with fire and a flint ax; then try an iron ax. Try to boil water by dropping hot stones into a tightly woven basket; then use a copper or brass kettle. Try staying warm in wet leather clothing, then try staying warm in wet woolen clothing. The trade goods saved time, they saved labor, they gave comfort.

And yet this is not the whole story. Trade goods were not always so functionally superior to native manufactures that Indians would bother to acquire them. A flintlock musket was not, for example, superior to a bow and arrow for hunting bison from horseback. The gun was unwieldy, hard to reload, and unable to bring down a bison with a single shot. Mounted nomads preferred to keep their old weapons for hunting, at least until the advent of repeating rifles.

## The Personality of Trade Goods

To fixate solely on the functional appeal of trade goods, however, is to miss an important aspect of their meaning to eighteenth-century Indians. Trade goods had other values that we do not see when we look at those simple and silent artifacts in museums. Once many of these trade goods were animate; their initial appeal was less utilitarian than divine. Some Indian peoples regarded kettles, which rang or sang when hit, as alive; some regarded guns as *manitous*—that is, as other-than-human, or supernatural, persons. Their roar was not *like* the thunder; it *was* the thunder, now at human disposal. The Taensa and Bayogoula on the Mississippi regarded glass as the equivalent of crystal and thus a tool in divination. Northeastern Indians may, at first, have so ardently desired mirrors because, even more than the fascination of seeing their own clear reflections, they hoped to catch a glimpse of the future. Mirrors, like water, which was the ordinary means of divination and prophecy, reflected images. But mirrors did so far more clearly, thus increasing, presumably, the power of the diviner. In museums mirrors, kettles, and guns are mundane; once they were miraculous.

In Indian society after society, material goods introduced by Europeans transcended their immediate utilitarian ends. Repeatedly Indian peoples put such goods at the service of honor. Indians honored other human beings or other-than-human persons by making them gifts. Indians honored those with spiritual powers whose aid they needed by making them gifts. Many Indian peoples honored the dead by burying valued goods with them or by distributing goods to mourners at the time of burial. The Algonquian-speaking peoples of the Great Lakes staged the most spectacular of these ceremonies: the Feast of the Dead. It involved a mass reburial of those who had died and been temporarily interred since the last Feast of the Dead. The ceremony was rapidly dying out in the early eighteenth century, but, while it had lasted, host villages might devote a year to gathering trade goods and native goods. They would then distribute all of these goods as grave offerings or as gifts to their allies who attended the feast.

A Delaware woman's blouse made of red trade cloth and German silver brooches and buttons, from the late nineteenth century.

*They lavish all that they possess in trade goods or other articles; and they reduce themselves to such an extreme of poverty that they do not reserve for themselves a single hatchet or knife. Very often they keep back for their own use only one old kettle; and the sole object for which they incur all the expenditure is, that they may render the souls of the departed more happy and more highly respected in the country of the dead.*

—NICOLAS PERROT, *Memoir*

## The Value of Indian Products

There was no single response to the fur trade. Indians could, and did, treat trade goods with wonder or with scorn. They could replace nearly their whole array of clothing and tools with European imports or they could change them hardly at all. At the end of the nineteenth century, Curly Chief, a Pawnee, told a story whose moral was the Pawnee's independence from the Americans and their goods. In various versions a Pawnee priest or a chief met Captain Zebulon Pike or the first Indian agent and took from a medicine bundle sticks to rub together to make fire, a flint to kill buffalo, and corn to give them food. They supposedly needed the Americans for nothing.

The story exaggerated an earlier reality, but its message of limited wants was accurate enough. Pawnees welcomed kettles, knives, and blankets long before Pike arrived, but they did not give up buffalo robes or bows and arrows. Plains horticulturists, like the Pawnees, and buffalo nomads, like the Lakotas, Crows, and Arapahos, had less use for European goods than other groups did. The buffalo supplied most of their wants. They needed guns to fight each other, but until the advent of repeating rifles, bows and arrows (with, as Curly Chief did not point out, metal points) were the most effective weapon for buffalo hunting.

At the other extreme were the Iroquois. They integrated the products of this European technology into their lives so thoroughly that in 1768 the missionary Eleazar Wheelock, looking for an item of native manufacture that was "perfectly Simple, and without the least Mixture of foreign Merchandise," could find only a "small specimen."

Look at an eighteenth-century painting of an Iroquois warrior. Virtually every piece of clothing, every weapon is of European or Euro-American manufacture. Yet the Iroquois was still fully Iroquois. He was at once distinct from the whites and inextricably connected with them through the very clothes he wore and the tools he used. He looked and lived far differently from his own ancestors even though in many ways he continued to see the world and behave in ways that they would have found familiar.

Neither Curly Chief nor the Iroquois warriors of the eighteenth century had yet lost control of their world, but it was a world, as Long Warrior realized, much changed. Most groups during the 1700s retained the ability to produce basic necessities: food, housing, and, if necessary, clothing. The loss of white goods might then be a grave inconvenience but not a disaster. When, after nearly a century of exchange, the American Revolution cut off supplies of powder and ball, blankets, and other trade goods from the Miamis, Piankashaws, Weas, and

*The man who came was from the Government. He wanted to make a treaty with us, and to give us presents, blankets and guns, and flint and steel, and knives.*

*The Head Chief told him that we needed none of these things. He said, "We have our buffalo and our corn. These things the Ruler gave to us, and they are all that we need. See this robe. This keeps me warm in winter. I need no blanket."*

*The white man had with them some cattle, and the Pawnee Chief said, "Lead out a heifer here on the prairie." They led her out, and the Chief stepping up to her, shot her through behind the shoulder with his arrow, and she fell down and died. Then the Chief said, "Will not my arrow kill? I do not need your guns." Then he took his stone knife and skinned the heifer, and cut off a piece of fat meat. When he had done this, he said, "Why should I take your knives? The Ruler has given me something to cut with."*

—CURLY CHIEF
(Pawnee), ca. 1860

OPPOSITE:
*Feast of the Dead*
by Fernando Padilla, Jr.
(San Felipe Pueblo), 1993.

*Hudson's Bay Trapper*
by Olaf Carl Seltzer.

other Indians along the Wabash River, they temporarily reverted to buffalo robes, bearskins, and bows and arrows. A shortage of trade goods brought discomfort, even suffering, but it did not usually bring starvation. A Sauk chief threatened with the loss of trade in 1779 replied that "he & all others had arrows for their living & . . . they were not alarmed by that."

In the short run, the Sauk chief was right, but in the longer run the Europeans had gained a sizable advantage. The Sauks would not starve without the trade, but if the traders disappeared, the Sauks would certainly suffer, and would welcome their return. For the Indian response to trade goods was different from their response to domestic animals or to the crops that whites brought. Given sheep, Navajos became sheepherders; given horses, Comanches became pastoralists; given cattle, Choctaws became cattle raisers. They were able to breed these animals themselves. But trade goods did not reproduce themselves; most Indian peoples could not reproduce them and did not wish to learn.

With some notable exceptions, the acquisition of trade goods brought a decline in Indian manufactures. Navajos and Pueblos wove their own blankets and cloth as did, in time, the Cherokees. But the Salish-speaking tribes of the Northwest Coast, who, before contact, wove blankets from a mixture of the hair of a dog bred specially for the purpose and mountain goat wool, abandoned their weaving altogether.

The Navajos and Cherokees learned to do exquisite work in silver, and the Sauk and Fox mined lead and made bullets, but few Indians outside of the missionized Indians made or worked in iron or brass except to turn scraps of those metals into weapons or, as the Iroquois did, to alter fowling pieces and muskets into rifles.

With relatively few exceptions, Indian peoples adopted the products of a new technology, but not the technology itself. And thus, to obtain hoes, axes, blankets, and shirts, to obtain knives and guns, to obtain vermilion and beads, they needed whites. In council in 1750 a speaker of the St. Joseph Potawatomis admitted that "without the French we would lack knives and the rest." It was an admission repeated in council after council by numerous Indians about numerous Europeans for the next century.

Two things kept this dependence in check. First, although the Indian demand for goods was real, it was limited. And second, Indians did not depend only on trade for the goods they required and neither did they usually depend on only one source of supply.

The French missionary and traveler Father Pierre de Charlevoix, writing in the 1720s, was struck by the Indians' relative indifference to wealth and European goods. He wrote that the Great Lakes Indians were "true philosophers, and the sight of all our conveniences, riches, and magnificence affects them so little that they have found out the art of easily dispensing with them."

The lesson Father Charlevoix sought to drive home to his eighteenth-century French readers is one that we are still reluctant to accept today. We tend to regard the way we buy and sell—and admit our own desire for wealth—as manifestations of universal human desires. It is still difficult for us to believe that most Indian peoples of the eighteenth century did not share them.

## The Indian View of "Trade"

It was the differences between Indian conceptions of wealth and exchange and those of Europeans that caused the trade to take the shape that it did. Almost a hundred years later, in the opening years of the nineteenth century, the French-Canadian trader Pierre-Antoine Tabeau came to trade among the Arikaras along the Missouri River. He recorded a conversation that, he felt, demonstrated the *unreasonableness* of the Arikaras.

> The Arikaras look upon the whites as beneficent spirits who ought, since they can, to supply all its needs and it looks upon the merchandise, brought to the village, as if destined for it and belonging to it. Besides, their minds not grasping our ideas of interest and acquisition beyond what is necessary, it is a principle with them that he who has divides with him who has not. "You are foolish," said one of the most intelligent seriously to me. "Why do you wish to make all this powder and these balls since you do not hunt? Of what use are all these knives to you? Is not one enough with which to cut the meat? It is only your wicked heart that prevents you from giving them to us. Do you not see that the village has none? I will give you a robe myself, when you want it, but you already have more robes than are necessary to cover you." All the logic and all the rhetoric in the world are thrown away against these arguments, and how hope for success in a nation, imbued with these principles and always destitute of everything?

What Tabeau recorded was a different logic, one that refused to make economic exchange either a separate sphere of human life or the purpose of human life.

> *Some day you will meet a people who are white. They will try always to give you things, but do not take them. At last I think that you will take these things that they offer you, and this will bring sickness to you.*
>
> —SWEET MEDICINE
> Cheyenne Prophet

## TLINGIT ACCOUNT OF FIRST CONTACT IN 1786

The Comte de la Pérouse, exploring the North Pacific for France, sailed into Lituya Bay in 1786. Tlingit living there a century later still maintained a tradition of their first encounter with Europeans arriving by sea:

*One spring a large party of men from the big village at Kaxnuwu went to get copper from the people at Yakutat. Four canoes were lost at the entrance of Lituya Bay and the first chief of the party drowned. While the survivors were still mourning, two ships rounded the bay. The Indians thought they were two great birds with white wings, perhaps Raven himself. They fled to the woods. After a time they came back to the shore and looked through tubes of rolled-up skunk cabbage leaves, like telescopes, for if they looked directly at Raven they might turn to stone.*

*When the sails were made fast, they thought the birds folded their wings, and they imagined they saw a flock of crows fly up from the ships, so they ran back into the woods again.*

*One family of warriors dressed in armour and helmets, and took their copper knives, bows and arrows, and launched a canoe. They were so frightened when thunder and smoke came from the ship that their canoe overturned and they scrambled ashore.*

*Then a nearly blind old man said his life was behind him, and he would see if Raven really turned men to stone. He dressed in sea otter furs, and induced two of his slaves to paddle him to the ship. When he got on board his eyesight was so poor that he mistook the sailors for crows, and threw away the rice that was offered to him thinking it was worms. He traded his fur coat for a tin pan and returned to shore laden with gifts of food.*

*The people were surprised to see the old man alive. They smelled him to make sure that he had not been turned into a land-otter man, and they refused to eat the food he had brought.*

*The old man finally decided that it must be ships and people he had seen, so the Indians visited the ships and traded their furs. Then the white men lost two boats at the mouth of the inlet and many were drowned.*

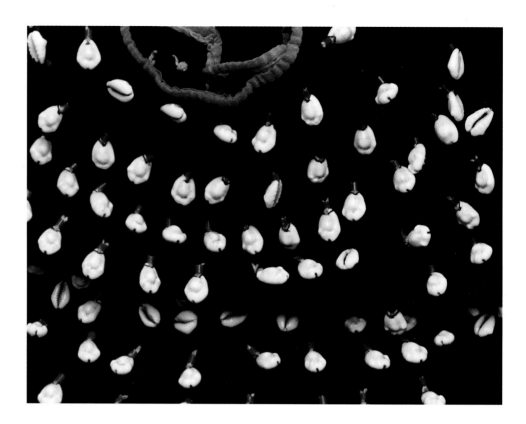

Shoshone dress decorated with cowry shells from the Indian Ocean.

Such reactions were common. More than a century earlier, the Fox, on first meeting French traders, thought "that whatever their visitors possessed ought to be given to them gratis; everything aroused their desires, and yet they had few beavers to sell." In such early encounters these expectations had sometimes arisen from deeper mistakes about the identity of Europeans. The Algonquians regarded the Europeans as well as their goods as manitous, and they took the customary stance toward such supernatural beings: they asked for pity and blessings. The Europeans did have miraculous otherworldly goods. And the Europeans were as unpredictable and arbitrary as one might expect supernaturals to be.

But the Europeans soon enough revealed themselves as not only fully human but often rather unpleasantly human. They seemed a crazy, unreasonable, greedy people with an insatiable lust for beaver skins, or buffalo hides, or sea otter in amazing quantities, but at the same time they sought to hoard their own extraordinary goods that the Indians themselves desired. In place after place across the continent Indian peoples and Europeans had to bridge the gap between their competing ideas of proper exchange. Remarkable compromises had to take place for the pelts to move one way and the blankets another.

For Indian peoples the idea that an economic relationship—giver and recipient, buyer and seller—could be separated from a social relationship—kinsperson, friend, enemy—was astonishing. It is as if outsiders should suggest to us that our relationship with our children should have no influence on our economic exchanges with them. Why not charge our children for their food, their clothes, their shelter? Why not make sure we get the largest possible profit from every ice cream cone we offer? And why not have our children, in turn, bill us for their labor? Indians extended the social logic we apply to immediate family to a wider array of social relationships. For them social relationships ideally determined the form of economic relationships. A person shared freely with kinspeople without immediate expectation of return. A person shared with friends or fellow villagers in the expectation that they would eventually reciprocate. A person traded, in the sense of seeking an even exchange, with allies or friendly outsiders. A person stole, not only with good conscience but with pride, from enemies or unfriendly outsiders. Determining the proper social relationship determined how goods would change hands. Within such conceptions the actions of Europeans seemed foolish and incomprehensible.

Traders noticed, without fully understanding, that the modes and ethics of trade varied according to the relationships between parties. The comments of the trader Peter Grant about the Chippewas could have applied to many others: "These haughty people, though uncommonly reserved among themselves, are, with their traders, the meanest beggars and most abject flatterers on earth, and though naturally honest in their dealings with one another, they often find many occasions to cheat their traders with impunity."

And so, in place after place, a basic logic of exchange worked itself out. If Europeans acted like enemies—if they sought their own gain at the expense of those they traveled and lived among or if they provided aid to a village's enemies—then they would be treated like enemies. They would be robbed and

*Trappers' Rendezvous*
**by Alfred Jacob Miller.**

From 1836 to 1844, *A History of the Indian Tribes of North America* by Thomas L. McKenney and James Hall was first published. The multivolume history was conceived as a permanent record of the features and customs of some of the more prominent native Americans, who were believed to be near extinction. It featured color engravings (including those above and opposite) faithfully reproduced from portraits painted from life, almost all of which were subsequently destroyed.

LEFT:
Red Jacket, a Seneca chieftain, in an illustration by Charles Bird King. The solid silver medal shown was presented to Red Jacket by George Washington.

RIGHT:
Yoholo-Micco, a Creek chief, also by Charles Bird King.

perhaps killed. If they acted like friends, they would be welcomed but expected to fulfill the duties of friends, for friends provided for each other's necessities. And if, as they increasingly did in the 1700s, they took wives from among their customers, they would enjoy the privileges of kinspeople. They would be expected to share with their relatives, but they would enjoy in turn protection and help.

The actual fur trade in the eighteenth century became a compromise between such logic and the European expectations of markets and gain. Parties gave gifts to validate their friendship, traded goods, usually at set or at least predictable prices, and then exchanged other gifts to create obligations and preserve the peace upon which exchange depended. Each side strained against the compromise. Indians pressed for greater gifts—they were "inveterate beggars" the traders said. Whites strained to limit gifts or to turn them into credit or loans that must be repaid. Traders cheated; Indians stole.

This compromised system of exchange repeatedly broke down; it was often marred by violence, but it endured through the eighteenth and into the nineteenth century. The fleets of French trade canoes that swept west from Montreal in the eighteenth century depended on such compromises. The long strings of packhorses and mules that wound their way through southern forests existed because understandings were reached. At Taos in the Southwest nomads and pastoralists poured into the town where European goods from Mexico now joined more ancient items of exchange. Ahead of this direct trade were Indian middlemen who carried European goods to people who had not yet seen white faces. The Mandan villages on the Missouri formed a mart on the Plains that included white goods before it included white men. By the late eighteenth century the trade had reached the Pacific Northwest with British and American ships trading in the harbors and rivers. The Chinooks acquired goods there that they carried upriver to trade along the Columbia.

## Wealth and Status in Indian Societies

The compromises Indian peoples made to get goods, the presence of new sources of wealth, and the increase in the hunting of animals for their furs, all had consequences for the societies that took part in the fur trade. That Indian peoples by and large limited their wants and desires did not mean that no one accumulated wealth. By the mid-nineteenth century the trader Charles Larpenteur thought it "a fine sight to see one of those big men among the Blackfeet, who has two or three lodges, five or six wives, twenty or thirty children, and fifty to a hundred horses; for his trade amounts to upward of $2,000 a year."

Larpenteur was not describing an ancient world he and other traders had found and exploited but a world still young and in the making. It was a world very much intertwined with the coming of Larpenteur and other Europeans. The horses Larpenteur counted with such pleasure were, of course, relatively recent acquisitions, but the prevalence of polygamy was probably also new. A big man and his wives existed in complicated relation to the trade. A big man loaned his extra horses to poorer men in return for the hides they took on the hunt. But to process the skins, he needed the labor of women. He needed more wives. It was the skins they processed that brought him the "trade . . . upward of $2,000 a year" that he needed to support so large a family. Such big men existed in symbiotic relationship with the traders who so happily calculated the proceeds when they saw the big men approaching.

By European standards, to be sure, the amount of personal wealth was not large. But some Indian people did accumulate wealth on a scale not seen since the Mississippian chiefdoms that preceded the Europeans. The big men among the Blackfeet with their $2,000 in annual trade had not only built up their horse herds, they had with considerable foresight also invested in other forms of

LEFT:
**Ledagie, a Creek chief.**

RIGHT:
**Thayendanegea, also known as Joseph Brant, in a George Catlin copy of an illustration by Ezra Ames. Before Brant, a Mohawk, became Great Captain of the Six Nations, he was a commissioned officer in the British Army and was largely responsible for maintaining the Iroquois League's alliance with the British during the American Revolution.**

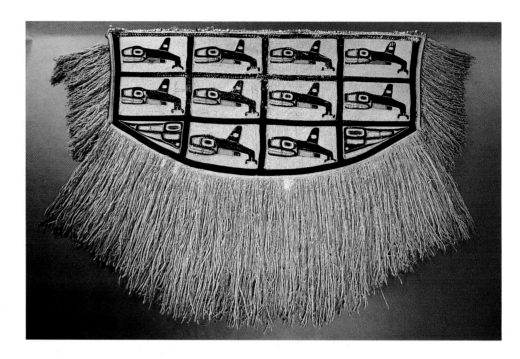

Woven from cedar-bark fiber and mountain goat wool, Chilkat blankets were highly valued by the Tlingit, and were often prominent in potlatches. The blanket's design, which usually depicted an animal associated with the owner's clan, was created and composed by the husband or father of the woman who wove it. The men paid high fees and provided the goatskin and the loom to the weaver, who might need six months or more to make a single blanket.

wealth. Three Calf, a descendant of Buffalo Back Fat, head chief of the Blood tribe of the Blackfeet confederation in the early nineteenth century, remembered his ancestor's advice:

> Don't put all your wealth in horses. If all your horses are taken from you one night by the enemy, they won't come back to you. You will be destitute. So be prepared. Build up supplies of fine, clean clothing, good weapons, sacred bundles and other valuable goods. Then, if some enemy takes all your horses, you can use your other possessions to obtain the horses you need.

There were functional equivalents of Blackfeet big men scattered across the continent, and in each case the scale of their riches had increased with the coming of Europeans. Navajo *ricos* measured their wealth in large herds of sheep, goats, and horses. Lineage heads and clan leaders on the Northwest Coast added to native measures of wealth—coppers, slaves, elaborately twined Chilkat blankets—large numbers of European trade goods.

All of this concern with gain and property traders could understand, approve of, and exploit, but ultimately the traders were frustrated with the attitudes toward property in most Indian societies. There were too many checks on the acquisition of wealth and too many pressures to give it away. James Adair, an eighteenth-century trader among the Indians of the Southeast, recounted what was a common Indian critique of whites as a selfish, greedy people.

> Most of them blame us for using a provident domestic life, calling it a slavish temper: they say we are covetous, because we do not give our poor relations such a share of our possessions as would keep them from want. There are but few of themselves we can blame on account of these crimes, for they are very kind and liberal to every one of their own tribe, even to the last morsel of food they enjoy.

# POTLATCH

Kaw-Ciaa, a Tlingit woman, dressed in potlatch finery (ca. 1906).

Of all the ceremonial occasions among the Tlingit, the greatest were the mortuary rites designed to honor or raise up the dead. These were the major potlatches, ceremonies marked by the lavish distribution of goods to guests from other clans, villages, and tribes. One of the earliest nineteenth-century descriptions of such a potlatch is by Sutkoff, an interpreter of mixed Tlingit–Russian descent:

*When the chief is dressed, he comes to the door and addresses the guests, viz., "You all know that my uncle was a great hunter, also my ancestors were great hunters, they killed a great many wild animals and*

*wounded a great many. The latter have gone back to the woods and are alive at the present time. And that he himself does the same as his ancestors, and that's how he became rich and owned many slaves."*

*After he has finished speaking he calls the slave that dressed him and gives him the end of the stick, and he tells him he is free and he can go, and so he frees all who dressed himself and his children.*

*After this they have a dance. They have no musical instruments save drums, and they keep time to singing. Head of drum [is] of deerskins.*

*They start in to dress the guests by*

*giving them pieces of blankets, and call each one's name as they make the gift.*

*They don't eat this day, but eat next day: hair seal, berries preserved in oil, eulachon grease, dried fish, and with feasting the festival ends. [Often] the guests eat so much that they vomit, for the host tries his hospitality by making his guests sick, and then it is to his honor afterwards that all got sick. And if no one should get sick, it would speak badly for the food. And those who vomit and get sick are made extra presents of blankets. All guests bring [with] them spoons and dishes, and they carry away all the food their dishes hold.*

The life of Two Leggings, a Crow of the Whistling Waters clan, born in 1844 at the end of this age of tumult and change, shows how, in a society without coercive power, people could be brought to conform to group ideals. Two Leggings is a valuable example because he was in no sense an extraordinary person. He was the Crow equivalent of guys we all knew in high school: ambitious, excitable, daring, and not real bright. He craved respect, honor, and standing, and his search for them made him a danger to everyone around him, but his needs also made him controllable.

Two Leggings grew to manhood wanting to be "brave and honored." If he survived his numerous raids against the Blackfeet and Sioux for horses, he would, he thought, "become a chief with many honors and horses and property." But to succeed, a man needed sacred helpers. To gain them, he needed either powerful dreams or visions, or, if he failed to procure powerful spirit helpers on his own, he needed to purchase a duplicate of a medicine bundle owned by a powerful holy man.

Channeling the ambition of young men such as Two Leggings was a constant problem in Plains Indian societies. Initial success as a raider or warrior led Two Leggings to think "I could do all these things alone." He "would not listen." "The old medicine men," Two Leggings remembered, "would shake their heads and say something bad would happen, but that was my worry." The transformation of rash young men like Two Leggings into responsible, wiser and more cautious men took place through a regimen of failure. For Two Leggings the critical event was the death of his friend, Young Mountain:

*Young Mountain had died because I had not followed the medicine men's advice. It was hard to have to learn this way. In the past I had met with some good luck and had also experienced many close escapes, but now I had lost my best friend. I began to see how reckless and foolish I had been.*

When young men failed, when their companions died, when they themselves were hurt or wounded, they sought the causes of their failure in their own lack of spiritual power. The evidence of their own deficiency drove them to older men who possessed greater power, knowledge, and understanding. Two Leggings bought a sacred bundle from Sees the Living Bull, giving him "a beautiful Hudson Bay blanket, a buckskin shirt, leggings, moccasins, and buckskin colored shirt. . . . I promised him everything I owned if only he would give me his powerful medicine." The dreams of older men, as the holy man Two Belly told Two Leggings, "had more truth than those of young men."

Coming to terms with life's failures put younger men under the partial control of their elders. It matured them and made them less reckless. "In time," Two Leggings admitted, "I realized the good example and valuable advice of these great holy men, and saw how reckless I had been." Chiefs and holy men replicated themselves by transforming rash and reckless men like Two Leggings into responsible people. He became a man who "decided to obey our tribal rules. When I broke them I never had any luck."

Far to the north at the turn of the eighteenth century, the French in a similar manner had reported that the Great Lakes Indians "would be exceedingly well-to-do if they were economical," but they refused to accumulate wealth.

In the majority of cases a person's status depended not on what he or she possessed but rather on what he or she gave to others. Riches mattered only as a road to generosity. To be rich when others were in need was to be a danger to the group. The accumulation in the hands of ricos, or big men, or chiefs thus often formed but a prelude to distribution. The carefully gathered wealth of a Northwest Coast leader disappeared in the lavish potlatches that astonished Europeans.

To validate their status, to honor and mourn a departed relative, to celebrate a marriage allying themselves with powerful outsiders, chiefs gave away mountains of blankets, as well as cloth, new and old clothing, animal skins, dishes, baskets, berries, beads, and, more rarely, slaves and coppers. Navajos distrusted those ricos who hoarded too much wealth, and were likely to regard them as witches. It was safer to be generous. From Iroquoia to the Northwest Coast, Indians created social systems that induced people to redistribute wealth and to reap status.

*Dividing the Chief's Estate*
by Joseph Henry Sharp, ca. 1901.

The motive for such redistribution—the respect and status that it secured, the religious sanctions that it fulfilled—astonished Europeans because so little authority accompanied that respect. Europeans also craved respect, but they associated respect with authority and the ability to command. But authority seemed to be exactly what was lacking in most Indian societies of the Eastern Woodlands and Great Plains. Only among a few eighteenth- or nineteenth-century Indian groups could a chief command. A late-eighteenth-century French traveler in the Ohio country observed with astonishment that chiefs could not "strike or punish the meanest warrior, even in the field, and at home nobody obeyed him, but his own wife and children."

It was a message Frenchmen had been sending home for nearly a century. The Sieur d'Aigremont reported in 1708 that the northern Indians "possess no subordination among themselves . . . being opposed to all constraint. Moreover, these peoples [have] no idea of Royal grandeur nor Majesty, nor of the powers of Superiors over inferiors." Father Charlevoix wondered how such people as the Algonquian nations of the Great Lakes could simultaneously be "so haughty and jealous of their liberty" and yet be "beyond imagination slaves of human respect?"

For those leaders whose authority depended on generosity, access to desired trade goods was critical, just as for traders seeking access into Indian societies

OPPOSITE:
*Honor and Thanks* by Fernando Padilla, Jr. (San Felipe Pueblo), 1993, depicts the Midewiwin ceremony.

connections with Indian leaders were necessary. Symbiotic relations between existing chiefs and traders often arose, but traders and European officials often sought to create their own trading chiefs, rewarding men who secured them a large trade with gifts and symbols of authority that could gain them influence among their own people. And some traders, such as the early-eighteenth-century French trader Peter Chartier, who was the son of a French father and a Shawnee mother, made themselves into chiefs.

In more hierarchical Indian societies—the Natchez with their Great Sun, the Pawnees with their hereditary chiefs and priests—such gifts flowed to an elite as tribute in ways that Europeans understood. Those seeking to benefit from the spiritual power of priests or shamans gave these holy people gifts. But priests and chiefs did not retain most of the goods they acquired. To maintain the status that procured the gifts, the priests and chiefs had to redistribute in turn. They had to validate their standing through their generosity.

## Taking from the Animal World

Just as trade goods altered the routes to leadership and status in Indian societies, so, too, did the fur trade itself alter the relationship of Indian peoples to the natural world. The change was not so simple as an abandonment of old beliefs.

In the eighteenth and early nineteenth centuries beaver vanished or was much diminished over all of North America. Sea otters virtually disappeared from the Pacific Coast. The range of bison dramatically decreased. White-tailed deer almost disappeared from southeastern forests. Indian peoples were not responsible for all of this decline, but as hunters in the fur trade they were implicated in much of it. What is interesting is that they were implicated not because they abandoned their old values, but because they retained them. These values no longer produced the results they once had.

The fur trade demanded that Indians kill animals for their fur and hides. Indians were already hunters accustomed to killing. Although killing for the trade often altered the pattern and the scale of the killing, the fact of killing was not new. Indian peoples took this killing quite seriously. The death of an animal was not a small thing. They understood the necessity to kill in particular ways.

Indian beliefs and customs with respect to animals varied enormously across North America in the eighteenth century, but there were common patterns. Virtually all Indian peoples regarded animals not as some subordinate order of beings put at the service of humans, but as persons, other-than-human persons, with whom human beings established relationships. The nature of these relationships had been richly charted in stories from a past when humans and animals communicated directly and even intermarried. And some of that fluidity, that ability to communicate, remained. A Nomlaki Indian of California captured the essence of this older world when she told an ethnographer that "Everything in this world talks, just as we are now—the trees, rocks, everything. But we cannot understand them, just as the white people do not understand Indians."

The profound nature of Indian identification with the animals and plants of their world was fundamental to their whole view of life. Animals could and did

## THE USES OF A BUFFALO

The buffalo was literally life to thousands of Plains Indians, providing the very basic elements of survival: food, shelter, and clothing. The hide alone had multiple uses: calfskin provided soft swaddling for newborn babies; the large, tough hides of fullgrown animals sewn together—often as a communal effort by the women—made a tipi for an entire family. The hide also provided the soles of moccasins, parfleches (bags), robes, and thongs.

The thickly padded neck pelt was used to make shields, a single hide a bull boat. The paunch was a useful cookpot; the sinews became thread. The bones were utilized as tools: they made handy scrapers, knives, and awls. Tied together with rawhide, the ribs made convenient sleds. Winter hides, with their heavy fur, provided both shelter and warmth. The fur itself could be used to stuff cradleboards and pillows, or it could be woven into rope. And this was all in addition to the bountiful meat the buffalo provided.

Not all uses of the buffalo were strictly utilitarian. Bone game dice, buckskin dolls, and toys made of horn were all common. Ornaments were created using buffalo hair, the animal's tail often appeared as a lodge decoration, and the buffalo beard embellished both clothing and weapons. Both horns and hair went into the making of headdresses. Medicine men used the first of the animal's four stomach chambers to combat frostbite and skin diseases, the bladder became a medicine bag, and the tail a medicine switch.

Rare yellow and albino buffalo hides were highly valued and often worn during rituals. Buffalo hooves and scrota would be made into rattles, and rawhide drums and drumsticks were also made for ceremonial purposes. Among the Sioux, Assiniboines, and Pawnees, the skull was used in prayer and in major ceremonies, including rituals designed to entice the buffalo herds to return and give of themselves again.

*Buffalo Hunt,* Chase by George Catlin, ca. 1844.

Headdress

Ceremonial rattles

A bone scraper used to clean buffalo hides

Water dipper

A winter count painted on a hide

HARPER'S WEEKLY.
JOURNAL OF CIVILIZATION.
Vol. XVIII—No. 937.] NEW YORK, SATURDAY, DECEMBER 12, 1874. [WITH A SUPPLEMENT PRICE TEN CENTS.

SLAUGHTERED FOR THE HIDE. [See Page 1022.]

An 1874 cover of *Harper's Weekly* depicts the slaughter caused by the trade in buffalo skins. A single green hide was traded for about $1.25. A processed robe, however, might fetch as much as $100 in the markets of Europe.

speak and communicate. In the Miami account of the founding of the Midewiwin religion, an old man, wandering in the woods while mourning his son, discovered an immense lodge. In it were animals who had taken human shape, and they gave him both the power to kill and cure. They gave him, too, instructions on how to found the Midewiwin lodge and share his powers. Followers of the Midewiwin north of the Ohio River made animals into healers, but south of the Ohio animals caused disease and plants provided the cure. But in each case animals and plants were persons with purposes of their own.

This was a world conceived as a biological republic in which relations between humans and other inhabitants had to be negotiated and not dictated. The negotiations were religious. Indians made hunting holy. Animals consented to die, and they or more powerful beings—holy people, keepers of the game, manitous, or other supernaturals—instructed hunters on the rules and rituals necessary to kill them.

Prayer, pleading, and reverence were as necessary to the hunt as the bullet, arrow, or spear. Unless honored, unless appeased by the proper rituals, unless the rules were followed, animals would not consent to their capture. But because the sanctions against overhunting were religious and ritualistic, the fur trade and Indian beliefs could, in fact, coexist rather easily.

Most sanctions against overhunting mandated only that the hunter kill to meet a real need and that he fulfill the proper rituals. As long as these conditions were met, the hunter could kill in good conscience, certain that animals would return. Shawnee hunters, for example, believed that each deer killed in a proper ritual manner had four lives. It would immediately reincarnate and return. The Lakotas believed that the buffalo issued out from a cave beneath the earth. As long as they were hunted in a proper and holy manner, they would return. Elsewhere, similar beliefs governed the hunt, and so gradually Delaware hunters in the Ohio Valley or Creek or Choctaw hunters in the Southeast could increase their annual kills to a hundred or more deer without any twinges of conscience. They needed the deer, and they killed them properly.

When confronted with a decline in game brought on by overhunting, Indian peoples thus first sought ritual explanations. And if they found their own consciences clean, they blamed their neighbors who, unlike them, did not follow the proper rituals. And everyone could, in time, blame the whites who also killed enormous quantities of game and followed no rituals at all. The whites, the Shawnees contended, killed deer improperly and that is why the deer did not return. The buffalo, the Lakotas believed, withdrew back under the earth because the whites slaughtered them without need and did not honor them.

Only rarely and relatively late did Indians see the fur trade per se as a cause in the depletion of game. In 1807 The Trout, an Ottawa holy man, conveyed to the Indians around Michilmackinac a message from the Great Spirit.

*You complain that the animals of the Forest are few and scattered. How should it be otherwise? You destroy them yourselves for their Skins only and leave their bodies to rot or give the best pieces to the Whites. I am displeased when I see this, and take them back to the Earth that they may not come to you again. You must kill no more animals than are necessary to feed and clothe you.*

*The Hide Hunters*
by Olaf Carl Seltzer, ca. 1930s.

But what was at issue here was the meaning of *necessary*. The Trout was defining need in terms of producing food and clothing from the animals themselves. He and the Shawnee prophet Tenskwatawa, who also denounced overhunting, explicitly connected the decline of game with the fur trade. They tried to introduce new ideological obstacles to halt the trade and preserve game, but they failed. The trade continued. Many, probably most, Indians continued to interpret a necessary kill in terms of trade and not immediate consumption. And under such conditions, Indian rituals and beliefs were insufficient to halt the decline of species with whom they had long shared the earth.

Incrementally in the decline of game, in the increase in the scale of gifts given at potlatches, in the substitution of blankets and woolen shirts for buffalo robes and deerskin clothing, the fur trade was changing both everyday life and the relations that maintained it.

But the change was not the alteration of Indians into Europeans. Instead, what it meant to be Indian, to be Cherokee, or Miami, or Blackfeet changed in significant ways, and, as Long Warrior and numerous others recognized, being Indian could now only be worked out in the presence of, in cooperation with, and in conflict with whites.

# CHAPTER FIFTEEN
# A PRECARIOUS BALANCE

TRADING WHISKEY FOR FURS, 1871

THERE EMERGED OVER SIGNIFICANT AREAS of North America in the eighteenth century a set of cultural accommodations between Indians and whites that might loosely be called a middle ground. Part of the process that created it was at work in the fur trade, and in other forms of accommodation. It arose not because Europeans became Indians, although this could happen, or because Indians adopted European culture, although this, too, could happen. It arose because Indians and Europeans, each confident of the rightness of their ways, had to deal with people who shared neither their values nor their assumptions of the appropriate way to accomplish necessary tasks.

The middle ground arose because, although neither side could muster enough force to make their opposites conform, neither side could do without the other. People had to find a means, other than force, to gain cooperation between opposing cultures. To succeed, those who operated on the middle ground had to attempt to understand the world and reasoning of others, and to assimilate enough of that reasoning to put it to their own purposes. People sought out congruences between cultures. The congruences did not have to be real, they only had to be accepted as valid by both sides, who then built on them to create whole new ways of doing things.

An analogy can be drawn in the creation of trade languages that arose during this period. These trade languages—Mobilian in the lower Mississippi Valley or Chinook jargon along the Northwest Coast and up the Columbia—were separate specialized languages made up of combinations of English or French words and

OPPOSITE: *The Trapper's Bride* by Alfred Jacob Miller, 1850.

words from various Indian languages. The grammar and pronunciation were largely from Indian languages. These trade jargons—neither fully Indian nor European—were a separate creation, but one that allowed people not only to move in and out of the various societies but to operate in a world of trade and negotiation that existed between them. Indian peoples, just as they might speak Chinook and their own language, could operate on the middle ground and in their own society.

## Sex and Gender on the Middle Ground

Central to the creation of the middle ground were questions of sex and gender. The women and men who met at the junctures between the various Indian and white societies of the 1700s had to come to terms with common sexual desires and profound cultural differences as to the best ways to fulfill such desires, and appropriate ways of acting for both men and women.

Whites, as well as Indian peoples, wanted to assume that certain physical acts were "natural" and the same the world over; they were fascinated and shocked when this did not prove to be the case. Bernard Romans, traveling in the Southeast in the late eighteenth century, informed his European readers that "a savage man discharges his urine in a sitting posture, and a savage woman standing. . . . I need not tell you how opposite this is to our common practice." Romans's interest was not scatological. It was the difference that fascinated him and his audience, for what Europeans took as the most "natural" thing in the world suddenly appeared as mere custom that varied from people to people.

And the difference that most often surprised Europeans in the seventeenth and eighteenth centuries was that they frequently encountered women where they expected to confront men. Where they expected biology to order the world, they encountered gender. Gender is a cultural coding through which various societies mark which actions and roles are appropriate for males and which are

appropriate for females. Although such roles actually are constructed and do change over time, people accept these roles not as social convention but as biological necessity. Thus when different societies with different roles collide, each initially tends to see the other not only as different but as unnatural. This is what happened each time Indians saw white men doing a task they deemed appropriate for women, and each time whites confronted women in a situation where they expected men.

Not everything was different, of course, but even when the division of tasks and roles between sexes seemed familiar, a closer look often proved otherwise. Thus the Pueblos, whose men worked in the fields, carried burdens, and dominated religion and politics, seemed outwardly familiar. But on closer examination this comforting predictability dissolved. Women not only owned the homes, they largely built them, mixing the plaster and erecting the walls. Men worked the cornfields, but the fields belonged to their female kin. Women preserved the sacred ritual objects of the clans. And it was through women rather than men that many Indian peoples, including originally most, if not all, the Pueblos, traced descent. Among the Iroquois, many southeastern peoples, and the

**Hopi women largely built their adobe homes and also owned them.**

OPPOSITE: **Weaving a basket.**

*After Auchiah*
by Kevin Warren Smith
(Cherokee), 1990.

OPPOSITE:
**Portrait of an Acoma Pueblo woman.**

*If the Indians go to war without the consent of the great women, the mothers of the Sachems and Nation, The Great Spirit will not prosper them in War, but will cause them and their efforts to end in disgrace.*

—JOHN ADLUM
Traveling among the
Seneca in 1794.

Pawnees, descent was traced through the mother, and property and titles descended through the female line.

Europeans recognized such differences—and judged them. Indians could not simply be different, they had to be better or worse than Europeans. Difference acted as a moral magnet: it attracted moral judgments. In being different, Indians had to be morally superior or inferior. And to eighteenth-century European eyes, the work done by Indian women combined with the sexual freedom they enjoyed marked the inferiority both of Indian women and of their societies. On the one hand, Europeans regarded Indian women as lascivious and wanton; on the other, they saw them as drudges and slaves.

William Clark, while on the Pacific Coast at the farthest reaches of the Lewis and Clark expedition, summarized the European attitude toward many Indian women pithily enough when he wrote: "Chin-nook women are lude and carry on sport publickly." And when, as among the Algonquian peoples of the Great Lakes, the relatives of unmarried women defended their right to regulate their own sexual activity on the grounds that women were "masters of their own bodies," Europeans thought these were societies without sexual restraint.

Europeans, seeing their own boundaries on sexual activity disregarded, tended to miss the boundaries Indian peoples created. Various groups banned sexual relations between members of the same clan; they barred sex during certain times of the year or following, or preceding, certain events such as childbirth or a hunt. And this was not a world without sexual violence or double standards. In groups as diverse as the Illinois, Sioux, and Blackfeet, adulterous men might lose property to an aggrieved husband but adulterous women might be mutilated, killed, or gang-raped, an activity recognized by the Indians as punishment.

Today we often reverse the judgments of early European observers. Some modern observers now make Indians superior. What was once denounced as wanton is now praised as sexually liberated. What was a sign of drudgery now becomes equality and independence. But both the early condemnations and the modern praise are based on white fantasies. That women performed work done by men in European societies did not make them drudges, but neither did ownership of land and matrilineality make them matriarchs. That women possessed a range of sexual choices not available to European women did not make them prostitutes, but neither did such sexual freedom make them independent of the wishes or violence of men. This was a more complicated world.

In thinking the labor of Indian women was a proof of their degradation, whites often misunderstood the nature of women's work. Work in the fields was not a mark of servility. Mary Jemison, a white captive intermarried among the Iroquois, recalled the pleasure of growing crops and laboring alongside other women. She thought their labor no harder than that of white women and their cares not nearly so numerous. Waheenee, or Buffalo Bird Woman, recalled from the vantage of her old age a youth where she and other Hidatsa women "cared for our corn in those days, as we would care for children. We thought that the corn plants had souls and that growing corn liked to hear us sing, as children like to hear their mothers sing."

The powers women possessed in matrilineal, agricultural societies were real enough, but this did not mean that women controlled these societies. Instead

these powers protected the female sphere against the demands of men. As the naturalist William Bartram observed among the Muskogees (or Creeks) and Cherokees, "marriage gives no right to the husband over the property of his wife." Among groups as diverse as the Iroquois, Pawnees, and Muskogees, women, not men, owned the lodge, retained custody of children when a couple separated, and had ownership of the fruits of their labor.

The fur traders who entered and described these Indian societies did not confront "gender roles," or "sexual freedom," or "matrilineal societies." These are abstractions. They confronted living women with corn or skins to sell, with sexual desires to fulfill, with curiosity to satisfy, with children to feed, with thousands of everyday human wants, needs, and desires organized and pursued in ways the traders did not initially understand.

## Trade Relations and Sexual Relations

As traders encountered the agricultural peoples east of the Mississippi, they entered societies where, as among the Iroquois and the Cherokees, women often controlled the crops their labor had produced. When traders bought corn among the Cherokees, they dealt with women. And elsewhere on the continent when traders sought furs and skins, they also often dealt with women. Among the Chinooks, the great traders of the Columbia River before smallpox ruined them, women dominated the actual trading of furs and fish because, the men said, "the women could talk with white men better than they could, and were willing to talk more. . . ." Among the Delawares and their neighbors, and in the Great Lakes region, women also dominated much of the trading in skins and furs.

In this exchange the line separating trade relations and sexual relations was often obscure. This, besides creating both delight and unease for white traders and travelers, expanded the boundaries of the middle ground. In the late seventeenth and early eighteenth centuries "hunting women" of the Ohio and Great Lakes region traveled and had sexual relations with French companions for whom they also cooked, cut wood, and made clothes. In return they received what amounted to wages. Later in the century Alexander Henry, a British trader in the upper Great Lakes, reported that trading sometimes ended with the women abandoning "themselves to my Canadians."

Europeans, too, blended exchanges of property and exchanges of sex, but they had only two categories for such exchange: marriage and prostitution. Combinations of property and sexual exchanges in the fur trade often fit neither pattern. Lacking an appropriate category, Europeans often labeled such sexual exchange prostitution. Father Carheil, a French Jesuit, denounced the hunting women as prostitutes. But their activities had little to do with prostitution as commonly understood. The women did not solicit customers and did not sell discrete sexual acts. They left the men when they chose. Indeed, it was the concept of Algonquian women as "masters of their own bodies" that most disturbed priests like Father Carheil. This is what he wrongly labeled prostitution.

In most instances, however, Europeans did not so much find prostitution as help create it. Sexual relations that accompanied the trade could themselves

## MARY JEMISON

Mary Jemison was a white girl who became Seneca. A French and Indian raiding party captured her as a teenager in 1758. They brutally murdered her family and then gave Mary to two Seneca sisters who adopted her to replace their own slain brother. They renamed her Dickewamis and, she recalled, rejoiced over her "as over a long lost child."

Living with the Senecas, she gradually lost her desire to return to the white settlements and came eventually to live in Iroquoia. She married and had children. And as she had wept for her murdered white parents, she would live to weep for her murdered Indian children.

Mary Jemison's account of her life as told to a New York doctor in 1814 has fascinated white readers ever since. In it, Indians cease to be two-dimensional figures, symbols of either savagery or nobility. She neither romanticized Iroquois life nor vilified it. She had become an Iroquois and she knew her people as varied and complicated human beings living by their own cultural logic. Jemison witnessed horrors and atrocities inflicted by both whites and Indians. She witnessed bravery and nobility. She saw incredible, dogged endurance, and people collapsing under the tragedies and horrors of life. She bore children, loved them, and buried them. She lived a fully human life, an Indian life, and through her white readers confronted the humanity of the peoples they dispossessed.

OPPOSITE:
Woman and child (1908).

The Chippewa woman painted by James Otto Lewis in 1827 shows her carrying her child, who is strapped onto a cradleboard and supported on the mother's back by a cord that wraps around her head. The board is made of wood, with a small projecting piece near the base covered with soft moss and designed to support the child when the board is upright.

The cradleboard was designed in such as way as to allow mothers to put it down, perhaps leaning it against a tree, without fear of the child hurting itself by falling. On the front of the board, a projecting hoop guarded the child's face and head in the event the board fell forward. These boards were generally used until the child was old enough to sit or walk alone.

Lewis's 1827 illustration below depicts a mother about to suckle her child.

become a trade. Sex, like beaver robes or deerskins, became a commodity. Women's bodies were available for purchase. Women became sexual objects. After a century or more of the fur trade in the Great Lakes, prostitution as such had been created, and it spread inland with French fur traders while American and British seamen carried it to the West Coast. Patrick Gass of the Lewis and Clark expedition noted an "old Bawd" on the Missouri who marketed the favors of younger women among the Americans, and on the Columbia he mentioned a Chinook woman who kept nine girls and "frequently visited our quarters."

By 1766 Delaware chiefs along the Ohio were condemning women who had sexual intercourse with whites in exchange for rum as "very bad." The women did not drink the rum but instead carried it back to their villages and towns and sold it at high prices to men. Sex had thus become a business venture in a double sense. As such women prospered in the liquor trade, however, they could eliminate sex from the exchange. Once they had a stock of goods, they began simply to exchange liquor for furs. The Shawnee chiefs, by 1770, were asking whites not "to sell [rum to] our women to sell to us again."

What was happening was that new patterns of behavior that developed on the middle ground were spilling over and changing the customary ways in which Shawnees acted toward each other. In this change, as Shawnee chiefs recognized, could be social dangers disguised as individual opportunities. But distinguishing danger from opportunity was difficult even in hindsight.

Not all intermingling on the common ground was centered on exchange of goods or sexual favors. Nor, by any means, were all Indian women free to enjoy, or sell, their sexuality as they wished. Many factors aside from sex and race went into determining whether the relationships that were being forged between white and Indian would open new opportunities or impose new burdens on the Indian. To a large degree these factors were rooted in personal characteristics and individual situations. Among the histories that have come down to us, the story of Marie Louisas, a woman anchored firmly in her Miami community, provides a stark contract to that of Rachel Mohawk, who lived most of her life among whites. Yet both women exemplify the struggle of complex individuals to meet the challenges of their changing world.

## Marie Louisas

When she reached middle age in the 1770s, Marie Louisas was still a striking woman; she had once been beautiful. She was of the lineage of Miami chiefs. Richardville, a French trader, had married her in the mid-eighteenth century. Her beauty no doubt attracted him, but like other white traders among Indians, he sought more than beauty in a wife. He needed her labor, and, above all, he needed to gain protection and aid from her kinspeople. Like so many other Indian women, Marie Louisas mediated between her white husband and her own community. In the process she gained status and influence.

But Marie Louisas was not just an "Indian" or just a "Miami" fulfilling a common social role. She was not simply a woman. She lived a particular life, and social roles and identities never fully contain any human life. She was, the whites who knew her thought, "a very clever" woman. While still married, she became a trader, accumulating "slaves, cattle, Indian corn, wampum, silver works, and axes." She had acquired skins from the Miamis, traded them in Detroit for rum, and then retailed the rum. She not only lived with a European, she had moved toward European modes of exchange. When her marriage to Richardville ended in squabbling and animosity, she retained her property and her trade.

Life was not made up of a series of stark choices for Marie Louisas. In marrying Richardville, in selling rum, in engaging in trade, she did not leave the world of the Miami towns. Her brother Pacane became her advocate against Richardville, and Pacane became a leading chief of the Miamis. Her son, Jean Baptiste Richardville, also became a Miami chief, and she, in an unusual role, acted as his speaker in council. He no more than his mother made simple choices. He joined with white traders in the Most Light Honorable Society of Monks, and the Monks celebrated Mardi Gras in his house. And his mother, as she had once mediated for her husband, continued to act as a mediator for French and English traders in the Miami towns.

Marie Louisas had constructed her life around the point where European and Miami life met, and it was a juncture where many Indian women found new ways of acting in the eighteenth and early nineteenth century. Some, like Marie Louisas, lived well at this juncture, but the lives of few women ended as successfully as did that of Marie Louisas.

A portrait of Hayne Hudjihini, or The Eagle of Delight, by Charles Bird King. She is identified as the favorite wife of an Indian named Shaumonekusse. In 1821 they visited Washington, where the young woman was admired for her "interesting appearance of innocence and artlessness."

## Rachel Mohawk

The Moravian congregation at Goshen on the Muskingum River in Ohio buried Rachel Mohawk on May 13, 1802. She had lived most of her thirty-one years among the Moravians, seeking salvation and sanctuary amidst a violent, rapidly changing frontier. She was a Christian Indian, and her life had been difficult.

Rachel had married at eighteen, and by twenty her husband, Levi, had deserted her as the Moravians prepared to move north to Canada, hoping to escape the bloodshed of the Ohio country. Rachel never discussed why Levi left, if she even knew, but the missionaries thought the episode emotionally scarred her. In any case, the Moravians reported, a young woman without a husband was in "a particularly trying situation."

Rachel did not remarry for years, and when she did, she chose a man as troubled as herself. Moses Mohawk was an Iroquois refugee who joined the Moravians in Canada, hoping to overcome his drinking. He feared, he told them, that "I might sometime be killed in a fit of intoxication, and my poor soul would be lost." Within a year of their marriage, Rachel left Moses for another man. Moses seized her by force and brought her to Goshen.

It was a strange journey. Rachel's brother, John Peter, accompanied them. So, too, did an Indian named Abel who had taught himself to write. Abel often refused to speak, but he sometimes secretly transcribed all that was said around him. On this journey, he is said to have recorded "every sentiment" expressed by Rachel, Moses, and John Peter. The party stayed only briefly at Goshen, leaving almost immediately. But within three months they were back.

The Chippewa woman pictured below grieves for her deceased husband by carrying a mourning bundle for a period of one year, during which time she cannot marry again. The 1827 illustration is by James Otto Lewis.

Rachel was pregnant. Moses wished to leave her at Goshen, return after the birth to claim the child, and "dismiss her [Rachel] forever." The Moravians did not really want the "adulteress" Rachel among them, but then, after an evening service, the couple reconciled. They agreed to remain at Goshen. Rachel gave birth to a son on March 11, 1800, whom she oddly enough named Levi, the name of her first husband.

The family would have only sixteen months together. On July 14, 1801, Moses died of tuberculosis. On September 12, 1801, baby Levi died. And on May 12, 1802, the Moravians put Rachel to rest beneath the oaks in Goshen's cemetery. The Moravians buried her as one of their own, and, in part, she was theirs. But she was more. In her husband Levi's leaving, in her checkered relationship with Moses, and in what Abel heard and recorded were signs of another complicated and uncharted moral universe. But Abel's transcription did not survive. And so Rachel only mutely gestures toward us, indicating a complicated human life, a complicated Indian life.

The middle ground could enable Marie Louisas, or the nameless Shawnee women who traded liquor, to advance their interests. Or it could lead to suffering and dislocation as it did for Rachel Mohawk. Yet misunderstanding did not always involve conflict or hostility. When each side had a need for the other and both pursued those needs with a modicum of sensitivity and decency, Indians and whites could still find much to admire and appreciate in each other.

The Lewis and Clark expedition of 1804–6 still stands as testimony to the ability of both sides to recognize a common humanity. Sponsored by Thomas Jefferson, whose instructions embodied his own intense interest in Indian peoples and their customs and beliefs, the expedition sought to find a water passage to the Pacific. Meriwether Lewis, Jefferson's private secretary, and William Clark, an experienced soldier and frontiersman, led the small expedition into the interior. It would not be the first expedition to cross the continent. Alexander Mackenzie had done that in 1793. And long before Lewis and Clark, French fur traders had penetrated the Plains and reached the Rockies. But the Lewis and Clark expedition was the first American expedition to cross over the Rockies and proceed on to the Pacific. And with the exception of a clash with the Blackfeet, it did so remarkably peacefully.

The expedition could not have survived without the aid of Indians, but in popular legend one Indian—the Lemhi Shoshone Sacajawea—has taken on the tasks performed by many different people. Sacajawea was captured as a young girl by Hidatsa raiders in the fall of 1800. Toussaint Charbonneau, a trader, purchased her sometime before 1804. She became his wife and accompanied him when he signed on as an interpreter for Lewis and Clark. She bore him a son while on the expedition.

Sacajawea did not in any sense guide the expedition; most of the country it covered was new to her. She did, however, help at critical points. Her aid as an interpreter among the Shoshones was invaluable, and she helped form the chain of interpreters by which Lewis and Clark communicated with Nez Perces and other Plateau peoples. Sacajawea died at Fort Manuel in South Dakota well before popular legend turned her into the expedition's guide. On December 20,

1812, the trader John Luttig wrote an obituary of sorts for this young woman whose brief life had bridged two worlds and many peoples: "This evening the wife of Charbonneau, a Snake Squaw, died of putrid fever she was good and the best woman in the fort, aged abt 25 years."

A quarter of a century later, in the early 1830s, when artist George Catlin journeyed into the Missouri River country, he, too, had a largely friendly reception. But he came under different circumstances. He came not to see and record what was unknown to white Americans and Europeans, but instead to record whatever he could of the western Indians before their lifeways and customs vanished forever. Catlin would even suggest the creation of a vast western national park to preserve the remnants of both Indians and the buffalo herds as reminders of what had existed before white settlement inevitably washed across the area.

Catlin was well intentioned. But the very fact that he already saw Indians as museum pieces instead of as formidable peoples whose friendship he needed to cultivate and whose skills might determine his survival showed how quickly the world was changing and how the middle ground was eroding.

The changes that the middle ground brought were often ambiguous. Tallying the losses and gains, assessing the results of change for women, or for men, is a difficult task. Then or now, non-Indian terms of evaluation would differ from those that Indian men and women would use to judge their own lives. We can be certain only that definitive and lasting changes were occurring.

In terms of lessening the labor necessary to live, the fur trade, at least initially, probably helped most Indians, male as well as female, but the gains were not uniform, nor was the fur trade functioning in a vacuum. Much else was happening, and many other changes were taking place. One of those changes was the introduction of the horse, which made potent differences in everyone's lives. The

*Archery of the Mandans*
by George Catlin, ca. 1844.

horse did lessen the burdens women bore; it did make travel easier. This was true on the Great Plains where, in 1724, a chief of the Skidi Pawnees complained that without horses their wives and children died under their burdens while returning from the winter hunt. And it was true in the Eastern Woodlands, although often here the burdens women bore were burdens imposed by the fur trade.

In the early years of the Carolina deerskin trade, Cherokee women often served "instead of pack horses carrying the skins of deer, which by much practice they perform with incredible labor and patience." Women carried sixty- to eighty-pound packs for fifteen or twenty miles a day. Even where the horse served as beast of burden, the woman's task was not necessarily lightened. There was a price for agricultural peoples to maintain horses, and women paid the price in extra labor. They took on part of the care and maintenance of horses, and it was their labor that was wasted when unconfined horses entered and damaged crops growing in the fields.

Horses that destroyed crops caused numerous quarrels among eighteenth-century Cherokees. Women threatened to tomahawk untethered horses and sometimes proved "as good as their word, by striking a tomahawk into the horse." Early nineteenth-century missionaries reported that care of horses among the Pawnees resulted in "more broils, jealousy, and family quarrels" between husband and wife than any other cause.

The preparation of skins and furs for the trade involved similar trade-offs. Men killed game for the fur trade, but it was usually women who tanned the skins. More labor went into processing a fur than went into killing the animal, and so the work of women tended to increase more than the work of men. The big man among the Blackfeet needed multiple wives to process the proceeds of the hunt. On the other hand, the clothing, knives, axes, and kettles that the trade yielded all worked to lessen the labor of women.

## The Seduction of Alcohol

In a world where constant change inevitably created tension within Indian societies as well as between Indians and whites, liquor proved, next to disease, perhaps the most dangerous element of contact. Obviously not all Indians drank, any more than all whites did. Whole peoples—the Pawnees, the Crows, and others—were once known for their abstinence. But liquor became a staple of the trade, particularly of the English and American trade, precisely because the Indian demand for it was at some level not rational or calculated. Captain Ouma, a chief of the Sixtowns Choctaw, compared the craving for liquor to a sexual desire. Rum, he said, was like a woman: "When a man wanted her—and saw her—He must have her." But the urge was not biological. Liquor was not always and everywhere a problem. The market had to be cultivated; desire had to be created and made habitual. And this was not always easy when liquor made people so foolish that, as the Arikara said, the whites should pay the Indians to consume liquor because the traders must wish to laugh at Arikara expense and should pay for the entertainment.

Yet when the desire was created, liquor became, as Duncan McGillivray of the North West Company realized, the ultimate inducement to the fur trade. Alcohol created wants where none existed before. Indians would hunt to procure

*I'm drunk now. I'm drunk now, and we have a pretty good time. I don't like to drink but I have to drink the whisky. Here I am singing a love song, drinking, drinking, drinking. I didn't know whisky was no good and still I was drinking it. I found out that whisky is no good. Come closer to me, my slaves, and I'll give you a drink of whisky.*

—Drinking Song (Sliammon, Northwest Coast), mid-1800s

**Drunken Frolic Among the Chippewas and Assiniboines** by Peter Rindisbacher, ca. 1820.

*Florida War, Whiskey Conquered the Indians* by T. P. Hunt, ca. 1830. The conversation between the two white men reads, "Well, I rejoice at the failure of these blood-hounds. It was cruel, unjust, & unchristian to employ them." And the reply, "It was unwise too, for you perceive they can be exterminated by other means, more certain and less revolting," refers to the casket, which reads, "N.E. Rum, or Indian Exterminator."

A cartoon appearing in *Frank Leslie's Illustrated Newspaper* from 1883. The caption reads, "Our Artist comes to the help of the Indian Department, which, according to a contemporary, 'is puzzled to know what to do with the captured Apaches.'"

liquor when they would not hunt for other goods. McGillivray concluded that "when a Nation becomes addicted to drinking, it affords a strong presumption that they will soon become excellent hunters."

Liquor brought release from normal social constraints, and it was often an invitation for violence. Among some peoples, a drunken person was initially treated as a person under the influence of a supernatural being and thus not responsible for his or her actions. Among the Cherokees if a drunken man, either accidentally or on purpose, killed another's horse, broke his gun, or destroyed anything of value, then the worth of the lost items in deerskins was determined by a Beloved Man. If the aggressor did not have the required skins, he either gathered them from his relatives or departed on a hunt to secure them. Among other groups, however, the harm done by liquor was attributed to the liquor rather than the drunken person, and he or she might not be held accountable.

But even in societies where drunks were culpable, when liquor temporarily crowded out other trade, absolute chaos could reign. In 1776 John Stuart estimated that among the Choctaws, "for one skin taken in exchange for British Manufacture, there are five gotten in exchange for liquor; the Effect of which is that the Indians are poor, wretched, naked, and discontented." Here was one way in which more animals died, trade increased, and Indians grew poorer.

Liquor often tore through the social fabric, as well. John Stuart's brother, Charles, reported in 1777 that he had come through the Choctaw towns and "saw nothing but rum Drinking and Women Crying over the Dead bodies of their relations who have died by Rum." That same year one Choctaw chief claimed, with probable exaggeration, that the liquor trade had cost a thousand Choctaw lives in eighteen months. Similar costs could be calculated across the continent.

Where liquor could not be banned, Indians sometimes found ways to confine its effects and integrate it into the rhythms and rituals of the trade. It was still dangerous; it could still bring death and destruction, but the potential for disaster could be confined and narrowed. In the Canadian West and on the Great Plains, some Indian peoples demanded liquor as gifts and as a necessary prelude to the trade, but refused to buy it, reserving their furs for other goods.

The consumption of liquor could be regulated in other ways as well, as the Iroquois proved. In the late seventeenth century an English officer, William Hyde, had described how seven or eight Iroquois warriors would "sitt Round upon the Ground all drunk, and to maintain fair Justice among them in drinking a young handsome Squa Sate in the middle with a Cagg of rum, & measur'd Each man's due proportions with her mouth into a dish and so it went Round." In the eighteenth century Iroquois life was punctuated by wild bacchanals that enveloped entire towns until the liquor was exhausted—then, with the liquor gone, life resumed its normal routines.

By making drunkenness sporadic, Indian peoples managed to engage in often violent and excessive dissipation while retaining intact a functioning social order. And, indeed, drinking by Indians was more sporadic and no more violent than that of the backcountry whites who bordered them or the voyageurs and packmen who came among them. Daniel Harmon, a British fur trader who had reason to know, said he would rather deal with fifty drunken Indians than five drunken Canadians. For all the damage it inflicted, for all the tensions it revealed, excessive drinking was not always either a cause, a result, or even a sign of social breakdown.

Between any two groups of people—no matter how different they may be—there exist basic similarities. As humans, both need to sustain life, and both need to procreate; both also need to make sense of the world and communicate that sense. Out of common needs and common humanity, Indians and Europeans tended, at first, to see what they believed to be common beliefs and practices. But the ways in which widely separated cultures perceive or interpret needs and behavior can also emphasize the differences between them—misperception leading to misunderstanding, and misunderstanding, all too easily, to hostility.

So the common world that mutual humanity created was always vulnerable. And when, in the 1800s, Indians no longer seemed politically or economically necessary, Americans tended to emphasize Indian difference, and to see that difference as inferiority.

Thomas Jefferson, the American president most fascinated with Indians, encapsulated the shift. He could, on the one hand, emphasize the similarities and invite the Delawares "to form one people with us, and we shall all be Americans" (although, as Jefferson envisioned it, becoming "Americans" meant drastic changes for Indians). He could, on the other hand, back ruthless war against recalcitrant Indians and seek to entangle them in debt and so deprive them of their lands. Jeffersonian philanthropy was as real as Jeffersonian animosity, but both in different ways envisioned the disappearance of the Indian.

By the mid-1800s, the precariously balanced middle ground would be actively abandoned.

## DRINKING AND TRADING AT FORT GEORGE

Duncan McGillivray, who traded for the North West Company out of posts on the Saskatchewan River during the 1790s, described the trading rituals and drunken revelry that characterized the Indians' visits to Fort George. The liquor was provided gratis by the trading company.

*On entering the house they are disarmed, treated with a few drams and a bit of tobacco, and after the pipe has been plyed about for some time they relate the news with great deliberation and ceremony relaxing from their usual taciturnity in proportion to the quantity of Rum they have swallowed, 'till at length their voices are drowned in general clamour. When their lodges are erected by the women they receive a present of Rum proportioned to the Nation & quality of the Cheifs [sic] and the whole Band drink during 24 hours and sometimes much longer for nothing—a privilege of which they take every advantage—for in the seat of an opposition profusion is absolutely necessary to secure the trade of an Indian. . . .*

# CHAPTER SIXTEEN

# THE SHEDDING OF BLOOD

EXPLOITS OF KILLS EAGLES (SIOUX)
PAINTED ON A BUFFALO HIDE, ca. 1875

IN 1712 THE TUSCARORAS OF NORTH CAROLINA attacked English and German colonists who had encroached on their land. They killed over a hundred of the colonists. North Carolina, a very weak English colony, called for aid, and South Carolina responded by sending two separate expeditions, one in 1712, the other in 1713. In both expeditions, the vast majority of fighting men were Indians—Yamasees, Cherokees, Catawbas, and the various groups who were coalescing to become the Muskogees or Creeks.

The mix of Indians from South Carolina destroyed the Tuscarora towns. They slaughtered most of the adult male prisoners and sold the women and children into slavery. More than a thousand Tuscaroras died; more than seven hundred were enslaved. The surviving Tuscaroras fled north, eventually finding shelter in Iroquoia where they joined the Iroquois confederation.

## Uneasy Alliances and the Indian Slave Trade

The Tuscarora War, a brutal little piece of slaughter, reveals two new forces that were influencing Indian–white relations in the early eighteenth century: the formation of new political alliances, and the growth of an Indian slave trade. Many of those who fought in the war did so as members of political entities that had not even existed in the recent past. North Carolina and South Carolina were new English colonies. But the Catawbas and the Muskogees were also new. The Catawbas proper gave their name to a new nation formed from the remnants of

*When Sioux and Blackfeet Meet* by Charles M. Russell, 1903.

groups decimated by the wars and epidemics of the seventeenth century. They were still in the process of creating their new identity when they joined in the attack on the Tuscaroras. After the war other remnant groups continued to join them, some freely, others under compulsion. James Adair reported that when he traded in the Catawba settlements between 1736 and 1743 he heard twenty different languages spoken there—an indication of the diverse peoples then being melded into a single political unit.

The Muskogees or Creeks (a term that did not even arise until the late seventeenth or early eighteenth century) were also an amalgamation of previously separate peoples, an initially loose alliance of Yuchis, Cowetas, Alabamas, Coosas, Tuskegees, some Shawnees (but not others), and numerous other groups. Inhabitants of the founding or mother towns of the Creek confederacy—Coweta, Kasihta, Coosa, and Abihka—spoke Muskogee, but most of the people who became Muskogees did not. Like the Catawbas, the Muskogees were very much in the process of creating themselves when they fell on the Tuscaroras.

As these new alliances illustrate, Indian societies, by and large, did not break down amidst the turmoil and change that created internal divisions and a growing reliance on European technology. Instead they forged new political structures that enabled them to retain their own independence and served to counteract the growing economic superiority of the Europeans.

To understand the power of these structures we need to shift our own focus away from what we tend to see as the central struggle of Indian peoples: their efforts to retain their lands. Land did indeed dominate the struggles of the seventeenth century along the East Coast, and land dominated the struggles of the late eighteenth and early nineteenth centuries, but for most of the eighteenth century the paramount issue of Indian–white relations was trade. Between 1700 and 1763 in Pennsylvania, in Georgia, and elsewhere, Indians continued to be dispossessed, but on the whole European evictions of Indians were relatively few compared with earlier and later periods.

The new Indian political organizations were not totally independent of and opposed to those of the Europeans. On the contrary, the two became intertwined. Politics, like trade, was part of the middle ground. Most warfare in the eighteenth century did not involve Indians fighting against whites; rather, as in the Tuscarora War, combinations of Indians and whites fought on the same side—often against other combinations of Indians and whites.

The Tuscarora War is also revealing because Tuscarora women and children were enslaved. They were turned into commodities available for sale. In the early eighteenth century, southeastern Indians confronted a slave trade basically modeled after the African slave trade. European traders, operating largely out of Charleston, armed Indian allies to raid into the interior and bring back slaves. The enslaved Indians labored either in South Carolina, where in 1708 nearly one-third of the slaves were Indians, or were sold to the West Indies. For some interior peoples these slave raids meant destruction. The slave raiders directly diminished the populations of their victims by seizing women and children and killing warriors. Equally important were the indirect losses. Fear of raids prevented the survivors from hunting; the raids disrupted the agricultural cycle, and the slavers often left behind impoverished towns that were easy targets for disease.

The slavers struck all the way to the Mississippi, but nowhere did they find a more inviting target than the Spanish missions that stretched from the Georgia coast through the Apalachee towns of the Florida panhandle. Here were tens of thousands of sedentary Indians living in towns and villages around the missions. To the English they were both an opportune source of slaves and plunder, and a danger. South Carolinians feared that in alliance with the Spanish, or worse, the French, they could destroy South Carolina.

In 1704, led by James Moore, the English, or rather fifty English and a thousand Muskogees, struck Ayubale, "the strongest fort in Appalachee." When it fell, Apalachee lay open to plunder. Besides those Indians dead in battle and those enslaved, the English accepted the surrender of entire towns and villages and relocated them near Savannah. English raids continued, and territories where Indians once lived became marked on maps with laconic notes of their passing. The mission villages of Timucua were now labeled "Wholly laid waste being destroyed by the Carolinians, 1706." And where there had been an Indian town on the west coast of Florida, south of Apalachee, the map now simply recorded: "Tocobogga Indians, destroyed, 1709."

Gradually, these lands would be occupied by people associated with the emerging Creek confederation. In time, these Muskogees would become the modern Seminoles. In an ironic turn, the area would become a haven for African slaves fleeing the English colonies. And some of these Africans would join the Seminoles and become Indians.

Meanwhile, the French, who had arrived on the Gulf Coast in 1699, settled in and began to expand; thereafter the Yamasees, Muskogees, Chickasaws, and other allies of the English slavers faced much tougher going. The French gradually began arming the victims of the raids; they resettled refugees around their own settlements. An alliance of French and Indians now confronted the alliance of English and Indians. The cost and difficulty of taking slaves soared. When coupled with the liabilities of Indian slaves as compared with African slaves, this sent the trade into decline. Indians, after all, were more likely than Africans to contract European diseases, and Indians were potentially more likely to escape. Those Indian peoples who had raided for slaves increasingly found hunting for deer a safer way to obtain English goods.

Deerskins, as a trade item, were moving onto the middle ground. English traders, eager for profits and disdainful of Indian methods of exchange pushed to make the trade in deerskins a market trade. When they advanced credit, they treated it not as a gift to be reciprocated when the recipient was able, but as a debt to be collected on demand. In extreme cases, English traders settled accounts by seizing the families of indebted hunters and selling them as slaves.

The Yamasees were allies of South Carolina and had helped subdue the Tuscaroras, but they now found the tables turned. As the power of South Carolina increased, the Yamasees faced the brutality of traders who beat them, who introduced rum to increase their profits, and who used rigged scales to give false measure. The Carolinians were busily using trade to reduce the Yamasees to debt peonage. The Indians remained nominally free, but the fruits of all their labor went to whites. Very soon they owed the Carolinians 100,000 deerskins— the yield of four or five years' hunting. In 1715 the Yamasees revolted.

*The sun was red, the roads filled with brambles and thorns, the clouds were black, the water was troubled and stained with blood, our women wept unceasingly, our children cried with fright, the game fled far from us, our houses were abandoned, and our fields uncultivated, we all have empty bellies and our bones are visible.*

—Account of a Chitmacha survivor of the slave raids along the Mississippi River, 1718.

Uniting with Muskogees, who had suffered similar abuse, the Yamasees slaughtered 90 percent of the traders and struck the border settlements. Only the decision of the Cherokees to join the Carolinians—in order to get, as they said, other Indians as slaves to trade for ammunition and clothing—saved South Carolina. The Yamasees and other tribes retreated farther into the interior, merging with the Muskogees.

## Balancing the Powers

The presence of competing groups of Europeans obviously posed formidable dangers for Indian peoples. The Apalachees suffered both because they were potential slaves and because they were Spanish allies who potentially threatened an English colony. Europeans sought, as the Yamasees and Muskogees knew all too well, to manipulate native peoples for their own purposes, and, when they were no longer useful, to eliminate them. This was not just a trait of the English. The French governor of Louisiana, Jean-Baptiste Le Moyne, sieur de Bienville, explained the policy of encouraging Choctaw–Chickasaw warfare in 1724 as one of putting "these barbarians into play against each other." It was, he said, "the sole and only way to establish any security in the colony because they will destroy themselves by their own efforts eventually."

But such logic could cut both ways. If Europeans found profit in Indian rivalries, Indians could find places to maneuver within European rivalries. Because competing European empires needed and sought Indian allies, Indians could find advantage in alliance or in a neutrality that played European off against

*Conference or Captain Bulgar's Palaver* by Peter Rindisbacher, 1825, depicts the Red Lake Chippewa chief making a speech to Captain Andrew Bulgar at an 1825 conference at Fort Douglas, Red River Settlement, Selkirk Colony, Canada.

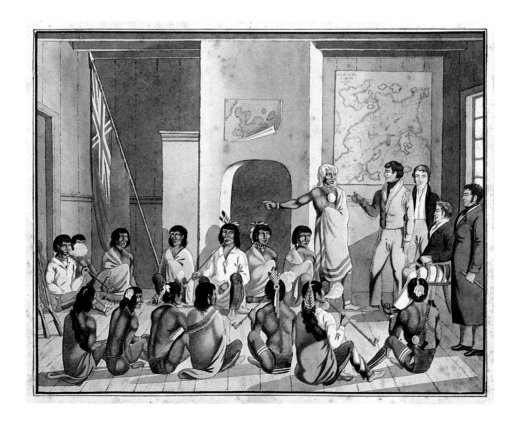

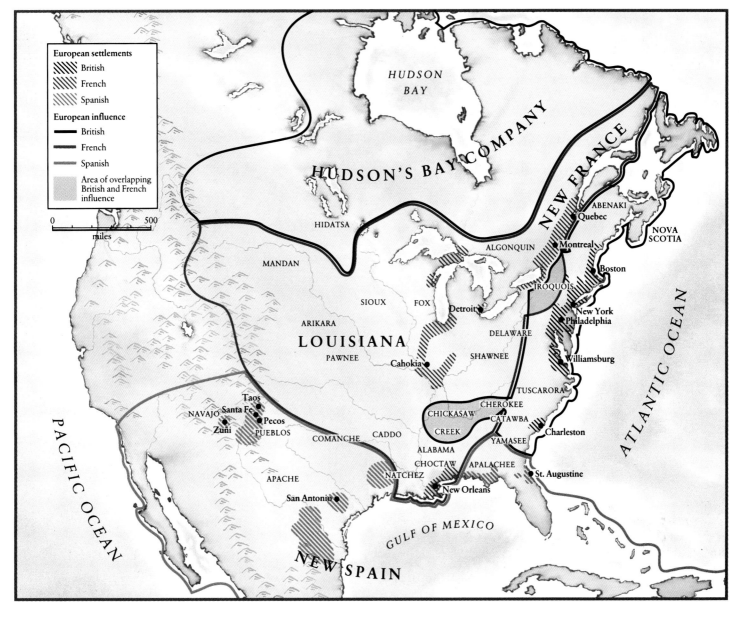

European settlements
- British
- French
- Spanish

European influence
- British
- French
- Spanish

Area of overlapping British and French influence

0     500
miles

HUDSON BAY

HUDSON'S BAY COMPANY

NEW FRANCE

HIDATSA

MANDAN

SIOUX   FOX

ARIKARA

LOUISIANA

PAWNEE    Cahokia

NAVAJO   Santa Fe   Taos
Zuni    Pecos
PUEBLOS

COMANCHE   CADDO

APACHE

San Antonio

NEW SPAIN

PACIFIC OCEAN

ABENAKI
Quebec
NOVA SCOTIA

ALGONQUIN   Montreal

Detroit

IROQUOIS

Boston

New York
Philadelphia

DELAWARE

SHAWNEE

Williamsburg

TUSCARORA

CHEROKEE
CHICKASAW   CATAWBA
CREEK
Charleston
YAMASEE

ALABAMA
CHOCTAW   APALACHEE
NATCHEZ    St. Augustine
New Orleans

GULF OF MEXICO

ATLANTIC OCEAN

European. And they could use their political importance to mitigate the excesses of European traders.

The Muskogees, caught between the English to their east, the French to their west, and the Spanish to their south, turned their position to advantage. James Adair sketched out how this playoff system worked:

> The old men being long informed by the opposite parties, of the different views, and intrigues of those European powers, who paid them annual tribute under the vague appellation of presents, were becoming surprisingly crafty in every turn of low politics. They held it as an invariable maxim, that their security and welfare required a perpetual friendly intercourse with us and the French.

The master of this political maneuvering among the Muskogees was Brims, usually called the Emperor Brims by the English and the French. Until his death

*European Settlement in the Early Eighteenth Century.* Though the actual European presence was still relatively small, vast territories of North America had been claimed in the names of England, France, and Spain. Despite the presumptions of the "discoverers," this was a period in which Indians often acted as powerful players in an evolving political landscape.

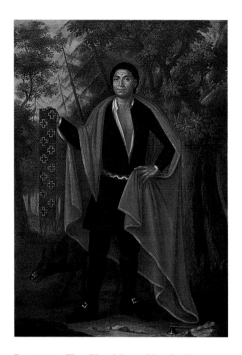

In 1710, Tee Yee Neen Ho Ga Row (ABOVE) and Sa Ga Yeath Qua Pieth Tow (BELOW), two Mohawk sachems, were sent by the colonists to England along with another Mohawk and one Mahican. They went in order to raise Crown support for their struggle with the French. While in England, Queen Anne commissioned John Verelst to paint their portraits in part-European costume.

in the early 1730s, he was the headman of the town of Coweta and the strongest advocate of neutrality in the emerging Muskogee nation. The fruits of the Muskogee policy were visible in the packtrains bearing gifts to the nation; and in the honor and presents delegations of Muskogee received from colonial officials when visiting Charleston and New Orleans. The new colony of Georgia tried, not always successfully, to check the abuses of the traders, fearing that the Muskogees might go over to the French or Spanish.

## Iroquois Diplomacy

What the Muskogees accomplished in the south, the Iroquois League outdid in the north. Following their defeat by the French and their allies in the wars of the seventeenth century, the Iroquois, in a masterful piece of diplomacy, carved out a position between the British and the French–Indian allies. They became the critical Indian group in the imperial wars of the eighteenth century.

Both the French and English believed that the Iroquois held the balance of power on the continent. Their allegiance could determine the fate of empires in North America. As the French governor at Quebec, Philippe de Rigaud, marquis de Vaudreuil, wrote in 1711: "the five Iroquois villages are more to be feared than the English colonies. . . . Twenty-four years experience has convinced me that war with them is bad for this colony. I know only too well how much it has cost us and how difficult it was for the people to recover from it."

After 1713 the English claimed sovereignty over the Iroquois, but it was a paper sovereignty, unacknowledged in practice by the Iroquois and unenforceable by the English, who continued to seek Iroquois support through negotiations and gifts. According to the New York commissioners of Indian Affairs, the "Five Nations are the balance of the continent of America." Should they go over to the French, it would prove to be "the ruin and destruction of the greatest part of this continent." The English cultivated the Iroquois, and the result was a complicated relationship that served the interests of New York and Pennsylvania rather than the English colonies as a whole.

Some Iroquois, particularly the Mohawks, would fight with the English in the imperial wars of the early eighteenth century, but the main service the Iroquois provided New York was to create a barrier that deflected the attacks of the French and their Indian allies into New England. The Iroquois closed their lands to the armies and war parties of both combatants, and the French did not wish to alienate the Iroquois by crossing their lands to strike the English.

The Iroquois protected New York and they enriched it, but by the 1740s the pressure on their lands and the parsimony of the New York legislature in providing gifts to the Iroquois had begun to sour the relationship. Only the Herculean efforts of William Johnson, who emerged in the 1740s as the only real English equivalent to the French chiefs of the French–Algonquian alliance, maintained New York's influence with the League. The French never gave up their efforts to win over the Iroquois. They drew Iroquois converts off to their Canadian mission towns, and they influenced chiefs on the council, creating a strong French faction in the politics of the League.

The polity that achieved this power was impressive, but it was neither the empire nor the league of states that Europeans mistakenly thought it to be. The League of the Iroquois was a league of tribes whose original ambition was to halt blood revenge among themselves. Iroquois warriors terrified both European and Indian enemies, but in the eyes of its chiefs, the League existed for peace rather than war. And like other peoples, they equated the extension of their own influence with the extension of peace. Had not Deganawidah, the ancient founder of the League, promised them, "The white roots of the Great Tree of Peace will continue to grow, advancing the Good Mind and Righteousness and Peace, moving into territories of people scattered far through the forest"?

The mechanism for the League was fairly simple. In most respects Iroquois towns and villages, like towns and villages across the continent, were autonomous. Senior women nominated the men who represented the clans at the village and tribal councils. They also nominated the forty-nine council chiefs or *rotiyanehr* who met at Onondaga to conduct the affairs of the League as a whole. Both the women and the younger warriors had considerable influence on the conduct of Iroquois business, although neither was formally represented in council. The major political actors, however, remained older males. The council considered, but did not necessarily follow, the opinion of the women. Ultimately men dominated politics.

The neutrality of the League was not perfect, for it could not finally control its members. At times groups of warriors, or indeed entire tribes, would violate Iroquois neutrality and join the English or the French. But as long as the League itself stayed neutral, much of its bargaining power remained. And Europeans learned as the century progressed that even a neutral League could serve imperial ends. It was the Iroquois who intervened and forced the Delawares to recognize the fraudulent Walking Purchase of 1737 in Pennsylvania. And it would be the Iroquois who would cede the lands of their dependents in the Ohio Valley, lands they had only a marginal claim to and no practical control over.

## The Children of France

Although the Iroquois used it masterfully, the playoff system was an option only for large Indian confederations in crucial locations between competing empires. More Indian peoples entered into alliances with Europeans than held the balance of power between them. But these alliances, too, functioned on the middle ground. The most important and most extensive of the European alliances involved the French. For many Indians, particularly in hindsight, it was the model for all others. There was no single French alliance; instead there were a series of interlocking alliances that stretched from the Atlantic to New Orleans and even out onto the Great Plains. Central to this network were the Abenakis of Maine, the so-called domiciled or mission Indians of Canada, the Indians of the Great Lakes and Ohio Valley, and, finally, the Choctaws and the Alabamas, who allied themselves with the French of Louisiana. In addition, French traders, operating relatively independently, created a series of loose alliances with the Caddoan peoples bordering on the Great Plains.

*Connessoa, King of the Onondagoes . . . desyred . . . That, Hospitality be shown to all strangers, and suffer them to pass, for without the assistance of the 5 Nations neither Christian nor Indian could live here for the ffrench.*

—CHIEF DECANISORA
In treaty, 1710

## THE WALKING PURCHASE

In 1734 Thomas Penn, an heir of William Penn and the proprietor of Pennsylvania, needed to sell land in order to pay his family's creditors. The land he wanted was at the Forks of the Delaware River, an area that contained both Pennsylvania Delawares and refugee Delawares from New Jersey. Penn persuaded the Delawares that an old, incomplete, and unsigned 1686 deed was, in fact, a legally binding bill of sale for land around the Forks. The Indians misunderstood the area that the deed conveyed, and they accepted it, thinking the adjustment in boundaries would be relatively minor. The deed transferred to the Penns land bounded by a walk of a day and a half from a specified starting point, but it did not say in which direction the walker should proceed. In 1737 Pennsylvania determined the boundaries. The Penns hired axmen to clear a path for three strong walkers. Two stopped from exhaustion, but the third covered sixty-four miles in a day and a half. He carried the claim beyond the Forks of the Delaware. He carried it

*William Penn's Treaty with the Indians,* based on a painting by Benjamin West.

twenty miles beyond the Kittatinny Mountains. The claim embraced roughly twelve hundred square miles. It cost the Delawares at the Forks all their land, and it also dispossessed the Minisink Delawares. Soon afterward, the original "deed" disappeared,

although the Penns claimed to possess a valid copy. When the Delawares protested this obvious fraud and refused to leave, Pennsylvania persuaded the Iroquois, the supposed conquerors of the Delawares, to order them off.

Delaware Chief Lapowinsa, who signed the Walking Purchase Treaty, in an illustration made after a 1735 portrait by Gustavus Hesselius.

Taken together, the two French colonies of Canada and Louisiana encompassed a far greater area than the English colonies of the Atlantic Coast, but they contained far fewer Europeans. Without Indian aid, the French could not have held their own against the more populous and better-supplied English in the imperial wars of the eighteenth century. The Indians of the interior, in turn, whether victims of English-inspired slave raids in the south, or Iroquois aggression in the Ohio Valley and Great Lakes, looked to the French for protection.

The French and the Algonquian and Muskogean peoples of the interior together had accomplished what none of them could have done separately. In the south they turned back the slave raids. In the north the Algonquians and the French defeated the Iroquois and made peace with them in the Grand Settlement of 1701. And with these successes the once-desperate peoples of the interior began to recognize that the French needed them as much or more than they needed the French. By the beginning of the eighteenth century the Algonquian peoples of the Great Lakes region had come to have, as Nicolas Perrot, a leading French emissary put it, the "arrogant notion that the French cannot get along without them and that we could not maintain ourselves in the colony without the assistance that they give us." What particularly galled the

French about such statements was that they were in large part true.

The French would have liked to establish an empire along conventional European lines. The French king, through his governors, would have preferred to dictate to his supposed subject peoples, the Indians. Indian leaders would have been subordinates of the French state. But the French could not dictate. And so they created an odd empire in which rulers often paid tribute to subjects, in which the so-called subjects fiercely claimed their own independence, and in which matters proceeded through negotiation rather than dictation. It was an empire whose very forms reflected Indian language, customs, rituals, and understandings. French officials relied on wampum belts, calumets, and condolence ceremonies to conduct their business.

But above all, the organization of imperial relations between Indian peoples and the French depended on a shared cultural fiction of kinship. In Canada the French governor acted as a father to his children. His ritual title was Onontio ("Great Mountain," a Mohawk rendering, derived from the Iroquois, of the name of Charles-Jacques de Huault de Montmagny, an early French governor), and the Great Onontio was the ritual title of the French king. Like Onontio, all Frenchmen who represented him acted as and were addressed as fathers. The French, in turn, addressed the Indians as children, and the Indians were supposed to act like dutiful children. In Louisiana the fiction was the same. The French governor was a father to his Indian children.

Both the French and the Indians accepted this fiction, but they differed on what it meant to act like a father and to be a dutiful child. In the south, for instance, the Choctaws and other neighboring people were matrilineal, which meant that descent was traced through the mother and not the father. Thus a father did not stand as the most important male in his own children's lives; instead their eldest uncle—their mother's brother—did. For the Choctaws the French insistence on being their father—a person who was kind and generous but without authority—instead of their uncle was confusing, but it relieved them of any obligation of obedience to the French governor. And so a mongrel kinship relationship arose on the middle ground.

In Canada many of the Algonquian children of Onontio were patrilineal, but even here the role meanings of fathers and children were contested. For the French the basic logic of patriarchy was quite simple: fathers commanded and children obeyed. But for the Algonquians the basic logic was somewhat different: a father was kind, generous, and protecting. A son owed a father respect, but a father could not compel obedience. A good father supplied his children's needs. As Governor Charles de Beauharnois explained to the French court in 1730, "All the nations of Canada regard the governor as their father, which in consequence, following their ideas, he ought at times to give them what they need to feed themselves, clothe themselves and hunt." Good children, in turn, supported their father when he was in need.

The actual working of the alliance was a compromise between these views. The French might yearn to be imperial masters who exercised their will by force, and the Algonquians, Choctaws, and Abenakis might tire of what they regarded as unreasonable French demands for aid and French parsimony with gifts, but in the end they needed each other. The Abenakis in Maine needed French aid

*When the Governor of Canada speaks to us of the Chain, he calls us Children, and saith, "I am your Father, you must hold fast the Chain, and I will do the same. I will protect you as a Father doth his Children." Is this Protection, to speak thus with his Lips, and at the same time to knock us on the head by assisting our Enemies with Ammunition?*

—Seneca protest against French support for antagonistic tribes, 1684.

## THE CALUMET

The calumet was, according to the French missionary Father Hennepin, "a large Tobacco-pipe made of red, black or white marble [catlinite]: the head is finely polished, and the quill, which is commonly two feet and a half long, is made of a pretty strong reed or cane, adorned with feathers of all colors, interlaced with locks of women's hair. They tie to it two wings of the most curious birds they find which makes their calumet not much unlike Mercury's wand or that staff ambassadors did formerly carry when they went to treat of peace. They sheath that reed into the neck of birds they call huars [loons] . . . or else of a sort of duck who make their nests upon trees. . . . However, every nation adorns the calumet as they think fit according to their own genius and the birds they have in their country."

It sufficed, reported another missionary, Father Gravier, "for one to carry and show it to walk in safety in the midst of enemies who in the hottest fight lay down their weapons when it is displayed."

*Crow Indian with Peace Pipe*
by James Bama, 1984. Portrait of Henry Bright Wings (Crow) in a pre-1900 headdress and antique buffalo robe.

against the English just as the French needed Choctaw and Algonquian aid against the English. But the alliance went beyond mere military aid; the Algonquians, for instance, needed the French as mediators.

French mediation was particularly critical to Algonquian-speaking peoples because their own political organization, centered on towns and villages, often proved incapable of securing a wide peace that allowed, in the words of the councils, the warriors to smoke peacefully on their mats. Indian peoples created, and the French adopted, mechanisms for securing peace. In the late seventeenth and early eighteenth centuries, the Calumet Ceremony, which has come down in American common speech as the peace pipe, spread from the Pawnees to the Sioux and the Algonquians. The Iroquois eventually adopted it in the form of the Eagle Dance. The calumet created a ceremonial means for arresting the aggression of war parties, mediating a peace, and creating representatives among each warring party who would be responsible for maintaining the peace.

Indian means—the calumet, gifts to cover the dead, slaves to replace the dead—provided the mechanisms for making peace, but ironically these means were most powerful when in French hands. The French had more gifts to give; the French maintained a presence among far more people than any individual Indian group and thus could mediate more effectively; and the French, as leaders of the alliance, could bring to bear the power of that alliance on any group who refused to make peace.

What the Indians and the French together established within the alliance was a structure of mediation, of negotiation, and of linkage that worked remarkably well until the defeat of France in the Seven Years' War in 1763. They created a system of alliance chiefs—men who gained influence by moving between and linking the two societies.

Sometimes such chiefs held independent rank within their own society; sometimes their status came from their ability to mediate with outsiders. Using the calumet, bearing gifts often provided by Onontio, they made sure that the children of Onontio remained at peace with each other. They smoothed the paths; they negotiated differences. To sustain the system, the French awarded Indian alliance chiefs with medals as marks of office, and they bestowed annual gifts redistributed through these chiefs.

Within this structure the French ironically had the most power and influence when they exercised the normal trappings of European power the least. When the French threatened instead of mediating, when they divided instead of uniting, when they used force instead of making gifts, the alliance fractured and the

*Eagle Dance* by Woodrow W. Crumbo (Potawatomi-Creek), 1941. Many tribes, among them the Cherokee, Iroquois, Iowa, and Choctaw, performed Eagle Dances for many different reasons: to create or cement friendships, ensure a successful hunt or battle, cure sickness (particularly "eagle sickness"), or make peace between antagonistic tribes. The dances all had in common dancers who moved, and sometimes dressed, like eagles, usually carrying a wand with eagle tail or tailfeathers attached. The Eagle Dance was made up of a series of songs and dances, and often included a recitation of the brave deeds of the most courageous warriors.

French became drawn into expensive and dangerous struggles. Three times in the eighteenth century the French waged bloody wars against people who, provoked by mishandling on the part of the French themselves, revolted from the alliance.

The most ruthless and relentless of these wars was against the Natchez. The Natchez remained the closest of any eighteenth-century Indian nation in the Southeast to the Mississippian cultures encountered by the first Spanish explorers. Far more hierarchical than neighboring peoples, they were ruled by a priest-king—the Great Sun; they possessed a hereditary elite and had integrated once-independent peoples into their polity as a permanent lower class: the Stinkards. Although exotic in many respects, they seemed to many Europeans politically the most familiar of Indian peoples. As the French missionary Father Membre recorded on seeing them, they were "all different from our Canada Indians in their houses, dress, manners, inclinations and customs. . . . Their chiefs possess all the authority. . . . They have their valets and officers who follow them and serve them everywhere. They distribute their favors and presents at will. In a word we generally found men there."

But the creation of French settlements neighboring the Natchez towns initiated a cycle of European aggression, Indian retaliation, and war that would become all too familiar between whites and Indians later in the century. Finally in 1729 when the French demanded large uncompensated land cessions, the Natchez revolted. They killed hundreds of men, women, and children. They killed some French slaves and seized others. When the French and Choctaws counterattacked, the surviving Natchez fled to the Chickasaws, and that redoubtable people then bore the brunt of attacks from the French and their allies, north and south.

The trade that Stung Serpent, a brother of the Natchez Great Sun, condemned for altering the lives of his people could also work against the French. For the only real advantage the English held in their competition with France for Indian loyalty was that English goods were on the whole cheaper, more plentiful, and better made. French generosity in terms of gifts and French mediation had to offset the appeal of English goods. But when French supplies failed and the French promoted war rather than peace, then the alliance weakened.

In 1745 the Choctaw war leader, Red Shoes, tired of the failure of the French to supply the Choctaws adequately, tired of the wasting internecine war with the Chickasaws, and fearful of French attempts to reduce his own influence, tried to lead the Choctaws into an alliance with the English. He failed only after a bitter and bloody civil war. His success would probably have doomed Louisiana. This was a world where Indian actions could determine the fate of empires.

Just as the French fought the Natchez, they also fought the Fox in a pair of vicious and expensive eighteenth-century wars that came close to destroying the French alliance north of the Ohio. In this case, however, the wars ended in 1737 with the refusal of the French allies, who had originally urged the destruction of the Fox, to continue fighting. As Governor de Beauharnois reported to Paris, "the Savages have their policy as we have Ours, and they are not greatly pleased at seeing a nation destroyed for Fear that their turn may come." The French consented to peace, for they recognized that they dealt with allies and not subjects.

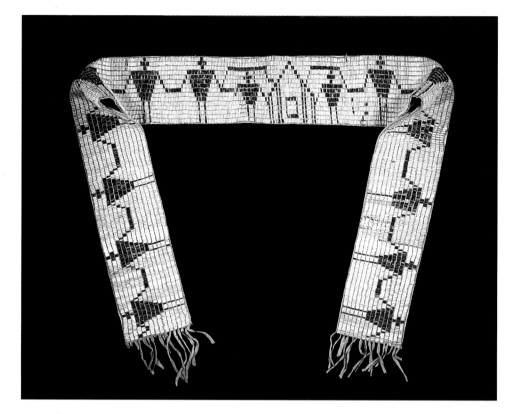

The Great Chain, or Covenant Belt, is generally thought to be a belt presented by the U.S. government to the Iroquois in 1794 at the Pickering Treaty at Canandaigua, New York. The human figures, each linked by a short line that may be a representation of a wampum belt itself, form a chain of friendship, which is believed to represent the alliance between the thirteen states and the Iroquoian confederacy. The central longhouse is frequently interpreted as the Iroquois Confederacy longhouse, and the large figures as the thirteen states.

## The English and the Iroquois

The English alliance never rivaled that of the French. In the south they relied on the Cherokees and the Chickasaws to counter French power, and colonial officials quailed when the allegiance of these peoples wavered. In the north they courted the Iroquois, who, even when neutral, could prove useful to particular English interests.

Among their other diplomacies, the Iroquois had instituted the Covenant Chain, a league of peace and friendship between the Iroquois and other groups, both Indians and European. It was not an alliance for war. The Iroquois strove to include new peoples in the chain and ritually to renew it with existing allies. The Iroquois came to play a particularly significant role in Pennsylvania and granted that colony a special place in the Covenant Chain. In 1736 Pennsylvania officials and the council of the Iroquois League agreed that the Iroquois should act as mediators and spokespersons for Pennsylvania's Indians in their dealings with the English. Although, in fact, the Iroquois had never conquered the Delawares, they became, in Iroquois diplomatic terms, "women," unable to negotiate directly with the English.

The Iroquois dispatched a half-king, the Oneida chief Shickellamy, to supervise the Pennsylvania Indians from Shamokin on the forks of the Susquehanna. As the decline of game and land cessions such as the Walking Purchase drove most Delawares and Shawnees west, the Iroquois appointed a second half-king, Tanacharison, for the western towns. It was a self-serving policy, one that would cost both the Iroquois and Pennsylvania dearly as embittered Shawnees and Delawares joined the French in the Seven Years' War (1756–63), and the Iroquois lost the allegiance of their supposed dependents.

Simple histories have no room for men like Soulouche Oumastabé, the Choctaw warrior who rose to be the Shulush Homa, the war captain of his town of Couechitto. The French and English knew him as Red Shoes. Soulouche Oumastabé moved from warrior to war captain to chief. But this was not a normal progression among the Choctaws. Europeans enabled him to rise, and Europeans caused his death.

Soulouche Oumastabé was not born into an iksa or clan of chiefs, and his status as Shulush Homa should have been the climax of his ambition. But Soulouche had a great skill. He could use others while making them think he was their tool. He manipulated Choctaw chiefs; he manipulated French and English governors; he manipulated traders. He recognized that lucrative opportunities lay in the rivalry between the French and English, and he played them adroitly for years. He recognized, too, that dangerous opportunities lay within the tensions of the Choctaw nation, in the divisions between chiefs and warriors. And Red Shoes rallied the warriors. He rallied them finally in a rebellion against the French and the chiefs that brought much of the nation into an alliance with the English. Of the forty-six towns in the Choctaw nation, the English traders thought only four remained pro-French in 1747.

It was in June of 1747, escorting an English packtrain with presents from Charleston, that Red Shoes died. A companion murdered him for the French price on his head at the very "time he seemed to have most triumphed in his measures." And with him dead, the chiefs and the French rallied. A bloody civil war followed. English supplies failed. English aid never appeared. And eight hundred of the warriors who had followed Red Shoes followed him in death. Other Choctaws brought their scalps in heaps to the French for bounties.

## Spain and the West

*When we arrived at the mission, they locked me in a room for a week; the father made me go to his habitation and he talked to me . . . telling me that he would make me a Christian . . . and Cunnur, the interpreter, told me that I should do as the father told me, because now I was not going to be set free, and it would go very bad with me if I did not consent in it. . . . One day they threw water on my head and gave me salt to eat, and . . . told me that now I was Christian and that I was called Jesus: I knew nothing of this, and I tolerate it all because in the end I was a poor Indian and did not have recourse but to conform myself and tolerate the things they did with me.*

—JANITIN, a Kamia Indian seized and taken to the Dominican mission at San Miguel, 1878.

The third European power on the continent, Spain, created a set of alliances that proved size did not necessarily equal strength. The destruction of the Apalachee missions cost the Spanish their major allies east of the Mississippi, and they did not regain influence there until after the decline of the French. West of the Mississippi, however, they were the dominant European presence for most Indian peoples during the eighteenth century.

Indian peoples entered into several different kinds of relations with the Spanish. In New Mexico a middle ground of a sort emerged. After the successful Pueblo Revolt of 1680 and the bloody reconquest twelve years later, the Spanish and the Pueblos gradually reached an accommodation. The Pueblos officially became subjects of the Spanish king, were baptized Catholic at birth and attended mass. But the Pueblos maintained their own native ceremonial cycles, and their clan and spiritual leaders continued to govern the internal life of the towns.

In California the situation was far different, for here the Spanish felt they had sufficient power to dictate and transform. California was, perhaps, the most densely populated section of native North America in the eighteenth century. It remained largely free of Europeans until, beginning in 1769, the Spanish established a string of missions, presidios, and towns along the coast from San Diego to San Francisco Bay. Missionaries, aided by soldiers, gathered up nearly the entire coastal population of Indians south of San Francisco into the missions. As Esselen, Salinan, Chumash, Gabrielino, Luiseño, Ipai, and Tipai peoples arrived, Spanish missionaries worked not only to convert them but also to "reduce" them from their "free and undisciplined state" to a life regulated and disciplined by the Franciscan friars. The missions formed a sort of Hotel California. Indians could check in any time they liked, but once baptized, they could never leave.

The initial attraction of the missions was partially material, and the world Indians created under Spanish supervision was impressive, even dazzling. Indian weavers, brick makers, blacksmiths, and farmers built the string of twenty-one missions and their churches. They created a vast agricultural wealth with herds numbering 400,000 cattle, 60,000 horses, and 300,000 sheep and goats.

But, in essence, this was forced labor. If Indians persistently refused to work, they faced the lash, stocks, or irons. The priests segregated unmarried Indian men and women from each other. Living in close quarters, with an altered diet, and subject to European disease, the California Indians died in huge numbers. During the mission period (1769–1836) the Indian population from San Diego to San Francisco declined from seventy-two thousand to eighteen thousand.

And so from the same missionary beginnings, the relations Indians carved out with the Spanish took different trajectories in New Mexico and California. In New Mexico the power of the priests and soldiers declined, and the Spanish came to rely on the Pueblos as necessary and largely independent allies against the nomadic tribes. The nomads raided both Spanish villages and the towns of the Pueblos, and were raided and enslaved in turn. Against raids from the Faraone Apaches, the Navajos, and the Comanches, the Spanish and Pueblos stood together, sometimes drawing the nomadic Utes into an alliance with them.

In California, too, the missions and ranchos faced raids from mounted Indians, but here the Spanish and later the Mexicans were often betrayed by mission Indians or Indians working on the ranchos. Some Indians found new technologies, new foods, and new sources of spiritual and secular power in the missions. But for many the missions were, at best, a life of bitter labor and, at worst, a death trap. Christianity meant, in effect, forced changes in their culture, and for most, the end of life itself. Some fled to join interior peoples such as the Yokuts and guided them on raids. A new period of often brutal conflict erupted.

## The Rise of the Nomads

By the nineteenth century, mounted horsemen dominated vast sections of the trans-Mississippi West. As they acquired the horse, they often changed their homelands, making the plains and prairies and desert lands of the Southwest a seething cauldron of peoples. The Comanches, Utes, Arapahos, Cheyennes, Crows, Sioux, Osages, Kiowas, and numerous other peoples changed their lives and their locations during the tumultuous eighteenth century.

Two groups in particular, the Comanches on the southern Plains and the Sioux on the northern Plains, signified the rising dominance of the nomads. The Comanches, advancing out of southwestern Wyoming, in alliance with the Utes, pushed the Plains Apaches from their rancherias. They attacked the Navajos, raiding their herds and pushing them farther west to what is now the Navajos' home. And although the Utes remained largely friendly to the Pueblos and Spanish, the Comanches raided both the New Mexican settlements and the string of missions that the Spanish established in Texas. Indeed, a major attraction of the missions for many Texas Indians was shelter first from Apache raiders and then from the Comanches.

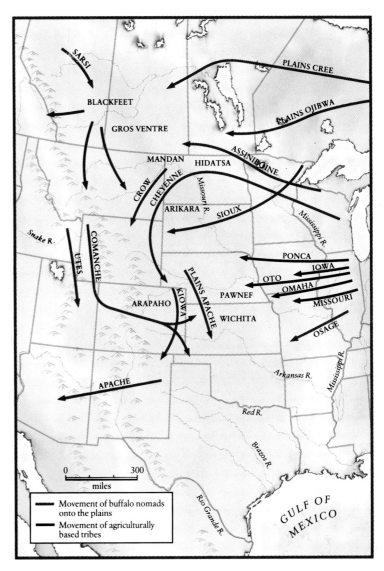

*Movement of the Buffalo Nomads Onto the Great Plains.*
The seventeenth and eighteenth centuries witnessed great
changes on the Plains as native peoples acquired firearms and
horses. Eastern tribes who had guns initially pushed their
neighbors to the interior farther west, while the arrival of the
horse spurred tribes such as the Comanches, Utes, Arapahos,
Cheyennes, Crows, Kiowas, Osages, and Sioux to take up new
nomadic lifeways on the Great Plains.

*The Buffalo Runners* by Frank C. McCarthy, 1985.

The raids of Plains nomads such as the Comanches might appear chaotic, but they masked a complicated set of relations between Europeans, settled horticultural villagers, and the nomads themselves. In the 1760s, for example, the Comanches under Cuerno Verde stripped New Mexico of horses. Such raids affected the Pueblos as much as the Spanish. The once prosperous Pueblos of Pecos and Galisteo went into dramatic decline and were eventually abandoned.

The Comanches, however, could attack the Spanish and Pueblos with virtual impunity because they had established a trade alliance with the Wichitas who were themselves in contact with French traders. The Wichitas, a settled horticultural group, thus managed to ally themselves with a dangerous nomadic group to their west who were simultaneously attacking other settled villagers, both Indian and European. But the Wichitas themselves had to confront a second group from the east entering into a seminomadic life: the Osages. The Osages, who had contacts with both English and French traders, used their superior access to guns to expand out onto the Great Plains. Osage attacks eventually drove the Wichitas from the Arkansas River valley.

The dilemma of the Wichitas and Pueblos in trying to come to terms simultaneously with expanding Europeans and expanding nomads symbolized the problem that horticultural villagers faced all over the Plains. In the north, the Sioux rather than the Comanches represented the great challenge.

*Following the Herds*
by Frank C. McCarthy, 1985.
Crow hunters and their families
follow the migrating buffalo.

When epidemics in the 1770s weakened the powerful horticultural villagers of the Missouri—the Mandans, Arikaras, and Hidatsas—the Sioux seized the advantage and spilled out on the Plains, leaving the villagers surrounded by nomads who raided or traded as conditions permitted. Some horticulturists such as the Crow, who split off from the Hidatsas, or the Cheyennes who, driven west by the Sioux, became nomads, gave up the attempt to maintain settled villages, but most persisted. Only on the central Plains, where the powerful Pawnee confederation maintained its territory against raids from both the east and west, did the villagers hold anywhere near their old power.

By the early nineteenth century a loose alliance among the Sioux, the Arapahos, and the Cheyennes dominated the northern Plains. They faced significant challenges only from the Blackfeet who were moving south from Canada and the still strong Pawnees of the central Plains.

Anywhere one went on the continent in the eighteenth century, Indians were playing vital and critical roles in constructing new political systems in the wake of the changes brought by contact. This was a time in which some Indian peoples gained and others lost, but it was still a world where Indians mattered a great deal. There was no understanding the balance of political and imperial power without reference to Indians like Red Shoes and Cuerno Verde and the Emperor Brims.

# CHAPTER SEVENTEEN

# INDIAN REBELLION

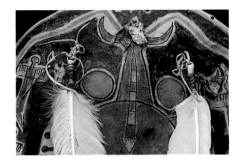

CROW WAR SHIELD (DETAIL)

IN HINDSIGHT THE POSSIBILITIES FOR Indian independence within the mixed political world of the mid-eighteenth century began to change in 1763 when England defeated France in the Seven Years' War. And such hopes as there might have been became virtually impossible to maintain after the War of 1812 when Great Britain abandoned attempts to support pan-Indian confederations that would serve to check the expansion of the United States. The roughly half-century between these events spelled the demise of the political middle ground, with Indian peoples fighting increasingly lonely battles to hold their own in the face of rising European and Anglo-American expansion and dictation.

## Caught in the Struggle of Empires

Although France had lost many of its Indian allies during the course of the Seven Years' War because of its inability to provide gifts and supplies as Great Britain cut its sea lanes, the actual cession came as a shock to Indian peoples. France ceded Canada to Great Britain and Louisiana to Spain. That these lands did not belong to the French king, that most had been occupied only with the consent of his Indian allies made no difference. The Shawnees demanded to know "by what right the French could pretend" to make such a cession. The news struck the Indians of the Ohio Valley like a "thunderclap," and according to the trader George Croghan "almost Drove them to Despair." The British, the Delaware

*Mystic Power of the War Shield* by Howard Terpning, 1984.

chief Netawatwees declared, had "grown too powerful & seemed as if they would be too strong for God himself."

Indian despair and outrage were matched by delight among most British military and colonial leaders. General Thomas Gage summarized their view nicely: "All North America in the hands of a single power robs them of their Consequence, presents, & pay." The time had come, the English believed, to dictate to Indians, and Sir Jeffrey Amherst was prepared to do so. He cut gifts, he restricted access to ammunition, he denied visiting Indians supplies. He treated Indians as a conquered people, although in the West, the British had suffered humiliating defeats.

The Indian allies of France, Amherst seemed to forget, had time and time again slaughtered British troops and created havoc on colonial frontiers. In 1755 two hundred French and Canadians and six hundred Indians repulsed a British expedition against Fort Duquesne (modern Pittsburgh) and defeated General Edward Braddock and a British force over twice their size. They left nearly five hundred British soldiers dead on the field at the Battle of the Wilderness.

In the fighting that followed, thousands of colonists had died as French and Indian raiding parties and colonial fighters had matched atrocity with atrocity during raids along the Pennsylvania and Virginia frontiers. General Forbes finally had taken Fort Duquesne in 1758 only when most of the Indians at the fort abandoned the French. And even then, in a last battle, they had helped slaughter Major James Grant's Scots Highlanders, whose severed heads lined the path to the abandoned ruins of the fort when the main British force arrived.

The Indians did not, George Croghan tried to remind Amherst, consider themselves defeated.

*The Forts and Battles of Pontiac's Rebellion.* Beginning in the spring of 1763 the Ottawa Chief Pontiac led the tribes of the Great Lakes into war against the British. Though the tribes were successful in taking many of the British forts, the siege ultimately ground to an indecisive halt. In the course of the siege on Fort Pitt, General Amherst ordered the distribution of smallpox-infested blankets among the Indians. The insidious strategy started an epidemic among the Indian attackers.

Pontiac's Rebellion, which had begun as an attempt to drive out the British and secure the return of the French, succeeded in creating the conditions for a British–Indian alliance, with the British adopting the more diplomatic ways of the French.

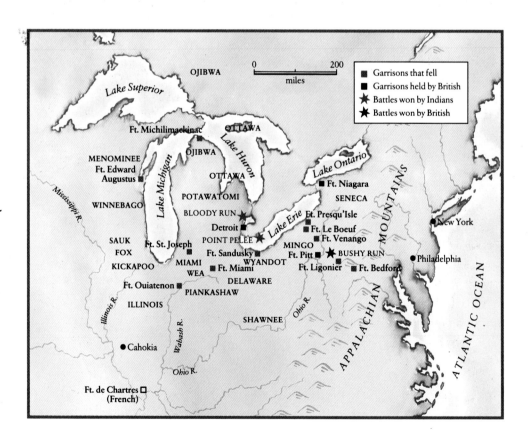

## Pontiac's Rebellion

The result of Amherst's attempt to make Indians into subjects, to replace the old French alliance with a British empire was Pontiac's Rebellion. The rebellion itself flared as a loosely coordinated series of attacks on newly occupied British posts west of the Appalachians. In 1763 the Indians of the Great Lakes and the Ohio Valley along with the Senecas (the westernmost group of Iroquois) took all of these garrisons except Niagara, Detroit, and Fort Pitt. With the relief of Detroit and the British victory at Bushy Run near Fort Pitt, the revolt dwindled to an inconclusive halt. The British did not so much crush the revolt as stymie it. And it was during the negotiations for peace that Pontiac, an Ottawa war leader who had led the siege of Detroit, emerged as the most critical figure.

It is easy to misinterpret Pontiac's goals and ambitions. He had adopted the doctrine of the Delaware Prophet, Neolin, who called for a general attack on whites and an abandonment of white technology and trade. But Pontiac had modified Neolin's teachings; he wanted an attack on the English, not the French, some of whom fought alongside the Indians. His goal was the restoration of his French father and not a return to a pre-European past.

He managed to achieve something very different. The French did not return, but the British, urged on by William Johnson, recognized that the only way to hold their lands to the west without endless expense and fighting was to mimic French methods. And so, incompletely and imperfectly, the British began to construct a replica of the old French alliance. This was Pontiac's great success, but he misread it. He began to believe that the individual power that the Europeans credited him with actually existed. He began to act as if he really did lead a united confederation that stretched from the Great Lakes to the Mississippi. And he began to act in ways that no Algonquian Indian leader could act. He lost

*Pontiac Greeting Rogers' Rangers, ca. 1766.* **At the time that the British took over from the French, most Indians assumed that friendly relations—and supplies—would continue. Colonial representatives who met with the Indians included Major Robert Rogers, Sir William Johnson, and trader George Croghan, all of whom also hoped and believed that peace would prevail.**

---

*Can ye not live without them? If you suffer the English among you, you are dead men. Sickness, smallpox, and their poison will destroy you entirely.*

—NEOLIN
Delaware Prophet, 1761

---

influence among the Ottawas; he stabbed, in council, a Kaskaskia chief. Few were surprised when, in 1769, a nephew of Makatchinga, a Peoria chief of the Illinois confederation to which the Kaskaskia also belonged, clubbed Pontiac from behind as he left a trading store and then stabbed him. Pontiac died ignominiously in the dirty street of the French village of Cahokia, his death a monument to the limits of chieftainship.

Pontiac's early success had, nonetheless, been an impressive one. In theory the British banned settlement on Indian lands west of the Appalachians, but in practice Britain was losing control of its colonies and pressure for settlement of Indian lands began to mount. It was abetted by the Iroquois, who cynically ceded western lands that they supposedly had conquered in the seventeenth century but which had long been occupied by their own allies and dependents, particularly the Shawnees and Delawares.

The repercussions of French defeat spread far beyond the Great Lakes and the Ohio region. In the south, the Muskogees began to feel serious pressure on their lands as the British demanded cessions to clarify the boundaries of Georgia and their new colony of West Florida. And squatters ignored even these boundaries to occupy and hunt on Muskogee lands. The Cherokees found their own lands under pressure from North Carolina speculators and squatters. Without fear of Indian defections to the French, the colonists seemingly were willing to act with utter impunity in the south.

Indians felt the consequences of the French defeat far to the west. With the cession of Louisiana to Spain, the Spanish could at last begin to bring under control the French traders who had supplied the tribes who raided Texas and New Mexico. By 1786 the Comanches came to terms with New Mexico. The son and successor of Cuerno Verde had died in battle, the Comanche alliance with the Wichitas was deteriorating, and the Comanches desired to resume trade with New Mexico. Comanche attacks on Texas continued, but New Mexico had won a long-sought peace. The Wichitas, with their own trade connections in decline, and under pressure from the Osage, now also sought peace with the Spanish.

## Confronting a New Republic

The outbreak of the American Revolution in 1775 seemed to promise a resurgence of the ability of Indians to create a stable political space between competing political powers, but the Revolution proved a disaster for previously powerful Indian confederations. The Cherokees eagerly joined the British cause to drive out the colonials who had been invading their lands, only to face invasion from revolutionary armies that killed their people, destroyed their crops, and burned their towns. Most of the Iroquois also joined the British, only to have their homelands invaded by an American army that methodically cut down their crops and orchards and left their towns in ashes. Most of the Iroquois became refugees dependent on British supplies. The Indians inflicted huge damage in turn, but the price the Cherokees and Iroquois paid was so heavy that they never again engaged in direct war with the Americans.

*Others declared that God had indeed given the bible or written book to the white people who could read it, but to the Indians or children of the forest He had given the hunting-grounds, sacrificial feasts, and had shown them another mode of life; the former could therefore seek to live up to what God had commanded them, while they felt it their duty to hold fast to that which He had appointed for them. Others again are of the opinion, which is not generally held among them, however, that the Indians did not come from the same source as the white people, but had been created separately, for which reason they were not allowed to adopt the customs of the white people and to regulate themselves according to their religion. Such declare that because of the acceptance of the white man's religion on the part of some, their gods had become angry and sought their destruction; that their deities wanted to take away from them their land and all customs and liberties, including the use of whiskey, which was the discovery of the whites, as well as their silver and their gold, and the practice of usury among them, all of which they regarded as an evil in the world, and as originally unknown among their race, and something that had been brought upon them by the white people.*

—ABRAHAM LUKENBACH
Moravian missionary to
the Delawares, late 1700s

OPPOSITE: **Iroquois Indians and a British Ranger prepare to attack the colonial militia (by Greg Harlin).**

## ALEXANDER MCGILLIVRAY

Alexander McGillivray was the son of a Scottish father and a Creek mother, Sehoy, who was herself of mixed French–Creek descent and a member of the Wind clan. Educated in Charleston, fluent in Muskogee and English, and with strong clan connections, McGillivray became one of the most accomplished diplomats of the late eighteenth century. Europeans regarded him as head chief, dictator, or *isti atcagagi thlucco* ["great beloved man"] of all the Muskogees, both upper and lower towns, although no such office existed ("most beloved men" was the general title by which advisory elders of the council were known to the Indians).

Until his death in 1793, McGillivray worked as hard (against considerable opposition) to centralize the Muskogees as to maneuver among the Americans, British, and Spanish. An excerpt from his letter of August 12, 1788, to Estevan Miró, the Spanish governor of Florida, conveys the magnitude of the difficulties he faced:

*In Short to Speak out my Sentiments at once, I am of the opinion that they [Congress] will not Compel the Georgians to restore our lands & if we take Strong Measures to obtain Justice, the force of the Union will be employd to reduce us to accept of their own terms of peace, which if they are permitted to effect they must have ourselves into the bargain.*

*I do not therefore hesitate to pronounce that the measure which the Governmt. [of Spain] adopted to Withhold from us the Royal Support to Induce us to treat with the americans is premature. A moments reflection would have foreseen the ill Consequences of compelling a Naked unarmed people to treat with a designing & incensd Implacable enemy. Such a mode of Interference Shoud have been reservd for the last, if it Shoud have been found that we woud not accede to Just & equitable terms of Peace.*

Cornplanter, one of the great Seneca chiefs, was a leader of the Iroquois in their war with the Americans during the revolution. He later played a principal role in making peace with George Washington, in which the League was given reservations and became subject to the new nation. This portrait was made by F. Bartoli in 1796.

The various Algonquian peoples who joined the British were militarily victorious north of the Ohio, but they failed to dislodge the Americans who settled Kentucky. And when the war ended, they found themselves once more betrayed, for the British had ceded their homelands to the Americans. The Americans had received as a British gift lands that their armies had not been able to conquer.

In the years following the American Revolution the Indian peoples east of the Mississippi made their final attempts to maintain an independent political role for themselves and to hold the middle ground they had created. These attempts took various routes. In the south the Muskogees and Choctaws divided, each nation, indeed often each town, containing various factions—British, Spanish, American. Their very divisions created what amounted to a playoff system within each nation. They maintained ties with all powers; they went over completely to none. But factionalism could harm as well as hurt the interests of the nation as a whole, and fraudulent land cessions and treaties plagued the southern tribes. Indian peoples still spawned leaders such as Alexander McGillivray, capable of navigating the tricky waters between competing powers, but the task grew more and more difficult.

The Cherokees took a different route. In effect, the Cherokees attempted to take the Americans at their word and act as if the American Revolution heralded a new republican revolution in which Indians would enter the United States as equals. For the Cherokees this meant the creation of a Cherokee republic to stand on equal status with the American republic that inspired it and to which it would be connected.

In many ways the Cherokees became a mirror of the American republic. Eventually they adopted a written constitution modeled after that of the Americans, and Sequoyah created a new syllabary that enabled them to become literate in their own language and to print newspapers and books in Cherokee.

Their elite, which was of mixed white and Indian descent, became slaveholders; the nation as a whole became farmers with men working in the fields. Christianity made large inroads among them.

To their north, the Algonquian peoples found accommodation with the Americans impossible. For the Americans stuck by their claim that the Indians, having been conquered, had forfeited their lands. They asserted that a series of rump treaties negotiated in the aftermath of the war had ratified American title. To resist, the Indians formed a confederation whose warriors opposed the American incursions.

Under Little Turtle, a Miami war leader, they inflicted two of the most disastrous defeats American armies would ever suffer. They first defeated General Harmar in 1790 and then in 1791 slaughtered General St. Clair's army. His casualties numbered fourteen hundred, two-thirds of his army, and he left six hundred men dead on the field. The victorious Indians, who lost only twenty-one men, stuffed the mouths of the enemy dead with dirt—symbolically satisfying in death the American lust for Indian lands.

These defeats caused the Americans to surrender their fiction of conquest, but they still rejected the Indian demand for an Ohio River boundary and so the war continued. It was a war in which the Indians, although betrayed in the past by the British, still had to depend on British support for supplies and aid. And when, following what would otherwise have been a minor defeat at Fallen Timbers, the British shut the doors of Fort Miami to the retreating Indians, the writing was on the wall. Without British support, the Indians came to terms, and made the first of their land cessions to the Americans in the Treaty of Fort Greenville, which secured the peace in 1793.

The treaty represented a pause before the climactic struggle in the region. In the early nineteenth century two brothers among the Shawnees, Tecumseh and Tenskwatawa, began a movement to reunite and reinvigorate the demoralized

## HANDSOME LAKE

Of all the prophets who arose with messages of salvation for Indian peoples during the years of turmoil between 1760 and 1820, the one with the most lasting impact was Handsome Lake of the Senecas, the westernmost of the six nations of the Iroquois confederation. In the cruel years following the American Revolution he witnessed the defeat and gradual dispossession of his people. He became a drunk. He grew depressed and melancholy.

In 1799, "but yellow skin and dried bones" as his daughter described him, he had a vision. Three angels appeared to him on a sky journey. They met George Washington. They met Jesus.

And Jesus told Handsome Lake, "Now tell your people that they will become lost when they follow the ways of the white man."

The visions and their message became the heart of the Gaiwiio, the "good word," the gospel of Handsome Lake, which, like the Christian gospel, is part history, part instruction for conducting proper ceremonies, part moral code, and part prophecy. But he grafted his teachings onto far more ancient ceremonies—the Midwinter Ceremony, the Green Corn Dance. And much of his teaching was new, incorporating Christian elements even as it preserved older Iroquois beliefs.

After 1801 Handsome Lake increasingly emphasized a second gospel, a gospel of this world suited to the new social conditions the Iroquois faced and aimed at social problems that he thought were sapping the strength of his people. He emphasized temperance, agriculture, peace, land retention, and the adoption of white technology. He gave fathers a centrality and authority in the family they had never had before. And in time, as the religion took hold, it ceased to be a new way. It became the Old Way of Handsome Lake. It became traditional.

**Tenskwatawa, the Prophet, painted by Charles Bird King in 1823.**

peoples north of the Ohio. From the beginning the movement was pan-tribal and religious, but it was also a movement that sprang from the middle ground of more than a century of contact and common life.

Tenskwatawa was one of numerous visionaries, male and female, among the Shawnees, Delawares, Ottawas, Muskogees, Cherokees, Iroquois, and others during the early nineteenth century who called for a religious renewal among the tribes. Their calls paralleled, and were in some ways connected with, the First Great Awakening going on among their American neighbors.

Before his vision, Tenskwatawa had been an inconsequential drunkard, a figure of ridicule named Lalewethika. Following it, he gave up drinking and took his new name, which meant "the open door." Although Tenskwatawa's teaching contained Christian elements, and at least one Shaker leader recognized the affinities as being close enough to consider him as being under the same divine inspiration as himself, Tenskwatawa came to emphasize the differences rather than the similarities between Indians and whites. His was an Indian religion, an Indian way.

Tenskwatawa and Tecumseh never attained great influence among the Shawnees, but they gained numerous followers elsewhere and created a series of pan-tribal villages. And to their religious teachings and demands that the Indians renounce drinking and their reliance on white tools and technology, they added an explicit political message: the lands belonged to all Indian peoples in common and no tribe, town, or chief had a right to make a cession. Tecumseh, who gradually took over the leadership of the movement from Tenskwatawa, moved to extend this new confederation beyond the Great Lakes and Ohio River valley and into the south. Capitalizing on another call for religious renewal among the Muskogees, he won a significant following there, but the Cherokees, Chickasaws, and Choctaws largely shunned him.

Tecumseh, for all his stress on Indian unity, knew that his only real chance for success was to secure British backing, and so, despite the two previous betrayals by the British, he once more cultivated a British alliance. Tecumseh regarded war as inevitable, but he sought to delay the advent of fighting until his alliances were complete.

During Tecumseh's absence in the south, however, Tenskwatawa allowed himself to be drawn into a premature fight when, in 1811, an American army illegally invaded Indian lands and marched on Prophetstown at Tippecanoe. He promised his warriors that his spiritual power would render the Americans dead or dying and easy victims, but the soldiers fought back and inflicted significant casualties. Tenskwatawa, who blamed the failure of his medicine on his wife's menstruation, precipitously lost influence, and Tecumseh took sole leadership of the movement.

The fighting had, however, begun and it merged into the War of 1812. Despite initial victories, the end result was defeat both for the Muskogees in the south, and Tecumseh's alliance in the north. When the Americans cut British supply lines on Lake Erie, the British retreated and the victories they and Tecumseh's warriors had won came to naught. On the retreat Tecumseh fell at the Battle of the Thames. His death was a merciful one. He would not live to see his people dispossessed nor to suffer the humiliations of American dictation.

*The Death of Tecumseh,* at the Battle of the Thames, October 18, 1813.

Tecumseh had never accepted the American claim that American freedom meant Indian freedom, that, in Jefferson's words, the two races would peacefully merge and spread together across the continent. He had recognized that the price of American freedom was the loss of Indian freedom, and that American prosperity would be built on Indian lands. He fought to prevent it; he fought to maintain an older world where the presence of Europeans did not mean the elimination of Indian freedom. He wanted a world where Indian polities were not simply mechanisms for conveying resources to Americans. He failed.

There would, of course, be continued resistance after Tecumseh. But when, following the War of 1812, Great Britain abandoned any further attempts to back independent Indian alliances as a buttress against American expansion, the Indians lost their last real chance to counter the Americans. They would still fight; they would still win military victories, but the chance for ultimate success was gone. And too often the result of resistance was only bloody tragedy.

One example of such tragedy was the slaughter of those Sauk and Fox who, under the Sauk war leader Black Hawk, resisted American attempts to take their lands under a treaty they regarded as invalid. The Sauk and Fox had successfully resisted Frenchmen; they had successfully fought the British; they had helped defeat American armies. They were a formidable people. But in 1832, divided

The Sauk warrior Black Hawk, in a portrait by Charles Bird King, 1823.

## HORSESHOE BEND

The religious renewal among the Creeks, or Muskogees, in the early nineteenth century, when coupled with Tecumseh's calls for pan-Indian resistance to the Americans, led to what amounted to a sacred revolt. But not all Muskogees rose against the Americans. The war against the United States was also a civil war. And when, at the town of Tohopeka on March 27, 1814, one thousand Muskogee warriors known to the Americans as "Redsticks" barricaded themselves in a horseshoe bend of the Tallapoosa River to face fifteen hundred Anglo-Americans and five hundred Cherokees, one hundred of their countrymen were with the attackers.

Only about a third of the Redsticks had firearms, but they possessed, they thought, a greater sacred power. They believed enemy gunfire could not harm them. They believed that their prophets would make the very earth oppose the invaders. Rifles and cannon did, however, prove more powerful. As a Redstick survivor recalled, the warriors dropped "like the fall of leaves." Eighty percent of them died on the fields or in the river trying to escape. It was one of the greatest defeats Indian peoples were to suffer in their resistance to the United States. It broke the rebellion.

among themselves, heavily outnumbered and without significant allies, they won early battles under Black Hawk only to be forced to retreat.

They fought the Battle of Bad Axe trapped with the Mississippi at their backs. They retreated into the river's sloughs. Soldiers lined the shores shooting at anything that moved. An American steamboat raked them with cannon. Men, women, and children died, their blood turning the waters that lapped the shore red and soaking the land they had lost forever. One band of about a hundred people made it across the river, but the Eastern Sioux, or Dakotas, allied to the Americans, struck them there, killing most of the fugitives. Perhaps three hundred Sauks and Fox died in the grim, hopeless fighting.

In the south, the larger confederations had by and large recognized that armed resistance to the Americans was hopeless. The southern Indians, even a majority of the Muskogees, modeled their governments after the new American republic. The Muskogees became commonly known as the Creeks, a name derived from their general habitat along waterways, and formed a confederacy. Their old politics of kinship yielded to more centralized governments, and a wealthy, educated elite gradually took control of their affairs. But as the American republic became increasingly enamored with doctrines of a racial nationalism and Anglo-Saxon superiority, the Indian republics recognized that the Americans had marked them as inherently inferior no matter what their accomplishments.

In reaction, they developed a nationalism of their own. Their old homelands became small nation-states existing alongside the American republic, which had treaty obligations to protect them. But the Americans did not observe these treaties, and by the 1820s the Indians found themselves under increasing pressure to surrender their lands and move across the Mississippi.

William Weatherford of the Creeks submitting to Andrew Jackson after the Battle of Horseshoe Bend at the Tallapoosa River, March 1814.

*The Trail of Tears*
by Troy Anderson, (Cherokee) 1992.
Removal—the government's solution
to the "Indian problem"—involved the
displacement of thousands of Indians
from the Southeast to Indian Territory
in Oklahoma and points west. The best
known, and perhaps the most infamous
of these forced marches, was the ordeal
suffered by the Cherokees on their
journey to strange lands.

## Indian Removal Policy

In May of 1830, President Andrew Jackson signed into law the Indian Removal
Act, thus putting teeth into the policy his predecessors had long advocated—the
"voluntary" exchange of lands by eastern Indians for territory that the federal
government would acquire for them west of the Mississippi. Jackson gave the policy immediacy and an assertion that existing Indian treaties did not constitute
federal recognition of Indian sovereign rights to the soil of their homelands. The
Indian Removal Act enabled the president to implement such assertions, putting
congressional support and appropriations behind the tragedies to follow.

The Removal Act did not authorize the use of force—but neither did Jackson
feel obliged to protect Indians from any force mobilized by the states and their
citizens. Moreover, the government had long before promised Georgia to eliminate Indian title to the lands within its boundaries in exchange for the state's
western land claims. The demands of Georgia, and of the white speculators,
planters, and farmers eager to take over Indian land, mattered far more to
Andrew Jackson than any guarantees made to Indians in treaties.

So, when Georgia unilaterally extended its laws over the Cherokee nation in
1829 (to be effective June 1, 1830), Jackson withdrew federal troops and denied
protection to the Cherokees. In 1830 Cherokees who held tribal office automatically became criminals. Georgia prepared to distribute their lands by lottery, and
seize their other property for debt. They had little recourse against fraud or theft
since, as Indians, they could not testify in Georgia's courts. The Cherokee government withdrew to the town of Red Clay in Tennessee. John Ross, the principal chief of the Cherokees, led a complicated legal fight against state usurpation
of their sovereignty and the federal government's refusal to enforce treaty provisions. And in *Worcester v. Georgia* they won a legal victory of a sort. In 1832 the
U.S. Supreme Court upheld treaties as "the supreme law of the land," and ruled
that Georgia's laws did not apply within the Cherokee nation. Federal marshals

*At the time of death,*
*When I found there was to be death,*
*I was very much surprised.*
*All was failing.*
*My home, I was sad to leave it.*

*I have been looking far,*
*Sending my spirit north, south, east*
    *and west.*
*Trying to escape death,*
*But could find nothing,*
*No way of escape.*

—Luiseño Song

# THE TRAIL OF TEARS

Years after the Cherokee removal, the ethnologist James Mooney interrogated participants, both Indian and white, and he condensed their accounts into one of his own. "Families at dinner were startled by the sudden gleam of bayonets in the doorway and rose up to be driven with blows amid oaths along the trail that led to the stockade. Men were seized in their fields or going along the road, women were taken from their [spinning] wheels and children from their play. . . .

"To prevent escape the soldiers had been ordered to approach and surround each house, as far as possible, so as to come upon the occupants without warning. One old patriarch when thus surprised calmly called his children and grandchildren around him, and kneeling down bid them pray with him in their own language, while the astonished soldiers looked on in silence. Then rising he led the way into exile. A woman, on finding the house surrounded, went to the door and called up the chickens to be fed for the last time, after which taking her infant on her back and her other children by the hand, she followed her husband with the soldiers."

But behind the soldiers came white looters who plundered the homes and graves the Cherokees left behind and stole their livestock.

The Cherokees fell sick in the holding camps. The main body departed west in the midst of a drought that made water and food scarce. They continued to travel into a viciously cold winter. People sickened and died and were buried along the way. The journey took an especially terrible toll of women and children. The road they traveled was the "road they cried": the bitter Trail of Tears.

*The Trail of Tears*
by Robert Lindneux, 1942.

Robt. Lindneux
1942 ©

could not act to enforce the ruling until a state judge formally refused to comply, and in this case the state just ignored the Supreme Court, which adjourned without ever reporting to the president Georgia's failure to conform. As a result, the decision had no practical effect.

This left the Cherokees and the other southern tribes at the mercy of the states. Alabama and Mississippi imitated Georgia in extending their laws over the Indian nations, and North Carolina and Tennessee followed. For the Choctaws, Chickasaws, Cherokees, and Creeks the result was disaster. From self-governing peoples living on their own lands, Indians became people pauperized by the government with no right to protect their lives or property. Tuskeneah, a headman of the Creek town of Cusseta, reported white marauders spoiling his lands and "taking possession of the Red peoples improvements that they have made with their own labor." Although whites stole Indian property, American troops refused to intervene. But when the Yuchis, "a small part of our Tribe," killed American livestock, the whites hunted them down "and shot them as though they were deer."

The federal government held out removal as the only realistic hope for renewed security and sovereignty, and in desperation and anguish southern Indians were left to "choose." The large majority of Indians in the south had no desire to remove, but after 1832 they had no effective way to resist. In each nation there came to be those who saw removal as inevitable. Some viewed it as a way of escaping whites; some saw personal or factional gain in cooperation; some simply resigned themselves to obtaining the best price they could. And beginning with the Choctaws at Dancing Rabbit Creek in 1830, federal negotiators, employing various degrees of coercion and fraud, obtained their removal treaties. The most blatantly fraudulent of all was the New Echota Treaty of 1835 with the Cherokees. Negotiated with the Ridge group, who represented only a small fraction of the nation, it was, as the Cherokee national council said, "a fraud upon the Cherokee people." The U.S. Senate ratified it by a single vote.

As an immediate aftermath of the removal treaties, abuse markedly increased. Although many of the treaties promised that Indians wishing to remain could obtain land allotments, white squatters invaded the nations, seizing land and improvements. Indians found themselves being stripped of property, including their homes, fields, livestock, and goods. Because no court could accept the testimony of an Indian against a white man, squatters could lodge fraudulent claims uncontested. Whiskey sellers appeared in droves. They advanced credit, which became debt, which then provided a spurious excuse for claiming the Indian land allotments supposedly protected under the treaties.

Fraud, violence, and drunkenness were the immediate fruits of the treaties. For Indians, chaos would be the ultimate result, with uprooted, homeless, displaced thousands trailing slowly west. Resistance was futile. When, in desperation, some Creeks, led by Eneah Emathla, an elder, retaliated for an attack by Georgia militia by killing whites and destroying their property, federal troops at once stepped in and, together with the Alabama militia, subdued them in the "Creek War" of 1836. The "hostiles" were rounded up, manacled, and chained together (including the eighty-four-year-old Emathla) and marched west. The state of Georgia gained twenty-five million acres of Creek land.

This letter of patent signed by President Martin Van Buren in 1838 in conjunction with treaties of May 6, 1828, February 14, 1833, and December 29, 1835, conveyed as a "gift" from the United States to the Cherokees two tracts of land comprising some fourteen million acres in Arkansas, with a "perpetual outlet west and free and unmolested use of all the country west of the western boundary . . . to have to hold . . . with all rights thereto belonging to the Cherokee Nation forever. . . ."

These treaties granting title to land remained unviolated. The treaties included clauses reserving rights for the United States to establish post and military roads and forts anywhere in the Cherokee nation as well as "the free use of as much land, timber, fuel, and materials of all kinds, for the construction and support of the same, as may be necessary."

The Seminoles mounted a far more effective resistance. Fraud and intimidation had produced the Treaty of Payne's Landing in 1832, and most Seminoles rejected it, but for the United States it served as a pretense for removal. The Seminoles did not possess prime cotton lands, but for years black slaves had fled to them, living in separate villages under the protection of Seminole chiefs. They spoke the same language as the Seminoles; they shared their customs; and to some extent they intermarried. The Americans initially not only demanded Seminole land, they demanded the right to retrieve escaped slaves.

As a result, the Seminole War, fought by both Indian and African-American

*Murder is murder and somebody must answer, somebody must explain the streams of blood that flowed in the Indian country in the summer of 1838. Somebody must explain the four-thousand silent graves that mark the trail of the Cherokees to their exile. I wish I could forget it all, but the picture of six-hundred and forty-five wagons lumbering over the frozen ground with their Cargo of suffering humanity still lingers in my memory.*

*Let the Historian of a future day tell the sad story with its sighs, its tears and dying groans. Let the great Judge of all the earth weigh our actions and reward us according to our work.*

—JOHN G. BURNETT
United States Army
and interpreter on the
Trail of Tears, ca. 1890

warriors, was as much a slave war as an Indian war. And to complicate it further, some Creeks joined the Seminoles while others fought with the Americans against them. The war dragged on from 1835 until 1842. In 1837 the Americans captured Osceola, the greatest of the Seminole war leaders, who had come in to parley under a flag of truce. He died the next year in prison. Gradually, through such treachery, surrender, and capture, more than four thousand Seminoles were forced to move west. Having spent twenty million dollars and having lost fifteen hundred soldiers, the United States gave up further attempts to seize the relative handful of Seminoles who still remained in the fastness of the Everglades.

Some Cherokees, Creeks, and Choctaws, like the Seminoles, would survive in their old homelands, but for most the treaties meant a long trek west to Indian Territory. Some went voluntarily; others went under armed escort. Virtually all went with a deep sadness. And virtually all suffered, for the journeys were grim. In 1831–32 the Choctaws, without blankets, shoes, or winter clothes, traveled through one of the worst winters the south had ever seen. American incompetence, more than malice, left them sick, hungry, and exhausted. In 1836–37 the *hillis hayas*, or medicine men, of the Creeks extinguished the sacred fires in the town squares. They preserved the ashes and flints used by the fire makers, wrapping these and other sacred objects in deerskin bundles that they strapped to their backs, and without a word began the procession westward. American troops conducted about twenty thousand Creeks west, and white settlers gathered en route to watch this exodus of a forlorn nation that they had reduced to misery.

The Cherokees endured the most deadly migration. Like the Creeks, the Cherokees departed late, and like the Creeks, they had offered resistance, albeit in the courtroom; now they suffered and died in even greater numbers. How many died remains unclear even now. The most careful estimates guess that of the sixteen thousand who set out, two thousand died during the 1838 journey itself. But losses continued to mount during the following years as epidemics ravaged the weakened survivors. By the highest estimates, a quarter or even more of the Cherokees died in the wake of removal.

The Cherokee and Creek removals were perhaps the most dramatic, but during the 1820s and 1830s, the majority of Indian peoples east of the Mississippi found they had to move west. Given a poor choice, some disagreed among themselves, some moved voluntarily, some went under duress. It was a time of tremendous upheaval, of profound dislocation. And entering, as they were, onto lands already occupied by people farther west, their removal sparked a new wave of intertribal conflict on the prairies and Great Plains. The removals affected many more Indians than those physically deprived of their homelands.

Across the Ohio, the northern tribes, too, found themselves forced to choose between exodus and life on individual allotments surrounded by whites. Some chose to stay, and small Miami, Wyandot, Potawatomi, and Ottawa communities survived in a sea of whites. More departed across the Mississippi. Along the northern border from upstate New York, through upper Michigan and across northern Wisconsin, the Iroquois, the Menominees, and the Ojibwas fought against the tide of removal. Eventually, they managed to retain some remnants of their old territories as reservations.

The attachment of some people to land and home persevered through extraordinary adversity. The Winnebagos lost their lands in Wisconsin in 1837 through a blatantly illegal treaty. About half the tribe refused to move. The government hunted them down, rounded them up, and shipped them west. Even so, some Winnebagos filtered home and managed to reestablish themselves in their ancestral lands.

Such minor victories only served to emphasize the massive human devastation wrought among the Indian peoples by the removals. Opponents of removal could view it as a conspiracy between the federal government, the state governments, and large numbers of their citizenry to defraud Indians. Supporters of removal claimed it was in the best interest of the Indians. Faced with the apparently overwhelming strength of the invaders, the native Americans endured.

In Oklahoma the Cherokees, Choctaws, Chickasaws, Seminoles, and Creeks began painfully rebuilding their republics. The exiled peoples north of the Ohio began rebuilding their lives. To their west powerful independent nations remained, but the context of Indian lives had altered. The Americans had the power to dictate, and the force and patience to impose their will. As they boldly annexed Texas in 1845, it was clear they no longer needed Indian peoples as Europeans had once needed them, and Indians lacked other Europeans to play off against them.

Mexico, the heir to Spain, would soon be forced from the Southwest. And outside of Oregon, which would be ceded the following year, the English had already withdrawn from the competition. Indian peoples faced a new and challenging world. Their successes of the eighteenth century seemed behind them.

—RICHARD WHITE

## WILLIAM APESS

As Indian removal proceeded and Indian power diminished, white Americans pushed claims of Indian racial inferiority and white superiority. Whites proclaimed themselves the darlings of God, destiny, and history. But nonwhite voices, too, embraced the language of race.

William Apess was a Pequot Indian whose parents were laborers. He lived in New England, a society where Indian peoples survived only on the margins. Deserted by his parents, abused and beaten by his often drunk grandparents, indentured to neighboring whites, he overcame his own problems with drink. He sought not to escape his own broken past, but to build upon it, to ally it with other pasts, to turn it into a weapon.

He became a Christian and a Methodist minister, but he maintained a strong sense of his Indian identity, and he came to live in the Indian town of Mashpee on Cape Cod. In 1833 as a literate, Christian Indian, he addressed a white audience in print:

Now let me ask you, white man, if it is a disgrace for to eat, drink, and sleep with the image of God, or sit, or walk and talk with them. Or have you the folly to think that the white man, being one in fifteen or sixteen, are the only beloved images of God? Assemble all nations together in your imagination, and then let the whites be seated among them. . . . Now suppose these skins were put together, and each skin had its national

crimes written upon it—which skin do you think would have the greatest? I will ask one question more. Can you charge the Indians with robbing a nation almost of their whole continent, and murdering their own women and children, and then depriving the remainder of their lawful rights, that nature and God require them to have? And to cap the climax, rob another nation, to till their grounds and welter out their days under the lash with hunger and fatigue. . . . I should look at all the skins, and I know that when I cast my eye upon that white skin, and if I saw those crimes written upon it, I should enter my protest against it immediately and cleave to that which is more honorable.

PART FOUR

# LONG THREADS

*In order to become sole masters of our land
they relegated us to small reservations as big as my hand
and make us long promises, as long as my arm; but the
next year the promises were shorter and got shorter
every year until now they are the length of my finger,
and they keep only half of that.*

CHIEF PIAPOT, CREE, 1895

Cheyenne and Arapaho gather for a
Ghost Dance at the North Carolina River
near Fort Reno, Oklahoma Territory, 1889.

# CHAPTER EIGHTEEN

# NATIVE AMERICA AT MID-CENTURY 1846–1861

A CHIEF FORBIDDING THE PASSAGE
OF A WAGON TRAIN THROUGH HIS COUNTRY

## October 1846

WHEN TWENTY-FIVE-YEAR-OLD U.S. Army Lieutenant James W. Abert rode his mule out of the pueblo of Laguna in central New Mexico early that crisp autumn morning, his exploratory party bade goodbye to the crowding Laguna Indian children, who were fascinated by the light-eyed whites. These inquisitive youngsters, along with their blanket-wrapped elders and moccasined mothers drawing bread out of beehive-shaped outdoor ovens, were "our new fellow citizens," as Abert reminded himself in his diary.

For the first six miles Abert's group moved swiftly westward on a "very hard and good road," but then at some Indian cornfields they bogged down in soft sand. Soon a train of Mexican "donkeys laden with peaches, watermelons and dried fruits" passed by, making for the command of another U.S. military officer, Colonel Jackson, who was recently stationed at the sleepy town of Cubero. All this activity bespoke the brand-new United States presence in the formerly Mexican Southwest.

*Acoma Pueblo* by Lloyd Townsend.

Around noon Abert's party suddenly topped a ridge to confront a spectacle of landscape "to exceed anything I have ever yet beheld." In the fifty-mile panorama below, looming up from the yawning expanse of the still-verdant San Jose Valley stood a prodigious sandstone mesa that supported the pueblo of Acoma, its low-lying mud walls almost camouflaged against the buff-colored rock. To its Keresan-speaking inhabitants, this was the very "center of the world."

Perhaps the most commanding townsite in all of North America, the community of some seven hundred souls was perched atop a 367-foot monolith surrounded by rocky spires and huge boulders as if protecting a sacred sanctuary. Along with a diversity of different tribal settlements dotting the rest of the vast Southwest—what today constitutes California, Colorado, Utah, Arizona, and New Mexico—this ancient native American community was on the brink of becoming the latest real estate prize of the United States.

One can imagine these American decades in the middle of the nineteenth century as a sort of continental hinge, creaking as great doors opened to admit the last major expansion of pioneering families and town builders into the West. For the newcomers these years would be memorialized as the climax of a God-given national destiny to bind a new union from sea to shining sea. For the epic told in this book, however, the problem with that national "master narrative" is that other human families, with their own cultural varieties and much longer histories, were living there already, with different worldviews and other stories to tell.

The numerous and contrasting Indian cultures west of the Mississippi had been interacting with Euro-Americans for nearly three centuries. But now they were on the cusp of that decisive, disastrous change that had already turned the world upside down for the Indians to the east. In the next seventy-five years the West might be "won" for the Anglo-American newcomers, but it would be decidedly "lost" for these Indian societies whose lifestyles, based on hunting, fishing, foraging, gardening, and trading, had been developing for more than ten thousand years. The latter half of the nineteenth century would see those cultural patterns, and the religious worldviews that supported them, disappear or, at best, be driven underground. Part IV tells the story of that turbulent transition, when the North American Indian world came to the brink of extinction.

For the cause of welding the United States into the Western Hemisphere's most powerful nation, the 1840s and 1850s were watershed decades, as vast new landholdings fell under American control in an astonishingly brief period.

After the Republic of Texas finally broke free from Mexico in 1836, a local newspaper editor assured his readers that "the giant arms of the United States will soon sweep the few bands of hostile Indians from our borders." Aggressive settlers began immediately to do just that, whether the Indians were belligerents or not. Texas did not actually attain statehood until its annexation in 1845, following ten years of debate, but between 1845 and 1861 ferocious attacks on Indians by Texas irregulars and land-hungry settlers virtually eradicated from the state its longtime native occupants, such as the Hasinai and the Caddo. Land-grabbing settlers also swept out relatively recent Indian immigrants, such as the scattered groups of Cherokees and Kickapoos, who were already refugees of earlier pressures to evacuate their old eastern and Great Lakes homelands. By the

*Approaching Chimney Rock* by William Henry Jackson, 1931.
Located near present-day Bayard, Nebraska, Chimney Rock served as a reminder to
travelers heading west that the more treacherous terrain of the mountains was near.

OVERLEAF: *Watching the Wagons* by Frank C. McCarthy, 1982.

1860s, bands of Comanche and Kiowa raiders, who had been freely marauding against Texas ranches while en route to or from Mexico, were among the few native peoples who remained—an active but diminishing threat.

Ultimately, the only Indians who held on to any Texas lands, ironically, were out-of-state native communities who quietly ensconced themselves well away from the frontier violence. These included one settlement, dating back to the seventeenth century, of Tewa-speaking Pueblo Indians from New Mexico who resided in West Texas and would call themselves the Tigua tribe, and another the Alabama-Coushatta, former affiliates of the Creek confederacy from the Southeast, who hid from prying eyes in the Big Thicket swamp of East Texas.

In 1846, one year after Texas became a state, England ceded its claim to Oregon, and that territory, too, was absorbed into the United States. Wagon trains had been rolling westward over the Oregon Trail since 1841, but now their numbers increased dramatically. This infuriated Plains Indians all along the route, who watched metal-rimmed wagon wheels cut ruts across their free range while hairy-faced strangers killed thousands of their buffalo with powerful guns. Disease added its ugly toll to the stresses upon native existence caused by desperately reduced food and water resources. Soon the invasion of white newcomers began exerting pressure on the resident Plateau Indians and the Pacific Northwest peoples as well, who watched these aliens damming creeks, clearing land for farming, and erecting permanent towns.

Only three years after Texas became a state, the 1848 Treaty of Guadalupe Hidalgo ended the bloody war between the United States and Mexico, bringing the largest of the new landmasses under U.S. dominion, and propelling government survey teams across the mesas and valleys of the Southwest. Lieutenant Abert's party that inspected Laguna and Acoma was but one of many to fan out into the juniper and piñon desert in order to assess what natural resource treasures it might hold for the land- and wealth-hungry republic.

Among these southwestern surveys was that of Lieutenant J. H. Simpson, who in 1849 brought back to Washington, D.C., the first descriptions of the great ruins of Chaco Canyon. American contact with the Hopi villages situated on fingers of Black Mesa to the northwest of Chaco was made by U.S. Army surveyors P.G.S. Ten Broeck and J.C. Ives in the 1850s. Very soon, however, the underlying motive for such surveys was based less on establishing goodwill with Indians than on expeditiously wrapping up rights-of-way; after 1853 the official search was seriously on for routes, both north and south, by which transcontinental railways could link the old and new parts of the United States.

Initially, the reception given by Pueblo Indians like the Acoma villagers to Abert and others in this first generation of Anglo-American delegates was not uncongenial. These blue-uniformed newcomers seemed less domineering and greedy than the gold-seeking Spanish, who had leveled Acoma with their cannons in 1599. After that rude awakening the Acoma people had enthusiastically participated in the all-Pueblo Revolt of 1680 against Spanish domination, hurling their Catholic priest off the mesa top. Soon after, however, they had accepted the Church once again, as witnessed by the adobe bell towers of San Estevan, which the villagers proudly pointed out to Abert. Yet as the women of Acoma fed Abert's men their traditional flaky blue corn bread, they were unaware that here

A wagon train crosses the Washita River near present-day Anadarko, Oklahoma.

In the short time span between 1845 and 1860 the map of non-Indian North America changed forever. Through the rapid-fire succession of land transfers with England (1846), Mexico (1848), and the Gadsden Purchase (1853), the United States extended its dominion to the western ocean. Had it not been for the gold strikes in California, however, its far-western landscapes might have remained isolated behind their reputation as forbidding desert and impenetrable mountains.

But the lure of fast fortune started a mad dash; in 1849 some 25,000 expectant newcomers headed for the West Coast, swelling California's population to more than 100,000. Another 45,000 arrived the following year, and 105,000 more would show up by 1852.

Invigorated by the western influx, the U.S. Congress even boosted it with the Oregon Donation Act of 1850, which advertised generous land grants for new homesteaders. The only trouble was some 200,000 Indians who were already residing west of the Mississippi. Nonetheless, the number of pioneers becoming settlers and of crossroads becoming towns continued to skyrocket.

En route to the 1849 Gold Rush, some sharp-eyed travelers noticed potential gold-mining at the foot of the Rockies. Salt Lake City became a boom town as new travelers—about 15,000 in 1850—exchanged their covered wagons for packhorses. Eight years later many miners returned from the Rockies to stake claims near present-day Denver. The following summer saw the Pikes Peak gold rush. Over the following three years it would attract an estimated 80,000 hopefuls to mining camps in Continental Divide country.

Such tremendous traffic affected the subsistence economies of Indian foragers and hunters on both sides of major western wagon routes. Tender grasslands were trod under hoof, traditional access to seed and root gathering areas was hampered, and firewood was depleted. Many of the ensuing conflicts between Indians and whites must be understood as struggles over the basic necessities of life.

Meanwhile, mounting behind the earliest westering settlers was another wave of newcomers hailing from Europe: in 1860, the U.S. foreign-born numbered 4,136,000; many of these immigrants had disembarked in America in the 1840s and '50s and now looked west with high hopes for a shining future on lands that Indians were losing right and left.

was a new crop of conquerors who were fast learning that it was cheaper to control Indians with presents and strokes of the pen than with guns.

However, relations between Pueblos and the early Americans pioneering into New Mexico and Arizona territories as settlers were not always so harmonious. For the theft of Indian food supplies and brutality toward their women, the territorial families faced a bloody revolt in 1847. Initiated by a combined force of Indians and Hispanics drawn from the Santa Fe–Taos axis, the uprising led to the killing of territorial governor Charles Bent. In swift retaliation, American troops sped north from Santa Fe and wound up executing fifteen of the Indian rebels, restoring an uneasy peace along the Rio Grande.

Farther into Arizona, where the Athapaskan-speaking Apache and Navajo people held sway in dispersed, hard-to-reach clusters of hogans or *wikiups*, Indian lifestyles that intermixed hunting, gardening, and rustling livestock from white ranchers did not change overnight just because the cattlemen now spoke English instead of Spanish. As one Apache forthrightly explained, "We must steal from somebody; and if you will not permit us to rob the Mexicans, we must steal from you or fight you." And steal and maraud the Apache and Navajo increasingly did, against the incoming miners, freight wagonmasters, and homesteaders, whose ranks were growing with each passing year. In order to save time and money and avoid bloodshed, the Americans signed a treaty with the Bear Springs Navajo in 1848, and with the Canyon de Chelly bands a year later. What rendered these documents rather irrelevant, however, was the nature of Navajo social organization, which was less that of a tribe with a unified political structure than one of loosely knit, quite independent clans composed of far-flung, semi-nomadic extended families. Consequently, a peace accord signed with Navajos near Shiprock carried little weight with Navajo families who seasonally resided near Fort Wingate.

A Navajo hogan, built in keeping with its creation myth—the Blessingway—when Talking God made the first hogan. The entrance faced east, to honor the sun, and bits of shell, obsidian, abalone, and turquoise would be set in the earth at the base of the support poles. Inside, men lived on the left, or south side, while women lived on the north side. Everyone moved clockwise around the central hearth, in imitation of the movement of the sun. The hogan—like all things Navajo—was a mode of worship.

*Sod House* by William Henry Jackson, 1936. On the treeless prairies lumber was at a premium, so pioneers often used densely packed sod for building their homes.

Still farther west, throughout the foothills overlooking the hot valleys that stretch south to north beyond the towering Sierra Nevadas, the year 1849 spelled catastrophe for the manifold California Indian peoples, some of whose populations were so miniscule they are sometimes designated as *rancherias* or *tribelets*. For coastal and other California Indians from San Diego north to San Francisco, the Spanish mission era had already delivered the first blow to Indian persistence. The native population, estimated to have been around 310,000 when the Spanish constructed their first Catholic mission at San Diego in 1769, had been reduced by at least 50 percent by 1834. Foremost among the factors causing this cataclysm were epidemic diseases such as smallpox, measles, and diphtheria.

Then there was the hard labor at the Catholic missions and the Spanish mines and ranches, backed up by corporal punishment for misbehavior. And for those California Indian resisters, the "bravos" who tried to survive in the wild outside the Spanish colonial system, there was the constant threat of brutal warfare with bows and arrows against horses and guns, and the loss of natural food supplies as hogs ate their acorns and cattle trampled their foraging lands.

With the discovery of gold at an old Maidu village site along the American River on January 24, 1848, a second blow struck the California Indians. Already white farming and ranching barons had retained Indians as semislaves after the Catholic missions were secularized in 1834. Unthinkably, Indian living conditions now got even worse, with thousands of gold miners descending upon the Sierra streams. As more efficient mining techniques developed, less dependent on native muscle, Indians found themselves gradually demoted from cheap laborers to expendable nuisances. By 1870, it has been estimated, outright killing of increasingly fragmented and traumatized Indian families had left a population of between thirty and fifty thousand Indians in the state, a reduction of 90 percent in less than a hundred years.

*Then white men began to fence the plains so that we could not travel; and anyhow there was . . . nothing to travel for. We began to stay in one place, and to grow lazy and sicker all the time. Our men had fought hard against our enemies, holding them back from our beautiful country by their bravery; but now with everything else going wrong, we began to be whipped by weak foolishness. Our men, our leaders, began to drink the white man's whiskey, letting it do their thinking.*

—PRETTY SHIELD
(Crow), ca. 1930

Of all Indian regions in America, California, with its medley of different native groups peopling diverse eco-regions, suffered the most after the United States won these lands from Mexico. In village after village, rampant brutality became commonplace as gold miners, ranchers, and townsfolk swarmed into river valleys throughout the northern half of the state.

It was not uncommon for the government to effectively reward the "volunteer armies" who cleared out unprotected Indian villages. In one year, 1851–52, California authorized over one million dollars to reimburse vouchers submitted by loosely orga-nized miners and new settlers for expenses incurred during their terrorizing raids. The Sinkyone Indians were one group stunned by these assaults.

Before the Gold Rush there were over four thousand in the Humboldt County villages; then, as one victim from Needle Rock later remembered, they were ruthlessly set upon. "About ten o'clock in the morning, some white men came. They killed my grandfather and my mother and my father. I saw them do it. I was a big girl at that time. Then they killed my baby sister and cut her heart out and threw it in the brush where I ran and hid. . . . I didn't know what to do. I was so scared that I guess I just hid there a long time with my little sister's heart in my hands." At the close of the 1860s all that was left of the Sinkyone was a handful of survivors with ghastly memories of what had happened.

In the period between 1855 and 1870, such brutality was the rule rather than the exception. By 1865 the Wintu, for instance, numbering over fourteen thousand a quarter century earlier, were reduced to fewer than one thousand weakened, wholly disoriented survivors. The story was repeated throughout the foothills, as community after community experienced the same nightmare.

Federal policy, meanwhile, was fraught, as always, with ambivalence. A visiting group of federal Indian commissioners phrased the options (as they saw them) regarding Indians at this critical juncture: *As there is no further West to which they can be removed, the General Government and the people of California appear to have left but one alternative in relation to these remnants of once numerous and powerful tribes, viz: extermination or domestication.*

And both approaches were underway. In 1851 and 1852, while gold miners and ranchers exploited state laws to rip Indian children from their families for indentured servitude, and Indian scalps were harvested for bounty, these same federal commissioners, seeking the somewhat gentler alternative, talked eighteen California Indian groups into signing treaties that would create model reservations for "domesticating" the Indian. But, as often happened, anti-Indian attitudes frustrated the progressive proposal. Meeting in secret session in June 1852, the U.S. Senate went along with white Californians opposed to giving lowly Indians prime plots of agricultural land and mineral resources, and the treaty drafts went unratified.

Even as they rejected the California treaties it was dawning on Washington politicians and administrators that the practice of bodily displacing unwanted Indians ever westward was not going to work much longer. Although a few Indian communities like the California Cupeño and the Black Mountain Navajo were forced to resettle well into the twentieth century, the country by and large had already run out of space in which to dump tribes. With no real solution in view, U.S. Indian policy throughout this mid-century period vaccilated between using the carrot and using the stick to deal with western Indians.

In order to protect American citizens pushing west, strings of military posts were set up throughout the trans-Missouri frontier. Authority over Indians had shifted in 1849 from the War Department to a special section of the newly established Department of Interior, the Bureau of Indian Affairs. Yet the hope for

*Hydraulic Gold Mining*
by William Henry Jackson, 1936.

*Fort William on the Laramie*
by Alfred Jacob Miller, 1851.

peaceful, civilian solutions to handling Indians embodied in this transfer was premature. To lessen the likelihood of incessant, expensive warfare with Indians who were reluctant to give up their homelands without a fight, the government sought other approaches to resolve what was bemoaned as the "Indian problem."

In 1850 the commissioner of Indian Affairs, Luke Lea, publicly promulgated an old solution on a more massive scale than ever attempted before: set aside special Indian reservations at safe remove from both frontier towns and the travel routes used by emigrants heading west. Backed up by soldiers on call to quash potential Indian "uprisings," but administered by federal agents selected through the Washington bureaucratic process, these reservations could both eliminate Indians as impediments to the white domestication of the West and simultaneously provide safe arenas for transforming them into law-abiding, God-fearing ranchers and farmers. To coax Indians to accept this program, frontier diplomats were dispatched to beg, threaten, bribe, and cajole them into signing a new raft of treaties.

One of the problems with this policy was that very often there was no clear-cut "tribe" to negotiate with. Undismayed, the government proceeded to create tribes, and to arbitrarily appoint chiefs to represent them. In such circumstances it was relatively easy for an aggressive U.S. negotiator to win the consent of Indians to agreements they could only barely understand.

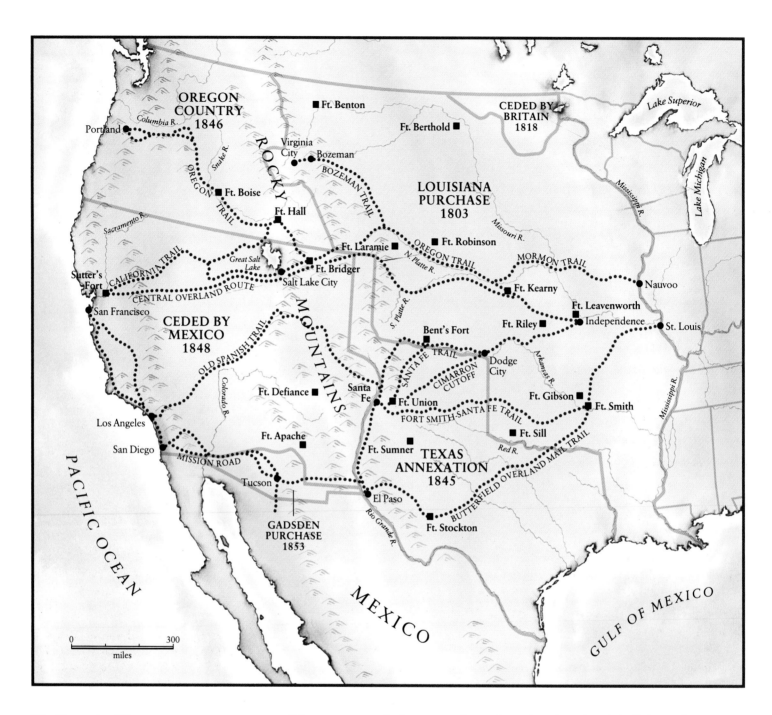

*The Expansion West.*
**As western lands were absorbed into the United States, traffic across the country increased dramatically, creating the need for extensive trails and railroad and communication lines, all of which crisscrossed Indian homelands, interfered with traditional hunting grounds, and furthered the breakup of native lifeways.**

This was particularly true in the early and mid-1850s. Of all the Indian treaties signed between 1621, when the Massachusetts Pilgrims won land concessions from the resident Wampanoag, and 1871, when the United States finally declared treaty making outmoded—few were as rapidly and successfully negotiated as the treaty councils held in the Northwest in the summer of 1855.

Ramrodding the first council at Walla Walla, Washington, in early June, and fresh from his triumphs of successfully negotiated agreements with the coastal fishing "tribes" of Puget Sound, was thirty-seven-year-old Isaac Ingalls Stevens, recently appointed both Washington Territory governor *and* territorial Indian commissioner. In the urgency to provide homesteads for settlers swelling into lands recently acquired from England, any conflict of interest between those two

assignments was overlooked. Stevens's mandate was simple: free up as much Indian land as quickly as possible. His former job surveying for the transcontinental railroad was proved good training for his new role as an agent for the burgeoning nation's Manifest Destiny.

To Walla Walla, Stevens had summoned the Cayuse, Umatilla, Yakima, Walla Walla, and twenty-five hundred Nez Perce Indians. After much feasting, Stevens, along with Oregon Indian superintendent Joel Palmer and a small military force, settled down to business with leaders of the thousands of Indians. Stevens swept aside the local linguistic and social distinctions that had maintained ethnic balance in this multitribal region. By a clever combination of bullying, bribing, and factionalizing of the tribal representatives, he coerced the group into accepting three treaties that, together, turned over sixty thousand square miles for an estimated three cents an acre. (In like fashion, between 1852 and 1856, the United States negotiated some fifty-two treaties with tribes of the trans-Mississippi West that transferred over 170 million acres of Indian land.)

Meanwhile, realizing they had been duped into disastrous concessions, some Washington coastal groups around Puget Sound, along with the Cayuse, Yakimas, and Walla Wallas farther inland, angrily struck back at incoming whites. But by hammering the natives militarily, removing troublesome groups to reservations, and encouraging loyalty among wavering tribes, the government succeeded in quelling the rebellions. By the late 1850s the Northwest was safe and secured as white man's territory.

As for that scattering of fragmented native communities east of the Mississippi that had managed to avoid the wide net of Andrew Jackson's eviction notices during the removal era of the 1830s, mid-century was a time to lie low. They had already been through the traumas in store for the western tribes. In nonfederal enclaves, mountain hollows, swampy outbacks, or well-nigh invisible

(ABOVE) The arrival of the Nez Perce Indians at the Walla Walla Council of 1855, and (BELOW) Governor Isaac Ingalls Stevens in conference with the Indians to discuss land concessions.

One of the most dignified office-holders during the much-maligned Grant administration was a Seneca Indian from the Wolf clan who was known as "The Reader" to his own people. Born in 1828, Brigadier General Ely Samuel Parker was the son of a Tonawanda Seneca chief from upper New York State, and the grandson of the famous Red Jacket, an orator who opposed white takeover of Iroquois lands.

During Parker's youth those lands were still in contention. After his student years at local schools, Parker encountered Lewis Henry Morgan, a lawyer who was interested in helping the Iroquois protect what diminished acreage they had retained. With Parker's assistance Morgan, who was also an aspiring ethnologist, learned enough about Iroquois social life to write a famous study on the tribe.

With Morgan's encouragement the industrious and highly intelligent Parker attended law school, but was shocked when his Indian identity barred him from being able to practice. Although a native American and a sachem, or political leader, in the Iroquois League (which, some say, had inspired the Founding Fathers) he was still not a U.S. citizen.

Frustrated but nonetheless determined, Parker then put himself through Rensselaer Polytechnic Institute, and used his degree in civil engineering to construct government buildings in Illinois, where he first came to Grant's attention. When the Civil War broke out, Parker hoped to be recruited by the Army Corps of Engineers to fight for the North. Once again, however, the race issue raised its insulting head, as Secretary of State William H. Seward told him to his face, "The fight must be made and settled by the white men alone. Go home, cultivate your farm, and we will settle our own troubles without any Indian aid."

From his farm, however, Parker retained his patriotism, which was rewarded when he received an officer's commission in the Seventh Division. To the end of the war he served closely with Ulysses S. Grant, becoming his military secretary. Parker's penmanship produced the final copy of the surrender agreement that General Robert E. Lee signed at Appomattox. And after Grant assumed the presidency, he appointed his old friend commissioner of Indian Affairs—the first Indian ever to hold that position.

But the Grant administration was the target of ceaseless charges of corruption, some deserved, others not. Parker was charged with fraud. As he recalled in a letter to a close friend, "They made . . . the air foul with their malicious and poisonous accusations. They were defeated, but it was no longer a pleasure to discharge patriotic duties in the face of foul slander and abuse. I gave up a thankless position to enjoy my declining years in peace and quiet." When he died in 1895, Parker was buried alongside his grandfather in Buffalo, New York.

OPPOSITE TOP:
A Seminole woman bathing her child in a riverbank (1930s).

OPPOSITE BOTTOM:
*Daily Life Among Florida's Seminole Women* by Fred Beaver (Creek), 1962.

neighborhoods amidst the settled towns and even cities of the Atlantic seaboard, tiny Indian communities clung to survival and identity using diverse strategies of passive resistance, economic accommodation, and cultural disguise.

Behind log or clapboard walls there still dwelled enclaves of "eastern remnant" native peoples. Bereft of official recognition as tribes for the most part, nonetheless they still told stories of their Little People, still related the miraculous feats of legendary "powwows" (the Algonquian term for medicine men), still made traditional baskets, and even spoke some indigenous languages. Living unobtrusively to avoid the stigma and stereotyping that was attached to being Indian during these years, for the next half-century these groups—some, like the Narragansett and Wampanoag, sizable enough to constitute townships, others, like the Penobscot of Maine and Micmac of Nova Scotia, so substantial as to count themselves as full-fledged tribes—awaited the day when they might proclaim their identities and recover territories as recognized native peoples.

No such delay was necessary, however, for the cluster of Iroquoian-speaking peoples situated along the St. Lawrence River who still proudly proclaimed themselves as the Six Nations, or the Great League of the Iroquois. The fortunes of these Northeast tribes had stabilized after the fearful American retaliation they suffered at the end of the eighteenth century for their allegiance to the British.

Thanks to the redemptive message of their native prophet, Handsome Lake, these "nations" were quietly cohering again as a people.

Through the late nineteenth century, the Iroquoian sense of tribal autonomy would surface with increasing frequency, often to the disgruntlement of central governments in Canada and the United States. After the 1850s, in fact, at least to reading and thinking Americans, the Iroquois League became one of the better-known confederacies due to what might be the country's first anthropological classic, a study of Iroquois kinship by Lewis Henry Morgan, the "father of American anthropology." Actually the work resulted from close collaboration between Morgan and a remarkable Iroquois leader, Ely S. Parker, soon to be General Ulysses S. Grant's aide-de-camp during the Civil War and the nation's first native commissioner of Indian Affairs when Grant assumed the presidency.

Down the Florida peninsula lived offshoots of the former Lower Creek Indian confederacy that by now had gained a tough reputation under the name of Seminoles. Following the Seminole Wars of the 1830s, some had been forcibly removed to Indian Territory, where they occupied a reservation crammed between those of the Creek and the Shawnee. But a few hundred unfettered Seminoles isolated themselves within the subtropical fastness of the cypress and mangrove swamplands, building palm-roofed chickees, or stilt houses, and

# OSCEOLA

Born around 1804, the great Florida Seminole war strategist known as Osceola (or Assiola, "Black Drink Crier") was actually raised as a Creek in Alabama or Georgia. Like the upheavals of earlier Creek Indians a half-century before, which had produced this new Seminole tribe, unrest during the Creek War of 1813–14 drove the boy and his mother to flee for safety to the Florida peninsula. Quite possibly he fought in the First Seminole War of 1817–18, when Andrew Jackson's American troops invaded the Spanish domain ostensibly to recover escaped slaves; one story has the teenager Osceola briefly captured but released due to his youth.

As the United States promptly annexed the peninsula, Osceola was noticed by the hereditary Seminole chiefs who opposed the white American demand for fertile farms, pasture lands, and citrus groves owned by the resident Indians. Although Seminole resistance to the Treaty of Moultrie Creek in 1823 was ultimately broken, and Indians did exchange their prime acreage for hamlets further south, Osceola stood alongside those chiefs who refused to

OSCEOLA.

sign the subsequent Treaties of Payne's Landing (1832) and Fort Gibson (1833). For here they were being asked to quit the region altogether, and remove to Indian Territory within three years.

Osceola's antagonism toward whites became personal; he watched his half-black new wife, the daughter of a Creek chief, torn from his side and clapped in irons by professional slave catchers, who shipped her south.

When he next confronted a treaty demanding Seminole submission to removal, legend has Osceola angrily stabbing a dagger through the document. While the Second Seminole War raged, from 1835 to 1842, Osceola's hit-and-run warriors cost the U.S. government an estimated $20 million, as the Indians established hideaways in the everglade swamps.

Finally lured from hiding under a flag of truce in October 1837, Osceola was captured and hastily imprisoned in South Carolina, where he died of disease or poison three months later. His head was cut off and put on display in the Fort Moultrie "Medical Museum." After his death, the fighting continued, and many Seminoles were in fact removed to Indian Territory.

By the late 1850s, after the so-called Third Seminole War, fewer than two hundred Seminoles still occupied the southern Seminole wilderness. But there they clung, and—intermarrying with other Indian holdouts—they survived to become the founders of the Seminole and Miccosukee Indian settlements where their descendants still live today.

---

surviving on hunting and fishing. Their resistence had already cost the U.S. government fifteen hundred soldiers and an estimated $50 million, and they continued to maintain a war footing with Washington (a status that, officially at least, would obtain into the twentieth century).

Other pockets of quiet Indian endurance dotted the byways of the Old South. In Mississippi the Choctaw and Hooma survived by old-time subsistence practices and service work for local whites. In the tangled chestnut forests of the Great Smoky Mountains of North Carolina, in communities like Snowbird and Big Cove, Cherokees who had managed to avoid the removal sweeps still played old-fashioned stickball and visited their medicine men for plant cures even as most of them were acclimatizing to their own hybrid form of Christianity, complete with hymns written in the Cherokee syllabary.

In the Indian Territory across the Mississippi, the Indian Appropriation Act of 1851 legalized as official reservations those areas where the removal policies of the 1830s had forcibly resettled southeastern tribes. But that was by no means

OPPOSITE TOP:
*United States Marines Penetrating the Everglades* by John Clymer. Marines battle Indians during the Seminole Wars in Florida, 1835–42.

OPPOSITE BOTTOM:
An 1843 illustration shows Indians in Florida being hunted with bloodhounds.

the end of using Indian Territory as a sort of concentration camp for unwanted, dislodged, or belligerent tribes. By peaceful treaty or under armed guard, Indian Territory would receive bands or whole tribes representing fifty different native cultures before and after the Civil War.

North of Indian Territory, inhabiting the sprawling grasslands between the Mississippi and the Rockies, relatively recent immigrants to the Plains had established a brand-new, horse-based lifestyle. These were the Plains tribes, whose colorful image as warbonneted, bead-decorated freewheelers of the open prairies was already signifying THE INDIAN—alternately cast either as the "Bloodthirsty Savage" or the "Noble Red Man"—to avid consumers of popular fiction about the American West, who could already be found around the world. By the first half of the nineteenth century these new Plains residents, emboldened by their acquisition of horses, had developed high-spirited raiding patterns against each other to build up their horse herds, to establish warrior reputations, and, for some tribes, to aggressively expand their territory.

Thus an early government initiative on the Great Plains sought to quell this boiling cauldron of intertribal warfare, spirited independence and native expansionism. For this task the services of the current agent for the Upper Platte and Arkansas Indian agency were absolutely indispensable. Thomas "Broken Hand" Fitzpatrick was a fifty-two-year-old frontier legend, one of the famous mountain men of the Rocky Mountain fur trade since he arrived west in the 1820s, and he knew Indians well. Upon his invitation, about ten thousand tribesmen, drawn from the Sioux, Cheyenne, Arapaho, Crow, Gros Ventres, Assiniboine, Arikara, and Shoshone nations, convened at Fort Laramie in southeastern Wyoming in September 1851.

Although many of the participants were traditional enemies, the mammoth peace conference was among seemingly the last benign diplomatic rendezvous that government officials and the then-still-powerful western tribes would ever enjoy. Fitzpatrick's delegation of 270 nervous soldiers was vastly outnumbered, huge piles of presents were distributed to all comers, and the resulting treaty demarcated tribal domains for the first time, so as to lessen fears for the white pioneers rolling through.

While goodwill abounded, however, some Indians still saw the handwriting on the wall. "You have split my land and I don't like it," complained one Sioux chief at the sessions. "These lands once belonged to the Kiowas and the Crows, but we whipped these nations out of them, and in this we did what the white men do when they want the lands of the Indians."

Portrait of an Indian named Three Horses, photographed in 1905 by Edward S. Curtis, who compiled one of the most extensive catalogs of Indian images during the thirty years he spent documenting the life and culture of the Indian tribes west of the Mississippi River.

OPPOSITE:
*The Death of Jane McCrea*
by John Vanderlyn, 1804, was one of many depictions of an actual killing that took place on July 27, 1777, when a young New England woman wandered beyond the confines of Fort Edwards, New York. Stories such as these, which portrayed barbaric natives committing grisly acts, fed popular taste at the time and often served to justify white hostility toward Indians and the appropriation of their homelands.

# CHAPTER NINETEEN

# EMBROILED IN THE WHITE MAN'S WAR 1861–1865

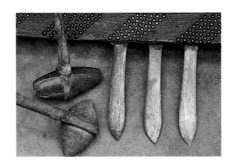

SIOUX WAR CLUBS

## April 1861

AS ALBERT PIKE STRODE into the plantation home of John Ross, the two men were a study in contrast. Pike, a Boston-born planter and lawyer, weighed close to three hundred pounds, and fairly burst with sheer physical size, boiling energy, and a lusty vanity so flamboyant that it pleased him occasionally to don the full panoply of Plains Indian attire: hide leggings, beaded moccasins, and feathered headdress. But now he was on an urgent and serious mission—to recruit the Indian Territory tribes to the pro-slavery cause.

Ross was part Cherokee, almost twenty-five years older than Pike, and at five and a half feet quite dwarfed by his ebullient guest. In waistcoat and tie, however, he looked every inch the wealthy, slave-owning, cultured politician and member of the landed gentry. Indeed, his colonial mansion, "Rose Cottage," could easily house forty guests. Ross was one of many important Indians with whom Pike had amicable relationships. For the moment, however, the two powerful men stood warily on opposite sides of the political fence: Pike had arrived with a wagon train of gifts and a promise of $100,000 to recruit the many thousand members of the Five Civilized Tribes (Creek, Chickasaw, Cherokee, Choctaw, and Seminole) in order to defend the Confederacy's western boundary. Ross, a veteran of the unsuccessful resistance against the federal government over removal thirty years

The Battle of Pea Ridge, Arkansas, in March 1862 saw the First Cherokee Regiment, led by Stand Watie, the First Cherokee Mounted Rifles, under Colonel John Drew, and the First Choctaw-Chickasaw Regiment, under Major O. G. Welch, assisting the Confederates against the Union Army.

## JOHN ROSS

It is doubly ironic that at twenty-three, this part-Cherokee soldier, whose keen strategy during the 1813 Battle of Horseshoe Bend is said to have won General Andrew Jackson's fight against the Creek Indians, would later find himself Jackson's bitter enemy, with his people suffering the same forced removal from their homelands as his old Creek foes. The remarkable John Ross, born of a Scot father and a part-Cherokee mother in 1790, was educated at white schools, but was perhaps the fiercest advocate for native Cherokee land and civil rights of his day.

After the Creek War, when Cherokees established their independent government, Ross became a member of its National Council. His obvious leadership talents propelled him to chiefly status by 1828. By then it was clear that no amount of accommodation to, or imitation of, white ways would protect the Cherokees from the anti-Indian sentiments that prevailed in state and federal governments alike. Resisting efforts to yield their rich plantation lands, Ross's followers took their case against the state of Georgia—which now officially dubbed them "tenants"—to the U.S. Supreme Court. Over the years Ross also pleaded the Cherokee case with leading politicians, winning over Henry Clay of Kentucky, David Crockett and Sam Houston of Tennessee, Daniel Webster and Edward Everett of Massachusetts, and Henry Wise of Virginia, among others. Despite such support, however, and the resounding Cherokee victory in the Supreme Court, President Jackson virtually ignored them all. The so-called Five Civilized Tribes, the vast majority of Cherokees among them, were forced on the greatest wholesale ethnic relocation in American history.

Following that ordeal, however, Cherokee trials were not over, and Ross remained in the thick of readjusting his people to their new eastern Oklahoma country. He participated in the drafting of a new constitution, and was again named chief, in 1839.

The Civil War presented Ross, himself a slaveowner, with a new challenge. As with removal, the slavery issue bitterly divided Cherokees. And while the war clouds were dissipating, Ross continued serving his people, dying in Washington on August 1, 1866, in his thirty-eighth year as principal chief, on a mission to watchdog one more threat to Cherokee rights.

before, was at this point leaning strongly toward the majority faction of his tribe, which sided with the North.

Prospects for this new national conflict were also pitting Ross against his old antagonist, the long-haired Stand Watie, known as Degataga, or "Standing Together" to his people, a stalwart supporter of the Confederacy.

As rumors of war flashed across Indian Territory in the late 1850s, many among the resettled tribes whose cultural lifeways were steeped in Deep South traditions sympathized with the Confederate cause. "In the event a permanent dissolution of the American Union takes place," the Choctaw National Council decided in early February 1861, "we shall be left to follow the . . . destiny of our neighbors and brethren of the Southern States." That same month, the breakaway Confederacy dispatched Pike to negotiate treaties with Indian Territory tribes. While the Choctaw and Chickasaw presented a nearly unanimous backing for the South, and soon summoned a regiment of ten companies, the Cherokee remained painfully divided on the issue, which left lasting scars within their communities.

To Pike, the dignified Ross expressed his people's desire to pursue a middle road, even as inwardly he realized that neutrality was a luxury few Territory

## STAND WATIE

A rather small man of strong, taut build, with wishbone legs from years on horseback; a man of a few explosively direct words; a man with an "Indian-looking" mien and absolutely fearless, known to his own people as Degataga, "the immovable," and to outsiders as Brigadier General Stand Watie of the Confederate Army—this was the archrival of John Ross.

Watie, sixteen years younger than Ross, had defied him once during the tribe's divisive internal debate over President Jackson's removal policy during the 1830s. A member of the Deer clan, Watie sided with his "progressive"-minded relatives of the so-called Ridge faction that agreed in 1835 to sign the government's controversial Treaty of New Echota, in which the tribe submitted to removal. In tribal councils in Indian Territory after removal, Watie and Ross often exchanged bitter words as they took opposite sides on many issues.

During the Civil War, however, Watie spoke mostly with deeds. His

legendary leadership of two companies of Cherokee Mounted Rifles saw his swift-raiding men fight in more battles than any other unit in the western theater of the war.

Given the freedom to turn his guerrilla skills where he saw fit, Watie managed to take personal revenge on Ross. While most of his pro-Confederacy tribesmen were in retreat from vengeful Union soldiers, he slipped his horsemen past the enemy lines to destroy the Cherokee capital at Tahlequah, in eastern Indian Territory, and put John Ross's famous Rose Cottage to the torch.

Seven months later his guerrillas captured a Union stern-wheeler supplying Fort Gibson across the Arkansas, and three months after that, with a consortium of Cherokee, Creek, and Seminole Confederate guerrillas, they descended by moonlight on a Union mule train. Indian Territory would never again witness such a Confederate victory.

When Watie finally rode into Doaksville in Indian Territory to lay down his arms to federal officers on June 23, 1865, it was a historic moment—the final Confederate holdout had surrendered and the Civil War, in the West at least, was over. Watie outlived Ross, dying at home at Honey Creek on September 9, 1871.

---

Indians could afford. If Ross and his Cherokees were split over Northern interests and their old allegiances to the South of their original homelands, so were the Creeks, and many others. And many would have preferred not to have to participate in the white man's war at all.

Yet, in the end, old rivalries in the ranks of Cherokee leadership stood Pike's cause in good stead, as Ross ran a sudden end run around his opponents during a climactic council to decide the issue, held at the Cherokee headquarters in Tahlequah. Surprising many of his assembled tribespeople, Ross declared, "Our general interest is inseparable from theirs [the Confederacy] and it is not desirable that we should stand alone." To establish a southern Plains protective zone between its forces and the Union, the Confederacy then negotiated looser treaties with southern Plains tribes.

But there was disaffection even in those tribes that were under active Northern control. From the new federal reservations of the West disturbing stories were leaking out about corruption by the very reservation agents who were delegated to domesticate Indians. In fact, the first generation of American Indian agents knew little about Indians and usually cared less. As one confessed in 1852, "Indian agents . . . are generally appointed for political services. Few of us are by

*Battle at Warbonnet Creek*
by Frederic Remington. In 1876, Dull Knife's large force of Northern Cheyenne was run down by the U.S. Cavalry as it attempted to reach the Powder River country where Sitting Bull and Crazy Horse were encamped.

nature better fitted to be an Indian agent . . . [and] have never seen an Indian." Presiding over a nation divided on whether to treat Indians humanely or to kill them off, President Lincoln sided with the humanists even while clearly advocating western settlement.

On the one hand, he promised that when the Civil War was over he would decisively eradicate graft within the Indian Bureau by rooting out those politicized Indian agents and their cronies in Washington and in the field—collectively known as the "Indian Ring"—who pocketed monies earmarked for Indian supplies. On the other hand, in 1862 he enthusiastically signed the Homestead Act, which inevitably brought pressure on reservations from whites clamoring for land. (A special Indian Homestead Act would be passed in 1875, encouraging Indians who had "abandoned tribal relations" to develop their individual spreads on unclaimed public lands.)

A year after the outbreak of the Civil War, the federal government was distracted by the August 1862 uprising of Eastern Sioux in western Minnesota. While hundreds of whites fled for safety to Fort Ridgely, when the tally of dead was taken, some four hundred Minnesota settlers had perished in attacks on isolated homesteads, settlements, and trading posts, leaving the state in turmoil.

At first even President Lincoln suspected that the killings were the result of a secret conspiracy of western tribes to assist his Southern antagonists. Then it became clear that this was an independent uprising. Long-simmering resentment over arrogant trespassing by homesteaders and gross corruption by agents and traders had touched off the killing of five settlers by four young Sioux hunters whose action, in turn, had sparked the series of raids. The short-lived Eastern Sioux War, led by a man known as Red Nation to his own people, Little Crow to the whites, ended with the brisk crushing of the Indians and the largest mass hanging in American history, as thirty-eight Indians—freedom fighters to their people, rebels to the whites—were executed on a freezing December morning.

This outbreak was a double omen: it anticipated the succession of bloody clashes between whites and Plains Indians—featuring the Sioux tribes—that would not cease until 1890, and, in its aftermath, it foretold the ultimate cost of Indian resistance as it provided the excuse for removing both the implicated Sioux as well as the uninvolved Winnebago to reservations farther west while homesteaders flooded into their Minnesota lands.

In the early years of the Civil War, hit-and-run marauding and full-scale battles flared between North and South throughout the Midwest. Indian Territory, that huge refugee camp for so many removed tribes, was not spared. Battles such as Honey Springs, Cabin Creek, and Prairie Grove, and incessant skirmishes in which Indian fought against Indian, devastated the territory; those who tried to remain neutral were caught in the crossfire. The bitterness of Civil War allowed no safe havens.

Meanwhile, the Indian horsemen led by Stand Watie served the Confederacy with distinction. In 1862 Watie was at the Battle of Pea Ridge, as a colonel under the command of General Pike—that same oversized Albert Pike, lawyer and poet turned military man, who had recruited so many Indians to the Confederacy, including a reluctant John Ross.

As troops were drained from the West to build strength in the East much of the northern Plains was left underprotected. This was no disappointment to some Indian tribes who construed the temporary absence of white military as a terminal victory. However, placing local volunteer troops on a quasi-military footing actually had the effect of strengthening the nation's punitive skills for the Indian wars just ahead.

Few troops were needed, in fact, to control Indians in California, where, far from the national bloodbath, native Americans were reeling from the combined sieges of epidemic disease and human cruelty that continued to destroy one community after another.

White visitors to Indian rancherias in the 1860s were aghast at the native suffering; in northern California, Charles Pancoast, a Quaker visiting the Hupa people, was shown a grove of trees and told that under each one lay the bones of many Indians who recently had died of cholera. And at the state's southern end, Albert Evans, visiting a Cahuilla village, overheard a smallpox survivor cry out, "The curse of the white man is upon us!"

Indians in the eye of this storm, the gold-rich foothills, eventually began to seek a spiritual rather than violent remedy to their desperation. In the early

Portrait of Little Crow, a Sioux chief, illustrated by Charles Bird King in 1824.

An 1864 recruitment poster promises volunteers "all horses and other plunder taken from the Indians."

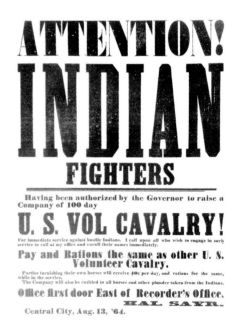

As the Civil War demanded fresh troop reinforcements, forts near vulnerable settlements up and down the western fringe were emptied of their protective soldiery. To fill the vacuum, many communities, states, and territories organized and armed their own citizenry. These undisciplined irregulars generally hated Indians and often overreacted to any Indian provocation.

Between 1862 and 1865, the number of these volunteer forces rose from fifteen to twenty thousand men. Along the Texas frontier, where response to Indian resistance was especially swift and harsh, the irregular Confederate regiments were joined by locals with a rough and ready "minuteman" mentality.

In the far west of Nevada and Utah territories and eastern Oregon, the Civil War drain on troops initially saw regional militias such as Mormon citizen companies and the Humboldt County "Star Rangers" organized to protect stagecoaches carrying mailbags and wagon trains bearing emigrant families. But soon more forceful western volunteers from California mobilized into cavalry and infantry units.

When such units joined up with western Confederate forces, as happened when the Apache-fighting Arizona Guards were absorbed by Lieutenant Colonel John R. Baylor's command in 1862, it meant the native Americans faced two bitter enemies, no matter whether they were officially involved in the white man's war or not.

Baylor, who was once charged with killing Indians with poisoned flour, expressed local sentiment when he called for exterminating all adult Apaches and selling their children "to defray the expense of killing the Indians."

1870s, as the death toll mounted and personal tragedies multiplied from cruelty and dislocation wrought by miners, ranchers, new diseases, and loss of habitats, a wave of native prophets began preaching apocalyptic messages of redemption. The so-called California Ghost Dances, foreshadowing the better-known Plains Indian Ghost Dance by twenty years, were less a single doctrine promulgated by one charismatic individual than a contagious message of divine hope that was reinterpreted by local curers and shamans in hamlet after hamlet throughout north-central California. Its basic message was that true believers who danced, prayed, and received visions of their dead relatives would experience a world purged by fire or flood, after which whites would be gone and Indian life would be better than ever.

It is hard to guess how governmental handling of tribes might have developed had Lincoln not been assassinated. If his treatment of the Pueblos provides any clue, tribal sovereignty might actually have been invigorated. For in 1863, the president publicly repaid the Pueblos for their assistance during the Civil War, when they had volunteered scouts and couriers, by ordering silver-crowned canes of office presented as a formal gift to each village, carrying on a tradition begun by the Spanish. Today these "Lincoln canes" are treasured symbols for each pueblo, embodying its "deed" to territorial and cultural sovereignty.

To the Pueblos' neighbors, however, those still free-ranging bands of Apaches, the Lincoln administration extended no such political favors, as Apache armed defiance of American authority was unrelenting throughout the Civil War period. Western Apache marauders struck against white settlers and defied whatever federal troops were available to subdue them. Knowledgeable of terrain by night or day, trained to endurance and stealth from boyhood, the Chiricahua and Mimbreño fighters consistently outfoxed their Union pursuers. Aside from their general antipathy for the miners and pioneers encroaching on their lands, and their resistance to attempts to halt their raids in Mexico, the Apache would soon have personal reasons, as well, for resenting Americans.

## The Apache

At no time after 1500 did all the Apache tribes together exceed six thousand people (excluding the Navajo who, before that, had broken away and developed a wholly separate culture). First occupying the southern Plains, by 1500 the Apache had become mountain and desert dwellers, their loosely shifting population of some three dozen major bands ranging locally over territory that extended from what are now the southern borders of New Mexico and Arizona up as far as Colorado. In central Apache country, the heart of Arizona, the people lived largely off wild foods—mescal, beans, acorns, prickly pear, sunflower seeds, piñon nuts among others—as well as hunting and some farming. The bands east of the Rio Grande relied more on buffalo. All habitually raided the most likely sources —Tonkawa, Pima, or (later) the Spaniards, New Mexicans, and Pueblos—for captives and livestock. And many Apaches were slaves both in Spanish settlements and in New Mexico.

The Apache were independent, untouchable, even unseeable, men and women so at home in their wild habitat that the "White-eyes" (their name for the invading Europeans) had trouble even detecting their presence. Moreover, an Apache man or woman could walk forty miles a day—day after day—and on horseback could cover seventy miles if necessary, knowing a remount was easily obtained from the nearest ranch. These qualities made Apaches formidable enemies, as was well known.

It was therefore particularly ill-advised for some gold miners to take offense at an older Apache who was near their camp, and, in order to discourage him, tie the man up and lash his back to ribbons. His name was Mangas Coloradas; he was sixty years old and an important Mimbreño Apache chief, holding kinship ties with the chiefs of the White Mountain and Chiricahua bands. Coloradas had been a peaceable man.

Similarly, Cochise, chief of the Chiricahua, and son-in-law to Coloradas, was at peace with the Americans, even helping them build a station at Apache Pass, the white man's gateway to the West. Then an over-eager lieutenant attempted to "arrest" him on a false charge. With a hidden knife, Cochise slit the army tent where he was being held and escaped. He and Mangas Coloradas set out to wage a fairly successful wipeout campaign against white settlements. During the Civil War, Arizona was almost swept clean of non-Indians.

After the Civil War, a policy of extermination was set in motion, carried out by General James H. Carleton, with three thousand volunteer Californians, plus miners, and returning settlers. The Papagos and Pimas, long enemies of the Apache, were now offered arms and expenses to kill as many as possible. (At one time, earlier on, an Apache scalp was worth $250.) As simple extermination was the object, all methods of killing were acceptable: under flags of truce, with traps,

*Cochise's Wrath*
by William Sampson, Jr. (Creek).

*Apache Devil Dancers* by Wilson Dewey (San Carlos Apache), ca. 1946. Also known as the Mountain Spirit Dance, the ritual depicted above is intended to protect Apache people. The painting shows Mescalero Apaches, dressed in black cloth masks and wooden headdresses, performing during a traditional puberty ceremony.

by hostage taking, and by deception—and including women and children.

As Apache bands withdrew to their mountain hideaways, their lives became increasingly precarious. But they continued to raid, and Apache country remained the most dangerous frontier for white settlers and travelers. Ten years of extermination policy, a thousand American lives, and some $40 million later, the government decided to try a peace policy, and sent in General George Crook to conciliate. Crook was a man of uncompromising honesty, one the Apaches quickly learned they could trust. He employed Apache scouts to mediate and negotiate with hostiles, and by 1874 he had brought most Apaches onto reservations. Even Cochise agreed to a truce for a while.

But once Crook departed, the agreements, as usual, were abrogated, and living conditions on reservations were allowed to become untenable. For another fifteen years, there were sudden breakouts, led notably by Geronimo, Victorio, and an ancient named Nana (he walked with a cane) who, with fifteen Chiricahua followers, led a thousand American troops and a frantic countryside on a wild chase for two months.

Outside of Apacheria, the toll of the Civil War on Indians was especially harsh in Indian Territory. Native homesteads were torched, food granaries were pilfered, and barns were robbed of their livestock by nonuniformed guerrillas. Some families sympathetic to the South sought sanctuary in the Red River region near Texas, while those backing the Union fled to Kansas.

For siding with the Confederacy, the Five Civilized Tribes were punished by losing the western portion of their lands, which were henceforth assigned to dislocated Indians from Kansas and other states. Nor, from their weakened position, could these tribes present any opposition to a raft of new treaties demanding land rights for railroads and new forts to garrison the increased military force needed to quell still rebellious southern Plains tribes.

But Indian casualties were not limited to those who chose sides in the white man's war. Even before the peace was signed at Appomattox in 1865 the fate of a band of peaceful Cheyenne Indians camped at Sand Creek in eastern Colorado suggested that Indian lives were not worth much on the ever westward shifting frontier. When the Colorado territorial governor ordered all native groups within his jurisdiction to collect at military forts, a Cheyenne chief named Black Kettle complied. After living on government rations at Fort Lyon for a while, the Cheyennes were instructed to shift their camp to Sand Creek, some thirty miles from the military post, where they could hunt for themselves.

There, on a late November dawn in 1864, seven hundred Colorado troops under Colonel John M. Chivington descended without warning upon a sleeping camp of men, women, and children. Quickly Black Kettle ran up an American flag and a small white banner, but to no avail. Babies and mothers, warriors and grandparents—all were slaughtered with bullet and bayonet for more than two hours until over a hundred Indian bodies, three-fourths of them women and children, were strewn along the stream.

And Sand Creek was but one of a number of atrocities as the cycle of postwar Indian raids, retaliatory military expeditions, and occasional outright massacres flared up throughout the West. Four years later Black Kettle's tragically diminished group suffered what was almost a repeat performance of the Sand Creek

Mangus, the son of Apache war chief Mangas Coloradas, photographed around 1884, a year after he gave up his life as a raider and settled down on the San Carlos reservation, where he was soon joined by Geronimo's band.

In 1885, however, Mangus, Geronimo, and several other Apache leaders led their followers away from San Carlos and returned to Mexico and their Sierra Madre stronghold. Once again in 1886, Mangus and his small band surrendered without resistance. They were sent to Fort Marion in Florida to join other Apache prisoners, including Geronimo.

*When I was young I walked all over this country, east and west, and saw no other people than the Apaches. After many summers I walked again and found another race of people had come to take it. How is it? Why is it that the Apaches wait to die—that they carry their lives on the fingernails? They roam over the hills and plains and want the heavens to fall on them. The Apaches were once a great nation; they are now but few, and because of this they want to die and so carry their lives on their fingernails.*

—COCHISE
(Chiricahua Apache), 1872

We have photographs of many famous warrior chiefs, but a few—the mysterious Sioux leader Crazy Horse and the great Chiricahua Apache Cochise—escaped the camera's eye. Based on fragmentary accounts of his deeds, Cochise, whose name meant "hardwood" in his own language, was a formidable and charismatic leader.

Born around 1812 in southern Arizona, initially Cochise was not unfriendly toward Americans trickling into the Southwest in the 1850s. In fact, in 1856 Cochise personally negotiated with a U.S. Army major to permit California-bound travelers to pass through Apache land. Then things changed. As Cochise himself is said to have recalled, years later, "When I was young I walked all over this country, east and west, and saw no other people than the Apaches. After many summers I walked again and found another race of people had come to take it."

The events of 1861—the false accusation that Cochise had stolen a child, his arrest, and escape—quickly escalated into bloodshed, with Apaches killing three whites and the army retaliating by executing Apache warriors. Eventually Cochise and his father-in-law, Mangas Coloradas, sealed off Apache Pass, whereupon General James Carleton's American irregular troops, several thousand strong and dragging deadly howitzers, showed up to reopen it. At first the Apache force of five hundred warriors staved off the California volunteers but their ordnance and their numbers proved too strong. More importantly, Mangas had been severely wounded.

Cochise carried him a hundred miles south, to a doctor in Mexico, where he recovered. In 1863, attempting a truce and supposedly under the protection of a white flag, Mangas was seized. By now an old man in his seventies, he was tortured by his guards who held heated bayonets to his feet and shot him to death for "attempted escape." Cochise was left to lead the rebellious Apaches in sporadic raids from his hideout somewhere in the impenetrable Dragoon Mountains, of which he said, "I have drunk of these waters and they have cooled me: I do not want to leave here." Nevertheless, he did so, in September of 1871, in an attempt to bring about a truce. Even though he had surrendered, when Cochise got wind that the Americans were planning to move his people to a new reservation in Tularosa, New Mexico, he broke for freedom again, with two hundred tribespeople, and six hundred more Apaches shortly following. Only when General Oliver O. Howard promised that the Chiricahua could remain in Arizona did Cochise give up for good. After he died on June 8, 1874, his body was secretly buried in a craggy area known today as the Cochise Stronghold.

*Nothing lives long.*
*Only the earth and the mountains.*

—Death song sung by White
   Antelope (Cheyenne) before
   he died at Sand Creek, 1864.

massacre when Lieutenant Colonel George Armstrong Custer's Seventh Cavalry fell upon their tipis, pitched along the Washita River in western Indian Territory. Again women and children, perhaps 40 all told, were slaughtered, with many men and Black Kettle himself dying alongside them. But when warriors from neighboring Comanche, Kiowa, and Arapaho villages came to the rescue, Custer rapidly withdrew, leaving 19 troopers who had been sent prisoner-hunting to their bloody fate.

This was Custer's first major "engagement" with Indians.

In January 1870, federal troops launched a similar surprise attack in Montana upon another nonbelligerent Blackfeet encampment, leaving 173 men, women, and children dead in the snow. The following year, in Camp Grant in Arizona Territory, 85 Apaches—mostly women and children—were killed by ordinary citizens eagerly joined by Papago warriors, traditional enemies of the Apache.

The Indian response to these tragedies was predictable. One southern Plains leader put their feelings into words, "What do we have to live for? The white man has taken our country, killed our game, was not satisfied with that, but killed our wives and children. Now, no peace. We have raised this battle ax to the death!" Following the Sand Creek massacre, the central Plains were aflame again, with Indian war parties tearing into vulnerable ranches and farms and committing their own atrocities. Such raiding, in turn, inspired greater vigilantism and telegrams calling for troop reinforcement.

At the same time, the reports in eastern newspapers of such brutalities as the Sand Creek and Camp Grant massacres aroused a humanitarian outcry. From the Atlantic seaboard came magazine editorials and speeches castigating frontier folk as barbarians and ruffians, while western newspapers saw this reaction as rank sentimentality from high-falutin liberals who loved Indians without knowing anything about them. This split in popular attitude was echoed in the polarized governmental policies, the swing between assimilationist "peace" and militaristic "force" approaches, which would vie for dominance until 1890.

*Sand Creek Battle* by Robert Lindneux, **1936. In the early dawn of November 29, 1864, Colonel John M. Chivington led the attack on a village of Cheyenne and Arapahos at Sand Creek.**

# CHAPTER TWENTY

# BETWEEN VIOLENCE AND BENEVOLENCE 1865–1879

INDIAN AGENTS GROW RICH WHILE INDIANS
RECEIVE "STARVATION" RATIONS, FROM AN 1890 CARTOON

## August 1865

THE NAVAJO HEADMAN known as Atsidi Sani ("Old Metal Smith") to his own people, and Herrero Delgadito to the U.S. officers who were imprisoning him, was a natural choice for conferring with the visiting dignitaries from Washington who were investigating rumors of horrendous living conditions at the Bosque Redondo, a reservation in southeastern New Mexico where over eight thousand Navajos, a major portion of the tribe, were being held against their will. Born around 1830, Herrero was a member of the Black Sheep People clan. He was twenty-eight years old when his people appointed him a major spokesperson for dealing with the white officials who were moving into the newly built Fort Wingate. Herrero had even signed an 1858 agreement with the United States promising not to make trouble; a white-designated "headman," however, his word probably meant little to other Navajo clansmen hundreds of miles away.

On this day Herrero was especially despondent, for, as he told the Senate investigators, his people were "dying as though they were shooting at them with a rifle." He himself had just lost three sons and two daughters to disease. "Some of the soldiers do not treat us well," Hererro complained. He described the ravages

---

*Attack at Dawn* by Charles Schreyvogel, 1904. In 1868, George Custer led the
Seventh Cavalry on a morning raid into Black Kettle's camp of sleeping Cheyenne.

Frank Starrs TEN CENT American Novels Number 139.

THE FIGHTING TRAPPER,
KIT CARSON TO THE RESCUE.

The American News Company. New York

Kit Carson (TOP). His exploits as a trapper inevitably resulted in his becoming a tabloid hero of the times, as in this Albert Johannson cover from *Frank Starrs American Novels* (ABOVE).

OPPOSITE: *Evicting the Navajos from Canyon de Chelly* by Narda Lebo. Carson led the assault that forced the Navajos to abandon their traditional homelands and ended with the destruction of all their property, including their cherished orchard of peach trees.

of venereal disease, alkaline water that caused stomach cramps, spoiled food, and the depression of being cooped up so far from their piñon and juniper uplands on the distant Colorado Plateau to the west.

The previous year had seen a ruthless burn-and-imprison campaign against the Navajo led by Colonel Christopher "Kit" Carson and his Ute mercenaries, traditional enemies of the Navajo. To punish them for cattle rustling and general marauding against new Anglo-American settlers, Carson was ordered by General James H. Carleton (over protests from both the Indian Bureau and Carson himself) to consolidate the entire body of Navajo clans to the arid lowlands of southeastern New Mexico, thereby forcing them "to abandon their nomadic, marauding way of life, to settle on a reservation away from their cherished mountain homes, and to devote themselves to the pursuit of industry as their means of support." Carleton was unpopular even among his own men, and in trouble throughout the Civil War. A stickler for protocol, extreme in his views, he was almost a caricature of the tyrannical military martinet.

Rounding up the dispersed Navajo from desert canyons and rimrock caves had consumed Carson during the winter of 1863–64, as his manhunters searched and destroyed their isolated hogan encampments. At the Canyon de Chelly, troops hacked down two to three thousand peach trees; three hundred men attacked the many cornfields. Having destroyed what they could not carry away, they confiscated flocks of sheep and herds of cattle, leaving a barren waste in place of a prosperous community. On the infamous trek still seared into Navajo memory as "The Long Walk," the tribe was escorted by armed troops to the Bosque Redondo. There it was General Carleton's vision that the Navajos, under watch from the garrison at Fort Sumner, would turn inside out, changing from raiders and heathens into settled Christians.

However, as Herrero's testimony implied, this transformation never took place. At Fort Sumner, the Navajo families resisted concentrated housing, preferring their own dugout shelters with brush roofs. Refusing to cultivate crops, they did accept training in carpentry, leatherwork, and metalsmithing. The fort hospital held special terror for them: "All who go in," said Herrero, "never come out." They preferred their own curing rituals, despite the army's ban on them. So while soldiers and others sought to turn the Navajos into whites, the Indians prayed only for release from this living hell. And isolated bands remained free, or slipped away from the fort to pursue their own form of guerrilla warfare.

Even before this experience, Herrero's life had been affected by white culture; he was the earliest silversmith of preeminence among his people, learning ironsmithing in the early 1850s and then crafting horse bridles from beaten-out Mexican silver coins. Although also known as a ritual chanter, his place in history derives from his contribution to the beautiful and, eventually, lucrative techniques and designs of Navajo silverwork. The resistence of Herrero and his fellow headmen to their abysmal conditions at Fort Sumner eventually helped to end that experiment in cultural conversion. In 1868 he was among the Navajo tribal leaders who signed a major treaty that granted the tribe the largest reservation in the United States, back in their old hunting and corn-growing grounds. But after the Navajo survivors retraced their long walk back home, they mourned almost a quarter of the tribe who had died during the entire Fort Sumner ordeal.

# WALK IN BEAUTY

Until the 1870s the Navajo had a reputation for banditry, raiding into Mexico, as well as among the Pueblos and Spanish colonials of New Mexico. At the same time, many hundreds of Navajo women and children were numbered among the slaves in the New Mexico settlements, so the raiding could not have been one-way.

The Navajo shared a much changed but Athapaskan-based language with the Apache, and they called themselves Diné, or Dineh, the People. They had few permanent settlements, living for the most part in movable, extended family-and-clan village groups in their spectacular homeland of high skies, brilliant ocher buttes, mesas, painted desert, and the occasional deep canyon that might allow the planting of peach trees. Spanish and Pueblo captives made them a varied people and favored a high population—their numbers exceeded all the other Apache tribes put together.

The Spanish settlements also yielded sheep whose value the Navajo quickly learned to appreciate. They became skilled sheepherders and their women learned to weave magnificent blankets. Their lives were permeated with religious feeling, with an exuberant joy in the richness of living; they believed in the Beauty Way. One of the sacred songs of their chanting tradition strongly images their identification with harmony and beauty:

*Now I walk with Talking God*
*With goodness and beauty in all things*
  *around me I go;*
*With goodness and beauty I follow*
  *immortality.*
*Thus being I, I go.*

After the four bitter years at Bosque Redondo, the Navajos were returned to part of their native lands, along with thirty-five thousand sheep and goats, so that they might take up sheepherding again. This they were able to do, albeit with years of hardship and struggle. Their religious dedication to the beauty of life never changed and became known to the world through the unique designs of their weaving and their exquisite silversmithing.

*Navajo Washing Hair* by Harrison Begay (Navajo), 1949.

## The Great Treaty-Making Boondoggle

The Navajo treaty of 1868 had resolved one major Indian headache, so government officials hoped more diplomacy that same year would ease the Indian situation in the northern Plains caused by the Red Cloud War along the Powder River and consequent Indian outbursts. As the U.S. Indian Bureau regrouped after the debilitating Civil War, a slew of peace delegations forayed among Plains Indian tribes to hassle over the wording of new treaties, whose intended consequences were clear in the minds of the white diplomats if intentionally vague as communicated to Indian leaders. At this time the U.S. government, economically exhausted by the War Between the States, was discussing whether to "feed Indians or fight them." So-called Friends of the Indian argued that at a probable cost of a hundred thousand troops and an estimated $1 billion it was far more practical to try the treaty approach, which had clear budgetary advantages as well as being the Christian thing to do.

First, these treaties inevitably asked for a restriction of the Indian land base to reservations, with promises of rations and presents always held out to sweeten the pill of this obvious loss of freedom. Second, in these post–Civil War treaties, white peacemakers acquiesed to Indians hunting in their traditional ways, so long as they did not turn their weapons on whites—yet privately they were not unhappy that the extinction of the buffalo would shortly deprive the Indians of this ancient source of life. Third, these treaties established the necessary conditions for changing Indians into model whites, and in certain cases for eligibility as U.S. citizens (the irony of possibly bestowing citizenship upon the country's native inhabitants appears to have escaped the participants).

The treaty approach, overall, finally united those whites who thought they were helping Indians with those who only desired Indian lands. Thus the stage was set for an ultimate assault against Indian sovereignty—the eventual

LEFT:
U.S. Indian Peace Commissioners at Fort Laramie, Wyoming, 1868. Left to right: Generals Alfred H. Terry, William S. Harney, and William Tecumseh Sherman, a Sioux woman, John B. Sanborn, Samuel F. Tappan, and General Christopher C. Augur.

RIGHT:
General Sherman and Indian commissioners meet with Sioux leaders at Fort Laramie.

*My heart is as a stone; there is no soft spot in it. I have taken the white man by the hand, thinking him to be a friend, but he is not a friend; government has deceived us; Washington is rotten.*

—Statement made by Kicking Bird (Kiowa) after the U.S. violated the Treaty of Medicine Lodge in 1873.

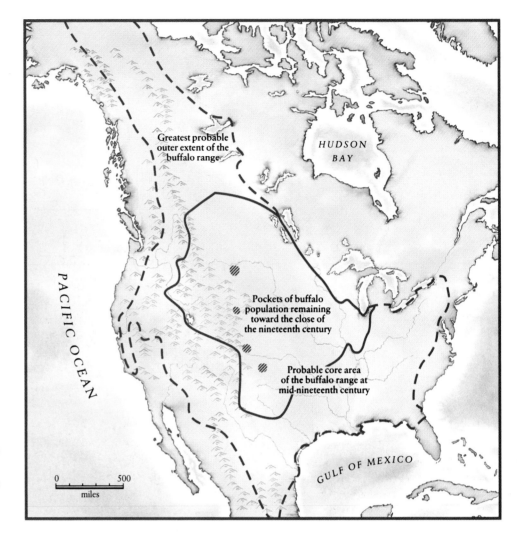

*The Extermination of the Buffalo.* The buffalo, which had been so essential to the life of the Plains Indians, were virtually wiped out by the end of the nineteenth century. The near-extinction of the buffalo was caused by a combination of the trade in buffalo skins, the sport of buffalo hunting, the building of the railroads, and diseases carried and spread by cattle. While it is estimated that at mid-century there were as many as twenty million buffalo roaming the Plains, by 1895 less than one thousand remained.

Map labels:
- Greatest probable outer extent of the buffalo range
- HUDSON BAY
- PACIFIC OCEAN
- Pockets of buffalo population remaining toward the close of the nineteenth century
- Probable core area of the buffalo range at mid-nineteenth century
- GULF OF MEXICO
- 0    500 miles

abolishment of tribally held territories through the process of allotting homesteads to individual Indian families.

The long-range vision of the treaty proposers would have aroused instantaneous Indian resistance, except for the fact that it was presented to them only in bits and pieces over time. The ten Sioux subtribes who, together with the Arapaho, signed the second Fort Laramie Treaty in April 1868, for example, thought they had negotiated a considerable victory. For while they had agreed to back out of Nebraska and Kansas, leaving the territories to the thousands of squatters and settlers who had flooded into the prairies during the previous decade, they had been promised supplies, security in their own holdings, and most astonishingly, the abandonment of military forts along the Powder and Bighorn rivers. For a moment, it was as if the clock had been turned back, as the Indians celebrated by burning the newly evacuated Fort Phil Kearney.

But as Red Cloud and the other Lakota chiefs learned, they had failed to read the fine print. Said Red Cloud two years later, "When I saw the treaty and all the false words in it I was mad. . . . I am not hard to swindle because I cannot read and write." The traders, missionaries, mixed-bloods, and frontiersmen married to Indian women talked them into agreeing; they had not realized that what they thought was only a peace and trade agreement had obligated them to relocate

# RED CLOUD

Few Indian leaders were as embroiled in the key events of their time as Red Cloud, the Oglala Sioux chief who was born at Pine Ridge, South Dakota. On the day of his birth, September 20, 1822, a red meteorite flashed across the sky; some say that inspired his name. As an adult, Red Cloud shared his people's anxiety over the mounting traffic on the overland wagon trails carrying settlers, gold miners, and townsfolk to the Montana gold fields and beyond. Ultimately, his warriors closed down the Bozeman Trail. When the federal government tried hiding its intent to increase military forces and build more forts under the cover of a peace conference, Red Cloud was not taken in; increased Sioux skirmishing finally forced the government to admit partial defeat.

In 1868 Red Cloud savored his greatest victory, the Fort Laramie Treaty, which guaranteed white withdrawal from the Bozeman Trail forts. Actually, he waited for the stockades to stand empty before signing the document. But then George Armstrong Custer broke agreements with the Sioux by leading mining experts into the sacred Black Hills, and the great Sioux War erupted.

Although Red Cloud counseled peaceful negotiation, his wise advice was drowned out. Yet Red Cloud kept fighting for Indian rights, mobilizing for the ouster of unfriendly Indian agents, initially resisting consolidation on reservations, and advising the non-Indian National Indian Defense Association on its assimilationist approach. But desiring accommodation with whites while fighting mistreatment placed Red Cloud in the midst of many controversies. In 1890 Red Cloud reviewed his people's treatment at government hands as he tried to explain the Plains Indian Ghost Dance movement of 1889.

"When we first made treaties with the Government, this was our position: Our old life and our old customs were about to end; the game upon which we lived was disappearing; the whites were closing around us, and nothing remained for us but to adopt their ways and have the same rights with them if we wished to save ourselves. . . . We looked forward with hope to the time when we could be as independent as the whites, and have a voice in the Government.

"[But] an Indian Department was made, with a large number of agents and other officials drawing large salaries. . . . Then came nothing but trouble. These men took care of themselves and not of us. . . . I was abused and slandered, to weaken my influence for good and make me seem like one who did not want to advance. . . . You who eat three times each day, and see your children well and happy around you, you can't understand what starving Indians feel. We were faint with hunger and maddened by despair. . . . The Indian Department called for soldiers to shoot down the [Ghost Dancing] Indians whom it had starved into despair."

from their Platte River lands to agencies along the Missouri River, implementing a plan to clear a path for the projected Union Pacific Railway. And while the Sioux were eager for the awls, blankets, axes, knives, and other rations the government had promised, these goods often turned out to be of poor quality—sometimes manufactured expressly for this Indian treaty market, with the savings from government appropriations going into private pockets. Finally, like Indians everywhere, the Sioux surely sensed that their growing dependence on such items spelled the end of their old way of life.

In the decade after the Civil War, behind-the-scenes corruption in the Indian Bureau went from bad to worse. Civilian Indian agents, often in cahoots with scoundrels in Congress and unscrupulous suppliers of the food and hardware promised in treaties, skimmed off hundreds of thousands of dollars through a wild

*Once there was an Indian who became a Christian. He became a very good Christian; he went to church, and he didn't smoke or drink, and he was good to everyone. He was a very good man. Then he died. First he went to the Indian hereafter, but they wouldn't take him because he was a Christian. Then he went to Heaven, but they wouldn't let him in—because he was an Indian. Then he went to Hell, but they wouldn't admit him there either, because he was so good. So he came alive again, and he went to the Buffalo Dance and the other dances and taught his children to do the same thing.*

—ANONYMOUS
(Fox)

variety of schemes. On the reservation an agent could thrive as a tyrant, with no one to check his authority or scrutinize his account books. "When the white man wants to raise wheat," a Sioux named Fire Cloud complained, "he plants wheat, when he wants to raise corn, he plants corn. But he says he wants to raise good Indians and he plants bad white men among us who plant bad seed."

President Lincoln, and Grant after him, were increasingly aware that scandals within the Indian Bureau were not only costing the government money, they were frustrating the crucial task of making reservations congenial incubators for Indian transformation. In 1871 President Grant tried to put some teeth into his "peace policy" approach by naming a civilian body, the Board of Indian Commissioners, to oversee the conduct of the U.S. Indian Bureau.

At the same time, since remaking the Indians meant converting them to Christianity, it was natural for Grant to replace the corrupt civilian agents on reservations with men picked from various church groups. The denominations divided up their potential flocks, Episcopalians taking the Lakota tribes, Presbyterians assigned to the Navajos, and Quakers working with the southern Plains tribes that were willing to relocate to reservations in Indian Territory.

To many of these humanitarian agents and eastern liberals, the responsibility to educate Indian children was just as vital as the task of civilizing Indian adults. With adults, after all, the reformers could only hope to change the outward, everyday habits—to make them plow fields, to put them into pants, shirts, boots, and hats, to encourage them to attend church.

Children, on the other hand, presented a much better opportunity for genuine reform—provided they could be cut off for a prolonged period from their "savage" environment. Thus was developed the notion of government boarding schools for Indians in which native children could be safely ensconced during their formative years. Today this approach strikes us as invasive to an outrageous degree, but we must remember that the reformers were arguing against strong public opinion that considered Indians to be an inferior and, as Secretary of State Henry Clay put it, "not an improvable breed," destined to an extinction that "will be no great loss to the world." (The term *ethnocide* had not yet entered the language, but the tragic cultural losses it denotes would soon be experienced throughout the Indian world. It would take whites much longer to wonder whether the loss to Indians might also be a terrible loss to all humanity.) But under the circumstances, one must actually regard the reform movement as the liberal approach of its day.

The year 1871 saw one more drastic setback for Indian autonomy as Congress changed the entire basis of government–Indian relations. Many Congressmen had long felt that treaty making, which allowed Indians some measure of self-government, was an obsolete process, serving only to uphold what they saw as a fiction: that Indian tribes were the equivalent of European nations. Now they had a powerful financial argument to back up their view: treaty making was proving quite expensive. The rations to supply Red Cloud's Sioux alone, based on the 1868 treaty, would amount to over $700,000 a year by 1873 (and never mind who really ended up with the money). Thus the guiding motivations behind national Indian policy—which had previously swung between military control and the negotiated treaty approach—now rested definitively against negotiation.

# LIFE ON THE RESERVATIONS

Shifts in federal policy drastically affected the quality of life on Indian reservations. Until the late 1860s, reservation existence was grim, even deadly, as a Winnebago named Little Hill described in 1865: "Before we left Minnesota [for Nebraska] they told us that the superintendent had started on ahead of us, and would be there before us, and that he had plenty of Indians, and would have thirty houses built for us before we got there. After we got there they sometimes gave us rations, but not enough to go round most of the time. Some would have to go without eating two or three days. . . . We got some goods now which the Great Father sent us. They are lying in the Omaha warehouse, and we don't know but that the rats have eat them. There are a good many women and children that are naked and cannot come out of

their tents."

Monstrous conditions like these were the result both of disorganization in the emerging reservation system and of outright fraud on the part of suppliers who stole and resold hardware and clothing that had been promised tribespeople in their treaties. In 1871, however, as part of President Grant's "peace policy" to keep Indians on reservations and transform them into

whites, a new practice was initiated: church groups were encouraged to appoint reservation agents throughout the West.

As an Arapaho Indian artist named Carl Sweezy remembered this new regime in his native Oklahoma, "There was more than one white man's road that we might take, and President Grant wanted us to take the right one. He sent Brinton Darlington to be our first Agent. . . . He brought assistants there, many of them Quakers like himself, who built good buildings and started schools and opened trading posts and laid out farms. He planted an orchard and a garden, so that our people might learn how fruits and vegetables grew. He was patient and kind; he managed like a chief."

Accordingly, by an act of Congress on March 3, 1871, the government formally ended the era of treaty making that had begun in 1778 and had produced 372 treaties. From then on, "agreements" (74 of them by 1902) and special laws (5,000 by 1948) were passed for handling the convoluted relationships between the federal government and well over a hundred American Indian tribes who were trapped in a legal limbo, not yet recognized as American citizens but no longer fully independant nations.

Meanwhile, both the Indians and the government continued to suffer the consequences of the treaties already signed. Following the 1868 Sioux treaty, a state of uneasy tension marked relations between Plains Indians and incoming whites for about five years.

In 1872, the Modocs, far away in California, nevertheless managed to rivet national attention on a costly uprising that lasted eight months. The tribe, though small, had always been respected, even by Indian neighbors, for their ready defiance. They had reluctantly agreed to join a reservation with their long-time enemies, the Klamaths, but within a year, led by a young man by the name of Kintpuash, they had left and settled back on Lost River, part of their original homeland at the eastern base of the Cascades. After seven increasingly tense years, and at the insistence of the many white settlers who had since moved in,

TOP: Kiowa women waiting for their rations in front of a government commissary in Anadarko, Oklahoma.

ABOVE: Tickets used to procure weekly rations. While treaties made with Indians promised them ample supplies of staple items—like beef, flour, and blankets—rations were frequently scarce and often suspended entirely at the whim of the agent, many of whom used their position to cheat the Indians and increase their own wealth.

Kintpuash of the Modocs. This photograph of the Modoc leader, also known as Captain Jack, was taken shortly after he was taken prisoner.

George Armstrong Custer, in addition to being called "the Chief of Thieves" by the Indians, was known as "Long Hair," "Hard Backsides," and "Son of the Morning Star."

the government authorized military removal of the Modocs to the reservation.

A minor skirmish sent the tribe, about three hundred strong, including families, slipping south along Tule Lake, destroying the scattered homes of settlers as they went, and killing the white families. Their objective was the broken land of lava beds at the south end of the lake, where a complex of volcanic caves provided perfect cover. Here they holed up, and here no more than fifty fighting men held off a thousand U.S. regulars and militia, with results so disastrous that the government elected to try peace talks.

The young leader Kintpuash, known to the whites as Captain Jack, was willing to accept a reservation provided it was in the Modoc homeland. But, strongly mistrustful of any terms offered by the government, other chiefs disagreed and argued Kintpuash into a plan that involved killing the peace commissioners. At the negotiation in April 1873, Kintpuash shot Brigadier General Edward Canby in the face and then stabbed him to death, while the other Indians killed or wounded the rest of the peace commission.

As Kintpuash had anticipated, the murders only incensed their enemies. Moreover, despite other victories over the U.S. military as the band moved deeper into the inhospitable lava labyrinth, dissension continued among the Modocs themselves. The band broke up into smaller groups, each individually pursued and picked up by an outraged military, led by a new, aggressive U.S. commander, Colonel Jefferson Davis (no relation to the Confederate president).

Eventually an exhausted Kintpuash, with his starving family, gave up on June 1, 1873. He and five other leaders were immediately tried by a military tribunal, and four—Kintpuash, Black Jim, Boston Charley, and Schonchin John—were hanged. The remnants of the Modocs, 155 in all, were sent east to Indian Territory, as far from home as the government could relocate them.

The tide of white humanity that tormented the natives did not consist solely of settlers. In the spring of 1874, word of gold sightings in the Black Hills—the sacred Paha Sapa of the Sioux—spread through the bars and banks of fledgling South Dakota towns. That summer Lieutenant Colonel George Armstrong Custer was dispatched on what was billed as a purely military expedition into the region to hunt for a future fort site.

For sixty days Custer's column of mules and twelve hundred troops, including trained gold prospectors, snaked through crusty boulders and evergreens, secretly eyeing the abundant timber, mineral, and potential farming resources available in the Hills. To the Indians, Custer would be known as the "chief of thieves" for this flagrant violation of the 1868 treaty. On his return, Custer let it get out to financial interests and poor miners that there was gold in the Black Hills "from the grass roots down." By 1875, knowing it could not keep the whites out, the government ordered Indian hunting parties—the "hostiles"—to report in to agencies by January of 1876.

For the Sioux, the winter of 1874–75 was one of bitter cold and scarcity; those with on-again, off-again ties to reservations along the Missouri tried to augment their rations by hunting, but the buffalo herds were noticeably sparse. In fact, that winter would mark their last tribal hunt. Their kinsmen—the more independent Sioux, Cheyenne, and Arapaho groups, still strong in numbers and

Sitting Bull, in a photograph from 1884. As leader of the Hunkpapa Sioux, he was at the Battle of the Little Bighorn, although he may not have taken an active part due to his age. After the Indian victory, he led his band into exile in Canada. Five years later he returned to give himself up and was killed by reservation guards.

in pride under the experienced leadership of Sitting Bull, Crazy Horse, Black Moon, Hump, and Gall—were not ready to give up their freedom without a fight. The government's dictum to report in, predictably, was ignored.

In March, General George Crook took the field and surprised a village of Oglalas and Cheyennes in winter quarters, but was nevertheless defeated at the Battle of Powder River. He managed an orderly retirement, but the winter battle served to alert the Indians that the Great White Father was serious. So were the

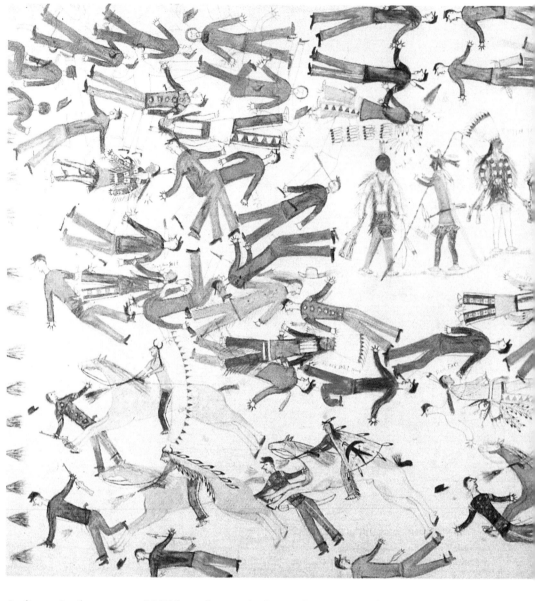

*The Battle of the Little Bighorn,*
painted on muslin by Kicking Bear, an
Oglala Minniconjou Sioux, from
around 1890.

Indians. In the spring of 1876, at the yearly Sioux Sun Dance, the Hunkpapa
Sioux chief Sitting Bull scarified his flesh in ritual prayer, and envisioned many
dead U.S. soldiers "falling right into our camp."

The imminent storm partially broke on June 17, 1876, when the combined
forces of Cheyenne and Lakota groups under the leadership of Crazy Horse,
struck hard against General Crook at the Battle of the Rosebud. When the
Indian forces, with their overpowering numbers, pulled back, Crook claimed victory and this time beat a hasty retreat. But the full fury of the Indian gathering,
and the main expression of their outrage, fell seven days later, on the banks of a
Montana stream called the Little Bighorn.

Assembled there was one of the largest combined Indian fighting forces ever
seen on the Plains, twelve hundred tipis strong, constituting nearly two thousand
warriors. And there Colonel Custer's isolated company of 210 was surrounded on
June 25 and wiped out in one hour.

The two arms of Custer's split command, under Major Marcus A. Reno and

Curley the Crow (ca. 1877), one of four Indian scouts who led Custer to the area where the "hostiles" were gathered. Curley left Custer's command before the fighting started but is nonetheless remembered as the only "survivor" under Custer's immediate command.

Captain Frederick W. Benteen, fought off attacks while suffering heavy losses. Altogether, 268 white men and officers died at the Little Bighorn. Indian losses are unknown. But by the time the supporting columns under General Alfred H. Terry and Colonel John Gibbon arrived, the main body of Indians, alerted to their arrival, had already scattered—seven thousand men, women, and children, some on horseback, some leading ponies dragging travois, slipping away over hills and down coulees, headed for the Bighorn Mountains.

The shocking discovery of the bodies of Custer's group, and of Benteen and Reno with their survivors, precluded an immediate pursuit. But the spectacular defeat of its golden-haired hero enraged the nation. In the bitter aftermath, during the fall and through the depth of the winter of 1876–77, the U.S. military relentlessly pursued the tribes.

In November, Colonel Ranald S. Mackenzie, one of the aggressive young officers under Crook, surprised Dull Knife's Cheyenne camp, inflicting a terrible retribution that sent a thousand Cheyennes into the winter without food or

shelter. They joined up with Crazy Horse and his Oglalas, themselves hard-pressed, having little more than courage to share.

In January, Sitting Bull led his people in an exhausting escape up into Canada. That same month, in the midst of a raging blizzard, Crazy Horse fought the battle of Wolf Mountain against Brigadier General Nelson A. Miles, who had tenaciously remained in the field the whole winter with a small, relatively mobile and well-equipped force of five hundred, harrying the Indians, determined to avenge Custer, his own personal hero.

Through the remainder of that bitter winter and early spring, groups of Indians drifted into the Red Cloud agency near Fort Robinson, Nebraska. By May, almost all had returned, quietly, in small groups. Then on May 6, three hundred warriors led by Crazy Horse, chanting war songs and followed by a thousand Cheyenne and Oglala herding twenty-five hundred ponies, arrived at the agency. It could hardly be called a surrender.

On the reservation, the presence of Crazy Horse made the authorities uneasy. They saw him as a focal point for the disaffected, his influence a potent force for trouble. Eventually, the army decided to arrest him, but did not dare to do so

OPPOSITE:
The place where Custer fell, photographed by John H. Fouch in early July, 1877. The view is from Last Stand Hill, where Custer was killed. In the valley beyond is the Little Bighorn River, past which stood the enormous encampment of Sioux and Cheyenne Indians that swarmed over Custer and destroyed his band of some two hundred soldiers.

*Conflicts in the West, 1854–82.*
The sites of the major U.S.–Indian battles west of the Mississippi River.

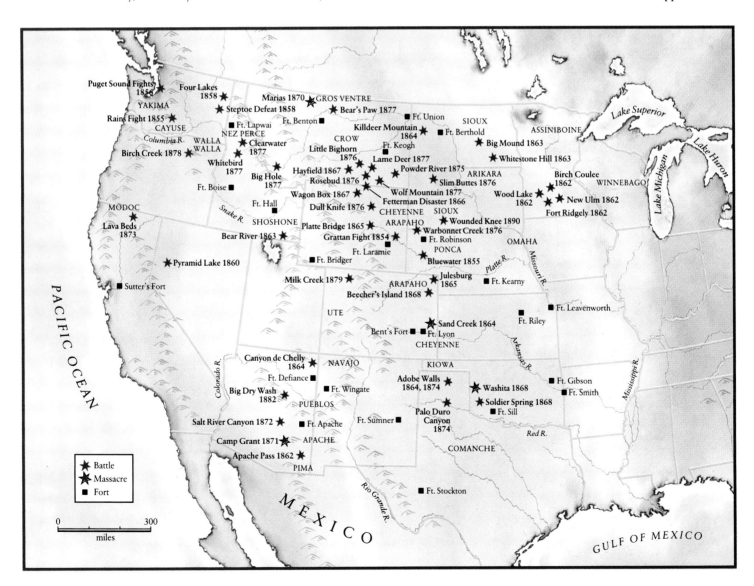

openly. Invited to the agency offices, he was led into the guardhouse instead. When he resisted, he was bayoneted and died later that night. Various official explanations were offered for the manner of his death, but no Sioux ever forgot the real reason for the shameful betrayal in that guardhouse. The spirit of Crazy Horse remains a symbol of defiance to this day.

The Sioux had to yield the Black Hills, and were eventually forced onto five separate and greatly reduced reservations stacked up along the west bank of the Missouri.

Throughout the 1870s, as treaties previously made were broken, and as further compromises were not adhered to, as the degrading miseries of reservation life thrust Indians to extremes, and as white settlers and miners flooded across the Plains and on into Oregon and California, there was a continuing threat of Indian reprisals—and ongoing efforts to subdue the dissidents, whether by military force or by sequestering them on reservations.

The northwest Columbia Basin was home to several tribes—the Yakima, Walla Walla, Cayuse, Flathead, and Nez Perce, although the Cayuse lands had already been confiscated in retribution for the tribe's murderous attack on a pair of arrogant missionaries back in the late 1840s. Most of the tribes were by now settled on reservations. However, the Nez Perce, who had held staunchly to their friendship with white men for some seventy years, were now torn among themselves on this issue of removal to reservations. Those who had been unwilling to sign the original treaty surrendering their lands included the Wallowas, led by young Chief Joseph, backed by chiefs Eagle from the Light, White Bird, Looking Glass, and the medicine man Toohoolhoolzote.

The negotiator assigned in 1877 to parley with the dissident Nez Perce was the new military commander of the Northwest, General Oliver O. Howard, a deeply religious man whose sympathies, in fact, lay with the Indians. Nevertheless, his plan was to buy out the Nez Perce. At stake was their homeland valley of Wallowa, rich grazing land now coveted by white settlers. Both Chief Joseph and the elderly Toohoolhoolzote spoke eloquently against the proposed sale, the latter so vehemently that Howard became angry and had the old man thrown into the guardhouse. Finally, the general declared that Joseph's band had no alternative but to pack their belongings and, without delay, move to the Lapwai reservation in Idaho with the rest of the Nez Perce.

Feeling betrayed and bitter, yet recognizing they had no chance in an immediate and all-out military confrontation, the chiefs agreed. On the way to the reservation, however, young men in White Bird's band killed four whites. The violence rapidly escalated, involving 100 cavalrymen from Fort Lapwai—who were cut to ribbons. As a result, General Howard himself took off in pursuit, with 400 men against the 300 warriors under Chief Joseph, who was encumbered by the weight and care of 500 women and children and all their possessions. Howard caught up with and defeated the Indians at the Battle of the Clearwater in July, but failed to implement his advantage. The chiefs decided to slip away, trek

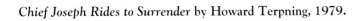

*Chief Joseph Rides to Surrender* by Howard Terpning, 1979.

Chief Joseph's brilliant generalship in leading his people on a seventeen-hundred-mile running battle against U.S. forces that heavily outnumbered the Nez Perce won the admiration of his opponents, generals Miles and Howard, and of the public at large. But General Sherman saw elimination as the best solution to the Indian problem. Despite the protests of Miles and Howard, the four hundred surviving Nez Perce were shunted from fort to fort, ending up in an unhealthy, miasmic location at Fort Leavenworth where many immediately contracted illnesses that generally proved fatal. From there, in 1878, Joseph began his unremitting twenty-six-year effort to get better treatment for his people. His gallantry and dignity won him many friends and a high profile of public recognition. As a spokesman for the Nez Perce, Joseph was an even more impressive leader than he had been a warrior. In 1879, when he was invited to speak before cabinet members, congressmen, and diplomats, themselves curious about this Indian "Napoleon," his moving appeal was published in the

*North American Review:*

*I cannot understand how the Government sends a man out to fight us, as it did General Miles, and then breaks his word. I do not understand why nothing is done for my people. I have heard talk and talk, but nothing is done. Words do not pay for my dead people. They do not pay for my country, now overrun by white men. They do not protect my father's grave. . . . Good words will not give me back my children. Good words will not give my people good health and stop them from dying. Good words will not get my people a home where they can live in peace and take care of themselves. I am tired of talk that comes to nothing. It makes my heart sick when I remember all the good words and all the broken promises. . . .*

*If the white man wants to live in peace with the Indian he can live in peace. Treat all men alike. Give them all the same law. Give them all an even chance to live and grow. The earth is the mother of all people, and all people should have equal rights upon it. You might as well expect the*

*rivers to run backward as that any man who was born free should be contented penned up and denied liberty to go where he pleases.*

*We ask to be recognized as men. We ask that the same law shall work alike on all men. Let me be a free man—free to travel, free to stop, free to work, free to trade, free to choose my own teachers, free to follow the religion of my fathers, free to think and talk and act for myself—and I will obey every law.*

But this and other appeals were to no avail. It was not until 1885 that the Nez Perce were removed from Fort Leavenworth, and even then they were split up. The Looking Glass and White Bird bands (recaptured as they straggled back from Canada) were sent to Lapwai, while Joseph's band, now reduced to 150 worn survivors, finally made a home for themselves along Nespelem Creek on the Colville reservation in Washington, far from their own rich valley. And even here, as late as 1900, Joseph was still fighting to prevent encroachment on the land his people now occupied. There he died in 1904.

OPPOSITE:
This portrait of Chief Joseph, taken in 1877 by John H. Fouch, is the first photograph made of the Nez Perce leader following his surrender.

across the Bitterroot Mountains and the high plains of Montana, to seek refuge among their sometime friends, the Crows.

They fought several battles along the exhausting route, at one point crossing the newly formed Yellowstone Park and just barely missing contact with an official tourist group that included General William Tecumseh Sherman. But on reaching Crow country, they discovered Crow scouts were part of the U.S. command. The Nez Perce decided to take their depleted band the remaining two hundred miles to Canada where they hoped for sanctuary with Sitting Bull, still evading the vengeance occasioned by the victory at the Little Bighorn.

Chief Joseph's people desperately needed rest; even so, he thought they should not stop. However, the other chiefs believed they had eluded the pursuing Howard, and Howard, counting on just this, sent a fast messenger to Fort Keogh. From there, General Miles swiftly swung northwest to cut off the Nez Perce.

Only forty miles short of the Canadian border, he caught up with them. The chiefs were able to organize a defense, but they lost old Toohoolhoolzote and Ollakot, Joseph's younger brother. Chief Joseph urged surrender. White Bird and Looking Glass wanted to continue to resist, and went their own way, slipping off

OPPOSITE:
Three Pueblo boys—Watte, Keise-te-Wa, and He-Li-te—posed in traditional dress (LEFT) and in Carlisle School uniforms (RIGHT).

In the same year, 1886, that Geronimo surrendered for the last time and was sent as a prisoner to Fort Marion in Florida, all the Chiricahua Apache children between the ages of twelve and twenty-two were taken from their families and sent to the Carlisle Indian School in Pennsylvania. Below, four months after arriving there, this photograph was taken of a group of Apache children in school uniform and dress.

with three hundred of their people and making a dash for safety to Canada (Looking Glass never made it—he was killed by a stray bullet).

Chief Joseph formally surrendered on October 5, 1877, the occasion of the famous speech that ended with his heartbreaking words, "From where the sun now stands, I will fight no more forever."

As the military pursued their strong-arm methods for domesticating Indians throughout the 1870s and 1880s, proponents of the "peace policy" were nonetheless claiming success. Despite eruptions by those temporary consortiums of different rebellious tribes in the Plains and the more furtive Apache guerrillas in the Southwest, easterners argued that their crusade to "civilize" Indians was bearing fruit; the Indian Bureau press releases claimed that 1875–76 had witnessed 42,500 male Indians "undertaking self-support" and 329,000 reservations acres being plowed and sown by Indians.

In concept, the Indian reservation was to function as a sort of laboratory for social change. Indians there would be indoctrinated into the white way of life by specially assigned farmers, craftsmen, teachers, and clergymen. But not only was

this vision not applied to all reservations, it was often not consistently applied within a single community. As Longbear, a Crow tribesman from Montana, complained, "One man comes and he is a farmer and wants every one of us to be farmers, etc. for four years, and he calls that government policy. [Then] another man comes who is a stock raiser, and we must all be stock raisers, too . . . and do in a tip-top manner all their work."

As for Indian children, here the white reformers looked to train the hearts and minds of tomorrow's Indians. But the reformers were divided between those who could envision only a factory or handicraft future for these youngsters and those who felt that the sky was the limit for youthful Indian aspirations. In either case, though, boarding school was the first step.

Overlooked in these white debates, of course, were the intellectual strides Indians had already made in the white world, the books written by Great Lakes Indian authors, the tradition of Indian journalism that had been developing ever since publication of the *Cherokee Phoenix* in 1828, the countless contributions by Indian go-betweens and translators to the infant discipline of American anthropology, and the Indians' demonstrated conceptual and oratorical skills in treaty-making debates where sheer survival was at stake.

While educating native youth had been a priority for Indian sympathizers

*Tuesday, April 4th, 1860—If will die my father, then will very poor my heart 4 my brother all die: only one Shooquanahts save, and two my uncle save. I will try to make all things. I want to be good, and I want to much work hard. When we have done work, then will please, Sir, Mr. Duncan, will you give me a little any thing when you come back.*

—Diary of Shooquanahts,
a Tsimshian boy sent to a British
Columbia missionary school.

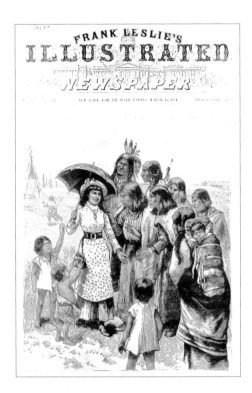

The caption with this illustration from 1884 reads: "Educating the Indians—A female pupil of the government school at Carlisle visits her home at Pine Ridge Agency."

*I went back to school in the fall. . . .*
*We read a history book about "the sav-*
*ages." The pictures were in color.*
*There was one of a group of warriors*
*attacking white people—a woman held*
*a baby in her arms. I saw hatchets,*
*blood dripping, feathers flying. I*
*showed the picture to the Sister. She*
*said, "Rose Mary, don't you know*
*you're Indian?" I said, "No, I'm not."*
*She said, "Yes, you are." I said, "No!"*
*And I ran behind a clump of juniper*
*trees and cried and cried.*

—ROSE MARY (SHINGOBE) BARSTOW
(Ojibwa), 1976

ever since 1775 when the Continental Congress appropriated funds for Indian freshmen at New Hampshire's Dartmouth College, the drive to "civilize" native Americans now took a new tack as an essential part of the Indian reform movement. Removing children from family and tribal influences was critical to the boarding school program that was initiated at Hampton Institute in Virginia, a government institution that, up to that time, had exclusively serviced black students. And it was primarily one man, Army Captain Richard H. Pratt, who developed the vocational-manual labor school that gained such a positive reputation within the humanitarian movement.

In 1875 Pratt had been assigned to St. Augustine, Florida, to guard seventy-four southern Plains Indian prisoners in the old Spanish-built fortress of Fort Marion. When Pratt struck off their chains, trusted the Indians to guard themselves, apprenticed them to nearby sawmills, railroads, and farms, and gave them pencils and paper, he was impressed by their innate abilities and responsiveness. At his own request in 1879 Pratt was allowed to open the government's first official boarding school at Carlisle, Pennsylvania, where he instituted a rigorous, no-nonsense approach to instill the work ethic into Indian boys and girls.

His first class comprised eighty-two Sioux, Pawnee, and Kiowa students. As with the old California Indian missions, self-sufficiency was desired as a cost-cutting measure; so Indian boys maintained the school's dairy barns and Indian girls stitched their school uniforms. They occupied separate dorms, marched to class, and their packed days were timed by hourly bells. Half the time was spent on the three R's, the other half in print or machine shops or working the fields—useful, "vocational" skills.

Discipline was harsh; children who whispered in their native language or ran off or talked back were often whipped or starved. To the humanitarians, the industrial school approach was perhaps their most clear-cut success; by 1900 over twelve hundred students representing seventy-nine tribes had attended Carlisle alone.

As this strict regimen was adopted by off-reservation Indian schools in Indian Territory, Arizona, New Mexico, and points west, it divided Indian families in bitter ways. Foremost was the sheer anguish aroused by such long separations—often lasting years—with little communication between parents and children of cultures where family and extended family ties were the heart and soul of their lifestyle. With this loss came the poignant irony—after mounting tolls from disease, devastation from the Indian Wars, and the disintegrating conditions on the reservations—of parents who were relieved that their beloved offspring would at least have food and shelter.

There was great irony and ambiguity in the children's situation as well. Quite aside from the terror any child feels at being torn from family and familiar surroundings, these children suffered personal humiliation when their long hair was hacked off and their bodies were physically abused; and certainly there was irreparable harm done when their Indian heritage and languages were suppressed. Yet in shared suffering there was sometimes the discovery of common strength, and it was here that they began the friendships that later linked them in multitribal networks based on intermarriage and pan-Indian religious movements. Moreover, these linkages strengthened political unity among the former students

# SARAH WINNEMUCCA

In 1883 a remarkable book was published by an unusual woman, then nearly forty years old. Her name was Sarah Winnemucca, but at birth she was named Tocmetone, or "Shell Flower." Her book, entitled *Life Among the Piutes*, detailed the sufferings of her people, the Paviotso Paiute of northern Nevada. Sarah's family had participated in the "opening of the West"; her grandfather, the first Winnemucca (probably meaning "One Moccasin"), escorted Captain John C. Frémont through the Sierras into California in the mid-1840s.

Sarah had visited the San Joaquin Valley in her early teens, lived with a white family for a while, and attended Catholic school briefly. That was where she first confronted racial prejudice. Other parents complained about their children sitting alongside an Indian. Throughout her life Sarah had similar experiences: she lost her mother, sister, and brother in the violent aftermath of the Paiute War of 1860.

Her keen intelligence and language skills kept Sarah mediating between her people's needs and unsympathetic Indian agents. In Nevada she was an official translator, often pleading for more food on behalf of the Pyramid Lake Paiute. When the tribe was forcibly moved to Oregon she soon found herself at odds with an especially brutal Indian agent there. Yet when her father joined Bannock Indian rebels against whites in 1878, Sarah remained neutral, and even undertook a peace mission to bring her father and his followers out of hiding.

Finally, her recounting of such experiences prompted her to follow the lecture circuit, arousing East Coast support for her people. But her personal life suffered. Married four times and known as Sarah Winnemucca Hopkins after her fourth marriage, she never was able to solicit adequate recognition from the government for her Paiute. She died in October 1891 of tuberculosis while living in Montana.

Toward the end of her 1883 autobiography, Sarah wrote in her own defense, and on behalf of her own tribe, "It is true that my people sometimes distrust me, but that is because words have been put into my mouth which have turned out to be nothing but idle wind. Promises have been made to me in high places that have not been kept, and I have had to suffer for this in the loss of my people's Confidence. . . . My people are ignorant of worldly knowledge, but they know what love means and what truth means. . . . They do not know anything about the history of the world, but they can see the Spirit-Father in everything. The beautiful world talks to them of their Spirit-Father. They are innocent and simple, but they are brave and will not be imposed upon."

when, as adults, they entered the struggle to help their people.

Yet for all the advantage the Indians managed to take from the situation, there was always that heartbreaking time when they returned home, often semi-strangers among their own people, no longer fluent in the language of family members and old friends—and frequently to learn that all the loved ones they looked forward to seeing were dead and gone forever.

# CHAPTER TWENTY-ONE

# THE CLOSING IN
# 1879–1895

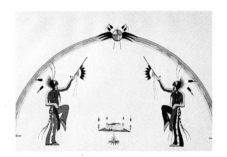

*PEACE PIPE DANCE*
BY ACEE BLUE EAGLE (CREEK-PAWNEE), ca. 1946

## April 1879

THE OMAHA COURTROOM was hushed as a fifty-year-old Ponca chief named Mochunozhin, or Standing Bear, told the sad story he had already related to the town's newspapers, which he would recollect repeatedly to rapt audiences in the East. His was the climactic testimony in a ground-breaking American Indian civil rights case: *Standing Bear v. General George Crook*. The ordeals he recounted had happened to Standing Bear's own particular people, but they were symptomatic of Indian sufferings throughout the nation.

"I want to save myself and my tribe," Standing Bear told Judge Elmer S. Dundy, who had instigated the trial to discover by what right a U.S. Army general was holding Standing Bear and his band of sixty-six followers under armed guard. Why couldn't they return to Indian territory? "If a White man had land," Standing Bear went on, "and someone should swindle him, that man would try to get it back, and you would not blame him. . . . I need help."

The trial was a consequence of years of mistreatment of the Poncas at the hands of the U.S. Army and the government. Through the early 1870s Standing Bear's Ponca tribe had clung to their Nebraska homelands, despite Sioux attacks to dislodge them. After Custer's defeat, however, the Ponca were slated for consolidation with the Sioux as part of the government's strategy of relocating "troublesome" northern tribes to Indian Territory. First, a delegation of Ponca chiefs was escorted to look over their prospective reservation. Finding the

---

OPPOSITE: *Walk Through the Great Mysteries* by Jerome Tiger (Creek-Seminole), 1967.

*Standing Bear* by Arthur Amiotte
(Oglala Lakota), 1978.

southern landscape dank and ugly, they made it clear they would not let their people move there. Infuriated, government officials made Standing Bear and his party walk the five-hundred-mile return journey to Nebraska, with one blanket and only a few dollars among them.

Then, although one Ponca contingent caved in to relocation, Standing Bear's followers held fast and he was imprisoned. Upon his release, armed soldiers forced Standing Bear and five hundred followers to walk back south to Indian Territory. During the fifty-day trek, and through the ensuing year, over a hundred Poncas died from disease and inclement weather, including Standing Bear's own children. To bury his son, Standing Bear once more broke out for the north, finding sanctuary among the Omaha Indians. That was where General Crook found this group putting in an early spring crop, and Standing Bear was thrown into the Fort Omaha brig.

After considering the U.S. attorney's argument that Indians were not "persons within the meaning of the law," and Standing Bear's account of his personal travails, Judge Dundy returned to the bench to rule that "an Indian is a person within the meaning of the law." The military, he concluded, had no special privileges in peacetime to deny Indians the basic constitutional protection against imprisonment without due cause. While Standing Bear and his followers were thereafter allowed to resettle in their old haunts, the southern Ponca were not allowed back, and the commissioner of Indian Affairs quickly made it clear that Judge Dundy's ruling had no bearing on other tribes.

The Standing Bear episode was among the earliest instances of an Indian leader shifting from the battlefield to the legal arena to stand up for native rights. Standing Bear's successful lecture tour of the East, underwritten by key activists in the reform movement, also ushered Indians into the court of public opinion. The experiences of Indians for nearly three hundred years became powerfully personalized through this saga of one uprooted people yearning for their homeland.

The main thrust of federal policy remained on eliminating "Indianness." Along with putting Indian parents to work and their children into boarding school, the government's campaign to civilize the native inhabitants also targeted traditional Indian beliefs and rituals with a harsh new prohibition. In 1883, the Bureau of Indian Affairs further insinuated itself into the Indian heart and home by issuing throughout its growing reservation network a circular entitled *The Code of Religious Offenses.*

Now Indian ceremonies were declared to be crimes punishable by imprisonment. Singled out were Plains Indian Sun Dances—practiced by upwards of twenty tribes—and medicine men's curing rites. After this, tribes like the Kiowa, Comanche, Ponca, and others either discontinued these summer religious festivals or held them clandestinely in secret locations.

On the Northwest Coast the Canadian government was undertaking a similar purge of the social-religious exchanges of goods known generally as the potlatch, which was officially outlawed in 1885. Other traditional practices also fell under this new rubric of "Indian offenses," such as the not-uncommon practice of a man's having two wives (who were often sisters), the direct Indian solution to providing a home and sustenance for extra women within the tribe; "giveaways,"

*Cheyenne Sun Dance,*
*First Painting of the Third Day*
**by W. Richard West**
**(Cheyenne), 1949.**

in which social groups honored each other with presents; and so-called animal dances, a loose cover term for any occasion featuring native dance regalia festooned with feathers or furs. As late as 1913, Indians at Fort Berthold in North Dakota had to beg the Bureau of Indian Affairs for permission to teach songs to their children or record them for visiting anthropologists. (Permission was granted, provided the songs did not "retard the moral, social and industrial welfare of the participants.")

Fortunately, Indian agents lacked the manpower to enforce such rules in all nooks and crannies of their reservations. And although similar circulars restricting dances and traditional activities would emanate from the Bureau of Indian Affairs through the 1920s, Indians subverted them in ingenious ways. Their gettogethers during the white man's Fourth of July celebrations were often an appropriate venue for performing old warrior society dances. Windowless roundhouses were built to seclude old-time rituals from the suspicious eyes of the local Indian agent and his spies. Nonetheless, a new atmosphere of constant surveillance and coercive assimilation pervaded Indian life throughout the reservation system.

Ironically, during the onset of this cultural clampdown, military men, such as Lieutenant James H. Bradley, Captain John Bourke, and Dr. Washington Matthews, among others, were contributing to the first scholarly accounts of tribal life for the newly instituted Bureau of American Ethnology, the govern-

Published MONTHLY. BEADLE'S DIME NOVELS Novel Series, NUMBER 71. THE CHOICEST WORKS OF THE MOST POPULAR AUTHORS. THE LOST TRAIL. NEW YORK: BEADLE AND COMPANY, 118 WILLIAM ST. General Dime Book Publishers.

Dime store novels had a field day with melodramas based on lurid images of the West.

ment's research center for the study of American Indians. Others at the bureau, such as Alice Fletcher, who conducted fieldwork among the Omaha, and James Mooney, who documented the old customs of both southern and northern Plains peoples, would advocate fiercely on behalf of Indian rights in the years ahead.

Meanwhile, turning Indians into self-sufficient farmers and ranchers continued to be a prime goal of liberal reservation officials. While a number of Plains Indian tribes were reluctant to adopt an exclusively farming economy (although the government forgot that many Plains peoples were part-time gardeners of corn, beans, squash, tobacco, and sunflowers before whites ever arrived), they often found the activities of ranch life to their liking. Whichever they tried—raising crops or grazing herds—the arid soils and threadbare grasslands left to them presented quite a challenge.

Despite the obstacles, after the first cattle were issued to the Sioux in 1879, they survived severe winters and actually quadrupled their herds between 1885 and 1912. Similarly many southern Plains and Apache groups initially displayed a knack for running cattle. Undermining Indian success at such self-help efforts, however, was an ominous retreat from support for Indian collective ventures as the 1890s drew near, and authorities showed greater interest in making it easier for Indians to lease their individual holdings so white ranchers could piece together large spreads.

Although the drama of bloody Indian warfare was largely relegated to sensational dime novels and the popular Wild West shows that, toward the end of the nineteenth century, were showcasing formerly "hostile" Indians throughout the eastern United States and Europe, one hotbed of Indian unrest remained—the Apache desertlands of southern Arizona. In 1876, U.S. authorities had tried to inhibit Chiricahua Apache raids against their old enemies, the Mexicans, by relocating them from the Apache Pass to the San Carlos reservation and thus distancing them from the Mexican border. Half the Chiricahuas complied, but a breakaway contingent, led by a forty-seven-year-old war chief named Goyathlay ("One Who Yawns"), escaped to Mexico where they harassed haciendas and rustled cattle to barter back in New Mexico.

Over the next decade Goyathlay, more popularly known and feared by the name Geronimo, kept up this breakaway and recapture scenario. Although San Carlos Apache police shortly corralled his insurgents back on the San Carlos reservation, Geronimo burst loose again in 1881. When General Crook managed to sequester the band's womenfolk and children, a trumped Geronimo accepted reservation life in 1884, and his warriors proved skilled cowboys on their own successful spreads. But stifling reservation life denied young Apaches an opportunity to spread their warrior wings, and in the spring of 1885, Geronimo and 134 followers broke for freedom one last time.

Raiding into Mexico, Geronimo soon had General Nelson A. Miles close on his heels, with a force of nearly five thousand troops and four hundred Apache scouts hunting down fewer than forty Apache renegades. Like many late-period Indian conflicts, this was in part a "newspaper war," with wild rumors arousing citizens to theatrical panic, which the military in many instances used as an excuse for retaliatory overkill. In this case, however, thanks to General Miles's considerable negotiating skills, the human toll was kept to a minimum.

Still, once Geronimo surrendered on September 4, 1887, Miles made good General Crook's old threat that this time the unruly Chiricahua would be exiled. In chains, Geronimo and thirty-four followers were sent by train to Fort Marion, in Florida. Although most were repatriated to Arizona, the state banned Geronimo forever. He died a Dutch Reformed Christian and a vegetable farmer in Fort Sill, Oklahoma, in 1909.

Goyathlay, known to white men as Geronimo, sat for this portrait a few days before he participated in President Theodore Roosevelt's inaugural procession in 1905.

*The whole world is coming,*

*A nation is coming, a nation is coming,*

*The Eagle has brought the message to*
*    the tribe.*

*The father says so, the father says so.*

*Over the whole earth they are coming.*

*The buffalo are coming, the buffalo*
*    are coming.*

*The Crow has brought the message to*
*    the tribe.*

*The father says so, the father says so.*

—Sioux Ghost Dance Song

Praying for supernatural aid and release was a common impulse for western Indians everywhere in the face of cultural annihilation and personal suffering. So-called nativistic religions, blending old-time Indian beliefs with Christian concepts and driven by a hopeful vision of an Indian tomorrow—whether in this lifetime or in an afterworld where whites did not exist—predated the California Indian Ghost Dance of 1870 and would continue long after it.

In the 1870s, for example, in the Plateau culture area of Washington Territory, the Dreamer Cult was promulgated by a Wanapum medicine man, Smohalla, who espoused a doctrine based on the authority of "Mother Earth" and the utter rejection of farming and the white man's wares. In the following decade, in the Puget Sound region, the prophet John Slocum attracted followers to his new all-Indian Shaker Church.

Although the Plains region yielded a number of messianic movements, in the 1880s one cult, inspired by the Paiute prophet Wovoka, gained prominence. The son of a visionary named Tavibo, Wovoka's message of salvation held special appeal. His "Ghost Dance" adherents gathered for many days, praying, chanting, and dancing in large open-air circles. Do this, Wovoka preached, undergo ceremonial purification, reject alcohol, and do not mourn. Then the old world will return, dead relatives will embrace their surviving kinfolk, the landscape will look as it did before the white man, buffalo will thicken the plains, and whites will disappear.

The compelling message was personally experienced, as closed-eyed Ghost Dancers earnestly swayed, sang, and eventually fell into trances where these future promises were vividly envisioned. Through letters written by boarding school–trained intermediaries and personal pilgrimages, Wovoka's desperate word of hope spread from tribe to tribe across the Plains, but found fertile ground especially among the Sioux, Arapaho, and Cheyenne. For some his message of nonviolence was downplayed, and specially blessed and symbol-covered muslin shirts were said to stop soldiers' bullets in the event of coming strife.

In the fall of 1890, when local towns got word of restless, "wild and crazy" Indians talking about a world free of white men, they wired for military help. The agitation was only heightened when Indian police killed Sitting Bull in a botched attempt to arrest those considered the ringleaders of the incipient religious rebellion. The building tragedy came to a head two days before the close of the year, a deplorable moment memorialized in the poet Stephen Vincent Benét's elegaic line, "Bury my heart at Wounded Knee."

Along Wounded Knee Creek on the Pine Ridge reservation, Seventh Cavalry troops, having rounded up a band of Hunkpapa Sioux suspected of potential trouble (fully two-thirds of them were women and children), herded the Indians for the night into a tight group surrounded by five hundred soldiers, their normal armament reinforced with four Hotchkiss guns. In the morning, the Sioux men were culled out, lined up, and disarmed. Someone is said to have discharged a weapon. Immediately, the Hotchkiss guns opened fire, and most of the men were killed in the first five minutes.

The Hotchkiss guns, carefully trained on the milling, terrified people, continued to fire. Some Indians fought back with whatever they had, stones or sticks or bare hands (leaving twenty-nine soldiers dead), while others tried to flee. Within an hour some two hundred Indians were dead or dying. A few women got as far as

Big Foot's Minniconjou band at the Grass Dance on the Cheyenne River, August 1890. Four months later, nearly all would be killed by the U.S. Cavalry in the massacre at Wounded Knee.

A mounted soldier surveys the battle-field at Wounded Knee, South Dakota.

OPPOSITE TOP:
A blizzard prevented soldiers from removing the dead until a few days after the killing occurred. When they returned to the scene, they loaded the frozen corpses into wagons and buried them in a mass grave.

three miles away before being caught and killed. The rest, about one hundred souls, fled and later froze to death in the hills.

It is unfortunate that the infamous Wounded Knee massacre, as sadly commemorated in American literature, seemed to validate the "myth of the vanishing Indian" by implying that an entire way of life had ended symbolically in this terrible finale. It served the dramatic needs of popular Indian history, but the reality was very different. For one thing, revitalization movements like the Ghost Dance survive in diverse forms throughout Indian America right up to the present day, still providing succor and hope to native peoples caught between the often contradictory creeds of two cultural worlds. For another, it was not so much sensational battles and deplorable inhumanities that, in the long run, cost Indians their autonomy after the Civil War, but rather the devastation wrought by disease and the expropriation of their land through the bloodless process of treaty making and anti-Indian legislation. Indeed, a vote in the U.S. Congress two years before the slaughter of innocents at Wounded Knee Creek probably created more widespread Indian suffering and left a more destructive legacy for Indians in the future than that infamous massacre. This far-reaching legislation was the General Allotment Act, also known as the Dawes Act, passed in 1887.

Ever since the early nineteenth century, when Secretary of War William Crawford had advocated property deeds for Indians, this notion of subdividing Indian land into single-family plots had found favor with Washington officials,

Gathering up the Dead at the Battle Field at Wounded Knee S.D. Copyrighted by the North Western Photo Co Jan 17 1891. Chadron Neb.

land-hungry private interests, and pro-Indian sympathizers alike. It seemed to satisfy everybody's agenda, regardless of whether that agenda was pro-Indian or anti-Indian. For one thing, it was consonant with the value white men placed on private ownership of property as a civilizing force. As one Indian agent expressed it, "The common field is the seat of barbarism . . . the separate farm [is] the door to civilization." Allotment also appealed to the Indian Bureau, which envisioned not only ridding itself of ever-larger bills for treaty-obligation rations and services but even turning a nice profit by auctioning off surplus reservation lands. Indian reformers liked the idea because they felt it would hasten the day when Indian families would feed themselves, sing hymns in church on Sunday, and behave like everyone else—the day when they would appreciate, as one Indian official put it in 1886, the importance of saying "'This is mine' instead of 'This is ours.'"

Over the years, a number of Indian spokespeople were also persuaded that land owned in common by the tribe was a standard of the past, that only with a property deed in hand could Indians defend themselves against a poverty-stricken future. In 1870 Seneca Indian Commissioner Ely Parker himself strongly urged "giving to every Indian a home that he can call his own," an understandably seductive prospect in a shrinking Indian world.

Some, however, doubted that allotment could actually be made to work as intended. In a nation where aggressive, homesteading newcomers were swiftly

An advertisement from the Department of the Interior (ca. 1911) luring individuals to purchase land designated as surplus after tribal allotments were made to Indians. The Indian pictured in the ad was a Yankton Sioux named Not Afraid of Pawnee.

The opening of the Cherokee Strip, September 16, 1893. The end of the nineteenth century saw huge land transfers in which Indian lands were sold off. The money obtained from these sales technically belonged to the Indians, but the commissioner of the Bureau of Indian Affairs was responsible for its disbursement.

outnumbering Indians, no reservation was free of land sharks ready to snatch Indian acres by any means necessary. Moreover, what if the allotted parcels—each of 160 or more acres—proved too barren or too arid to support their new Indian owners and their families? Or, supposing it was good land, what if greedy, well-heeled interests tried to lease or outright purchase whole blocks of parcels in order to run large cattle and agricultural operations? Above all, what if the Indians stopped dying out?

The entire allotment mechanism was premised on the expectation that the Indian population would continue the steep decline it had suffered from the combined effects of warfare, disease, and what one writer called the "natural" result of one race supplanting another. But with the improved conditions that allotment would supposedly bring about, this decline might be halted, the downward trend might reverse itself, the Indian population might actually begin to grow.

If that happened, the parcels would eventually be chopped up and "checkerboarded" (as it was called when those smaller bits were leased to outsiders) into increasingly smaller lots distributed among many sons and grandsons—or, more likely, among many daughters and granddaughters, as property rights traditionally passed through the female line in many parts of Indian America. How, then, could allotment hope to fulfil the reformers' visions of a new generation of happy Indian farm families since none would have sufficient land to support them?

Such doubts and warnings went unheeded. Despite the fact that early allotment experiments among the Omaha and Chippewa showed how easily outsiders might grab private Indian landholdings, the U.S. Congress made this policy the law of the land on February 8, 1887. Surveying parties shortly ranged across Indian country, computing the total acreage and dividing it into 160- or, sometimes, 320-acre plots—the sizes for an average Indian family allotment. Census takers tallied the number of Indian heads of households in the same tribe. After the lands were assigned to all Indian allottees, most of the remainder was generally available on the auction block to the highest bidder.

In Indian Territory a succession of massive land transfers was arranged

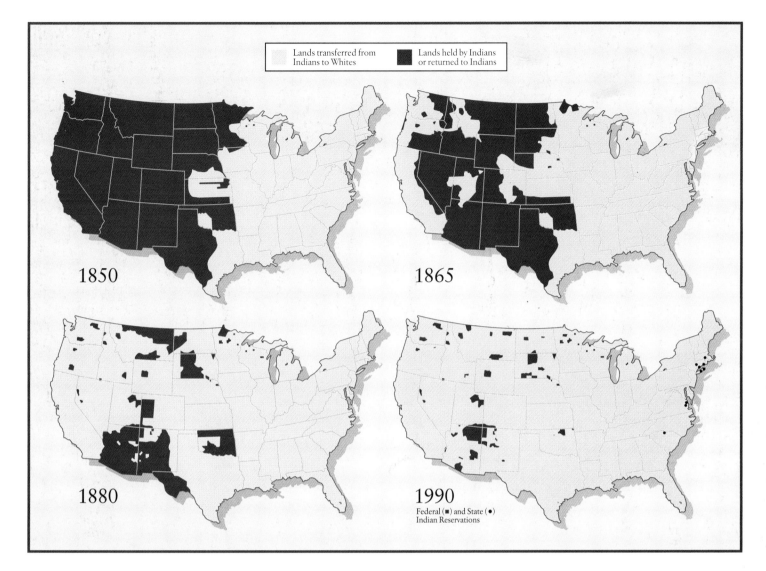

Lands transferred from Indians to Whites    Lands held by Indians or returned to Indians

1850

1865

1880

1990
Federal (■) and State (●) Indian Reservations

through lotteries, sealed bids, and frantic "runs." In 1889 alone, whites—racing from starting gates in buckboards or riding horses and mules—staked claim to two million acres of formerly Indian landholdings. Almost overnight the territory's non-Indian population exploded, from 60,000 in 1890, when it officially became Oklahoma Territory, to 400,000 a decade later. And each passing year the government boasted about how much land it had acquired through the allotment process: 13 million acres by 1890, 23 million acres by 1891, and over 30 million acres by 1892. Pressure on Indians to cede ever more acreage would remain intense as the allotment policy—what President Theodore Roosevelt termed "a mighty pulverizing engine to break up the tribal mass"—continued to rumble across Indian country.

*The Progression of Land Loss.*
**An astonishing amount of land had been transferred from Indian to white control by the close of the nineteenth century. Through treaties, purchases, and outright theft, claim to the continent was wrested from the native peoples. Today, many native Americans are trying to reclaim lands that were illegally expropriated in the past.**

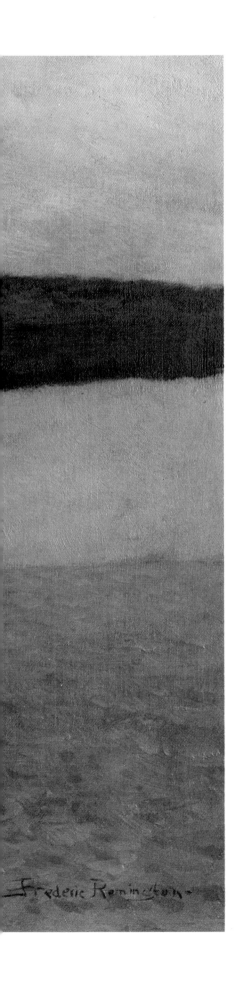

# CHAPTER TWENTY-TWO

# AT THE EBB POINT
# 1894–1915

WARRIOR AT NIGHT BY GINA GRAY (OSAGE), 1991

## Summer 1894

AS THEY WERE DEER HUNTING near Mill Creek, one of hundreds of narrow feeder streams penetrating the eastern flank of California's Sacramento Valley, a teenager named D. B. Lyon and his brother noticed what at first glance seemed to be a bear track. Bending down, however, they saw a human footprint. Almost the same jolt of recognition had occurred five years before when Lyon was hunting at Red Antelope Creek not far away. At that time, hearing crashing in the brush, he threw a rock at the sound and heard a human grunt. But when Lyon pursued he found only a complete Yahi Indian arrow-making kit (now in Berkeley's Phoebe Hearst Museum). Now, however, Lyon and his brother followed the tracks only to glimpse a running Indian hurl himself from the top of a bluff, snatch a supple treetop, which bent with his weight, and drop into the brush like a ghost.

Such sightings of phantomlike "last" representatives of native groups were emblematic of the general public's sense of Indian existence at this time. Whether as wishful thinking or pseudoscientific projection, the "vanishing Indian" theory still prevailed. Within a very few years the very last representative of this Yahi Indian group, who had been hiding in the California scrub, would make himself known to the world.

Indeed, the tragic extinction of this one Mill Creek tribelet would epitomize the plight of Indians up and down California who had suffered from white "Indian hunts." And since the U.S. Congress had not ratified any of their treaties, they were landless and defenseless. Over these years, to be Indian in

*Indian, Horse, and Village* by Frederic Remington, 1907.

*They who are the white soldiers killed almost all the Sioux in a battle. It was then that the woman, Tail Feather Woman, is said to have hidden among the reeds; in order to breathe there she parted the leaves of the reeds. She probably lay in the water for four days. When four days had passed it is said that the Spirit then came to her. He told her everything; he told her how the Indian should perform the Dancing Rite; he gave her to understand how to do everything that is good. He told her the way everyone should act; that they should not be the way they still are—people harming one another, killing one another—no! That was what the Spirit told her. . . . Everything good was explained to her: that they should pity each other, that they should be good to each other, that they should help each other in everything.*

—Menominee story from 1878 as told by Johnny the Thunderer Comes With Noise of Thunder, ca. 1950.

California was to be vilified as a "Digger" (a stereotype derived from the importance to the traditional California Indian diet of digging for roots and other edible plants), and so it was no wonder that many Indians preferred to identify themselves as Hispanic. They eked out meager livings as seasonal workers on the fruit and vegetable picking circuit, or they did odd jobs on farms as domestic servants, augmenting their subsistence wages with furtive hunting and foraging. In a state where nearly 300,000 Indians had been alive 125 years before, hardly more than 15,000 Indians could be found by 1900.

With most Indian freedom-fighters like Geronimo captured, killed, or incapacitated, a phenomenon of this transitional period was outbursts of outlawry on the fringes of western reservations by hot-blooded, angry, and confused younger Indians. From 1890 through 1915, brief outbursts led by these isolated young upstarts—Swordbearer in Montana, Almighty Voice in Canada, the Apache Kid in Arizona, Willie Boy and Shoshone Mike in Nevada, and the youthful leaders of the short-lived Navajo (1913) and Ute (1915) wars—underscored the human cost to the powerless tribes of having no authority figures to channel the warrior impulses and incipient leadership qualities of the next generation.

Aside from the general public's momentary amusement at newspaper items about such distant evocations of a bygone frontier, what made these turn-of-the-century years especially distressing for Indians was that, as a people, they were virtually invisible. As America industrialized and her leaders reached for new roles on the world's stage, the spotlight was off its first inhabitants. As if to exemplify this turn away from its Indian population, in 1899 the federal government authorized its final appropriation for religious organizations to operate Indian schools. Now Indian affairs were relegated to the routine federal bureaucracy. The humanitarians' crusade to "Americanize" the Indian also languished for lack of financial support and national interest.

New epidemics of trachoma, influenza, pneumonia, and tuberculosis within native communities, aggravated by malnutrition and abysmal living conditions, went unreported in national media and unaddressed until the Federal Indian Health Program was instituted in 1908. The ravages of tuberculosis were especially widespread, decimating Indian families in the Pacific Northwest, amounting to 95 percent of all deaths within the Mohave tribe of southern California in 1907, and 66 percent of Pima Indian fatalities in Arizona.

The trachoma scourge, an eye infection leading to blindness, put an estimated seventeen hundred Indian boys and girls in boarding schools "in danger of complete blindness," warned the Society of American Indians in 1913, with five thousand definitely infected.

Moreover, a major white-collar crime wave in Indian Territory was defrauding Indians of their last allotments and natural energy leases. At the same time, police state–like conditions, repressing Indian rituals and social gatherings, persisted on many reservations. Together with a pervasive sense of bleak hopelessness, these forces led to the plummeting of the national Indian population in 1900 to 237,196 men, women, and children.

And while the general public was disinterested in Indian people, the crusade to slice up Indian lands advanced relentlessly. Once male heads of households received their assigned tracts, what was left over invariably fell into white hands. At the same time, new laws kept loosening the Indians' grip on the fractioned parcels they still kept. Through an act passed in March 1901, for instance, if a road was surveyed across an Indian's allotment, the owner would find his acreage automatically condemned. The thrust of government policy remained aimed at negating any sense of cultural wholeness; in 1907 the Interior Department was allowed to distribute funds earmarked for tribes to individuals instead.

It was upon Oklahoma Territory, which would gain statehood in 1907, that the second front of the allotment process focused in the early 1900s. In 1887, nineteen of the area's Indian tribes had voted against allotment. Attempting to forestall the dreadful fate in store, the Five Civilized Tribes fought now for an all-Indian state, no longer named Oklahoma, as had been proposed in 1861, but Sequoyah, in honor of the Cherokee who had invented their unique syllabary.

As Oklahoma approached statehood, however, these nations resigned themselves to the inevitable, surrendering their ancient rights to self-government and accepting the state constitution. But it was a deeply painful loss, as one Cherokee woman who refused to attend the statehood ceremonies recalled. "I went to bed and cried all night long. It seemed more than I could bear that the Cherokee Nation, my country and my people's country, was no more."

Over the dozen years after 1898, surveyors, working on allotting out Oklahoma lands to the Indians, divided up some twenty million acres. But once

**Portrait of a Mosa Mohave girl (1903).**

## LIZETTE DENOMIE

Lizette Denomie was a Chippewa allottee who died in 1897. Her 80-acre parcel was split up among nine heirs: twenty years later six of them had died, subdividing the land further so that fourteen of these third-generation heirs had only patches of between four-and-a half acres to three-quarters of an acre apiece. Finally, in 1935, the original tract had been splintered among thirty-five heirs, seventeen of them expected to make a living on less than an acre each.

Indians were granted their own individual parcels (and the rest sold or leased to white towns and farming), whatever security they felt on their homesteads was soon at risk again. First, the inheritance problem, which some had predicted, became a reality, as the generational splitting of land had the effect of depriving the original owner's descendants of sufficient land to make a living.

As a bailout from this type of incremental land loss, the Burke Act of 1906 smoothed the way for those Indians whom the government approved as "competent" to decide for themselves how they wished to unload their diminishing holdings. Now a host of cunning deals and illegal inducements blossomed, devised by con artists wise in the way of acquiring assets cheap, especially from people whose wretched prospects and trusting ways made them easy targets.

To complicate matters, oil was found on the lands of the Osage, Creek, Seminole, and Delaware, arousing a feeding frenzy to buy or otherwise steal Indian deeds. False wills were drafted, Indian family members were bribed, beatings and even murder were not uncommon.

The decades immediately following allotment witnessed such an assault on Oklahoma Indian land rights that of the thirty million acres originally deeded to individual Indians, twenty-seven million were lost to them forever.

On August 9, 1911, barking dogs in a corral in Oroville, California, fifty miles northeast of San Francisco, drew attention to a frightened, emaciated Indian with burned-off hair, a wooden plug in the septum of his nose, deer thongs in his earlobes, and a ragged piece of covered-wagon canvas over his loins.

After a while scholars from the University of California's Berkeley campus who rescued the man from local gawkers learned that he was probably the very last member of the Yahi Indian band that D. B. Lyon had pursued up the canyon seventeen years before. Never learning his real name, they dubbed him Ishi, or "man" in his native tongue. The eagerness with which Californians read about the discovery of Ishi, and flocked to see him at the Berkeley campus, where he became something of a living exhibit, revealed the astonishing grip that the "noble savage" and "vanishing Indian" images held—and still holds—on the American popular psyche.

At Berkeley, Ishi demonstrated for sympathetic scholars the survival technologies of his people, flaking arrowheads from bottle glass, teaching linguists his difficult language, and taking one poignant field trip back to the old haunts where his entire tribelet met its tragic end. When Ishi died on March 25, 1916, the collective experience of his tribe died with him, and another native American worldview was irretrievably lost. Other lesser-known deaths of traditional holdouts like Ishi before the turn of the nineteenth century had already spelled the end to Indian cultures that had evolved over many thousands of years.

Yet most native American groups across the country were hanging on despite "vanishing Indian" myths, new outbreaks of disease, unreported crime waves, and against tremendous economic odds. In this new era of behind-the-scenes corruption and official neglect, small native communities continued quietly to fend for themselves in time-honored ways. At the Wind River agency, for example, the Northern Arapaho still subscribed to a "Help Your Neighbor" policy when it

Ishi demonstrating how to chew sinew for making arrows (LEFT) and chipping a stone implement (RIGHT).

came to such rudimentary tasks as cutting and hefting logs for simple reservation dwellings, or assisting the elderly in planting and watering ten-acre wheat fields and home-use vegetable gardens grown from seeds obtained from the agency. Buffeted by incessant demands that they remake themselves in a white image, it is striking how Indians heeded deeper voices, acting upon words said to have come from the lips of Sitting Bull himself: "Take the best of the white man's road, pick it up and take it with you. That which is bad leave alone, cast it away. Take the best of the old Indian ways—always keep them. They have been proven for thousands of years. Do not let them die."

Some high-profile Indians who also followed this dual cultural road were graduates of the boarding school system that had tried to eradicate their Indianness and separate them from their heritage. To a degree the assimilation campaign had created a gulf between the reservation communities and the first generation of Indian adults whose lives and outlooks had been transformed by boarding school indoctrination in non-Indian patterns of worship and work and the desirability of seeking prestige and creating a meaningful personal, rather than tribal, life. But as the graduates of the early classes at Carlisle and Haskell reached maturity in the first decades of the twentieth century, some also sought out each other to share ideas about creating a more hopeful Indian future for their children. Often the prize students of the assimilation campaign, they had the intelligence and skills to make a real impact on behalf of Indian causes. Among the organizational results of this new professional Indian generation was the Society of American Indians, which, despite its short life span, would galvanize the best Indian writers, physicians, artists, and thinkers of the day.

Crumbo

# CHAPTER TWENTY-THREE
# GLIMMERINGS OF SOVEREIGNTY
# 1915–1924

CORN MOTHER, *THE HARVEST OF LIFE*
BY FERNANDO PADILLA, JR. (SAN FELIPE PUEBLO), 1987

## September 1915

WHEN THE TALL, UNSMILING Yavapai Apache physician named Carlos Montezuma strode toward the podium during the fifth annual conference of the Society of American Indians, some of his Indian colleagues in the audience braced themselves. Representing the upper crust of the professional American Indian world, the society had recently been grappling with factional disputes over a number of basic issues. For one thing, there was dissent over the use of peyote, the hallucinogenic cactus that was the sacramental food for a popular form of Indian ritual that blended old and new religious beliefs. To some this ritual was only another form of debilitating intoxication while to others it served as a positive and vital bridge between the tribal and modern worlds. Montezuma, however, was concerned with a more urgent matter. Indian autonomy was at stake, and his impatience with the society's fence-straddling had made him boycott earlier meetings. Montezuma was consumed by the continuing stranglehold of the Bureau of Indian Affairs over Indian freedoms, and he even suspected Indian Bureau influence over some of his society colleagues.

---

*Sunset in Memoriam* by Woodrow W. Crumbo (Potawatomi-Creek), 1946.

*The Indian Bureau system is wrong. The only way to adjust wrong is to abolish it, and the only reform is to let my people go. After freeing the Indian from the shackles of government supervision, what is the Indian going to do: Leave that with the Indian, and it is none of your business.*

—CARLOS MONTEZUMA
(Apache), ca. 1916

Other notables in attendance included the Winnebago Henry Roe Cloud, the Seneca Arthur C. Parker, the Arapaho Rev. Sherman Coolidge, and the Sioux writer Charles Eastman. Recruiting talent largely from graduates of the government boarding school system, the Society of American Indians boasted native intellectuals from all the professions and arts among its elite membership. They shared the vision of a "race consciousness" that would consolidate "all lines of progress and reform, for the welfare of the Indian race in particular, and humanity in general." For the past four years the society had met annually, re-dedicating its members to the virtues that their reform-minded teachers had instilled: self-help, personal initiative, the importance of education. Occasionally they highlighted sharper positions regarding legal rights and improved health care. By and large, however, they could agree only on moderate planks, and Montezuma was about to call them on it.

Montezuma's own background was most unusual. A Yavapai Apache, he was stolen by Pimas in Arizona when he was only five years old. Then he was sold to a Chicago photographer who raised him in the Midwest. After he finished high school, Montezuma put himself through the University of Illinois, graduating in 1884, and four years later completed Chicago Medical School. Angry over government mistreatment of his mother, who had died trying to locate him, and furious that, although African-Americans had been granted citizenship in 1868, Indians were still disenfranchised, Montezuma's passionate campaign against the Indian Bureau could not be activated under the society's mild charter.

"The iron hand of the Indian Bureau has us in charge," he proclaimed in the fiery speech he had dramatically entitled "Let My People Go." His point was that this first pan-tribal organization for Indian rights had disintegrated into "the mere routine of shaking hands, appointing committees, listening to papers." Montezuma left that meeting wholly dissatisfied, and the following year published his own monthly newspaper, *Wassaja*, which lashed out at the Indian Bureau in editorials and cartoons. He also targeted for scorn middle-of-the-road society members like Arthur C. Parker, nephew of Grant's Indian commissioner,

Photographer Frank Palmer, of Spokane, Washington, made widely distributed postcards of Nez Perce and Yakima Indians posed in western vehicles or against other "amusing" backgrounds (ca. 1916).

Ely Parker. To Montezuma, Parker's campaign for a national American Indian Day was ludicrous so long as Indians were not freed from the constraints of government meddling in their business.

Among the items on the society's lengthy agenda for improvement of the Indians' lot was winning citizenship for America's first inhabitants, a cause to which their 1919 annual conference was dedicated. Charles Eastman declared in his opening address, "We Indians started the whole basis of Americanism. . . . [The Indian] will save this country. The day when an Indian becomes leader of this country will be the day when civilization may come on a stable foundation." When one invited bureaucrat maintained that only Indians judged "competent" should be awarded citizenship, Omaha member Thomas Sloan countered that "The Indian is a native of this country and it is a universal rule of civilization that a person shall be a citizen of the country of which he is a native. . . . The backward subject Indian needs citizenship more than the advanced Indian." Unfortunately, when an Indian citizenship bill—authored by Representative Charles Carter of Oklahoma, himself a Chickasaw Indian—was introduced in Congress, it called for a ranking system that would separate Indians into classes. This prevented the society from uniting behind it, and helped to doom it.

Since the general American public had largely put Indians out of sight and mind, it came as a surprise when, shortly after the onset of World War I, an Indian presence made itself conspicuous by demonstrating enthusiastic support for the government's war effort. Even before the United States entered the international conflict, hundreds of young Indians slipped across the border to sign up with Canadian military units leaving for the European front. And once America did declare war, another 10,000 Indians saw active service in the U.S. Army, while 2,000 more joined the Navy. Meanwhile, on the home front, approximately 10,000 Indian members of the Red Cross sewed over 100,000 items of clothing for the troops overseas and sent 500 Christmas boxes to them. And digging into their own rather shallow pockets, Indians across America came up with an estimated $25 million to spend on war bonds.

On the killing fields of France and Germany, the exploits of a full-blood Choctaw named Joseph Oklahombi from Bismarck, North Dakota, were exemplary of this unexpected outburst of native patriotism. Engaged in the horrendous trench warfare on the eastern front, Oklahombi, only a private, dodged 210 yards through rolls of barbed wire and under withering German fire. Reaching the German positions, he overpowered the machine-gun nest and single-handedly captured 171 prisoners. After this, Oklahombi gained a reputation for crossing the cratered no-man's-land between the combatants, taking surprised Germans prisoner in sections of their own trenches, pinpointing enemy positions, and rescuing wounded comrades. For these acts of bravery Marshal Philippe Pétain, the French commander in chief, awarded Oklahombi France's highest honor.

Despite glowing examples of Indian bravery overseas, the "ward" status of Indians on the home front left them vulnerable during such times of national crisis. As Sioux author Vine Deloria, Jr., describes the impact of World War I on the Pine Ridge reservation of his father's day: "Many of the Sioux families had developed prosperous ranches. Then the Government stepped in, sold the Indian

Blackfeet Indians from Montana, in New York to publicize Glacier National Park in 1913, view the city from the roof of the McAlpin Hotel, billed at the time as "the tallest hotel in the world."

*Kennee Krooked Arrow*
by Roger Perkins (Mohawk), 1992.

*At last I see that which I have always longed for, to see my race dissatisfied with themselves and the conditions under which they live. It pained me to see the stoical indifference, the lethargy, the masklike countenance with which they viewed their condition. I longed to see the flicker of the old spirit, the spark of the old-time flint and the breakneck speed of the chase and the battle.*

*A sleeping nation is a hard nation to help. The awakening has come; the war has done its work.*

—EDWARD AHENAKEW
(Saskatchewan Cree), 1920

cattle for wartime needs, and after the war leased the grazing land to whites, creating wealthy white ranchers and destitute Indian landlords."

At the same time, a sea change was taking place in the Indian world's sense of itself. A new Indian assertiveness was building, and a growing national responsiveness soon to match it would galvanize the strongest pro-Indian sentiment since the post–Civil War reform movement. What would differentiate this new coalition of whites and Indians, however, was that it was less assimilationist than live-and-let-live in its dogma. In the 1920s, Indians and non-Indians alike began to take serious stock of earlier philosophies of forced cultural transformation, the costs of misguided government policies, and the current well-being of Indians. While the older generation of reformers had dreamt of "killing the Indian and saving the man," this new attitude exhibited respect for those traditional Indian ways that government policy had discouraged. An appreciation for what today would be labeled "multiculturalism" lay on the horizon; soon it would revolutionize Washington's attitude toward the Indian past, present, and future.

Demographic changes were also in the air. From that alarming all-time low point in 1900, the national Indian population had crept up to nearly 277,000 by 1910. Though it slid back to 244,500 in 1920, due in large measure to the worldwide influenza epidemic of 1918, it would recover with a 40 percent increase by 1930. More interestingly, whereas in the late nineteenth century very few Indians could be found in the nation's cities, by 1920 some 6 percent of the country's Indians were urban dwellers, and their numbers were on the rise.

Although the Society of American Indians was gone, its legacy remained as throughout the 1920s new local Indian organizations kept appearing. The more moderate groups were content to publicize Indian self-awareness, while the more militant mobilized against particular abuses of native rights. Formed in 1912, the Alaska Native Brotherhood and Sisterhood networked with both native and sympathetic white groups to watchdog the rights of Indian and Inuit peoples in the north. Various California Indian rights associations would come and go until 1926 when native Californians organized the all-native California Indian Brotherhood, which lobbied for more lands for Indians, better schooling, emergency health relief, and compensation for those 1851–52 unratified-treaty lands that had been confiscated by the federal government but never paid for. In the Midwest the Grand Council Fire of Chicago, beginning with both Indian and non-Indian members in 1923, continued the quieter call for Indian reform, while farther east the long-standing fight for sovereign rights for Iroquois tribes who lived on both sides of the U.S.–Canadian border led the outspoken Tuscarora leader Clinton Rickard to form the Indian Defense League of America.

Indians also contributed to revelations of scandalous graft and exploitation in eastern Oklahoma. In 1924 an old Indian advocacy group, the Indian Rights Association, dispatched an investigative team that included Sioux writer Gertrude Bonnin (an author of short stories under her native name, Zitkala-sa). Among their case studies of fraud and corruption was the sad tale of seven-year-old Ledcie Stechi, a Choctaw girl who had inherited her dead mother's oil leases and was being raised by her grandmother. After a local banker insinuated himself into the family fold as her guardian, he supplied her family with $15 a month while he tried to sell ten of her acres—appraised at $90,000—for a quick $2,000. Although he was stymied at this, the meager allowance was continued, and the malnourished little girl eventually died in her guardian's home under mysterious circumstances. Her emaciated body was not even buried before other speculators besieged the mourning grandmother with deals for the dead child's valuable property. As the Rights Association exposé made clear, this sort of graft and exploitation had become rampant among "Oklahoma's Poor Rich Indians."

Meanwhile, in 1921, a bill was introduced in the U.S. Senate that threatened to undermine the Pueblos' autonomy and land base in the Southwest. Although the independent nature of their rural village-states had traditionally insulated the Pueblo from the economic uncertainties that beset the rest of Indian country, now they were attacked by anti-Pueblo interests that sought to legitimize the land claims, amounting to many thousands of acres, of some three thousand non-Indian families who had been squatting illegally on Pueblo territories over the years. This grave threat—embodied in legislation proposed by Senator Holm O. Bursum, which also proposed injunctions against traditional Pueblo religious practices—actually galvanized rival Pueblo communities into uniting for the first time since their 1680 revolt against the Spanish. In November 1922, at Santo Domingo pueblo, in part energized by a rising white organizer on behalf of Indian rights named John Collier, their All Pueblo Council convened to draft a resounding objection to the proposed scheme. Ultimately the Pueblo peoples prevailed and the Bursum Bill was defeated.

Back in Washington, debate over the bill had helped to focus the new pro-Indian awareness. In 1923 Secretary of the Interior Hubert Work convened an advisory panel known as the Committee of One Hundred. Composed of quite a few former associates of the old Society of American Indians, this distinguished group was charged with reviewing the net effects of government Indian policy over the preceding half-century.

As they began their work, the terribly discouraging facts of Indian land loss, and associated social, educational, and medical privations, began to emerge. In tribe after tribe, in the aftermath of allotment, Indians had become dependent, landless paupers, not the happy self-sufficient ranchers and farmers envisioned by the reformers. Without adequate safeguards or federal support to sustain them during the government's great experiment in wholesale cultural transformation, Indians had sacrificed over half of the territories that, in treaties negotiated since the 1850s, had been promised them in perpetuity.

By 1880 those treaties had left Indians nationwide with roughly 155 million acres. One way or another, by the end of the 1920s over 85 million acres—more than double the territory in all of Oklahoma—had been stripped, or "alienated" as officials put it, from them. Furthermore, of the lands that did remain in Indian hands, about 30 million acres were retained by tribes as a whole, primarily in the mesa and canyon Southwest, where large tribes, such as the Navajo, had largely escaped the ravages of allotment. Finally, a close inspection of those allotments that Indians had managed to retain quickly revealed why no one else wanted them: more often than not they were on parched desert, in rugged mountains, on range that was poorly watered or whose alkaline clay slicked in rain and hardened in the sun, or they lay deep in mosquito-ridden swamps.

*Anasazi Blues*
**by Roger Perkins (Mohawk), 1992.**

*Many of our young men volunteered and many gave their lives for you. You were willing to let them fight in the front ranks of France. Now we want to tell our troubles to you—I do not mean that we are calling on your governments. We are tired of calling on the governments of palefaced peoples in America and Europe. We have tried that and found it was no use. They deal only in fine words. . . . We have a little territory left—just enough to live and die on. Don't you think your governments ought to be ashamed to take that away from us by pretending it is part of theirs?*

—DESKAHEH
Cayuga chief of the
Younger Bear clan, 1925

Ever since the mid-nineteenth century, limited opportunities had been open for Indians to enjoy the legal securities and voting privileges of U.S. citizenship. Since the days of the great removals, some treaties and statutes were baited with the promise of citizenship if Indians complied with their terms. Usually, when this was adjudicated on an individual-by-individual basis, the new Indian citizens had to verify their status through dossiers they were supposed to carry around whenever they expected to interact with government officials. Still, it is estimated that by 1917 almost two-thirds of all American Indians, largely through their acceptance of allotments, had become U.S. citizens.

While the Indian Rights Association lobbied for forty years for Indian citizenship, not all Indians, it must be pointed out, were panting for the opportunity. Some Iroquois of upper New York State, for instance, continued to think of themselves as citizens of their own nation, voting on their own declaration of war in 1917, and later sending representatives to the United Nations and designing their own passports for use by their citizens commuting between Iroquois communities in Canada and the United States. And it was also true that some congressional advocates of Indian citizenship, as with earlier proponents of allotment, had the ulterior motive of getting Indians off the government's back and lifting the skimpy protections on Indian land that remained.

With the gallant Indian performance in World War I, the issue of Indian citizenship, still dear to the heart of many Society of American Indian followers, was resurrected. In 1919 Congress passed a special law granting any Indian who had fought alongside the Allies permission to apply for citizenship. But as the majority of Society of American Indian members expressed at their gathering that year, this was not enough. Too many of their people remained under the status of "wards," in which their lands and finances were held in trusts administered by the federal government, and they were denied voting and other rights.

At long last, on June 2, 1924, the Indian Citizenship Act was passed—in large measure because Congress had become embarrassed over the obvious discrepancy between Indian status at home and Indian courage overseas. Actually the deed granting citizenship seemed a slight maneuver, only a paragraph in length. Legally Indians were now a unique sort of 200 percent American, enjoying full standing in the country at large as well as in their own tribal communities—many of which still clung to a fundamental sense of their semisovereign status within the political confines of the United States. At the same time, since states retained the power to confer voting rights, Indians in Arizona, New Mexico, and Maine had to wait until the mid-1950s, after fighting many court battles, to exercise their full franchise as American citizens.

This almost offhand shift in status for native Americans was observed by the *New York Times* with some irony, demonstrating the degree to which the country's sympathy for Indians had evolved in the half-century since the Custer debacle, when most newspapers clamored for Indian blood. "If there are cynics among the Indians," wrote the *Times*, "they may receive the news of their new citizenship with wry smiles. The white race, having robbed them of a continent, and having sought to deprive them of freedom of action, freedom of social custom, and freedom of worship, now at last gives them the same legal basis as their conquerors."

That *Times* editorial was right and wrong. For what Indians had really retained, which was perhaps of more precious value than the legal status of U.S. citizenship, were their own special historical, cultural, and legal bases as indigenous North American nations.

First, as historical survivors, despite one of the most sustained assaults against any collection of ethnic groups in the history of humankind, American Indians had not been eliminated by weapons, extinguished by disease, or "vanished" by wishful thinking.

Second, as cultural survivors, Indians had not lost all their languages (58 still existed in 1924) or their lifeways (there were 193 federally recognized tribes in 1924) or their beliefs about the proper relationships that should prevail between native peoples, their traditional spirits, and their natural environments.

And third, as legal survivors, many Indian tribes still clung to the unique nation-to-nation relationships embodied in their treaties, whose enduring authority would resurface within another two generations to recover for many of them a degree of the sovereign status they had enjoyed back in 1850.

Against all odds, native Americans had survived into the twentieth century.

—PETER NABOKOV

*Osage Friendship Blanket*
by Gina Gray (Osage), 1988. According to Osage custom, traditional dances are held for four days in the summer of each year. The final day is known as the Giveaway Day, when gifts such as blankets and shawls are exchanged. The painting above is based on a design of a blanket made in the late 1800s.

# PART FIVE

# THE TWENTIETH CENTURY AND BEYOND

I am purified and free.
And I will not allow you to ignore me.
I have brought you a gift.
It is all I have but it is yours.
You may reach out and enfold it.
It is only the strength in the caress of a gentle breeze,
But it will carry you to meet the eagle in the sky.
My name is "I am living." I am here.
My name is "I am living." I am here.

ANNA LEE WALTERS, PAWNEE-OTOE
From *I Have Bowed Before the Sun*

Stan Jones, Sr., Tulalip tribal chairman, presides over the
ceremonial blessing of the first salmon—called Big Chief King Salmon—
caught in the new fishing season, Tulalip reservation, Washington (ca. 1986).

# CHAPTER TWENTY-FOUR
# BEING A TWENTIETH-CENTURY INDIAN

PAINTED HARDHAT
BY RICHARD GLAZER-DANAY (MOHAWK), 1982

IN THE 1920S, the members of the Caughnawaga Mohawk tribe made their living through an exclusive and risky profession—the high altitude, precision steelwork crucial in the construction of skyscrapers and bridges.

Like many Caughnawaga Mohawks, Paul Diabo migrated back and forth across the Canadian border, returning to the Kahnawake reservation for holidays and hard times, moving to New York or Philadelphia for a season or two of lucrative work as a skilled structural steelworker. Diabo's brothers lived in New York with other Mohawk steelworkers, in a Brooklyn neighborhood they called "Downtown Kahnawake."

The Brooklyn Caughnawagas maintained tight bonds with friends and family back on their Canadian reservation, frequently returning for weddings, funerals, lacrosse matches, and the simple pleasure of being back home. On most Friday afternoons, groups of Mohawks piled into their cars for the all-night drive to Kahnawake. Money from steelwork paid for nice homes and community improvements on the reservation. Back in Brooklyn, neighborhood stores, bars, and a church contributed to cultural unity among the two to three hundred Mohawk residents. Both places were essential to Caughnawaga community. As they traveled between the two, the steelworkers pursued a path of cultural integration, adjusting to modern-day life and, at the same time, making it part of a tradition that was particularly Mohawk.

---

OPPOSITE:
*Cloak of Heritage* by Kevin Warren Smith (Cherokee), 1991.

A Mohawk steelworker,
New York City (1980).

The Mohawks began working in steelwork in 1886 when an official with a Canadian bridge-building company noticed a group of teenage Caughnawagas playing on a bridge being built over the St. Lawrence River. Needing workers who would brave high winds, great heights, and precarious support systems, he hired a group of young Mohawk men. They proved adept at the job.

The original twelve taught the craft of high steelwork to friends and family members who, in turn, taught others. Soon, one could find Mohawks on construction sites across Canada and the United States. When a building boom came to New York in the 1920s, the Caughnawagas flocked to the city, banding together in the close-knit twelve-block neighborhood.

In New York, Mohawks worked on innumerable structures, including the Waldorf-Astoria Hotel, the Empire State Building, the Chrysler Building, and the George Washington Bridge. Mohawk steelworkers saw their dangerous and difficult occupation as part of a tradition that extended back to their nineteenth-century work as expert canoe guides, and beyond that to the warrior traditions of the eighteenth century and earlier. Values of family and community were sustained by the strong link to Kahnawake and the tight bonds of the Brooklyn neighborhood. Yet the Caughnawagas were employed in the most modern of wage-labor enterprises, and, indeed, their specialized skills were particularly sought after for the hazardous work. They had found an ideal way to participate in American society while maintaining the ties of tradition, kinship, and tribe.

But Paul Diabo and his community would confront an even greater problem of adjustment. In 1926, the United States arrested Diabo as an illegal alien working without a permit. The Caughnawaga community responded in terms that were both traditional and modern. Mohawks from Brooklyn and Kahnawake created a communal fund from which they hired a pair of non-Indian attorneys. Diabo's lawyers argued that he was not, in fact, a Canadian but a Mohawk and that his rights to "free intercourse and commerce" across the border had been established by the Jay Treaty of 1794, and confirmed by the Treaty of 1796 and the Treaty of Ghent signed at the end of the War of 1812.

In one of the first legal victories for modern Indian sovereignty—the legal right of tribal people to define themselves and to act as unique entities—an appeals court ruled that the Mohawks were a "separate dependent nation," rather than a simple part of either Canada or the United States. Diabo's victory allowed the Brooklyn Mohawk community to maintain its commuting relationship with Kahnawake and established that the independence of Indian self-rule could be worked out within the context of larger "nations." As a result, Mohawks continue to band together to face the rigors of structural steelwork today.

In the early twentieth century, many tribes began taking the legal path followed by the Mohawks in efforts to win back lost rights. But Indian people also found other ways to state their cases effectively. In January of 1923, even before the Diabo case, a group of Pueblo Indians visited the New York Stock Exchange seeking support for their struggle against legislation introduced by New Mexico Senator Holm Bursum. Bursum's Pueblo Lands Bill would have invalidated Pueblo land titles and water rights. So, dressed in feathered headdresses, blankets, and beaded moccasins, the Pueblos sang and drummed for the assembled brokers.

The Exchange went wild, and its members flooded congressional offices with telegrams urging the bill's defeat. Bankers and brokers who rarely thought twice about Indians suddenly and solidly lined up in their corner.

This show of support, however, did not spring from a reasoned consideration of the Bursum Bill's problems. It represented instead an emotional response to the display put on by the Pueblos, and this in turn was a result of the symbolic meanings Americans had progressively attached to their idea of "The Indian." While Indian people like Diabo and the Caughnawagas had decided for themselves what it was to be a twentieth-century Indian, white Americans had a harder time separating urban steelworkers from the painted savages galloping across their silver screens. On that day when the Pueblos danced in New York, the most significant exchange was cultural and symbolic. In order to understand it, we need to recognize the remarkable variety of roles that "Indians as symbols" have played in the continuing relationship between the newcomers to this continent and America's indigenous peoples.

The various roles that "Indians as symbols" have played reflect what was happening in the minds of observers at varying times. This proved to be the case at the

*A good ironworker is afraid of high places. I don't want to work with no fool who's not a little bit afraid of being up so high. It's the fear that gives you the edge, that keeps you alert. . . . No, a Mohawk is afraid of heights just like the next guy. The difference is, the Mohawk is willing to deal with it.*

—Mohawk Ironworker

*Reflections: Tribute to Our Iron Skywalkers* by Arnold Jacobs (Onondaga), 1983.

*Missing* by Frederic Remington, 1899.

"I saw the living, breathing end of three American centuries of smoke and dust and sweat," wrote western artist Frederic Remington in 1905, "and I now see quite another thing where it all took place, but it does not appeal to me."

What did appeal to Remington was the picturing of a nostalgic and romantic past full of rugged cowboys, masculine military figures, and savage Indians. At the turn of the century, Remington's images, along with those of artists such as Charles M. Russell and Henry Farny, were thought to be accurate representations of the era of western expansion that had supposedly just passed into history. Indeed, many consider these images to be equally truthful today, and they frequently appear in books and films that wish to present images of Indian people.

But the works of these artists better represent the fascinations, worries, and nostalgia that characterized the early twentieth century than they do

Indian people. Remington, for example, began his career picturing Indians as savage opponents for hearty Anglo-Saxon adventurers. By century's end, he adopted the figure of "The Indian" as a more sympathetic symbol of the twilight of the "old America." Henry Farny pictured Indians in an Eden-like natural harmony. Farny himself, however, lived amidst the urban industry of Cincinnati where he had hired a Lakota man to model for him and serve as the janitor of the city's art club. With experience as a Montana cowboy and continuing residence in the West, Charles M. Russell was considered among the most "authentic" of the western painters of the early twentieth century. But among his cattle-country influences, Russell also numbered the local theater where he saw stereotyped movie Indians projected like shadows onto a blank screen.

Various misperceptions of "The Indian" have long fulfilled an honored place in American thought. The

Puritans, for instance, came to the new land equipped with the concept that they were God's chosen and that all who did not believe as they did were spawns of the Devil. They saw Indians as the perfect foil to justify their own beliefs.

Later, during the revolt against Great Britain, many colonists forged a more positive image of "The Indian." Indians now symbolized the American continent and all it stood for—freedom, liberty, and not being British. This more sympathetic revolutionary image of Indians was hardly reflected in the new nation's dealings with real Indian people.

By the early nineteenth century, the new Americans came to believe that Indians were naturally and inevitably vanishing before American "civilization." The "vanishing Indian" provided a convenient cover for a harsher reality: most Indian vanishing was the direct result of cold-blooded American expansion.

*The Luckless Hunter* by Frederic Remington, 1904.

LEFT:
*Pehriska-Ruhpa, Moennitarri Warrior in the Costume of the Dog Dance* by Karl Bodmer, ca. 1834.

RIGHT:
*Indian After Bodmer* by Fritz Scholder (Luiseño), 1975.

turn of the century. Four hundred years after Columbus first landed on San Salvador, Americans gathered in Chicago to celebrate his achievement and its most obvious consequence—the United States of America.

The 1893 World's Columbian Exposition triumphantly proclaimed a rising American political and economic empire. The United States had seemingly fulfilled its Manifest Destiny, extending its political sway across the continent and offering Christian civilization to the remnants of the "primitives" whose land the burgeoning young nation now occupied. Yet the sensitive observer might have detected an undercurrent of anxiety in Chicago, an undercurrent expressed at the exposition itself by historian Frederick Jackson Turner.

American society and character, said Turner, had been formed on the frontier. Here, Americans had returned to their own primitive roots, lost their European backgrounds and history, and made themselves over as practitioners of local democracy.

This celebratory—if somewhat skewed—definition of American character, however, was Turner's only piece of good news. He also had bad news: much of the frontier area had already been settled, effectively erasing the line between wild and civilized that was so crucial in the remaking of Americans. The corollary was painfully obvious: if American character and society were formed by the

LEFT:
*Wak-Tae-Geli, A Sioux Warrior*
by Karl Bodmer, ca. 1834.

RIGHT:
*Standing Indian*
by Fritz Scholder (Luiseño), 1974.

experience of the frontier, and if there was no longer a frontier, what would guar-antee the future health of American social values?

Turner's pronouncement was a reflection of a more deeply rooted, and grow-ing anxiety: were the costs of America's transition from pioneering to the modern world simply too high?

In the years following the Chicago exposition, Americans confronted rapid social and cultural changes that made the alleged demise of the frontier doubly worrisome. For the first time in the country's history, more Americans lived in urban than in rural settings. Modern reality exchanged the frontier's ever-expanding elbow room for urban masses now jostling for living space. Accel-erating technological and industrial development combined with a continuing flood of foreign immigrants to create a work force in constant confrontation with profit-oriented management. Social critics worried that, in the context of com-petitive urban life, individuals were growing increasingly estranged from one another, and their sense of community was disappearing.

For the United States, the new century began as a time of unrest, of union wars bitterly fought, of breakdown and change in a shifting world, and eventually of a soul-destroying Great Depression. And all of these traumas would be re-flected in American attitudes about the land's native peoples.

Land of Enchantment
by Woodrow W. Crumbo
(Potawatomi-Creek), 1946.

OPPOSITE:
Blessing of the Deer Dancer
by Gilbert Atencio
(San Ildefonso Pueblo), 1964.

*Are you hot? Be an Indian and keep cool. Are you tired of work and sick of the city? What's the answer? Simply be an Indian. Cut out the work and take the first trail for the timber. No one knows how to enjoy the big outdoors like an uncontaminated redskin and no one better likes a prolonged vacation.*

—ARTHUR C. PARKER
Seneca anthropologist. This ironic injunction epitomizes the absurd quality of American views of Indians. From "Lure of the Woods: Joys of Camp Life on an Indian Reservation," appearing in *The Knickerbocker*, July 3, 1910.

## Modern Americans Meet the "Children of Nature"

In the first decades of the twentieth century, writers and artists fled the cities, seeking sanctuary in a variety of rural settings that included the Pueblo country of northern New Mexico. These intellectual refugees hoped that remedies for the ills of modern society might be found in places like Taos, a remote Indian pueblo that epitomized for them the opposite of bustling, harried urban life. They imagined native people to be content with simple technology, bound by organic community, and full of insight about "nature."

For those left behind to run urban businesses, factories, newspapers, and radio stations, northern New Mexico assumed an importance, not as a real location on the map, but as a magical locale to be imagined and idealized from a safe distance. Indians in general, portrayed as pagan savages during much of the nineteenth century in order to justify conquest, had now become positive symbols of a mythical American past, an easy oversimplification usefully juxtaposed against the rush of industrialization and modern life.

Yet obviously the Pueblos, and other Indian communities, had suffered through their allotted measure of turmoil. Indeed, nothing in the complex of modern social changes could rival the experience of Indian people who had witnessed powerful and deliberate attempts to destroy their ways of life. Native people were as capable as anyone of using and appreciating complex technology, even if they were perhaps not as eager to produce it themselves. Indians had for hundreds of years been involved in elaborate trade networks with other tribes and European nations. Any "harmony with nature" enjoyed by native people was the product of centuries of ecological trial and error that had also, in its time, produced environmental disasters. Soil exhaustion, overhunting, overfishing—all had caused massive movements of entire peoples, and even abandonment of centuries-old homes.

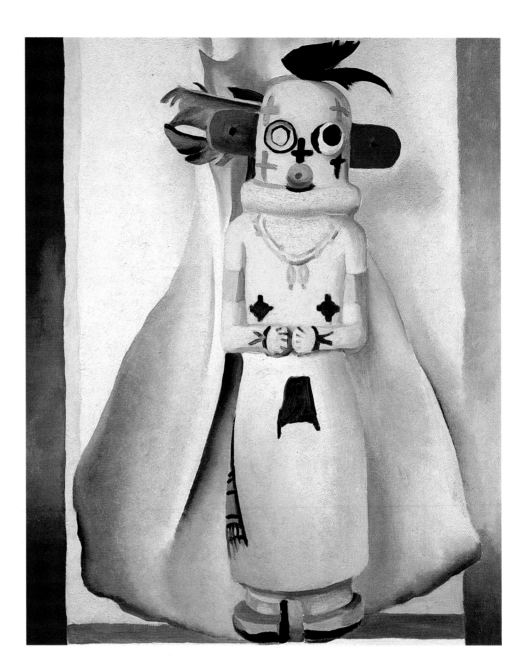

*Kachina* by Georgia O'Keeffe, 1931. O'Keeffe divided her time between New York City's artistic community and the romantic solitude of New Mexico, where she was joined by D. H. Lawrence, Oliver LaFarge, and many others seeking inspiration from the Southwest and its native peoples.

The "antimodernist" image of Indians said much more about America's own obsessions than it did about actual native people. One of those obsessions was "the return to nature." In search of Turner's lost frontier, well-to-do urbanites now indulged themselves in "Indian-style" outings in the newly created national parks and forests. Americans had for a long time regarded Indian hunting and fishing as leisure and sport activities. City dwellers now combined leisure and getting back to nature by going on hunting vacations that offered men a mock-wilderness experience that helped reaffirm ideas about their masculinity.

Symbolic understandings of Indians, whether as savage, noble, vanishing, or child-of-nature, could not help but affect the development of official Indian policies. Government policy, however, tended to lag well behind the current popular image. Perhaps nowhere was the disconnection between current understandings and Indian policy formulation as clear as in the 1920s attack on the Dawes Allotment Act of 1887. The Dawes Act had surmised not only that Indians were both literally and culturally vanishing but that the federal government could assist in the process by splitting up communal landholdings, assigning people their own allotted parcels of land, and teaching them to farm, thus creating "individuals" out of tribal people. These individuals, it was expected, would then dissolve into the rest of the population, the Bureau of Indian Affairs could be dismantled, and the "Indian problem" would be solved.

In the 1920s, a generation of white American intellectuals, disenchanted observers of the modern urban scene, began to challenge thirty years of federal Indian policy based on the Dawes Act. The leading actors in this effort were the New Mexico refugees—artists, anthropologists, and philanthropists who saw Senator Bursum's Pueblo Lands Bill as a direct threat to "their Indians." The Pueblos' white defenders focused primarily on Taos, a place that artist-socialite Mabel Dodge Luhan excitedly characterized as "a magical habitation of six hundred magical Indians."

The struggle catapulted the Pueblos to national attention and produced one of the most significant figures in the history of Indian affairs, John Collier. The son of a reformist Atlanta mayor, Collier had developed programs for urban immigrants in New York until discouraged by the outbreak of World War I and the subsequent collapse of the Progressive movement. In order to avoid a nasty political struggle, he had recently resigned as California's director of Adult Education and was planning a lengthy camping trip in Mexico when the family detoured to Taos. In December 1920, an exhausted Collier and his family arrived in Taos in response to Mabel Dodge Luhan's repeated pleas for a visit.

A few days after Christmas, the Colliers stood with Mabel Dodge, her Pueblo husband, Tony Luhan, and others on the pueblo's rooftops watching the Taos Deer Dance. For Collier, whose plans for healthy ethnic communities had played to mixed reviews in New York, the dance was a spiritual experience—a reawakening. "None has described adequately," he wrote later, "the great dances of the Pueblos. And I cannot describe any of them; but they entered into myself and each one of my family as a new direction of life—a new, even wildly new, hope for the Race of Man." The Pueblos, he thought, had developed the art of creating healthy personalities through community relationships and rituals. Suddenly rejuvenated, Collier vowed to protect Luhan's magical neighbors and the "wild new" antidote they offered mankind against the alienation of modern society.

His chance to act came soon after in the form of Holm Bursum's threatening attempt to end land title controversies in New Mexico. For centuries, the Pueblos had maintained political and cultural autonomy as small city-states. Their theocratic governments banded together in 1680 to oust Spanish priests and government officials from northern New Mexico. After the Mexican War, the United States reaffirmed long-standing Pueblo treaties with Spain and Mexico and established the usual "guardian–ward" relationship. Culturally, the Pueblo farmers already conformed to the agrarian standard that Americans used to measure civilization. Citing this background, the U.S. Supreme Court had ruled in 1876 that the Pueblos were "competent Indians" and capable of selling their land without federal government oversight.

Mabel Dodge Luhan, photographed in Taos around 1917.

An advertisment for The Pocahontas-brand chewing tobacco.

In 1913, however, the court overturned its previous decision, ruling that the Pueblos were, in fact, Indians who needed and were entitled to federal guardianship. More troublesome for New Mexicans, the court also ruled that the guardian–ward relationship between the Pueblos and the federal government had commenced with the Treaty of Guadalupe Hidalgo back in 1848. This determination threw the validity of claims based on the 1876 decision open to question and created turmoil in the state.

Bursum's 1922 legislation would have validated the land titles of most non-Indian claimants, restricted Indian water rights, and extended sweeping federal jurisdiction over the politically autonomous Pueblos. Although the Pueblos protested loudly through letters, petitions, and delegations their voices were soon overwhelmed—not by rival New Mexican land claimants, but by the public relations efforts of groups of sympathetic Indian policy reformers.

The elite intellectual refugees of New Mexico wielded disproportionate influence in the eastern media establishment, and their articles and editorials flooded a wide range of publications. John Collier methodically plotted a huge and effective propaganda campaign that included writings from many different reformers, a tour of Pueblo dancers and singers, celebrity endorsements, and blistering attacks on prominent government officials. Eventually, these efforts defeated the Bursum Bill and produced a more equitable legislative compromise.

Even in the midst of the campaign, Collier began setting higher goals for the future. He used the Bursum Bill struggle as a rallying point for the founding of the American Indian Defense Association (AIDA), a group that he headed for the next ten years. Through AIDA, Collier carried out similar aggressive public relations campaigns aimed at stopping appropriations of Indian land and resources and eliminating restrictions on Indian religious freedom.

The Bursum Bill fight marked an early and halting step toward a partnership between white reformers and Indians. Where older organizations—the Indian Rights Association, for example—had been content to meet annually at swank resorts devoid of Indians, Collier started to hold frequent meetings with Pueblo people. Where the Indian Rights Association acted out of a moral belief in the virtues of civilizing Indians, Collier and his friends believed that Indian cultures had their own intrinsic value and that America could learn something from native peoples. A new generation of Indian policy reformers had arrived.

Equally important, native people watched and learned how to manipulate America's rising symbolic respect for Indians to their own advantage. By drumming and singing at the Stock Exchange, the Pueblos tapped into America's modernist ambivalence in order to influence a political confrontation most Americans would have otherwise ignored.

But a still larger question loomed behind the Stock Exchange performance: how could native people—conquered, segregated, and removed from the mainstream—participate in American cultural and political dialogue as Indians? And if they must, through what channels could they speak meaningfully to the American people? The struggle over the Bursum Bill made it clear that their most influential and effective means of communication were the powerful symbols of "Indianness"—the only images that held meaning for a changing American society. Taking this path, however, meant that Indian participation

Clothing makes statements about both the personal identity of the wearer and the cultural setting in which he or she lives. In many Plains societies an eagle feather headdress initially signified an accumulation of brave deeds and community services. When worn to a white media event, it took on additional significance, communicating "Indianness" to a non-Indian audience in a way that made sense to them. As the headdress became accepted as a widespread symbol of "Indianness," other native people, like the eastern Cherokee, adopted it in order to convey a similar message. Ruth Muskrat's adoption of stereotypical "Indian princess" garb offers a similar example.

But Indians have also reversed the formula and adapted European dress to their own cultural contexts. Since the turn of the century, western tribes have enthusiastically adopted cowboy clothing. In the last several decades, beadwork has increasingly been incorporated into a variety of styles, as have turquoise and silver jewelry, ribbon shirts, and other pan-Indian markers of Indian identity.

ABOVE LEFT:
An Indian boy poses in full cowboy regalia in this 1907 photograph.

LEFT:
Ruth Muskrat Bronson, a Cherokee, photographed during her visit to the White House in 1923 as part of a committee presenting a report to the president on the state of Indian affairs.

ABOVE:
In a publicity photo sponsored by the local state tourist bureau, an honorary Cherokee "chief," wearing a symbolic Indian headdress, greets "model" tourists in Cherokee, North Carolina.

Rodeo is one of the most popular sports among Indians. The Navajo Nation alone holds thousands of small rodeos each year.

RIGHT:
The Navajo Nation Rodeo Cowboys Association is one of twelve Indian associations in the United States and Canada which sponsor rodeos (1990).

BELOW:
At the Navajo Nation Fair rodeo, the crowd watches a bareback rider (1990). The fair features one of the largest Indian rodeos. Over 100,000 people come to the fair to witness and participate in events including the rodeo, powwow, traditional song, traditional foods, horse shows, and arts and crafts show.

in the struggle was structured, defined, and limited by the ways in which white Americans had decided they could understand Indians.

The creation and use of symbols, a complicated affair at best, becomes even more complex when those symbols are built on the backs of living people. Throughout the twentieth century, native people have followed the Pueblo example, using "child of nature" understandings of "The Indian" to their own advantage. They have tried to shape American cultural ideas about themselves in ways that might in turn lead to positive political and social change. But at the same time that twentieth-century Indians have worked within the limits of American understandings, they have just as persistently sought to overcome those limits.

As native people entered the modern world themselves, they redefined what it meant to be Indian in that world. While undergoing their own process of self-definition, Indians have also tried to get non-Indians to develop a more complete and complex understanding of what it means to be Indian. This process of self-definition has often led Indian people to interact with white Americans through what are considered to be non-Indian "American" practices—wage labor, politics, mass media, art and literature, among others. For the most part, Indian participation in these activities does not signify "assimilation" into American culture. Rather, these "American" practices have themselves been assimilated—incorporated into living Indian cultures that are constantly being remade as native people interact with non-Indians.

## Change and Living Culture

As Indian cultures—like all cultures—have changed and adapted, they have also had to contend with coercive American policies. Taking advantage of the relative lack of military and political power held by Indian peoples, Americans have sought to impose alien frameworks they deemed superior or more appropriate. In the 1920s, despite the efforts of reformers like John Collier, this was still the case.

Entrenched government institutions and policies continued to lag years behind the new insights developed by reform elements. The Bureau of Indian Affairs (BIA), even though it recognized the disaster of allotment, continued to issue allotment patents, and Indian people continued to lose control over their land. Indian policy "experts" continued to advise native peoples, no matter what their environmental constraints or work preferences, to practice farming and stock raising. Missionaries and officials continued to denigrate and prohibit native religious traditions. Day and boarding school teachers continued to attempt to separate Indian students from their cultural supports.

In the meantime, the government's already ineffectual stewardship of Indian resources reached new heights of laxity and corruption. Native people faced threats from oil, gas, and mineral corporations that, with the help of the Interior Department, sought outrageously advantageous leases on Indian land. In Arizona, government agencies dipped into the Navajo tribal treasury to fund a bridge project on a road Navajo people never used. In Montana, the commissioner of Indian Affairs made deals with a power company to turn over Flathead lands without

The Intertribal Indian Ceremonial has been held annually in Gallup, New Mexico, for over seventy years. The event includes a powwow, rodeo, parade, marathon, queen contest, marketplace, and performing arts.

*It is little wonder that Indian peoples were perceived not as they were but as they "had" to be—from a European point of view. They were whisked out of the realm of the real and into the land of the make-believe. Indians became variably super- or subhuman, never ordinary. They dealt in magic, not judgment. They were imagined to be stuck in their past, not guided by its precedents.*

—MICHAEL DORRIS
(Modoc), 1987

## ROSA MINOKA HILL

Born on the St. Regis Mohawk reservation in New York, Rosa Minoka was adopted and taken to Philadelphia by a Quaker doctor. She graduated from the Women's Medical College of Pennsylvania in 1899 and, for five years, shared a medical practice with another woman doctor. After marrying in 1905, Rosa Minoka Hill moved to Oneida, Wisconsin, intending to give up medicine and concentrate on a family and farm. Instead, her practice simply became more informal. Relatives, friends, neighbors, and eventually strangers began to appear at the kitchen door asking for advice and treatment and offering chickens and squash in return. Hill was Oneida's only doctor, but eventually she realized that, in order to receive reimbursement for welfare patients and to order medicine, she would need an official Wisconsin medical license. In 1934, after years of unofficial practice, she took and passed the state exam.

Rosa Hill created her identity with elements from two different worlds. Although trained in Western medicine, she always respected the powers of Indian curing techniques. She simply encouraged patients using bear grease and herbal teas to try her prescriptions as well. At a time when few women or Indians became physicians, she was proud to be both an Indian woman and a doctor.

bothering to consult the tribe. In Nevada, Paiute water rights cases waited, ignored by federal attorneys, while non-Indians claimed western water.

These wholesale efforts to stamp out Indian lifeways and usurp Indian lands and resources had devastating effects. The destruction of native land bases eroded communal social structures and pushed many Indians toward a more self-centered individualism. People who had lost their land strained kin-based group support systems. Children returned home from boarding schools unable to speak their native languages and unfamiliar with their cultures. Strict prohibitions on religious practice drove ceremonies underground or extinguished them altogether. Indian agents hindered political and social unity by encouraging certain families or factions at the expense of others. Their languages, religions, communities, and identities under devastating attack, many Indians experienced an alienation more intense than any felt by the Americans crowding the cities.

But this gloomy story of coercion and corruption intertwined with another story—one in which native people like the Caughnawagas responded to pressures and new ideas with a continued reshaping of their worlds. The Plains Sun Dance reemerged as a Fourth of July celebration. Old warrior societies and women's groups reappeared as St. Joseph and St. Mary church societies. New traditions, like the pan-Indian Native American Church, spread across tribal lines.

On many reservations, Indian people worked out new and flexible subsistence patterns that relied not only on small gardening, fishing, hunting, herding, and livestock, but also on wage labor, and the leasing of allotments. For some, the church became an arena for developing social power, and Indian clergymen and catechists took strong leadership roles. As domestic and child-rearing roles often remained relatively unchanged, women maintained durable links with past traditions. Yet, they also participated in the ongoing creation of interactive exchange. In Nebraska, for example, an Indian woman ran for sheriff, promising to eliminate bootleggers, most of whom were other Indian women. Other Indians traveled off the reservation seeking work, training for professions, acting in films, or participating in professional and semiprofessional sports.

## The Ongoing Struggle

Native people, the government, and the reform groups all struggled (as they continue to struggle) to answer the same question: what is an Indian in twentieth-century America? Could Indians work on New York City skyscrapers and still be Indians? Americans have tended to view native cultures as either-or propositions. If Indians seem to use and enjoy the trappings of modern or non-Indian cultures, they are considered "progressive" and "assimilated," their Indian character diluted, contaminated, or lost. "Tradition" or "the old ways" validates one as a true Indian, but tradition also signifies (especially to non-Indians) the past, often a mythic "precontact" past of feathers and tipis.

Here, then, is one of the paradoxes of Indian country in the twentieth century: if Indians change, their culture is considered contaminated and they lose their "Indianness." If they do not change, they remain Indians, but are refused a real existence in the modern world.

# LUTHER STANDING BEAR AND FILM

Luther Standing Bear's life combined elements from both Lakota and American worlds. A graduate of Carlisle and a veteran performer with Buffalo Bill's Wild West Show, Standing Bear's skills in dealing with American society stood him in good stead when he returned to the Rosebud reservation. He became a local leader and eventually represented the tribe in Washington. In 1912,

Standing Bear went to Hollywood where he worked for filmmaker Thomas Ince, acting onscreen with Douglas Fairbanks and William S. Hart. His acting career eventually brought him to the New York stage and to tours, films, and lectures across the country. During these later years he recalled a conversation he had with Ince: "One day Tom Ince was talking with me about the making of Indian

pictures. I told him that none of the Indian pictures were made right. He seemed quite surprised at this and began asking me questions. I explained to him in what way his Indian pictures were wrong. We talked for a long time, and when I arose to leave he said, 'Standing Bear, some day you and I are going to make some real Indian pictures.'"

They never did.

RIGHT:
Filmmaker Thomas Ince poses with Luther Standing Bear and other Sioux Indians at his studio in Inceville, California, in 1914.

BELOW LEFT TO RIGHT:
Ricardo Montalban as an Indian warrior in *Across the Wide Missouri* (1951); Marisa Pavan in makeup for her Indian role in *Drumbeat* (1954); and Victor Mature, with Suzan Ball, portrays the legendary Sioux chief who defeated General George Custer at the Little Big Horn, in *Chief Crazy Horse* (1954).

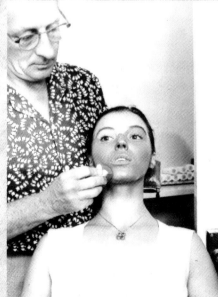

ABOVE: *Indian Ballgame* by Cecil Dick (Cherokee).

High-profile figures like football, baseball, and Olympic competitor Jim Thorpe and Olympic marathon runner Louis Tewanima tend to garner the bulk of attention paid to Indian athletes. But hundreds of Indians from across the country participated in professional and semiprofessional sports during the early twentieth century. In the collegiate ranks, the Carlisle and Haskell Indian schools consistently fielded national-caliber teams and sent players to the pros.

Indians all over the country celebrated when Carlisle's football team beat Harvard by using the "hidden ball trick." Their schedule included pigskin powerhouses like Yale, Army, Navy, Alabama, and Notre Dame. Non-Indian schools, including Notre Dame, Georgia Tech, Minnesota, Dartmouth, and many others, eagerly recruited Indian athletes themselves.

At a time when American athletics were closed to African-Americans, they were frequently open to Indian peoples. Professional baseball often bypassed the college ranks and recruited directly from the reservations. Well-known major league players like John Meyers (Cahuilla), Louis Sockalexis (Penobscot), and Charles "Chief" Bender (Chippewa)—a member of the Baseball Hall of Fame— joined numerous lower-profile players in minor and semipro leagues.

In addition to football and baseball, native Americans frequently found success competing in track and field and marathon running. Basketball players from the Dakota reservations formed the Sioux Travelers, an exhibition team that occasionally took on the Harlem Globetrotters.

Indians continue to excel at a variety of sports activities today. Reservation-based high schools often do very well in statewide contests. Running, road racing, and basketball have reached new heights of popularity, and one can often find tribal races and basketball tournaments on reservations. Contemporary athletic competition often serves to unify tribal communities. The Six Nations of New York, for example, fields an excellent lacrosse team and offers lacrosse training to tribal youth. Lacrosse provides an outlet through which the people of the Six Nations express Indian unity, pride, and identity.

ABOVE: The 1903 Carlisle Indian School football team. ABOVE RIGHT: Jim Thorpe during the New York Giants spring training camp in 1916. BELOW: The Red Cloud High School Crusaders during a football game in 1991.

# CHAPTER TWENTY-FIVE

# THE INDIAN NEW DEAL

*ONONDAGA MAN*
BY ROGER PERKINS (MOHAWK), 1992

DEFINING ONESELF AS AN INDIAN in the twentieth century has meant walking a fine line between the domination and allure of American culture and the resistance and resilience of one's own tradition. Nowhere has this tension been more apparent than in Indian efforts to enter the political arena. And perhaps no policy better illustrates this tension and ambivalence than the Indian New Deal, a component of the larger New Deal reforms initiated by Franklin Delano Roosevelt's administration in the 1930s. Although challenged by subsequent policy shifts, the political, legal, and economic innovations of the New Deal have shaped native American societies to the present day.

Many ideological currents in American society combined to make the radical changes of the Indian New Deal possible. Faced with severe economic depression, Congress continued to search for a way to make Indians financially self-sufficient. Intellectuals remained fascinated with the idea that "primitives" offered useful lessons for modern society. Appealing to both groups, eager reformers asserted that Indian people could best become self-sufficient not as individuals but in communal groups, and, moreover, that their example could provide a model for Americans.

Although these perspectives eventually coalesced around the Indian New Deal, it was native people themselves who developed one of the key formulas for New Deal Indian policy reform. In the mid-1920s, frustrated by the inefficient and paternalistic control of the BIA, many members of Oregon's Klamath tribe pursued a greater political and economic voice.

**Franklin D. Roosevelt with Chief Bird Rattler of the Blackfeet tribe in Montana (1934).**

Tired of watching their timber sold at bargain prices, Wade Crawford and a group of Klamaths approached Congress with a proposal to revert control over their land back to the Klamath people by transforming the reservation into a federally chartered corporation. All personal and tribal property would be owned by the corporation and members would be issued stock that could not be transferred to anyone outside the group. Crawford wanted a fifty-year federal trust period during which the corporation would be free from state taxes and controls. Guided by three court-appointed supervisors, a Klamath board of directors would manage Klamath resources.

Although his ideas met with opposition from some members of Congress and from other Klamaths, Crawford proposed a solution to what many policymakers had come to see as a central problem in Indian affairs: the absence of native legal and political bodies capable of interacting with business interests and with federal and state governments. This lack, so they thought, greatly hindered Indian efforts to establish self-sufficiency.

Congress, which generally despised the BIA for its costly and inefficient bureaucracy, was inclined to support the Klamath proposal. So was John Collier, who saw it as a model for a type of tribal self-government that might succeed in the modern world. But while the Klamaths—and other tribes with similar

*Drum Beats Keep Dancing in My Head*
**by Arthur Amiotte (Oglala Lakota), 1988.**

*Paper Dolls for a Post-Columbian World*
by Jaune Quick-to-See Smith
(Cree-Flathead-Shoshone), 1991.

complaints—simply sought greater control over the administration of their lands and resources, Collier saw in the apparent agreement an opportune political moment to redirect the relationship between tribes and the federal government.

Much of the philosophical underpinning of the Indian New Deal legislation came from Collier and his generation of reformers. Throughout the 1920s, Collier's AIDA group had assisted tribal people in fighting a variety of battles. With his savvy political sense and awesome ability to wage a propaganda war, Collier had kept the BIA on the run for a decade. His criticisms raised widespread concern and spawned a series of reports that sought to reevaluate the "Indian problem." The most publicly significant of these was the Meriam Report.

Issued in 1928, the report found allotment to be a dismal failure that had resulted not only in loss of Indian land, but in the creation of a huge Indian Office bureaucracy. The report recommended land repurchase, increased funding for tribes, and the establishment of tribal corporations—such as that proposed by the Klamath—in order to better manage natural resources. Its implementation would wait, however, until the 1932 election of Franklin D. Roosevelt who, after a round of intense politicking, appointed John Collier as commissioner of the Bureau of Indian Affairs. It appeared that Collier had at last been empowered to implement his reforms. But while his appointment can be seen as a triumph for Indian policy reform, in practice Collier's program was fraught with internal ambiguity and beseiged by outside attacks.

Although centered in Indian affairs, Collier and his allies were involved in a broader debate about the nature of modern society. Collier's philosophy attacked the "social Darwinist" belief that societies necessarily progress through an evolutionary chain—hunter-gatherer, herder, farmer, merchant—that ends in civilized

*Navajo Women with Blankets* by Rudolph Carl Gorman (Navajo), ca. 1962.

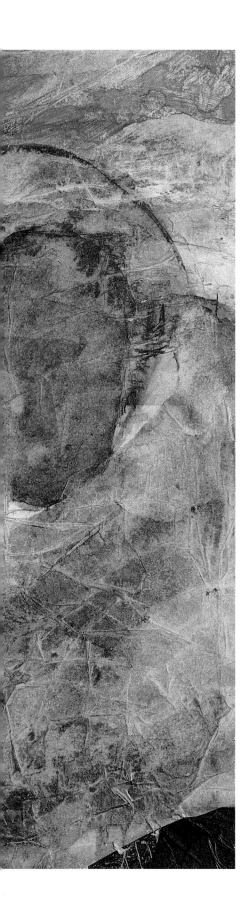

modern society. He espoused instead the concept of multiculturalism: Indian and American cultures simply viewed the world differently, and each had something to contribute to the other. But other, more powerful, forces were being generated by the Depression and, later, World War II. These two major crises tempered the multicultural ideal and emphasized instead the pressing need for national unity. Editorials and propaganda encouraged people of diverse backgrounds to celebrate the basic "Americanness" thought to be holding them together. This emphasis on unity created an idea of community far different from that which motivated Collier. Where he saw the organic community of the Pueblos as an antidote to the alienated modern individual, Depression-era Americans looked to community in a national sense for an alleviation of their own insecurity. And just as Collier's Indian policy emerged from his own cultural roots in modernity and Progressivism, a rising political generation rooted in national community, expert management, and fiscal restraint challenged Collier's efforts from the beginning.

But the Indian New Deal suffered from its own internal contradictions as well. As a result, the program faced conflicts with Indian people, Congress, and other government agencies. Perhaps the most acrimonious encounter of the New Deal took place on the Dineh (Navajo) reservation in Arizona.

One of the few tribes to maintain relative autonomy into the twentieth century, the Navajo farmed, herded sheep and goats, and produced weaving and jewelry for the crafts trade. By 1900, gradual increases in Navajo herds were coinciding with the beginning of a natural cycle of gully creation and erosion. At the same time, non-Indian cattlemen moved into the Navajo region and monopolized available off-reservation water and forage, leading to smaller and more restricted areas on which to graze the growing Navajo herds. Although subsequent Navajo overgrazing certainly played a part in the region's growing erosion problems, New Deal administrators placed the entire blame for the situation squarely on the Navajo sheep and goats.

The enormous dust storms that thundered across the overplowed Great Plains in the 1930s made erosion control one of the great obsessions of the New Deal. Other New Dealers had equally powerful fixations on dam building and water reclamation. West of the Navajo reservation, the Colorado River's Boulder Dam linked these two interests and provided the context for an assault on Navajo herds.

One of the greatest threats to dammed reservoirs is silt, and the Colorado River receives tons of it from tributaries that flow from the Navajo reservation. Haunted by visions of a useless, silted-up dam and the finely powdered dust that darkened the skies over large parts of Kansas and Oklahoma, administrators from the BIA and the Department of Agriculture's Soil Erosion Service spared no effort to get Navajos to reduce their herds. John Collier, who saw himself as a champion of Indian culture and development, took the lead in urging the scientific management philosophies of stock reduction on the Navajos.

In a series of poorly administered stock reductions, the government bought sheep and goats at below-market prices. Percentage quotas favored larger herders who could simply cull weak animals from the herds. Smaller-scale operators ended up eating their breeding stock and, in many cases, their herds never recovered. Poor planning led, in several instances, to animals being slaughtered and

Commissioner of Indian Affairs John Collier, surrounded by reservation officials, meets with Florida Indians in 1940 to discuss saving their deer from slaughter in an official drive against cattle ticks.

*[John] Collier comes across as enigmatic because there is a fundamental contradiction in his thinking and his politics. Collier was content to uphold and celebrate and honor our expressive life, our cultural life, namely, the arts and religion. At the very same time, he was also content to deliver our more fundamental freedoms such as sovereignty and tribal self-government into the hands of the federal government. These two things seemed to work simultaneously in his life, and so both are true.*

—ALFONSO ORTIZ
(San Juan Pueblo), 1986

left to rot, a situation that psychologically devastated many Navajos.

Although he had acted with good intentions, Collier's paternal treatment of the independent Dineh contradicted his belief in the validity of Indian decision making. He became the most reviled figure in recent Navajo history, a man whose name has evil connotations even for those who never experienced the stock reductions.

Despite his heavy-handed encounter with the Dineh, Collier did improve conditions for many Indian peoples. He spent his initial days in office forging links between the BIA and other New Deal programs. Indians were among the people hardest hit by the Great Depression. The new BIA saw to it that Indians benefited from government service projects and relief programs, soil erosion and conservation services (including an Indian wing of the Civilian Conservation Corps), farming and ranching cooperatives, and many other New Deal efforts.

Collier meanwhile was readying legislation—which would be passed in 1934 as the Indian Reorganization Act (IRA)—designed to reverse the Dawes policy and to provide for Indian self-government and corporate business councils modeled on the Klamaths' plan.

Assimilation still had powerful adherents, however, and his proposals met with immediate resistance from both Congress and many Indian people. "Why segregate [us] on the reservation and not let us be with white people?" asked a California Indian named Costa. "Is that the way to make American citizens of us?" After a turbulent round of hearings in the House Indian Affairs Subcommittee, Collier sought Indian opinions and support through a series of regional "Indian Congresses" in which he explained the legislation and answered questions.

Collier's congresses represented the first widespread use of Indian input in formulating policy—a gesture much appreciated by the tribes. Nonetheless, the meetings often proceeded in a tense, suspicious atmosphere and were marked by frequent attacks on Collier. Obsessed with political maneuvering designed to bring about a new tribalism, Collier displayed a serious lack of understanding of the extent to which many native people had begun adapting to their situations.

In Rapid City, South Dakota, representatives from the northern Plains tribes grilled Collier for four days. Their criticisms reflected persistent concerns that appeared at other Indian Congresses. Many Indians had no interest in a communal land ownership system in which tribal shares replaced individual patents. George White Bull, from Standing Rock reservation, argued that most of Collier's supporters were mixed-blood Indians who had already sold their allotments. Not only did he like owning his own land, other full-bloods who had held on to their allotments also resented being equated with those who had sold. White Bull questioned, as well, the legislation's failure to clarify the situation surrounding pending and future Indian claims against the government. Others, like Joe Irving from Crow Creek, labeled Collier's proposals as "communistic."

The truth was that Collier's Pueblo-based model of close-knit communal life did not apply to many native groups, and certainly did not relate to the lives of most Indians in different parts of the country at that time. Thus for some Collier opponents, Indian communities as self-governing entities were romantic relics. For others, the constitutional governments proposed by Collier's model threatened still-vital "traditional" forms of leadership. Many Christian Indians voiced concern over Collier's desire to remove the privileged position of missionaries and churches on their reservations.

At the Rapid City meeting, Francis Red Tomahawk offered perhaps the most trenchant observation: like the Dawes Act, Collier's proposals were too influenced by non-Indian perspectives and moved too fast. But Collier had at least given Indian people a voice. And while Collier's charisma, sincerity, and respect for Indian people eventually won over many supporters, the meetings also demonstrated the variety, sophistication, and depth of Indian dissent. Perhaps no tribe better exemplifies the complexity of that dissent than the Seneca.

The sovereignty of the Seneca nation was recognized and guaranteed by the Treaty of Canandaigua, signed by George Washington in 1794. In 1848, the tribe developed an elective self-government to represent its sovereign interests. Keenly aware of this history, many Senecas perceived the Indian New Deal as another assault on an independence already established by treaty. After lobbying for exemption from the Indian Reorganization Act itself, the Senecas and other Six Nations tribes overwhelmingly voted to reject the offer of additional BIA help.

The Seneca political activist Alice Jemison rose to national prominence as a critic of the IRA and an opponent of the very idea of an "Indian" Bureau. "The Wheeler-Howard Act [IRA]," she observed, "provides only one form of government for the Indian and that is communal or cooperative form of living. John Collier said he was going to give the Indian self-government. If he was going to give us self-government he would let us set up a form of government we wanted to live under. He would give us the right to continue to live under our old tribal customs if we wanted to."

## ALICE JEMISON

Alice Jemison came from a long line of prominent Senecas. After working as a legal researcher and secretary, as an assistant to Seneca political leaders, and as a newspaper correspondent, Jemison helped found the American Indian Federation, a group that testified and lobbied extensively against Collier's reform efforts. Jemison's arguments against the IRA, rooted in ideas of Indian sovereignty and cultural separatism, influenced a wide group of congressional critics that included the legislation's sponsor, Senator Burton K. Wheeler. Her understanding of the diversity of adaptations and opinions in Indian country and her ability to bring these dissenting voices before Congress and the public made her an enemy of the new Indian Bureau. But just as Collier had come under attack for his role as resident BIA gadfly, Jemison found herself attacked (ironically enough, by John Collier) as a fascist "Indian Nazi." Her resistance to Seneca participation in the Selective Service Act, for example, was characterized as unpatriotic, when in fact it stemmed from the belief that the Seneca nation's sovereignty extended to the declaration of war. It should take a Seneca decision, she thought, rather than an American mandate, to send Seneca men off to fight. Alice Jemison's insistence on Indian sovereignty represents both a continuation of "traditional" tribal understandings of sovereignty and a prefiguring of the struggles over sovereignty still to come.

## Imposing a Foreign Political Framework

The White Indian is too susceptible to wrongdoing. He always wants the money. That is the reason for such poverty. What is being left for our children—for the future generation? And what then will they live on? All these allottees have sold their 160 acres and I don't believe any of them possess even a twig of a tree and I don't believe that they have as much as one shot of gunpowder or a parcel of land!

—GEORGE WALTERS
(White Earth Chippewa), 1934

About the half-breeds on the Flathead reservations, a lot of them want to be turned loose—to get paid off and I see things here that most of the other tribes have got that same idea. And if you turn them loose and take them off of the reservation and if they go broke, I wish they wouldn't come back to the reservation—back to their old grandmothers and grandfathers because their old grandmothers and grandfathers might have a little something to eat yet.

—ENEAS CONSO
(Flathead), 1934

Three major initiatives survived scrutiny and rewriting by Congress to become the Indian New Deal. The Johnson-O'Malley Act of April 1934 provided federal credit to Indian communities and allowed tribes to contract independently for health care and other services previously provided by the BIA. A few months later, the Indian Reorganization Act formally ended the Dawes allotment policy, extended federal trust relationships with tribes indefinitely, restored tribal lands that had been expropriated as surplus, and set up provisions for purchasing land for Indian communities.

Following the Klamath example, the IRA also allowed and encouraged tribes to set up written constitutions (subject, however, to the approval of the secretary of the interior) and it set up a fund that advanced economic development loans to tribes. Finally, the Indian Arts and Crafts Board, authorized in the following year, was to assist in the marketing and promotion of Indian cultural expression.

Collier thought that modern Indians needed to create social structures meaningful in both Indian and American terms, and he hoped that the Indian New Deal programs would aid in making such bicultural adaptations. Tribal governments were to make Indian people competitive in the modern world while allowing them to retain traditional beliefs. But, as Collier's effort reaffirmed, policy—even the best intentioned—cannot simply dictate the course of cultural change. Even as the IRA reversed Dawes and proposed a new formula, it repeated the same larger patterns that had characterized the older policy. The differences in American cultural assumptions that had appeared between 1887 and 1934 simply made Collier's policy look new.

Collier's blind optimism over the economic potential of communally owned Indian land echoed the Dawes reformers' equally optimistic claims for the civilizing benefits of individual landholding. Where Dawes had sought to replace native forms of government with eventual individual membership in the American body politic, Collier replaced them with separate constitutional assemblies modeled on American governments. And Collier, like earlier Dawes administrators, often ignored Indians in order to implement a system of bureaucracy, paternalism, and control based on his own philosophical beliefs.

Perhaps most dangerous for Indian peoples, Collier (like Dawes) sold his package to legislators as a solution to the "Indian problem." With Indians self-sufficient on their reservations, Collier hinted, the functions of the BIA could be reduced and eventually Indians would be able to sever their connections with the federal government.

But the Indian New Deal was, of course, not the Dawes Act. At the same time that Collier's policies echoed the past in form, in specific content they pointed many Indian people toward uncharted cultural territory and a form of government in which most simply did not believe. For many, adapting to the Indian New Deal would present a more formidable challenge than adjusting to the Dawes Act. Under Dawes, reservation life buffered contact with American society. With BIA agents handling Indian–federal administrative concerns, older styles of leadership, often based on example rather than power, maintained a precarious footing. In this setting, theocratic governments that blurred the lines between civil and religious authority, and consensual governments that relied on the consent of all participants could survive—with a few strategic modifications.

The IRA's constitutional form of government was radically different and perfectly attuned to create problems within many tribes. Rejecting older decision-making methods and adopting majority vote guaranteed the creation of factions based, at the very least, on the question of whether the new or old style of governing was most appropriate. When tribes debated, and later voted, on accepting the IRA, the nature of this factionalization became clear.

Typically, the new policy had its strong adherents. These were opposed both by assimilationists who saw the Dawes policies as successful and by "traditionalist full-bloods." "Full-bloods," like George White Bull, argued (usually correctly) that older tribal leadership would be supplanted by educated, landless, mixed-bloods because many full-bloods distrusted the government and would simply refuse to participate in IRA elections. Given this divergence of opinion, many elections were closely and hotly contested. The Oglala Lakota, for example, voted in 1935 to accept an IRA constitution, but the vote was 1,348 to 1,041—hardly a mandate, even by American standards.

The Oglala vote demonstrated and reinforced a deep split within the tribe. Authority that was vested in individuals based on their character, behavior, and demonstrated leadership now came to reside in the abstraction of political office. And, in a profoundly antidemocratic change, many tribal decisions now turned not on the voices of all the people, but on a few individuals elected by simple majority. The acceleration of factional struggles turned consensual tribes, like the Oglala, into groups that had trouble arriving at, and supporting, tribal decisions.

Many tribes mustered the votes to turn down the IRA. Others participated only in part. Only 96 of the 181 tribes that voted to accept the legislation had their constitutions approved. Only 73 tribes accepted business incorporation and thus became eligible for the economic development credit fund.

Ironically, the Klamaths numbered among those who voted to reject the Indian Reorganization Act.

## The Basis of Indian Sovereignty

Even with their many flaws, IRA governments did give tribes a political and legal voice in American Indian policy. The more loosely woven consensual governing of the Plains tribes or the culturally foreign theocracies of the Pueblos had not really looked like governments to non-Indian observers. By mirroring American constitutional structure, however, IRA constitutions established Indian tribes as governments, and as autonomous societies, in ways that white Americans could see, understand, and accept. Equally important, the IRA allowed tribes to rescue the idea of tribal sovereignty and their status as "dependent domestic nations" from the dustbin of federal policy.

Most significantly, the IRA redefined the nature of the political relationships between the United States and Indian tribes. IRA policy asserted that Indian rights to sovereign self-government and political autonomy were inherent. That

*I am a woman and you might think it funny that the Colvilles elect a woman for a delegate but the capacity of an Indian woman's head has the same amount as a man or a white man. To those people who are not in favor of the bill, there is always a place for them. If they want to keep their allotments and their land they can ask the government for them. John Collier could take every foot of land, if they wish to, with the stroke of the pen according to law and we would lose every bit of ground we have. He has given us this privilege to find what kind of people we are.*

*We have been driven. We have been led by the white people for 122 years since the white people came into this country. We have never been given the choice of our leaders. We have no voice in anything. And now you are opposed to this bill of Collier's. He has worked for fifteen years for the Indian's cause. You want to be driven to it because you are not accustomed to lead your people. Your people as a people, industrious and self-governing, can do just what you want if you have the Federal court to back you in your cause. Let us hope that this new form of government will not be imposing on our old people, that you younger men and women will have a voice in the government of the U.S. Let us try a new deal. It can not be any worse than what it has been.*

—CHRISTINE GALLER
(Colville), 1934

is, such rights were not *granted* by the United States as part of the guardian–ward relationships, but had been *retained* by the tribes through their treaties. The concept of Indian sovereignty had been severely eroded during the nineteenth century. Although it has taken some sixty years for the ramifications of this basic concept to unfold in subsequent legal and policy decisions, the idea of inherent tribal sovereignty has come to serve as the basis for contemporary Indian–American political developments. It is, after all, a recognition in law of the fact that Indian societies were here first.

Less obvious, but perhaps equally significant was the Indian New Deal's introduction of widespread wage-labor opportunities to the reservations. From 1933 to 1942, eighty-five thousand Indians participated in Indian Emergency Conservation Work programs on thirty-three reservations. They received $30 per month as well as vocational and leadership training. Full-time wage labor introduced economic concepts that proved difficult for some tribes to integrate into their cultures. While these New Deal programs saved many Indians from near-starvation during the Depression, they also prepared native people for the profusion of off-reservation wage work soon to be required by the war effort.

Although Collier and his staff got the New Deal off to a quick start, they never managed to consolidate its initial gains. Senator Wheeler, sponsor of the initial legislation, sought the IRA's repeal only three years after its passage.

The ambiguity of the Indian New Deal sprang, in part, from its internal contradictions. Collier used the words "corporate" and "communal" almost interchangeably, confusing his romantic ideals with his awareness of the business realities of industrial capitalist society. Perhaps the program that best defined

Navajos, in job training at a federal Indian school, learn new methods of construction.

*Maple Sugar Time*
by Patrick DesJarlait (Chippewa), 1946.

these contradictions was the Indian Arts and Crafts Board. The board institutionalized the concept that one way of preserving and invigorating Indian societies lay in linking Indian products to the American market—thus attempting to achieve two laudable objectives with a single stroke.

Congressional attacks on Indian programs intensified with America's entry into World War II and the development of a very different set of funding priorities. Led by New Mexico Senator Dennis Chavez, conservative congressmen charged that the Indian Office had spent too much money in Washington and not enough in the field, had failed to make native people self-sufficient, and had expanded rather than pared down the bureaucratic apparatus. In 1944, Chavez and Wheeler coauthored a proposal that amounted to a complete repudiation of the Indian New Deal. Under this proposal, the government would close all government Indian schools, turn over Indian health and land management to other government agencies, dissolve the BIA, make per capita payments of all tribal funds, and eliminate federal trust status over Indian lands. The Chavez-Wheeler

## New Deal Ambiguity: The Arts and Crafts Board

Until the late nineteenth century, most Indian people did not share American ideas about art and crafts. European-based cultures celebrated art largely "for its own sake," occasionally for its ability to offer social commentary, and historically as religious decoration. They viewed crafts—and this included Indian weaving, basketry, pottery, and many other objects—as an expression of old-fashioned individuality, far removed from modern mass production; and they were fascinated by the artistic form of "primitive" objects, forms that often anticipated their own explorations in abstraction.

Native peoples had generally produced objects—even very beautiful and highly decorated objects—for utilitarian or ceremonial uses. Most Americans regarded these objects as crafts—albeit extremely attractive in their own "primitive" way. But if policymakers—many drawn from or affiliated with the New Mexico intellectual refugees—appreciated Indian expression for its "primitive" elements, they also perceived that this very quality made it marketable.

By establishing standards of authenticity and developing market strategies, the Indian Arts and Crafts Board helped accelerate Indian crafts production to provide an additional source of income for Indian people. In doing so, however, it also curtailed the expression of individual Indian artists who wished to speak to non-Indian Americans through the artistic medium. Personal expression took a back seat to the production of objects that resonated for Americans attuned not to the artistic but to the "primitive."

ABOVE:
**A Skokomosh Indian from Washington decorating a carved box (1990).**

BELOW:
**An Eskimo woman from Brooks Range, Alaska, decorates a caribou skin mask (1988). These masks have been made for about one hundred years and are not "traditional." They have been a stock-in-trade and source of outside income for the residents of this small mountain Eskimo village for about thirty years.**

OPPOSITE:
*Navajo Woman Weaver*
by Andrew Tsinajinnie (Navajo).

proposal, while politically out of reach in the mid-1940s, laid the groundwork for the policy initiatives of the next decade.

Meanwhile, the House mounted its own attacks on the Indian New Deal. Through severe and continuous funding cuts, it effectively hobbled the efforts of the BIA. Collier's direct manner and political skills had made him many enemies. He sensed that a significant portion of New Deal opposition was directed not only at the policies but at himself. Realizing his ineffectual position, the commissioner submitted his resignation in January 1945.

# CHAPTER TWENTY-SIX

# TERMINATION

STRUT YOUR STUFF BY JOHN BALLOUE (CHEROKEE), 1989

IN NOVEMBER 1944, the city of Denver hosted eighty Indians who had gathered, in the words of the *Denver Post*, "to tell America that Chief Big Feather is a good Joe." When the dust cleared three days later, delegates from more than fifty tribes had founded the National Congress of American Indians (NCAI). The group's first president, Napoleon Johnson, articulated its central aim: "Indian leadership should contribute to the formulation of Federal policy and should take the leading part in inquiring into the needs of the Indians and in making those needs vocal."

Although the Indian New Deal had offered tribes a political voice, it was a voice that had remained local and specific. Native people developed the political skills required to operate the local council and to deal with specific tribal–federal relationships. The possibility of political alliances between tribes, however, had gone largely untested. By the early 1940s many of the Indian people working for the BIA (during his tenure John Collier hired over three thousand Indian employees) were ready to inaugurate a national pan-Indian organization that could address the problems native people had in common.

The NCAI mixed the formal constitutional structures to which IRA tribes had grown accustomed with a nonpartisan, nonbinding neutrality reminiscent of older Great Plains–style tribal governance. It was a forum in which Indians could agree to disagree and then proceed to work together. Although planned and organized by native BIA employees Gary Burns and D'arcy McNickle, the convention quickly moved to distance itself from the Indian Office. Only two "BIA Indians" served on the first board of directors. The remainder came from tribal councils, noncouncil factions, religious societies, and the Indian community at large.

---

*Stronghorse* by Jesse Cooday (Tlingit), 1984.

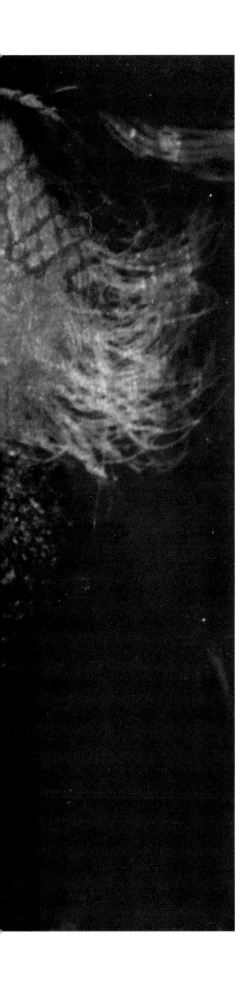

Charged with presenting recommendations for the future course of the Bureau of Indian Affairs, the Committee of One Hundred had met for a long weekend in December 1923. When the time came for the committee to present its reports to President Calvin Coolidge, however, the group and the president simply stared at each other, unable to open a dialogue.

Ruth Muskrat, at the time a student at Mount Holyoke College, broke the impasse by approaching the president in archetypal Cherokee Indian princess costume. Perhaps her garb appealed to Coolidge, who was also known to favor outfitting himself in Indian regalia. Muskrat delivered a short speech and offered the president a book prepared by a Protestant missionary group. The book, which outlined troubled conditions on the reservation and then called for continued support for the Indian Office, captured the essence of Muskrat's subsequent long career.

Already experienced in reservation social work through participation in YWCA programs, Muskrat became a BIA teacher immediately upon her graduation. Intelligent and articulate, she moved quickly through the bureaucracy, eventually becoming a guidance officer and overseeing government loans and scholarships for Indian students. As executive secretary for the NCAI, she worked with tribal groups across the country, stalked the halls of Congress as an Indian lobbyist, and published *Indians Are People Too*. In 1957, she returned to Indian service in the field of community health.

ABOVE: **Ruth Muskrat Bronson with President Calvin Coolidge (1925).**

In its second year, the NCAI prohibited BIA employees from serving and guaranteed that at least one board position would go to a woman. Ruth Muskrat Bronson, a Cherokee from Washington, D.C., became the first executive secretary and the group's primary organizer and lobbyist.

Indians needed a national organization to unite opposition to the termination policy outlined by Chavez and Wheeler. Crucial to the growth of both the policy and the NCAI opposition to it was the experience Indian people gained in World War II. The "Good War" changed the lives of all Americans. Indians proved no exception.

## The Indian Experience in World War II

Native people may have participated in the war more completely than any other group in American society. Almost one-third of the pool of able-bodied Indian men joined the military. Another one-fourth found work in war industry and related services. Indian women participated both in military auxiliaries and in war-related work. Many men and women left the reservations for other varieties of urban employment. They gained technical skills and, more important, skills in dealing with American society outside the reservations. After the war, many Indian veterans augmented those skills by attending college on the GI Bill.

It seems surprising that Indians would flock to defend the nation that had taken their lands and attempted to destroy their societies. But, in fact, the Indian response itself makes it clear that native cultures had not been destroyed but were simply cutting it both ways—across and along the grain of American culture. Many Indian people saw themselves defending their own geographic homelands as much as the American state. Others noted with pride the existence of a still-vital warrior tradition in their cultures. Tribal elders and spiritual leaders frequently performed ceremonies for departing or returning servicemen. But Indians all over the country also expressed a genuine and deeply held sense of American patriotism. Even though they had trouble making ends meet, native people bought disproportionately large numbers of war bonds and supported the country in every way possible.

Unlike African-Americans, Indian soldiers were scattered throughout the military in integrated units. Indians served as pilots, navigators, and gunners in the air corps, machinists, signalmen, and spotters in the navy, and regulation GIs in the army. The Forty-fifth Army Division had perhaps the greatest concentration of Indian soldiers—approximately one-fifth of the "Thunderbird" division was native American. From June 1943 until the spring of 1945, the division experienced 511 days of combat. They fought from North Africa through Italy and southern France to the Forest of Ardennes, encountering some of the worst

*When I went to Germany I never thought about war honors, or the four "coups" which an old-time Crow warrior had to earn in battle. Those days were gone. But afterwards, when I came back and went through this telling of the war deeds ceremony, why, I told my war deeds, and lo and behold I completed the four requirements to become a chief.*

—JOSEPH MEDICINE CROW
(Crow), 1972

The 297th U.S. Marine Platoon—the second all-Navajo platoon—at San Diego in 1943.

RIGHT: In this publicity shot, Chief White Bull stands in traditional garb, brandishing bow-and-arrow, next to a jeep filled with modern Sioux warriors.

BELOW: Private Floyd Dann, one of several Hopi Indians in the Signal Corps.

## NAVAJO CODE TALKERS

Perhaps the most familiar instance of Indian participation in the war effort is that of the Navajo code talkers. Although other branches of the military used native language speakers to encode and decipher communications—Oneidas, Chippewas, Sauks and Foxes, and Comanches all served in the Army Signal Corps—the Marine Corps developed the largest program, recruiting over four hundred code talkers by the end of the war.

The Dineh (Navajo) developed a specialized military dictionary in which Dineh terms were used to describe military maneuvers and hardware. A submarine became an "iron fish"; a machine gun, a "fast shooter." Many of the Dineh marines served in the Pacific theater, seeing action at Guadalcanal, Iwo Jima, and Okinawa.

fighting of the war. Both Indian winners of the Medal of Honor came from the Forty-fifth, as did the winners of numerous Purple Hearts and Bronze Stars.

Although the war featured new military technologies and tactics, many Indian soldiers continued to practice traditional rituals, integrating older martial heritages into a very new type of conflict.

In one of his last stories, war correspondent Ernie Pyle described the confidence of Dineh code talkers who had conducted a ceremony before leaving for Okinawa: "The Red Cross furnished some colored cloth and paint to stain their faces. They made up the rest . . . from feathers, sea shells, coconuts, empty ration cans, and rifle cartridges. In their chant they asked the [gods] to sap the Japanese of their strength for this blitz. And then they ended their ceremonial chant by singing the Marine Corps song in Navajo." Correspondent Walter Wood noted other ceremonials by Lakotas, Comanches, Apaches, Pimas, Kiowas, Crows, and various Pueblo people.

Indian women played their part in numbers that proportionally equaled or surpassed non-Indian female populations. Thousands signed up for military auxiliaries, nurses corps, Red Cross work, and the American Women's Voluntary Service. The Standing Rock Lakota reservation alone put at least fifty women in military uniform. Thousands more took over men's jobs both on the reservation and at urban and war industry production sites. In Alaska, over five hundred native women manufactured mittens, mukluks, snowshoes, and other traditional cold weather apparel for troops serving in winter campaigns. Others engaged in a wide variety of craft industries in order to buy war bonds and stamps.

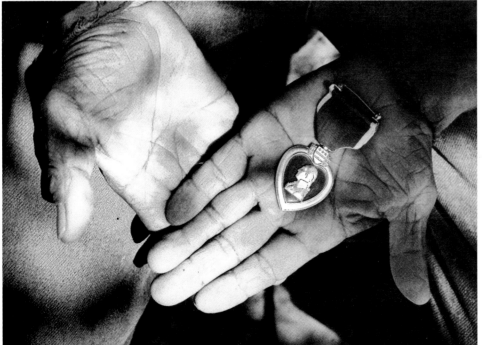

ABOVE:
The Special Warriors Celebration was held in the summer of 1991 in Window Rock, Arizona, to honor all Navajo veterans and welcome home Navajo fighters from Operation Desert Storm. Here a group of World War II Navajo code talkers waits for the parade to start.

LEFT:
The Purple Heart, which is awarded for injuries sustained in combat, was bestowed upon Navajo Johnnie Alfred, who served with the Sixth Marine Division in Tarawa, Saipan, Okinawa, Tinian, the Ryukyu Islands, and the Mariana Islands.

A Chippewa family settles in to watch television in their Oakland, California, home (1955). Families like this presented the white ideal of the urbanized Indian but told little about the effects of cultural loss experienced by many others forced off their homelands and into America's urban centers.

## Postwar: Making Indians into "Americans"

Many Indians hoped that their participation in the war would lead to greater American respect and tolerance for tribal life. But most Americans saw things differently. To them, Indian participation in a unified, if not fully integrated, American society suggested that complete assimilation into mainstream American culture was not only possible but imminent. This wishful thinking interlocked neatly with the fortress mentality of the cold war. After World War II, Americans cherished the illusion of a happy, homogeneous America devoid of serious racial or cultural divisions.

This notion came as an abrupt turn from Collier's emphasis on valuing other cultures for their differences and it led to yet another shift in federal policy toward Indians—this time back to assimilation, that is, absorption into the national whole. In 1946, Congress began to implement the new "termination" policy with a commission to resolve Indian claims. The call for an Indian Claims Commission had its roots as far back as the Meriam Report of 1928. Its meaning, however, had changed with subsequent shifts in American culture and policy.

Although native people could go to court—or could request the government to file suits on their behalf—they could not sue the United States itself without a special congressional enabling act. (The Lakota, for example, had requested and received such an act in 1920 in order to file suit against the government for violating the treaty of 1868.) In the first decades of the twentieth century, hundreds of tribes had sought enabling acts. The Meriam Commission hoped to streamline this bureaucratic procedure that produced excessive paperwork and delayed tribal appeals for justice.

Five years later, in 1933, the Indian New Deal had taken up the proposal to grant Indians the same legal rights enjoyed by other Americans. But by the time Congress approved the Claims Commission in 1946, thirteen years after the New Deal proposal, the project reflected yet another set of motives. Congress now hoped to use the Claims Commission to "clear the decks" of any possible Indian claims in order to expedite the government's rapid departure from Indian affairs.

Like latter-day Dawes advocates, postwar policymakers saw termination, the Indian Claims Commission, and the relocation policy—which removed Indians from the reservations and transplanted them to cities—as creating an urban style of assimilation. Although the policies addressed different dimensions of Indian life, termination and relocation complemented each other in mounting a devastating attack on Collier's notion of revivified Indian cultures.

The relocation policy evolved out of postwar urban job-placement programs and addressed worries that returning veterans and workers would strain the capacity of the reservations. Bureau of Indian Affairs Commissioner Dillon Myer (who gained expertise in moving people as the supervisor of wartime Japanese internment) saw urban integration as the ideal solution to the problem. In the cities, Indians could finally be incorporated into American society. Given initial assistance and training, urban Indians would be left to sink or swim, the same as any "foreign" minority.

Many native people eagerly accepted the relocation program's offer of a bus ticket, an apartment, and an alarm clock (for punctuality on the job). Conditions on many reservations had deteriorated during the war and many returnees found their hometowns limited and confining. Across the country, Indians had returned to the postwar reservations as confirmed wage laborers with no place to work.

Still haunted by IRA–accelerated factionalism, tribes now had to confront generational gaps between the young who had left and returned and the old who had stayed behind. Many mixed-bloods, stung by American racial prejudice, disavowed their native heritage altogether. Worst of all, perhaps, were the dashed hopes of those who had believed the rhetoric of "Americans all," who had been taken in by yet another false promise of equality.

In this setting, perhaps the best one could hope for was a bus ticket out. Unfortunately, relocation frequently involved nothing more than a trade of rural for urban poverty. Many relocated Indians soon made their way back to the reservations where poverty could be ameliorated to some extent by extended family

## POSTWAR ADJUSTMENT

Putting on the uniform of the American armed forces had given Indian people a crucial ingredient missing from both assimilation and cultural pluralism—sincere respect. Americans reverenced the men and women who were fighting the war, and Indians in the service found that, despite their nonwhite status, they could command the same respect. From America's train stations, bars, and army bootcamps to the bunkers and foxholes of the Pacific islands and European forests, Indians, many for perhaps the first time, felt valued and appreciated by non-Indians.

American society had never before conferred such respect upon Indian people, and native servicemen and women came to like the resulting feelings of self-worth and national worth. When the war ended, however, and the uniforms came off, Indians found that America's respect had vanished as well. Indian people, even the most "assimilated," would seemingly always be second-class citizens, kept in their places by both the subtle snub and the sign reading "No Dogs or Indians Allowed." After the liberating experience of wartime, America's return to prewar discrimination proved doubly humiliating for many Indians and raised the level of frustration in Indian country to new heights.

relationships. Others stayed in the cities, forming substantial urban enclaves in places like Denver, Los Angeles, Minneapolis, and Chicago. These urban Indians banded together in pan-Indian groups, generating new cultural forms that intermingled the characteristics of many tribes.

The relocation program also served the larger agenda of terminating both the federal trust relationship with Indian tribes and the institution of the tribe itself. As John Collier had understood, reservation land bases encouraged Indian tribal identity and political status. Termination reversed this—if Indians could be moved off the reservations and encouraged to devalue their traditional ties, the goal of terminating tribal political entities could be more easily accomplished.

Congress formally implemented the termination policy in 1953, through House Concurrent Resolution 108 and Public Law 280. Termination sought to turn the "Indian problem" over to the states. Under Public Law 280, state agencies would take over both federal services and jurisdiction and the local role of IRA–based tribal councils. After termination, Indians would no longer be recognized as Indians by federal, state, or local governments.

By attacking tribal landholding, political existence, and the very notion of "Indianness," termination created a climate of fear in Indian country. That fear intensified when it became obvious that tribes had no voice in the new matter of state jurisdiction and that Congress would apply extreme pressure to tribes to accept the full termination of federal trust relationships. Getting rid of its responsibilities to the tribes was, after all, the primary aim of the termination policy.

The kind of pressure the government could bring to bear was demonstrated on the Menominee, a Wisconsin tribe with a successful lumber and sawmill business. In 1947, when the BIA had recommended certain tribes that it deemed "ready" to be terminated, the Menominee appeared near the top of the list. The government used money and threats to pressure the tribe into agreeing to termination, and then pursued the reluctant Menominees throughout the 1950s.

In 1951, the tribe was awarded a $7.6 million judgment as compensation for BIA mismanagement earlier in the century. Senator Arthur Watkins visited the reservation in 1953, praised Menominee industry, and then threatened to distribute the award only if the tribe voted in favor of termination. The advisory council—a small percentage of Menominees—voted 169 to 0 to accept the program.

Doubts and difficulties arose almost immediately, and the tribe spent most of the decade trying to develop a termination plan and asking for a series of extensions. Originally scheduled for 1958, Menominee termination finally took place in December of 1961.

Under the termination plan, the tribe was reorganized into a corporation, the members became shareholders, and the reservation became a county. Although termination was supposed to leave the Menominees "free," they were subjected to a set of government restrictions never placed on a non-Indian corporation. The Menominees could not take out a mortgage on their property. They were supervised by a board of local non-Indian businessmen, and the bulk of shares in the Menominee trust fund were controlled by white bankers.

Although the tribe tried its best to make termination work, creating a brand-new county proved no easy task. Per capita distributions, state and local taxes, and the need to provide and pay for services to county residents dried up the

Menominees' settlement money and sent the people into a downward spiral of poverty. Within a few years, a group of Menominees began a long struggle to restore their federal trust relationship.

With its denial of the very idea of being Indian, termination sent psychic shock waves reverberating across Indian country. Indians nervously watched the progress of the Menominee termination program and began to formulate political responses. Individual tribes, many led by college-educated veterans, issued their own protests.

On a national level, the NCAI took a leading role in speaking against termination, arguing for a dual Indian identity that encompassed *both* tribal membership and American citizenship. In 1958, Congress decided not to terminate any tribe against its will. By bringing leaders of diverse tribes together to fight a common battle, the NCAI paved the way for a host of national Indian organizations that formed during the 1960s to demand the rights guaranteed Indians by their treaties and by their American citizenship.

George Gillette, chairman of the Fort Berthold Indian Tribal Business Council, weeps as Secretary of the Interior J. A. Krug signs a contract confirming the sale in 1948 of 155,000 acres of the North Dakota reservation's best lands to the government for the Garrison Land and Reservoir Project. Of the sale, Gillette said, "The members of the tribal council sign this contract with heavy hearts. . . . Right now the future does not look so good to us."

# CHAPTER TWENTY-SEVEN

# SOVEREIGNTY

*CLOAK OF THE EAGLE*
BY MIKE LARSEN (CHICKASAW), 1992

THE FOUNDING OF THE National Council of American Indians and the national scope of the fight against termination marked one of the first milestones in the development of Indian participation in American politics. As tribal leaders became used to working together in the NCAI, they developed other national organizations focused on more specific aims such as health, education, economic development, and resource use. Gathering at conferences and conventions, putting together proposals and task forces, these leaders created a new Indian political arena that centered not only on tribes and tribal relations to the federal government, but also on the idea of national Indian leadership itself. The developing political skills of these leaders would have national impact on Indian and non-Indian alike.

One of the clearest tests of Indian political skill came with the struggle over Alaska native land claims. In 1959 legislation granted Alaska statehood and allowed the state to select 103 million acres of federal land. Seeing state ownership and rapid resource development as the primary pathway to economic success, Alaskans selected commercially viable lands with little or no regard for the land-use patterns already established by Alaska natives. With their subsistence hunting areas threatened, Alaska natives filed Indian Claims Commission land claims for most of the state, and in 1966 convinced the secretary of the interior to place a freeze on state land selections until land claims issues had been resolved.

The freeze stopped the region's largest economic project, the Trans-Alaska Pipeline, dead in its tracks.

---

OPPOSITE:
**Portrait of James Holy Eagle, Oglala Sioux, at age 102 (1992).**

A woman from a village on the Kobuk River in North Alaska lays eulachon out to dry on outdoor racks.

A member of the Quinault tribe catches salmon near Taholah, Washington (1981). The traditional method of gill netting has been practiced since before contact with whites.

That same year, three hundred representatives from existing native organizations met in Anchorage to form the Alaska Federation of Natives (AFN), a group created specifically to deal with the Department of the Interior and to lobby the land claims bills being drafted in Congress. Most of the main players in the AFN had significant experience in non-Indian society. Some, like AFN president Willie Hensley, had been involved in the Alaska state senate. Many came from groups like the Haida and Tlingit of southern Alaska. These tribes had a long history of political activity in Alaska and had been in contact with non-Indians since the first Russians had arrived in 1741.

The AFN quickly learned the techniques necessary to nurse a major piece of legislation through Congress. They nurtured relationships with key figures like Senate Interior Committee member Henry Jackson of Washington, and forged alliances with groups like the Ford Foundation, the National Council of Churches, and the United Auto Workers. A media campaign in the lower forty-eight states helped win over the general public. Perhaps the most significant achievement of the AFN, however, was the unification of eighty thousand Alaskan native peoples with disparate interests and economies that ranged from pure subsistence hunting and fishing to pure urban wage work. Congress demanded a unified position and the AFN responded. The Alaska Native Claims Settlement Act (ANCSA) of 1971 was the landmark result.

Meanwhile, back in the lower forty-eight, Indian leaders continued to politic with one another, honing their skills and expanding their political interactions with the federal government.

Many native people found BIA work on their reservations in the fields of education, administration, and law enforcement. More important, however, was the policy of the major domestic plans of the 1960s—the New Frontier and the Great Society programs—that allowed Indian tribes to sponsor federal programs and to administer the accompanying funding. The War on Poverty program, for example, brought countless Indians into bureaucratic and political relationships with a variety of federal agencies. Slipping through the maze of paperwork to come home with funding and programs required both knowledge and connections. Tribal leaders learned, in effect, how to function in the manner of pork-barrel congressional representatives. Yet even when they did bring home the bacon, Indian leaders still faced heavy expectations and more political struggle back in Indian country.

By administering federal money, tribal councils often became the major employer and provider of services on reservations. And since tribal leaders controlled federal funds, it was not surprising that tribal elections frequently became struggles among factions, each of which desparately needed better access to employment and social services. Some leaders, like Oglala Sioux tribal chairman Richard Wilson, took shameless advantage of the position. Wilson knew exactly how to play politics both in Washington, where he was a BIA favorite, and at home on the Pine Ridge reservation, where he wielded almost absolute power. As chairman, Wilson handed out choice jobs to family members and supporters, plundered tribal accounts, bypassed the elected tribal council, and terrorized political opponents with a group of enforcers known as the "GOON Squad" (Guardians Of the Oglala Nation).

Under ANCSA, native people were given $962.5 million and forty-four million acres of land, making them the largest private landowners in the state. But the act also reflects the problems inherent in a non-Indian approach to politics. The people who helped design the act and who pushed it through Congress established a structure based not on native forms of governance and management but on an American business and politics model.

ANCSA created thirteen regional for-profit corporations charged with selecting native land holdings. These corporations retained complete title to sixteen million acres and subsurface rights to the remaining land, and channeled settlement money and profits to individuals and more than two hundred village corporations.

But, because they seek a profit, the corporations remain inherently unresponsive to the needs of natives who live largely or partly through hunting or fishing. The corporations must make money. To do so, they often pursue mining and logging projects that destroy the subsistence resources used by their own shareholders. Since the corporations hold the land privately rather than under government trust status, the possibility exists that native people may one day lose their land to corporate bankruptcy or tax liability.

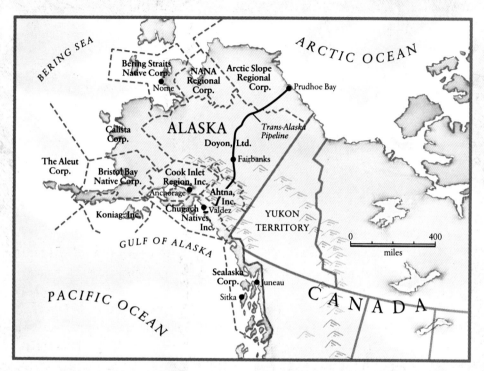

*Native Land Holdings in Alaska.* The twelve regional landholding corporations of the Alaska Native Claims Settlement Act. The thirteenth regional corporation was established for Alaskan natives who were eligible to share in the treaty but who lived outside of the state. The corporation was not allotted any land but received a share of the monetary settlement.

Wilson's ironclad totalitarianism proved to be something of an aberration in Indian country. But even in its extremes, the Wilson regime can be recognized as a logical product of the IRA reforms that substituted American-style tribal governments for the older Indian forms of governance by consent. Wilson's government bore a close resemblance to a number of American administrations also plagued by nepotism, patronage, deficit spending, perquisites, sloppy bookkeeping, suppression of democratic representation, spying, and intimidation.

While some tribal governments followed Wilson in succumbing to the possibilities of corruption, others integrated less-distasteful elements of American political culture into their own societies. Parliamentary procedure, legalistic language, and legislative strategy appeared quickly on many reservations after the IRA. By the 1960s, American-style politics had become a vehicle not only for tribes to speak within American society, but for individual Indians to speak within their own societies. An obsessive awareness of politics came to permeate many tribes, spanning all levels from the local to the federal. Although political maneuvering often created dissension within tribes, many of its more skilled participants were also able to help their people in significant ways through social and economic development programs.

But if the tribal administration of Great Society money helped people at the same time that it intensified reservation political struggles, it also pointed toward yet another shift in government policy. By the late 1960s, it appeared that tribes had started living Collier's dream of more efficient—by American standards—corporate management.

In 1970, President Richard Nixon recognized this development by formally repudiating termination, a policy that—thanks to Indian protest and political activism—had been dying a slow death since the late 1950s (the Menominees succeeded in winning the repeal of their termination act in 1974). In place of termination, Nixon supported a new policy—"self-determination."

Formally articulated by young Indians as early as 1961 and foreshadowed by the IRA and the programs of the Johnson administration, self-determination emphasized tribal control over social programs, law enforcement, education, and other services traditionally controlled by the federal government. Now, *when tribes deemed themselves ready*, they were to take over or administer contracts previously supervised by the BIA. Self-determination has been a frequently invoked cornerstone of federal Indian policy ever since.

By participating in the American political system at an opportune historical moment, Indian leaders established greater autonomy on many reservations and promoted a more empowering federal policy. Although Indians remained among the poorest people in America, government money—now sometimes controlled by native people rather than by distant bureaucrats—improved Indian living standards and health appraisals during the 1960s and 1970s. Indians had achieved a measure of control over the programs directed at them. This relative autonomy, however, depended entirely on the availability of federal money. What would happen if the government withdrew its support? Indian politicians liked to believe that their skill at lobbying Congress and the public would prevent such an occurrence. But many younger Indians sought a more substantive understanding of Indian autonomy. Material benefits aside, the increasingly sophisticated political relationships between tribes and the government struck these people as uncertain and humiliating exercises in colonial subservience.

In response, these younger Indians established an alternative—a noisy and aggressive politics of rebellion that celebrated Indian tradition, staged mass media events, and used non-Indian symbolic understandings of Indians to great effect. Strategic descendants of the Pueblo people who had drummed at the Stock Exchange in 1923, these "New Indians" also acknowledged their debt to other social movements that arose out of the widespread rebellions against cold war America's cultural conformity.

Indians were not the only American minority group to struggle with social inequalities after World War II. African-Americans and Latinos insistently pursued their rights to equal educational and employment opportunities. By the 1960s, black nationalist and Chicano movement activists had learned to create unity by emphasizing ethnic identities centered around shared culture and history. "White" Americans were no less immune to the allure of identity politics. Like the modernist refugees of Santa Fe and Taos forty years earlier, young white Americans began celebrating other cultures for their "authenticity" and insights into "soul," community, environmental awareness, and spirituality.

A small group of people, part of the Indian contingent that occupied Alcatraz Island in 1969, stands on the docks under signs repainted to express the Indians' message.

... white man's own standards. By this we mean that this place resembles most Indian reservations in that:

1. It is isolated from modern facilities, and without adequate means of transportation.

2. It has no fresh running water.

3. It has inadequate sanitation facilities.

4. There are no oil or mineral rights.

5. There is no industry and so unemployment is very great.

6. There are no health care facilities.

7. The soil is rocky and non-productive; and the land does not support game.

8. There are no educational facilities.

9. The population has always exceeded the land base.

10. The population has always been held as prisoners and kept dependent upon others.

Further, it would be fitting and symbolic that ships from all over the world, entering the Golden Gate, would first see Indian land, and thus be reminded of the true history of the great lands once ruled by free and noble Indians.

In this cultural milieu, many young Indians turned naturally to "traditional" practices. Some of those who sought to reestablish tribal identities were the disillusioned products of relocation programs or BIA schools. Others had grown up on the reservations and were fully aware of their heritage. But like the Mohawk steelworkers of the 1920s, all these young Indians defined themselves in the modern world by pulling their pasts into a twentieth-century present. They wore beadwork on their blue jeans, pulled buckskins over their cowboy boots, and grew their hair long—not to imitate white countercultural rebels, but to reclaim the Plains-style practices that had come to symbolize pan-Indian identity. Tipis and sweat lodges returned to common use. Young urban Indians scoured the ethnographies of the previous century for details of older rituals. They turned back to their homelands as well—back to the "full-blood traditionals" who had often quietly maintained older practices.

Sun Dance lodge, Montana (1986).

I set out to see if there were any resources and in time I began to see that the language was still alive, the songs were still there, and the ceremonies were still there but people were very hesitant. . . .

When I went back to the tradition . . . sweat ceremony, vision quest, Sun Dance . . . my own sisters and brother stepped back. They didn't stop me, but they just pulled back. They were deathly scared that I was doing something that was evil and that I shouldn't even consider it.

In 1973 I went to a Sun Dance. I remember that for four days they only sang three songs over and over. The next year there were two more. Today there are over twenty sun dance songs that have come back. Last summer or the summer before an old timer came to a sun dance and said "this is an old song that I remember. I'm going to sing it once so try and catch it." And he sang it once and the singers caught it. So that song was shared by every Sun Dance last summer and it's a very beautiful song. Every year one or two songs would come back just like people coming back to the ceremony.

We did some ceremonies that we read from books. We looked at written documents and tried to follow and as we did the older people would say, "That's not correct," and we went through a lot of criticism in the beginning, but we kept it up and finally one older person got up and said, "Here's how you do it."

An Apache Sunrise Ceremonial, a gift of spiritual blessings given to a young girl by her family on the occasion of her first menstruation. The ceremony is usually performed in the summer, to coincide with the time nature reaches full bloom.

But for many Indians, reclaiming "the old ways" also meant repudiating the "new." Regeneration of older traditions implied a rejection not only of American social and cultural dominance but also of the IRA form of governments and the "Indian politics" that had grown around it. The "traditionals" who had refused to participate in the IRA often provided the intellectual underpinnings for a "new politics." They continued to call for a return to the rights of tribal self-government recognized in treaties, rather than the "colonial" self-government of IRA councils. Taking their cue from the protests of the civil rights and antiwar movements, younger Indians provided the political method: they took Indian history and culture into the streets.

Perhaps the first manifestation of a new political approach came as early as 1961 with the formation of the National Indian Youth Council (NIYC). In the years that followed, NIYC leaders and other young Indians decided to shift their struggle for Indian autonomy from the mostly bureaucratic arena of the IRA–NCAI tradition into the larger battleground of American culture itself. By creating media events, Indians could tap into a large, sympathetic audience primed by concerns over U.S. social inequality, military colonialism in Southeast Asia, and increasing environmental degradation. Native leaders developed their own strategies for bringing their grievances and their resurgent societies before the American public. In 1964, the NIYC joined a series of ultimately successful "fish-ins" in Washington State, public protests against the callous long-term abridgement of treaty fishing rights.

Other organizations formed as well. In 1968, the American Indian Movement (AIM) organized in Minneapolis, where police routinely brutalized Indian people. AIM members patrolled the streets with cameras in a media-based assault on police brutality. One year later, a group of "Indians of All Nations" took over the deserted federal prison on Alcatraz Island, citing a vague agreement that unused federal property could be turned back to reservation status.

# THE TWENTY POINTS

"Indians have paid attorneys more than $40,000,000 since 1962. Yet many Indian people are virtually imprisoned in the nation's courtrooms in being forced constantly to define their rights," noted one of the Twenty Points. The authors sought to codify those rights by doing away with the accumulated policies and decisions that separated twentieth-century Indians from their original treaties, documents understood legally to be "the law of the land." Among the provisions were a comprehensive review of all treaties, including those that had not been ratified by the U. S. Congress, the reestablishment of treaty making between tribes and the federal government, the elimination of state jurisdictions, the abolition of the BIA, the restoration of Indian land bases, and the protection of legal rights and religious freedoms. Both Indian self-government and relations with the federal government would be defined not by federal edicts and decisions but by mutually agreed-upon treaties.

**1. Restoration of Constitutional Treaty-Making Authority.** The effect of this proposal would be the restoration of federal recognition of tribes as independent political entities.

**2. Establishment of a Treaty Commission to Make New Treaties.** This provision would reinforce existing treaties while establishing an agreement on the "national commitment to the future of Indian people."

**3. An Address to the American People and Joint Session of Congress.** Indian leaders wanted to combine both politics and cultural appeal in a nationally televised event with Congress and the President.

**4. Commission to Review Treaty Commitments and Violations.** With this provision, the authors recognized the limitations of treaty-based lawsuits: "Indians have paid attorneys more than $40,000,000 since 1962. Yet many Indian people are virtually imprisoned in the nation's courtrooms in being forced constantly to define their rights. . . . There is less need for more attorney assistance than there is for an institution of protections that reduce violations and minimize the possibilities for attacks on Indian rights."

**5. Resubmission of Unratified Treaties to the Senate.** Many tribes, especially in California, had made treaties that had never been ratified. Indian leaders wished to formalize treaty status with each of these groups.

**6. All Indians to Be Governed by Treaty Relations.** A general reaffirmation of points one, two, and five that would cover any possible exceptions to those points.

**7. Mandatory Relief Against Treaty Violations.** The authors asked for an automatic injunction against non-Indian violators whenever tribes petitioned for treaty violation relief. This provision would eliminate the use of legal delaying tactics.

**8. Judicial Recognition of Indian Right to Interpret Treaties.** Indians wanted a law requiring the Supreme Court to hear Indian appeals arising from treaty violation cases.

**9. Creation of Congressional Joint Committee on Reconstruction of Indian Relations.** This proposal would restructure Congressional committees dealing with Indian affairs into a single entity.

**10. Land Reform and Restoration of a 110 Million-Acre Native Land Base.** A request for restoration of land, permanent nonalienable status, consolidation of resources, the termination of leasing, and condemnation of non-Indian land titles on reservations.

**11. Restoration of Rights to Indians Terminated by Enrollment and Revocation of Prohibitions Against "Dual Benefits."** Blood quantum qualifications for tribal membership, while posing few problems for people with successive non-Indian parents, often deny tribal membership to full- or mixed-blood Indians with parents from different tribes.

**12. Repeal of State Laws Enacted Under Public Law 280.** This provision would eliminate tribal-state jurisdictional and sovereignty disputes by removing state controls over Indian land.

**13. Resume Federal Protective Jurisdiction over Offenses Against Indians.** In response to the continued inability of state and local court systems to convict non-Indians of crimes against Indian people, the authors wished to make crimes committed against Indians federal offenses and empanel a federal Indian grand jury with powers to indict violators.

**14. Abolition of the Bureau of Indian Affairs; A New Structure.** Unconvinced that the BIA as constituted could ever escape its past, the authors asked for a new agency that would operate according to the guidelines laid down in new treaty negotiations.

A woman draped in an upside-down flag, along with about five hundred other native Americans protesting the government's history of broken treaties, occupies the Bureau of Indian Affairs building in Washington, D. C., in November 1972.

15. Creation of an "Office of Federal Indian Relations and Community Reconstruction." This provision spelled out Indian ideas for a new agency. It would preserve equal standing between government and tribes, be responsible to the President, and have a maximum of 1,000 employees.

16. Priorities and Purpose of the Proposed New Office. It may be taken as an indication of the level of distrust of the BIA, that Indian leaders wanted to reiterate yet again that the new agency's main goal would be "to remedy the breakdown in constitutionally-

prescribed relationships between the United States and Indian nations."

17. Indian Commerce and Tax Immunities. This provision would eliminate the constant wrangling between tribes and states over taxation powers by removing all tribes from state taxation authority. Reservation taxes would be tribal and federal.

18. Protection of Indians' Religious Freedom and Cultural Integrity. The authors insisted that legal protections be given to Indian religious expression. (Although Congress passed the

American Indian Religious Freedom Act in 1978, it does not, in fact, offer such legal protections.)

19. National Referendums, Local Options, and Forms of Indian Organization. A general appeal to cut proliferating Indian organizations and to consolidate leadership at local levels.

20. Health, Housing, Employment, Economic Development, and Education. The authors asked for increased funding and better management of a variety of programs.

(Left to right) An unidentified woman, Dennis Banks, and Clyde Bellecourt, members of the American Indian Movement, at Wounded Knee on the Pine Ridge reservation, South Dakota, March 1973.

*The Great Sioux Reservation, According to the Fort Laramie Treaty of 1868, and Present-Day Sioux Reservations.* Though the takeover at Wounded Knee was primarily rooted in the politics of tribal government, the occupiers raised broader issues, arguing that the treaty affirmed Sioux political sovereignty over the area. This called attention to longstanding land claims struggles based on the 1868 treaty and it allowed them to assert that the United States had infringed on internal Sioux politics.

The most significant articulation of the new Indian position came in 1972, with the "Trail of Broken Treaties" caravan to the headquarters of the BIA. Native people from across the country drove to Washington in hopes of convincing the government to renew the treaty relationship and respect treaty rights. The demonstration was marred, however, by the takeover of the BIA offices—an action provoked largely by the government. In the flurry of media excitement at yet another radical protest, the conceptual foundation of Indian demands, encapsulated in a document called *The Twenty Points*, was lost. The authors of *The Twenty Points* called not for more social programs, legally enforced equality, or integration, but for a return to the terms of treaties. *The Twenty Points* proved to be an accurate indicator of Indian thought, for in the years that followed, Indian people repeatedly turned to Congress and the courts to force government administrators to uphold treaty responsibilities and to ratify the right to Indian sovereignty.

Driven by widely differing objectives, the old-line Indian politicians and the new radical-traditional alliance were on a collision course that finally exploded at Wounded Knee.

When the Pine Ridge contingent returned from the Trail of Broken Treaties, Richard Wilson and his backers met them with a gauntlet of intimidation that quickly led to a desperate takeover.

On the night of February 27, 1973, national activists from the American Indian Movement and local Oglala Lakota people seized the trading post and Catholic church in the reservation town of Wounded Knee, South Dakota. Hoping for a temporary platform from which to publicize a variety of grievances, the protestors instead found themselves besieged by hundreds of federal agents equipped with the latest military hardware. While planes and helicopters buzzed

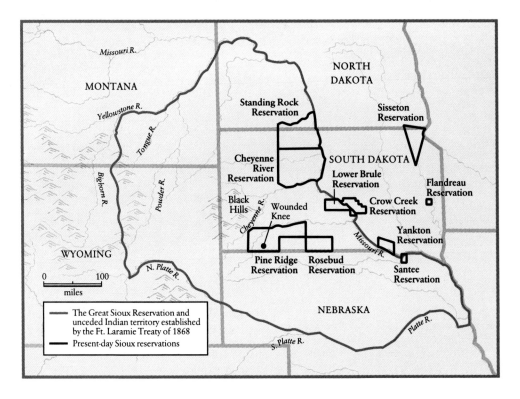

Indians stand guard outside the Sacred Heart Catholic Church during the occupation and siege of Wounded Knee.

overhead and armored personnel carriers circled the countryside, the occupiers dug bunkers with golf clubs and returned the government's high-powered weapons fire with shots from their hunting rifles.

The reporters and outside observers who flocked to the scene viewed the takeover in the context of the civil rights and antiwar struggles of the late 1960s. With its explicit historic and symbolic links to the original Wounded Knee massacre, the 1973 occupation offered American media a story that practically wrote itself. A small band of Indians was once again in danger of being slaughtered simply because they refused to acquiesce to continued American social inequalities. The involvement of AIM activists and government marshals reinforced the perception that Wounded Knee was a 1960s-style battle between angry Indians and the federal authorities. But at the core of Wounded Knee lay the more subtle conflict between Indian people who believed in working "outside the system" and those who had found success working within it.

## The Role of Indian Law

Ironically, the rift between politicians and radicals was at that very moment being bridged by another practice taken from American politics and culture: the emerging discipline of Indian law.

Indian lawyers helped create a middle ground often capable of uniting both parties. Like tribal politicians, Indian lawyers dealt closely with the political and legal institutions of American government. The suits they filed, however, most often originated from treaty rights violations, and thus represented the positions of the radical-traditional alliances. Many Indian people had retained comprehensive knowledge of the treaties signed with the United States and had for years sought redress in the courts for violations of those treaties. The Indian Claims Commission was created to deal with exactly that sort of claim. In the early years of the commission, however, Indian lawyers were in short supply and tribes often turned—with decidedly mixed results—to non-Indians for legal counsel.

This situation began to change in 1970 when a California group used a Ford Foundation grant to create the Native American Rights Fund (NARF), a national organization dedicated to providing free legal assistance to Indian people. NARF and lawyers for the Nevada Paiute tribe subsequently won several important victories in a protracted fight for Paiute water rights. The organization quickly grew into a sophisticated and omnipresent voice in Indian law.

Other native Americans also realized the crucial importance of law to the struggle of Indian peoples, and additional legal assistance groups came into being. The American Indian Law Center at the University of New Mexico assisted Indian law students, and the Institute for the Development of Indian Law and the Indian Law Resource Center offered aid to tribes pursuing legal remedies for treaty violations. One of the greatest victories in Indian legal history came in the mid-1970s when the Passamaquoddy and Penobscot tribes offered proof that, according to the laws of the United States, they retained legal ownership of the greater part of the state of Maine. The federal government was eventually forced to make a settlement that included awards of both money and land.

As Indian lawyers and their allies grew in sophistication and confidence during the 1970s, they won several key battles. In Washington State, a federal judge ruled that the state's native people had legitimate rights—guaranteed by treaty—to half of the state's salmon and trout fisheries. In the upper Midwest, courts upheld the treaty rights of tribes to regulate their own hunting and fishing. The Lakota Black Hills claim—contested since 1920—eventually ended up in the U.S. Supreme Court where the justices awarded the Lakota tribes $105 million as compensation. The Lakotas, however, want their land back. They have consistently refused the money, and it now sits, gathering interest, in the federal treasury. And when the Wounded Knee defendants went to trial, their lawyers (although non-Indian) were able to introduce and cite the 1868 Sioux treaty and a body of treaty law in making a successful defense.

After Wounded Knee, tensions between the Wilson faction and the traditional–AIM faction turned the Pine Ridge reservation into a battle zone. With time, however, tempers cooled and both sides began to look at the middle ground offered by the legal pursuit of treaty rights. Although still wracked by internal

Robert Fast Horse, chief tribal judge of the Oglala Sioux, in chambers at the tribal courthouse in Pine Ridge, South Dakota (1985). Rulings are made in accord with the Sioux Tribal Law and Order Code as drafted by the tribal council.

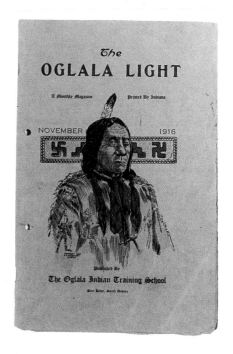

A 1916 cover of the *Oglala Light,* a monthly magazine published by Sioux Indians.

dissension and political game playing, many tribal councils began to use their treaties rather than the supervision of federal money as the primary means of defining their own autonomy.

## White Backlash and New Indian Strategy

In 1971, the Michigan Department of Natural Resources announced that it would no longer distinguish between Indians and non-Indians in its enforcement of state game laws—a clear violation of the Chippewa treaties of 1836 and 1855. Under those treaties, the Chippewa had retained the right to regulate their own fishing without the interference of any American government.

Shortly after the state's pronouncement, an angry Chippewa named Albert LeBlanc went fishing on Lake Superior to invite arrest and put Michigan's jurisdictional claim to the test of law. Non-Indians, mostly sport fishermen, gathered quickly under the politically correct banner of "conservation" and charged Chippewa fishers with "raping the environment." Despite the fact that sport fishing took 80 percent of the Great Lake's trout fishery and Indian fishing only 7 percent, the "sporting" activists blamed Indian fishers for a supposedly threatened trout population. They cut Indian nets, slashed tires, scuttled boats, and fired shots at Indian fishers. Threatening racist bumper stickers—SAVE A FISH–SPEAR AN INDIAN—and "Wanted" posters offering bounties for Indian fishers appeared across northern Michigan.

Seven years later, a federal judge added fuel to this gathering firestorm of white backlash by ruling that the state did *not* have the legal right to regulate Chippewa fishing. During the 1970s, such Indian legal successes often meant that native people were able to set their own regulations for hunting, to claim a certain percentage of a given fishery, to hold legal ownership of a share of limited

### INDIAN MEDIA

At the same time they created media events, native people were also developing their own media voice. In 1969, Vine Deloria, Jr., published a sarcastic attack on American Indian policy entitled *Custer Died for Your Sins* and Scott Momaday released his Pulitzer Prize–winning novel, *House Made of Dawn*. Both helped to bring Indian peoples and problems to the attention of non-Indian audiences. Newspapers like *Wassaja*, *Akwasasne Notes*, and the *Tundra Times* connected Indians from around the country to each other's struggles. In 1974, *American Indian Quarterly* and the *American Indian Culture and Research Journal* started to bring Indian voices into the academic study of Indian life.

Sympathetic non-Indian authors offered up a plethora of writings in which culturally potent Indian images spoke to American concerns about ecology, spirituality, and colonial victimization.

Fishing on the Deschutes River, Oregon, a traditional fishing ground of the Warm Springs Indians (1988). Fishing sites are controlled by individual families and are handed down through generations. Great physical strength is required to maneuver the long poles against the strong current and net the salmon, which can often weigh as much as sixty pounds.

## PASSAMAQUODDIES AND PENOBSCOTS

In 1980, the Passamaquoddy and Penobscot tribes each received $40.3 million to settle their claims to over 12 million acres in the state of Maine. Rather than simply distribute the money among tribal members, however, the tribes established sophisticated business and investment plans.

One-third of the money was committed to the acquisition of 300,000 acres of land. Another third went into conservative investments whose proceeds are distributed to the tribal members each year. The final third was invested directly in business enterprises through a tribal investment banking firm, Tribal Assets Management.

Holding the largest pool of capital in the state, the tribes began to consider business opportunities that met not only economic but also social and political objectives.

In the 1980s world of corporate raiding and leveraged buyouts, the tribes' fortunes diverged. The Penobscot investments—an ice hockey arena on the reservation and a venture making audio- and videocassettes—did not turn out as well as they had hoped.

The Passamaquoddies, on the other hand, bought Maine's third largest blueberry farm and recovered their investment in two years. They purchased two radio stations and, in 1983, bought the only cement plant in New England. When they sold the plant five years later, the Passamaquoddies turned an estimated $60 million profit and controlled the patents on a high-technology scrubber for reducing industrial sulphur dioxide emissions.

western water resources, or to exercise law enforcement jurisdiction over certain criminal activities on their reservations. Backlash groups like the Interstate Congress for Equal Rights and Responsibilities organized to fight what they regarded as "special privileges" given to Indian people.

The backlash against Indian legal successes was only part of a larger political shift in which white Americans attacked the gains many racial and ethnic groups had made in the 1960s and early 1970s. Rising conservatism led to renewed attacks on Indian treaty rights and the widespread pronouncement that affirmative action programs were "reverse discrimination" and that America should be a "level playing field." Just as this new conservative constituency ignored America's history of structural discrimination and physical and wage slavery of African-Americans, Latinos, and Asian-Americans, they also wanted to ignore the treaty agreements their nation had made in obtaining Indian land.

Once again, non-Indian symbolic understandings of Indians clashed with the real political gains made by actual Indian people. Americans loved Indians as a nonthreatening, historical group of people who could be easily romanticized and then forgotten. But Indians had always been far more troublesome as real people and never more so than during the period around 1970 when they developed the political skill and power to beat American citizens at their own game. As determined and articulate plaintiffs who threw real estate titles into question and went after valuable resources, Indian people were threats rather than icons.

After Wounded Knee, the FBI—already committed to an organized program of intimidation of native activists—intensified its efforts to neutralize Indian dissent. A long string of malicious prosecutions kept Indian leaders tied up in court. Undercover agents infiltrated domestic radical groups like AIM and provoked the organizations into acting against their own best interests. Eventually AIM found itself isolated, its confrontational tactics no longer appreciated in post-1960s America. Although Indian activists continued to organize protests, demonstrations, and boycotts, they failed to recapture the large sympathetic audiences they had won in the glory years of cultural rebellion. Americans had dedicated the 1980s to "getting theirs."

Tribal politicians also felt the effects of shifting American political and cultural values. The Reagan administration's slashing attack on social services budgets exposed the fiscal dependency of tribal politics on the federal government. As the historian Alvin Josephy has pointed out, the Carter administration's Indian appropriations made up a mere .04 percent of the federal budget. But in 1982, 2.5 percent of *all* federal budget cuts came entirely from that .04 percent. Indian programs provided a fiscal well that the architects of Reaganomics drained without any regard for the people affected. National poverty statistics showed the Pine Ridge reservation to be the poorest county in the entire United States. The nearby Rosebud reservation was close behind.

As programs that served tribes fell under the budgetary ax, tribal leaders had less to offer their constituents, and the sniping between factional groups intensified. Government jobs disappeared, reservation economies fragmented, and federal officials shrugged their shoulders and pointed Indians toward the supposedly revitalized "private sector." There, a host of multinational corporations waited, each eager to turn reservation land into strip mines or toxic waste dumps. Many

Interior of Brule Sioux Peter Swift Hawk's home on the Rosebud reservation, South Dakota (1976).

tribes found themselves in a painful dilemma, sorely tempted by the prospect of economic survival even if it came at the cost of their lands and resources.

Nor was their newly developed skill in law much help, for Reagan's judicial appointments policy tempered their most effective tactic—Indian claims on the American legal system. An increasingly conservative federal judiciary offered extremely narrow interpretations of Indian rights both under treaties and under the U.S. Constitution and Bill of Rights. Soon, Indian lawyers had to exercise great care in selecting the cases they would take to trial. An adverse ruling for an individual tribe often created a precedent that could be applied across Indian country, affecting the lives of all native people.

The tightening of restraints on Indian people extended far beyond issues of land and jurisdiction, ultimately infringing upon the very practice of religion, an area supposedly dear to Americans. The American Indian Religious Freedom Act of 1978 had established what appeared to be a freedom-protecting policy: "Henceforth it shall be the policy of the United States to protect and preserve for American Indians their inherent right of freedom to believe, express, and exercise [their] traditional religions, including but not limited to access to sites, use and possession of sacred objects, and the freedom to worship through ceremonials and traditional rites."

Unfortunately, however, Congress had provided no mechanism for implementing or enforcing the act, trusting the good intentions of various individual government agencies who were thereby freed to ignore its provisions. The *Lyng v. Northwest Indian Cemetery Protective Association* (1988) and *Department of Human Resources of Oregon v. Smith* (1990) decisions both struck directly at Indian rights to practice "traditional" religions under the First Amendment and the 1978 act.

*Lyng* interpreted the First Amendment in extraordinary terms. After agreeing that an Indian sacred site was indeed legitimate and that it was vital to the practice of tribal religion, the Supreme Court ruled that although the Bill of Rights did protect religious practice it did not protect a religious *area*, even if the destruction of that area meant that the religion could no longer be practiced.

In the *Smith* case, on the other hand, the court took an entirely different view of the First Amendment. This case involved two Oregon members of the Native American Church who were fired because they used peyote as part of their religious rites. Citing the alleged "war on drugs," the court threw out the traditional balancing test that weighed social imperatives against religious rights. The court now claimed that the First Amendment might be too strict in its protections of religious freedom and that, in a culturally diverse society, there was simply too much at risk not to restrict religious freedom to some degree.

The decision got an immediate reaction from mainstream religious leaders who quickly recognized it as a threat to themselves (many churches, after all, serve wine, often to minors, and on Sundays, in clear violation of many state and local laws) and immediately organized to seek congressional legislation that would restore the traditional American understandings of religious freedom for their beliefs. Ironically, Indians were not invited to participate in this effort. Native American traditions were considered too controversial.

The general assault on Indian activism, federal programs, and legal rights took a harsh toll. Although quality of life varied from reservation to reservation, the

*Medicine Man—Peyote Ceremony* by Cecil Murdock (Kickapoo), 1946.

OPPOSITE:
*Peyote Ceremony* by Herman Toppah (Kiowa).

*There are many things to be shared with the Four Colors of humanity in our common destiny as one with our Mother the Earth. It is this sharing that must be considered with great care by the Elders and the medicine people who carry the Sacred Trusts, so that no harm may come to people through ignorance and misuse of these powerful forces.*

—Resolution of the Fifth Annual Meeting of the Traditional Elders Circle, 1980.

(Back row, left to right) Sewel, Frank, Gladys Makes Room for Them, Linda Forgets
Nothing, Twila Makes Room for Them, and Elmer Bravebird; (front row, left to right)
Dominic, Junior, and Willard Makes Room for Them, photographed in their home in
Spring Creek, South Dakota (1974).

overall situation was almost unimaginably bleak. Unemployment on many reservations hovered between 70 and 90 percent. Despondent over the jobs and opportunities they would apparently never have, and given too much time to think about them, many Indian people grew increasingly desperate. Incidents of crime, vandalism, domestic abuse—the symptoms of individuals in despair—often soared.

Perhaps most harmful was an old nemesis, alcohol. Drinking compounded a variety of other problems. Reservation roadsides sprouted warning signs—sometimes as many as a dozen together—marking the multiple places where drunk drivers had crashed and died. Pregnant mothers gave birth to increasing numbers of babies permanently damaged by fetal alcohol syndrome. The sexual liberties that often accompanied weekend drinking parties raised concerns about the enormous potential impact of AIDS on tight-knit reservation communities.

The backlash that began in the late 1970s and the often desperate times that followed made it clear to many Indians that once again they needed to find new strategies for living within the larger American community.

Indians recognized that the failure of previous government–tribal relationships stemmed from their perennially one-sided character. Although the tribes had achieved a measure of greater autonomy, it was still white Americans, not Indians, who limited and defined what Indians needed, where they would go, and how they would get there.

Those non-Indian definitions had often developed from limited understandings and, more significantly, were always dangerously subject to the swings in attitude that characterized American society. The continuing problems surrounding Indian policy stem not only from these ambiguous cultural understandings but from similarly vague, and even conflicting, developments in the legal and political frameworks that define the status of tribes.

## The Shifting Ground of Tribal Status

Treaty provisions have long been interpreted as establishing a trust relationship between the government and tribes, a relationship that casts tribes and individuals as wards in relation to a government guardian. Among the responsibilities assigned to the guardian and exchanged for concessions of land were those of education and protection from hostile Americans. But, in an apparent contradiction, treaties and legal interpretations also establish tribes as "domestic dependent nations," sovereign entities in their own right.

So, as American Indian policy shifted from assimilation to cultural pluralism to termination to self-determination, these two possibilities—dependence as wards, and independence as autonomous tribes—have been emphasized in varying degrees. Assimilation and termination sought to integrate "wards" into American society and therefore ignored the concept of Indian sovereignty. The Indian New Deal and the ideal of self-determination stressed the independent and corporate nature of tribes. If tribes could assume their own unique social status, according to these latter policies, the guardian–ward relationship would gradually fade away in favor of tribal self-government.

# ALCOHOLISM AND ITS TREATMENT

While many tribes have shied away from drinking on religious or moral grounds, many others have been reluctant to develop effective sanctions against excessive drinking. For some Indian people, group drinking provides a joyous sense of community and "Indianness." Others drink to escape the seemingly insurmountable problems of isolation, discrimination, and grinding poverty.

But, as the toll exacted by alcohol has become more alarming, Indian people have responded not only with standard group support programs like Alcoholics Anonymous but also with more culturally based adaptations. The broader ideal of tribal sovereignty provides a crucial underpinning for these efforts.

The task of rebuilding Indian nationhood has helped restore community to those who have felt its lack, and pride to those who have been robbed of their self-esteem.

Even more important, treatments for alcoholism created by Indians often revolve around a return to native spiritual traditions. The original power of alcohol quite possibly stemmed from its evocation of spiritual experience. It seems only fitting that, centuries later, native spirituality should provide a path away from the destruction wrought by excessive drinking.

Painted buckskin playing cards made by Southwest Apache Indians from the nineteenth century.

During the 1980s, Indian people continued a long-standing attack on the either-or approach Americans traditionally took when confronted by these apparent contradictions. First of all, they argued, the nature of the tribal–federal relationship could not be defined by only one of the parties. If the United States really wished to solve its "Indian problem," then both Indians and non-Indians would have to be involved in equal measure in developing a solution. Second, they argued that tribal–federal relations would have to include a recognition of *both* federal trust responsibility and tribal sovereignty.

Self-determination had suggested an awkward balance between federal trust (in the form of funding) and tribal sovereignty (in the form of Indian administration). Ironically, the backlash against 1960s-style programs, personified by the Reagan administration cuts of the 1980s, destroyed that balance and encouraged tribes to consider the idea of tribal sovereignty even more seriously.

For the Reagan and Bush administrations, "self-determination" and "sovereignty" were largely buzzwords used to placate Indians and simply meant tribes ought to "take care of themselves" by signing expedient deals for waste disposal and resource extraction. Some tribes have, indeed, followed this route in varying degrees. The groups that refused, however, found themselves in a precarious, but exciting position. Federal trust, as it had been defined by the 1960s Great Society programs, had meant dependence on government funding. The cuts in that funding during the 1980s made tight tribal–federal political relationships less useful and, in effect, moved Indians further away politically from the federal government. Why visit Washington if no one ever answered the door? The funding cuts also forced tribes to consider other forms of revenue, social services, and administrative structure in order simply to survive and maintain their reservations.

The Reagan administration sought to dismantle the Great Society. In doing so, it bolstered (albeit unintentionally) the concept of Indian sovereignty in the form of self-imposed taxation on reservation property, sales, and resources, the strengthening of local jurisdiction in highway and criminal prosecutions, tribal license plates and automobile registration, Indian hiring preference rules for reservation construction, and, perhaps most significantly, the opening of various high stakes gaming industries.

Unlike the BIA–directed corporate thrust of the New Deal or self-determination policies, these were *Indian-based solutions* to the ever-present problem of survival in non-Indian society. In order to justify and defend such solutions against the challenges of Americans who inevitably regarded Indian initiatives as threats, tribes often called on the legal and political skills they had developed over the preceding decades. Taken together with the chilling of the tribal–federal relationship, these initiatives represented the most serious statements about sovereignty and nationhood that Indians had made in over a hundred years.

The Indian Gaming Act of 1988 followed Public Law 280 and other precedents in linking Indian independence to state law, thus highlighting once again the contradictions created by making sovereignty, or nationhood, subject to state, as opposed to federal, control. This conflict has occasionally led to heated battles as some Indian people, introducing gambling to reluctant states, have insisted on maintaining their own oversight and law enforcement.

In Connecticut, for example, a state provision allowing charity "casino night" gambling enabled the Mashentuckett Pequots to open a high-stakes casino in Ledyard, but only after a long war of words and legal briefs between Governor Lowell Weicker and tribal chairman Skip Hayward. The Pequot casino and bingo hall now provides employment for both Pequots and local non-Indians and generates a healthy regional cash flow.

Many Indians wonder, however, if gambling is a wise way to attempt to build a sustaining reservation economy. As tribes have initiated gaming industries, some states have loosened their own restrictions, allowing better financed non-Indian competition to dominate. Some gaming statistics appear to be falling, an indication that markets may be becoming saturated. In addition to incurring state hostility, the very idea of Indian gaming has come under attack from powerful and connected lobbyists for the Las Vegas and Atlantic City industries.

Despite these misgivings and challenges, on many reservations gaming has provided both Indians and non-Indians with jobs, reduced federal welfare rolls, and offered tribal councils a financial shot in the arm.

A game set, made by the Winnebagos of Nebraska, includes a wooden bowl, playing surface, five bone dice, and seed counters.

*Shawnee Playing Dice*
by Ruthe Blalock Jones
(Delaware-Shawnee), 1978.

## INDIAN GAMING ACT

During the 1980s, many tribes took advantage of the federal trust status of reservation land to bypass state gaming laws and open high-stakes bingo and gambling parlors. Indian gaming grew throughout the decade and tribes used the income to replace some of the social services lost to government budget cuts. State and regulatory agencies, however, launched vigorous protests against Indian gaming businesses and, as a result, Congress passed the Indian Gaming Regulatory Act of 1988. Under this law, if a state allows certain types of gambling, even for charitable purposes, then it *cannot prohibit Indians* from conducting the same games for profit. But, as states and tribes are to negotiate gaming compacts to govern the activity, the act again makes tribes subject to partial state control.

**Sign of Strength**
**by Jerry Ingram (Choctaw), 1981.**

*A hundred thousand years have passed*
*Yet, I hear the distant beat of my*
    *father's drums*
*I hear his drums throughout the land*
*His beat I feel within my heart*

*The drums shall beat, so my heart*
    *shall beat,*
*And I shall live a hundred thousand*
    *years.*
                    —SHIRLEY DANIELS
                    (Ojibwa), 1969

# The Pursuit of Sovereignty

As part of the new exploration of sovereignty, many tribal people are turning to each other, developing their own programs to combat problems ranging from alcoholism and family abuse to language loss. Tribal colleges, first organized in the early 1970s, have blossomed on many reservations. Locally controlled television and radio stations use modern media to offer a variety of "traditional" and "progressive" voices.

Much of the talk at these new venues centers around the developing idea of sovereignty—a concept with tremendous ramifications that Indian and non-Indian Americans have only started to consider. What does it mean to be a sovereign nation within the political bounds of American society? And what of the government's sworn treaty obligations to Indian peoples? Can one be sovereign yet dependent upon outside obligations? Grounded in five hundred years of historical contact, Indians are raising questions about the nature of international and internal political relationships that carry immediate implications for both the short and long term.

Indian efforts to articulate and develop a workable idea of modern sovereignty within the context of a larger state draw heavily on their past. The groups of native people who first faced the struggling American nation certainly had as much (or more) claim to sovereign nationhood—even by European definition—as did the fledgling United States. The new Americans needed those Indian nations at that time, and so their government recognized Indian sovereignty and made guarantees, payments, and promises to educate Indians and protect them from other Americans with less regard for the law. By the mid-nineteenth century, federal legal rulings—recognizing the shift in relative military power—had developed those promises into the idea of a government protectorate over tribes.

The recent tribal reaffirmation of trust responsibility wedded to nationhood marks a desire to return to the relationships that existed when many of the original treaties were made. If it does nothing else, tribes say, federal trust responsibility should at least protect Indian sovereignty from the encroachments of states, individuals, and private interest groups.

By the eighteenth century many native societies had been worn down—decimated by repeated epidemics, pulled headlong into the European market economy, threatened by intertribal conflict and the nascent American state. Nonetheless, Indian people survived and created new social, political, and spiritual orders out of the pieces of older cultures.

Two hundred years later, Indian people continue to survive in this land and find themselves facing an array of similar challenges. Where smallpox and influenza previously threatened Indian people, now AIDS, alcoholism, fetal alcohol syndrome, and diabetes haunt reservations and urban communities. Where the goods of European trade and technology once beckoned, now the commanding corporate dollars of waste disposal and mineral extraction interests seem to offer a path away from poverty. Where new political structures once developed in order to cope with the expanding European world, so too is a new political

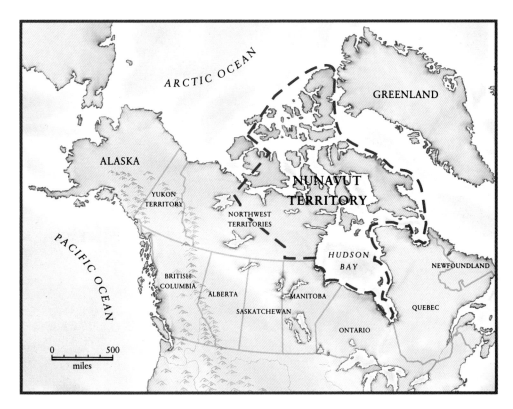

*Proposed Territory of Nunavut.*

## NUNAVUT AND CANADA

The native people of Canada have been waging a struggle for sovereignty that echoes that of Indians south of the border. In 1982, after a decade of sustained pressure, Canada finally recognized the constitutional existence of "aboriginal and treaty rights."

In 1991, Canadian and Inuit leaders may have taken a step toward furthering their relationship when they agreed to settle an Inuit claim to 800,000 square miles by creating a new territory in Northeast Canada. To be called Nunavut, the Inuit word for "our home," the proposed territory comprises 770,000 square miles, approximately one-fifth of Canada. Under the agreement, still to be ratified by the Inuit, native people would have title to 140,000 square miles of land, mineral rights to 14,000 square miles of their selection, and $580 million to be paid over fourteen years.

Equally important, the Inuit would administer a territorial government over the entire area. Although holding a clear electoral majority at the moment, Inuit leaders are pushing for a five-year residency requirement for voters in order to ensure Nunavut stays a native political entity able to combat boom-or-bust resource development.

Dance, as a medium of expression, celebration, and belief, is one of the oldest Indian art forms. In a tradition that continues to grow, members of tribes from all around the United States gather to dance and compete at annual powwows.

RIGHT: Male Fancy Dancers at the Rocky Boy Powwow in Montana (1986).

BELOW: Traditional Dancer at Milk River Indian Days in Belknap, Montana (1990).

BOTTOM: A Straight Dancer at the Cherokee Powwow in Tahlequah, Oklahoma, adjusts his roach headdress.

OPPOSITE: A dancer at the 1990 All Indian Idaho Expo held in Boise.

relationship in the process of being defined today, but now its larger context is that of a newly emerging global order.

As the world slowly digests the fragmenting of the Soviet Union and the rise of ethnic and nationalistic sentiment, the futility of attempting to maintain extended empires will come into sharper focus. To preserve external order, huge resources must be diverted to the military. In the meantime, the internal order degenerates as the government fails to provide for the needs of its people. Empire simply does not work in the modern world.

In the omnipresent and interconnected culture of the global village, people tend to reinforce—often violently—the boundaries of ethnicity, race, religion, sexuality, and nationhood simply to define who they are and how they are different from one another. The politics of group identity, whether political, cultural, or economic, thrives on attempted suppression. A new global order will have to take into account both the failure of unification through empire and the increasing tendency of people to split into diverse "tribalized" groups.

How might a richly diversified, mutually respectful new world look? The relationships that eventually develop between industrial and postindustrial countries and developing nations may bear affinities to those being called for by Indian people. Both developing countries and Indian nations remain financially dependent upon the highly developed economies of the United States, Japan, and the European Community. Yet the wealthier countries, despite their tendency to exploit the developing world, must also recognize the sovereignty of its nations.

Just as American experience administering tribal people within its own borders shaped its colonial policy in the Pacific, the decolonizing of tribes could provide useful lessons for defining America's postcolonial world relationships. By viewing its own tribes as the nations they are, the United States may conceivably learn something about participating in, rather than attempting to dominate, a new global order.

Even as they call for a new sovereignty, however, tribal people realize the enormous improbability of returning to the political relationships of the original treaties. But for many Indian people, the call for sovereign status is as much a tribal matter as it is a global, or even national, concern. It has to do with reestablishing the legal and moral roots of modern Indian identities. As native people reestablish their own governance, insistence on treaty relationships offers some tribes a good way to fuse new and old in creating effective ways of life.

Indian people now have an existing set of efficient political organizations that look very familiar to non-Indian Americans. They have offices, boards of directors, acronyms, budget oversight, and the like. But many Indians, especially grass-roots people who live outside the bounds of tribal governments, are beginning to think of ways to re-empower less familiar institutions—the still-existing shadow systems of "traditional" governance often pushed aside by the long buffeting of American policy experiments. On the Great Plains, for example, Lakotas and Blackfeet talk about how to build *back* to small "groups" of people, organized loosely and exercising leadership by example rather than by election. These groups question the very idea of organization. "What," they ask, "is the minimum amount of structure necessary for a group to act?" Other grass-roots people look toward the governance offered by religion or traditional clan relations, and almost everywhere Indian people are trying to keep threatened languages alive.

The changes of the 1960s demonstrated the close linkage between cultural revitalization and political activism. Doing this work for decades has given many Indian people a guarded optimism about the prospect of intentionally directing their cultures back to native languages, political structures, and social understandings. Although often imperfectly executed, this conscious determination to shape culture around reclaimed "tradition" may offer an example to an American nation worried about soaring crime rates, drugs, child abuse, corruption at every level of government, and the apparently steady decay of its value systems.

## THE SMITHSONIAN NATIONAL MUSEUM OF THE AMERICAN INDIAN

Theodor Adorno once pointed out both the semantic and the actual connection between the words *museum* and *mausoleum*. Both sites serve as the repositories for dead objects. Traditional natural history museums have proposed exactly this message with regard to Indian people. Indians almost always appear as dead relics: dioramas and mannequins of an idyllic past with no evidence of a present or a future. These presentations are pure ideology. They tell us that we can learn about "natural living" from Indians while they simultaneously deny that Indians are still around to teach us anything. So whatever it might have been that these dead Indians had to teach is automatically devalued—it did not seem to help them survive into the present.

In 1989 the Smithsonian Institution acquired the Museum of the American Indian collection of the Heye Foundation in New York City and decided to use the last available spot on the Washington Mall to build a new American Indian museum. Stung by recent Indian demands to release the thousands of Indian remains stored in the museum, the Smithsonian sought out Indian input for the new building and its displays. The end result will be a museum far more concerned with demonstrating living Indian cultures than with displaying the dead. It seems possible that the museum could be a site at which Indians and non-Indians realize their commonalities as humans rather than their differences as exotics.

ABOVE: **Eagle Staff with dream-catcher (1986).** OPPOSITE: **Eagle Dancer (1990).**

# CHAPTER TWENTY-EIGHT

# WHAT INDIANS CAN TEACH US

*WAYNE'S WORLD*
BY JESSE COODAY (TLINGIT), 1992

THE IDEA OF LEARNING from native Americans is problematic. Imposed upon the variety of Indian peoples are layers of historic oppression, ideological pandering, and symbolic oversimplification. During the nineteenth and twentieth centuries, white Americans methodically purchased, conquered, and swindled their way to possession of most Indian lands. Then, to justify the decision that another people's land was free for the taking, they developed the ideology of the "doomed and vanishing Indian," forever consigning Indians to a marginal and archaic position. When confronting their own modernist demons, even well-meaning reformers like Collier enshrined a mythical Indian past as a symbolic panacea for an uncertain present. In the twentieth century, the imaginary "Indian" came to symbolize those mysteries of community, spirituality, and harmonious relationship with the environment that the modern world has made increasingly difficult to find.

This is not to suggest that individuals who seek to understand and learn from native people are facile and foolish—far from it. Rather, they are people who participate in a familiar American ritual in which Indians represent the possibilities for something "other than what is." And Indians who participate in this ritual, telling non-Indians some of the things they would like to hear, are not necessarily cynical imposters. Like the Pueblos who sang and danced at the New York Stock Exchange in 1923, they are often people with an acute sense of cultural politics

*Different Generations* by Mike Larsen (Chickasaw), 1992.

Twelve-year-old Patrick Battees (Ojibwa), along with over three thousand others, protests outside the 1992 Superbowl in Minneapolis against the use of native American names and symbols as mascots for sports teams.

*I like living in this community, and I like being Choctaw, but that's all there is to it. Just because I don't want to be a white man doesn't mean I want to be some kind of mystical Indian either. Just a real human being.*

—BEASLEY DENSON
Secretary/Treasurer of the
Choctaw Tribal Council, 1988

who act in their group's best interest within the framework handed them by a dominating society.

This interaction, however, creates a symbolic "catch-22." As long as stockbrokers, past and present, open their hearts and their wallets when the mythic Indian pounds on the drum, real Indians will continue to act the part, and their actions will continue to reinforce American symbolic notions. With Indians supporting the framework, non-Indian Americans continue to find it meaningful.

Seeing Indians in primarily symbolic terms prevents non-Indian Americans from accepting them as flesh-and-blood people. When non-Indians do encounter actual native people, idealistically high expectations often leave them disappointed and annoyed. When Indians turn out not to be the sources of supreme understanding that those Americans have imagined, another form of symbolism often replaces the romantic image. Indians are lumped together as poverty-stricken social problems, people degraded by alcohol and disease—and possibly by an inbred unwillingness to "improve their lot." For most Americans, there have been few opportunities to view Indians simply as people trying to get by.

In 1991–92, the Atlanta Braves baseball team, its frenzied fans doing the "tomahawk chop," made it to the World Series, and the Washington Redskins football team, its followers clad in turkey feather headdresses, went to the Super

Bowl. When real Indians protested the theme of the riotous celebration—masses of people loudly promoting the idea that Indians were savage "others"—many Americans attacked them, demonstrating their clear preference for symbolic Indians over real people. When American self-interest and mythic memory are at stake, it is all too easy to sever the connections between symbol and reality, past and present, and come down on the side of the image.

Insisting on symbolic Indianness diverts Americans from facing the real problems of modern society. The things Indians stand for (and, in their own societies, attempt to practice)—family, community, spiritual experience, an affinity with "nature"—are difficult to obtain in America today.

Most of us already *know* the answers to the questions we put to our symbolic Indians; we simply have difficulty living out those answers in the modern world. How can we have ties of family and community when we pick up and move every few years? How can we exist in a closer relationship to the natural world when we depend on cities, automobiles, petrochemical backpacks and raingear, and artificially designated lines that tell us where "nature" or "wilderness" begin and end? It is far easier to think of Indians like Chief Seattle and get misty-eyed and nostalgic than it is to sell the car.

This is not to say that native people do not allow us to see alternatives. Indians have always made different choices and they continue to do so. But real learning from Indian people cannot be as easy as appropriating a religious ceremony, a symbol or two, or even an attitude. This sort of selective grazing in the multicultural garden is too painless to be worth much.

To learn something from Indian people, mainstream Americans need to question basic assumptions *they* hold precious—government, profit, progress, just to name a few. Once questioned, analyzed, and reduced, assumptions can be rebuilt—not as simply the Indian-tinged rhetoric of Chief Seattle, but as complex and complicated ideas that actually address the modern lives of both Indians and non-Indians. This is no easy task, but even a little success contributes to the reclaiming of a more legitimate cross-cultural exchange and a new and different view of the future.

How can non-Indian Americans create a respectful and meaningful cross-cultural dialogue? Most certainly *not* by packing up *en masse* and heading for the reservation to bother the medicine men.

But Americans can perhaps take a small clue from Indian peoples themselves. Almost every North American tribe has tales of trickster beings. Sometimes the trickster is a coyote, sometimes a spider, sometimes an undefined being. He is a slippery character, an ambiguous shapeshifter loaded with natural and sexual energy. He can be both man and woman, dog and cat, human and animal. He can regenerate body parts and send his phallus across a lake to impregnate a chief's daughter.

Not only does the trickster defy the flesh-and-blood boundaries of animal identity, he also refuses to fit into the mental categories we use to understand the world. Stupid and wise, reviled and respected, dangerous and clownish, the trickster reveals that the world is a confusing and mutually contradictory place. He is what we all hold in common—life itself.

## CHIEF SEATTLE

During the spring of 1992, while Americans prepared Columbian celebrations and debated the virtues and vices of five hundred years of European contact, the *New York Times* announced a stunning discovery: the Chief Seattle speech was a fraud! Perhaps the most overused document of the environmental movement, for decades the Chief Seattle speech has appeared in countless eco-pamphlets, calendars, children's books, fund-raising letters, and epigraphs. "How can you buy or sell the sky? the land?" asks Seattle rhetorically. "This we know: The earth does not belong to man, man belongs to the earth. All things are connected like the blood which unites us all. . . . When the last red man has vanished with his wilderness, and his memory is only the shadow of a cloud moving across the prairie, will these shores and forests still be here? Will there be any spirit of my people left?"

Produced by a Texas literature professor in the early 1970s, the beautiful sentiments of the Seattle speech have continued to strike resounding chords in the hearts of Americans. The vanishing Indian, never quite laid to rest, makes an obligatory appearance in the speech and offers the frail hope that his successors have somehow captured not only his land but his people's spirit as well. Only by capturing that spirit, in fact, can white Americans save themselves. It should come as no surprise that before passing on to the next metaphorical world, Seattle pronounces Americans his brothers: "One thing we know. Our God is the same God. Even the white man cannot be exempt from the common destiny. We may be brothers after all. We shall see."

## TRICKSTER TALE:
## IKTOMI IN A SKULL

Iktomi was off on a trip when he heard singing and shouting and dancing nearby. He stopped to listen. Immediately he wished to dance too, so much that his soles itched; and he tried hard to locate the source of the sounds. While he listened, it seemed as though the dancing and shouting grew louder and louder; and at last he knew that it came from a dry buffalo skull lying near his path. He saw that the interior was all cheerfully lighted up, and inside was great jollity.

When he peeped in through one of the eye socket openings, he saw that the mice were staging a great dance. So Iktomi knocked on the door and said, "My little brothers, take pity on me and let me enter. I want to dance too." "Aw, let's open for big brother!" they said and opened the back door for him. He thrust his head in and could go no further. Then someone said, "Look out! It's Ikto!" and soon they disappeared into the darkness. Ikto sat down with the skull on his head and began to weep. He sat by the road, and whenever he heard someone going by he wept loudly; and when they went on past, then he wept in a low voice.

He ran to a rock and said, "Grandfather, knock this loose from me." So the rock replied, "Very well. Swing your head this way." Whereupon Ikto swung his head so forcefully toward the rock that he shattered the skull to bits and bruised his head in the bargain. He was dizzy for days and went about vomiting, they say.

Trickster tales are often built upon layers of tricks. Even as he engineers a trick, the trickster himself is often the victim of an additional trick turned by others, by circumstance, or, perhaps unintentionally, by himself. In the stories, the figure playing the trick and the figure being tricked merge together. Cause and effect are called into question. The trickster Iktomi sought to sneak into the mouse dance and ended up being tricked, moaning through a skull stuck on his head. He is simultaneously the trick's victim and its perpetrator. Through the idea of the trick, Iktomi breaks down the distinctions between "self" and "other," between "us" and "them." Through the experience of the story itself, listener and teller become each other and thus become one and the same, while still retaining their differences.

Indians have lived the twentieth century as trickster peoples. Faced with repeated attempts to force them to conform, Indians have responded with a kind of cultural shapeshifting that blurs the boundaries between "us" and "them" so eagerly erected by white Americans. At century's end it has become clear that the question of what it means to be an Indian in the twentieth century is not nearly as difficult to answer as the question of what it means to be an American.

Indians have fought to be tricksters, to maintain Indian identities and social cohesiveness even as they live, work, and play in a society that prides itself on being a huge "melting pot." Americans love to bandy the phrase about, but in practice we have frequently reaffirmed *differences* of race, ethnicity, class, religion, gender, sexuality, and geography that have allowed us to hold meaningful group and personal identities. What too many of us have failed to do, however, is to accept the uncertainty that inevitably accompanies a society cherishing both the idea of shared values and of a diverse multiculturalism. Instead, as American Indian policy demonstrates, Americans have bounced back and forth between unity and diversity, one year trying to force its minorities to assimilate, the next recognizing and embracing their differences.

If Indian people have any great lesson to teach America, it is carried by a trickster history that speaks of the impossibility of holding on to rigid categories of understanding, of the necessity for both uncertainty and conviction, of the true meaning of "tradition" in a world that will never cease to change.

The Mohawk warriors hanging from New York skyscrapers, the Pueblo drummers at the Stock Exchange, the Indian volunteers in American wars, the Indian lawyer in court—all of these people have understood, sometimes out of necessity, the trickster essence of cultural interaction and coexistence: break down needless and harmful boundaries between people. Empathize. Respect. Become the Other while remaining Yourself.

—PHILIP J. DELORIA

OPPOSITE:
*Iktomi (Trickster)*
by Arthur Amiotte (Oglala Lakota), 1966.

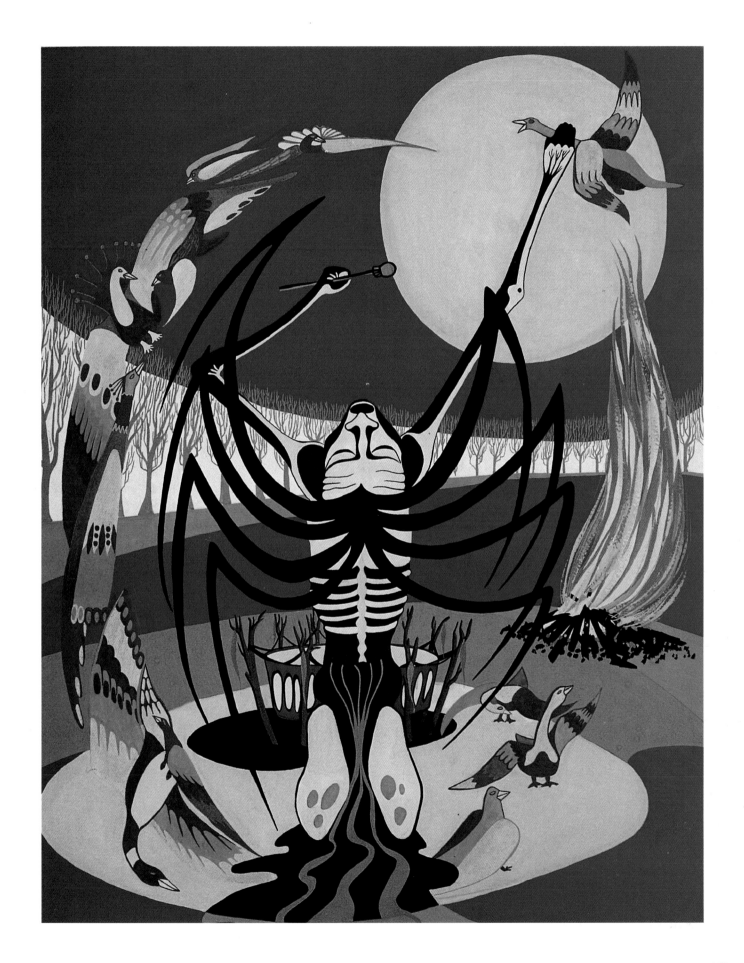

*In my half century of life, I've witnessed extreme poverty, poor health care, disorienting cultural loss, infant mortality levels that are twice the national average, the highest suicide rates in the U.S., and unemployment as high as 80 percent. But today there is a newly awakened pride and interest in tribal life and a new vitality in our communities. I see energy, determination, conviction, and vision among our tribal peoples. . . . My art, my life experience, and my tribal ties are totally enmeshed. I go from one community with messages to the other, and I try to teach and enlighten people. My paintings and my drawings are part of the conduit. They are my voice.*

—JAUNE QUICK-TO-SEE SMITH

*Indian Horse*
by Jaune Quick-to-See Smith
(Cree-Flathead-Shoshone), 1992.

# TRIBES BY CULTURE AREA AND LANGUAGE FAMILY

*List groupings derive from the comparative research and scholarly review of Jay Miller.*

## ARCTIC:

**ESKALEUT**
ALEUT
INUIT
YUPIK
  **Siberian**
  **Pacific (Alutiiq)**
  **Alaskan**
    Kogmiut
    Magemiut
    Kaialigamiut
    Kuskokwagmiut
    Togagamiut
    Nushagamiut
    Ogulmiut
    Kaniagmiut
    Chugachigmiut
INUPIAQ
  **Alaskan**
  **Canadian**
    Kinugmiut
    Malemiut
    Nunatagmiult
    Noatagmiut
    Kopagmiut
    Point Barrow
    MacKenzie
    Copper
    Caribou
    Netsilikmiut
    Aivilirmiut
    Baffin Island
    Kigiktagmiut
    Itivimiut
    Tahagmiut
    Sukininmiut
  **Greenlandic**
    Polar (*Thule*)
    West Greenlanders
    East Greenlanders
    (*Ammassalik*)

## SUBARCTIC:

**ATHAPASKAN**
  **Arctic Drainage**
    Bear Lake
    Beaver (*Dunne-za*)
    Chipewyan
    Dogrib
    Hare
    Sarsi
    Slavey
    Yellowknife
  **Yukon-Kuskokwim Drainage**
    Ingalik
    Koyukon
    Tanana
  **Cook Inlet**
    Tanaina
  **Cordilleran**
    Babine
    Upper Koyukon
    Kutchin (*Gwich'in*)
    Mountain
    Han
    Upper Tanana
    Tutchone
    Tagish
    Kaska
    Tahltan
    Tsetsaut

Sekani
Carrier
Chilcotin
**ALGONQUIAN (ALGIC)**
  **Maritime**
    Montagnais (*Innu*)
    Naskapi
    Algonquin
    Cree

## NORTHEAST:

**ALGONQUIAN**
  Pennacook
  Massachusetts
  Wampanoag
  Narragansett
  Niantic
  Podunk
  Montauk
  Wappinger
  ⌐ Mohegan
  └ Pequot
  Mahican
  Delaware (*Lenape*)
    Unami
    Monsey
  Nanticoke
  **Great Lakes**
  ⌐ Ojibwa/Chippewa
  ├ Ottawa (*Odawa*)
  └ Potawatomi
  Menominee
  ⌐ Sauk
  ├ Fox (*Mesquaki*)
  └ Kickapoo
  Shawnee
  ⌐ Miami
  └ Illinois
  **Maritime**
  Abenaki
  Penobscot
  Micmac
  Malecite
**IROQUOIAN**
  Erie
  Huron (*Wyandot*)
  Neutral
  Tobacco (*Petun*)
  Iroquois
    Mohawk
    Oneida
    Onondaga
    Cayuga
    Seneca
    Tuscarora [post-1712]
  ⌐ Susquehanna
  └ Conestoga

## SOUTHEAST:

**ALGONQUIAN**
  Powhatan
  Pamlico
**MUSKOGEAN**
  ⌐ Choctaw
  └ Chickasaw
  ⌐ Koasati
  └ Alabama
  ⌐ Hitchiti
  └ Mikasuki

⌐ Creek (*Muskogee*)
└ Seminole
Atakapa
Tunica
Natchez
Timucua
Chitimacha
**IROQUOIAN**
Cherokee
Tuscarora [pre-1712]
Nottaway
Meherrin
**SIOUIAN**
Tutelo
Catawba
Biloxi
Ofo
Saponi
YUCHI [Isolate]

## GREAT PLAINS:

**SIOUIAN**
  **Village Tribes**
  ⌐ Dakota (*Santee*)
  ├ Mandan
  └ Hidatsa
  ⌐ Iowa
  ├ Oto
  ├ Missouri
  └ Winnebago
  ⌐ Omaha
  ├ Ponca
  ├ Osage
  ├ Kansa
  └ Quapaw
  **Hunting Tribes**
  Nakota (*Yankton*)
  Lakota (*Teton*)
  Assiniboine (*Nakoda, Stoney*)
  Crow
**CADDOAN**
  **Village Tribes**
  Caddo
  ⌐ Pawnee
  ├ Arikara
  ├ Wichita
  └ Kichai
**ALGONQUIAN**
  **Hunting Tribes**
  ⌐ Arapaho
  ├ Gros Ventre
  └ (*Atsina*)
  Blackfeet
    Blood
    Piegan
    Siksika
  ⌐ Cheyenne
  └ Sutai
  Plains Ojibwa (*Bungi*)
  Plains Cree
**UTO-AZTECAN**
  **Hunting Tribes**
  Shoshone (*Numa*)
  Comanche
  Ute
  Kiowa
**ATHAPASKAN**
  **Hunting Tribes**
  Plains Apache (*Kalthdin*)
  Sarsi

## PLATEAU:

**PENUTIAN**
⌐ Klamath
└ Modoc
Cayuse
Molala
**SAHAPTIAN**
Nez Perce (*Numipu*)
Sahaptin
  Klickitat
  Kititas
  Tenino
  Umatilla
  Walla Walla
  ⌐ Yakima
  ├ Wanapum
  └ Palus
**ATHAPASKAN**
Nicola
**SALISHAN**
  **North Interior Salish**
  Shuswap (*Sexwepemx*)
  Thompson (*Nl'akapamux*)
  Lillooet (*St'at'imx*)
  **South Interior Salish**
  Coeur d'Alene
  ⌐ Flathead
  └ (*Selish*)
  Kalispel
  └ Spokan
  Colville (*Sweelpoo*)
  Okanagan
  Lake
  Sanpoil
  Nespelem
  └ Methow
  ⌐ Columbia (*Sinkiuse*)
  Wenatchee
  Chelan
  └ Entiat
KUTENAI [Isolate]

## GREAT BASIN:

**UTO-AZTECAN**
**NUMIC**
  **Western**
  ⌐ Northern Paiute
  ├ Bannock
  └ Mono
  **Central**
  Western Shoshone
  Goshiute
  Panamint
  ⌐ Lehmi
  ├ Wind River
  └ Comanche
  **Southern**
  Ute
  ⌐ Kwaiisu
  ├ Chemehuevi
  └ Southern Paiute
**HOKAN**
  Washo

## SOUTHWEST:

**HOKAN**
Quechan (*Yuma*)
Cocopa
Mohave
Walapai
Yavapai
Havasupai
**ATHAPASKAN**
Navajo (*Dene*)
Apache
  **Southern Plains**
  Llanero
  Mescalero
  Jicarilla
  Lipan
  **Western Plains**
  Tonto
  White
  Mountain
  San Carlos (*Pinaलños*)
  Cibecue (*Coyoteros*)
**UTO-AZTECAN**
**PIMAN**
Pima (*O'odham*)
Papago (*Tohono O'odham*)
**Puebloans**
**TANOAN**
**TEWA**
San Juan
Santa Clara
San Ildefonso
Nambe
Tesuque
Pojoaque
TANO [Southern Tewa]
Hano
**TIWA**
Taos
Picuris
Sandia
Isleta
**TOWA**
Jemez
Pecos
**NUMIC**
**HOPIC**
Hopi
  **First Mesa**
  Walpi
  Sichomovi
  Polacca
  **Second Mesa**
  Shimopovi
  Shipaulovi
  Mishongnovi
  **Third Mesa**
  Old Oraibi
  Kykotsmovi (*New Oraibi*)
  Hotevilla
  Bacavi
  Moenkopi
KERESAN [Isolate]
Cochiti
Santo Domingo
San Felipe
Santa Ana
Sia
Acoma
Laguna

**PENUTIAN**
Zuñi

## CALIFORNIA:

**HOKAN**
Palaihnihan
  Achomawi
  Atsugewi
Shasta
Karuk
Chimariko
⌐ Yana
└ Yahi
Pomo
⌐ Salinan
└ Esselen
Chumash
Diegeño
Kamia
Yumans
**PENUTIAN**
Yokut
Miwok
Costanoan
Maidu
Wintun
**ATHAPASKAN**
Hupa
Kato
Mattole
Tolowa
Wailaki
Sinkyone
**NUMIC**
Tubatulabal
Takic
  Serrano
  Cupan
  ⌐ Luiseño
  └ Juaneño
  ⌐ Cahuilla
  └ Cupeno
  ⌐ Gabrielino
  └ Fernandeño
Numa
**RITWAN**
Wiyot
Yurok
YUKIAN [Isolate]
Yuki
  Coast
  Huchnom
  Wappo

## PACIFIC NORTHWEST:

**NA-DENE**
EYAK
TLINGIT
ATHAPASKAN
  Kwaliokwa
  Tlatskanie
  Umpqua
  Chetco
  Tututni
  Tolowa
  Hupa
**PENUTIAN**
**CHINOOKAN**
⌐ Wishram
├ Wasco
Chinook
Klatsop

Kathlamet
Clackamas
OREGON PENUTIAN
Takelma
Kalapuyan
Coosan (*Coos*)
  Miluk
  Hanis
Yakonan
  Yaquina
  Alsea
Siuslaw
**CHIMAKUAN**
Chimakum
Quileute
**WAKASHAN**
NOOTKAN
Makah
Nitinat
Nootka (*Nuuchanuth*)
**KWAKIUTLAN**
  **Northern**
  Bella Bella (*Heiltsuk*)
  Xai Xais
  Owikeno
  Haisla (*Kitimat*)
  **Southern**
  Kwakiutl (*Kwakwaka'wakw*)
**SALISHAN**
COAST SALISHAN
  **Northern**
  Bella Coola (*Nuxalk*)
  **Central**
  Comox
  Pentlatch
  Sechelt
  Squamish
  Halkomelem
  Cowichan
  Musqueam
  Chilliwack
  Nooksack
  Lushootseed (*Puget*)
  Twana
  **Straits**
  Lummi
  Songish (*Lkungen*)
  Sooke
  Klallam (*S'klallam*)
**Tsamosan**
Quinault
Chehalis
Cowlitz
**Southern**
Tillamook
HAIDA [Isolate]
Kaigani
Masset
Skidegate
TSIMSHIAN [Isolate]
⌐ Coast
├ Southern
└ Niska
└ Gitksan

Years of research by anthropologists and linguists have established larger groupings of native Americans based on similarities of lifestyle and language. About ten geographical culture areas and a dozen language stocks have been identified. Each culture area represents a particular ecological adaptation sharing commonalities of technology, staple foods, kinship groups, and rituals. Language stocks are based on the detailed study of underlying grammar and essential vocabulary. Some unique languages are referred to as "isolates" because they have no close relatives. As arranged on the opposite list, each category begins with the culture area followed by the language stock (in BOLD CAPS), stock subdivisions (in CAPS), regional subdivisions (in bold lowercase), and then representative tribes (in lowercase). Since many tribes are best known by the names given to them by outsiders, their own names for themselves, as of current usage, are given in italics between parentheses. Tribes that speak closely related languages or dialects are indicated by a bracket.

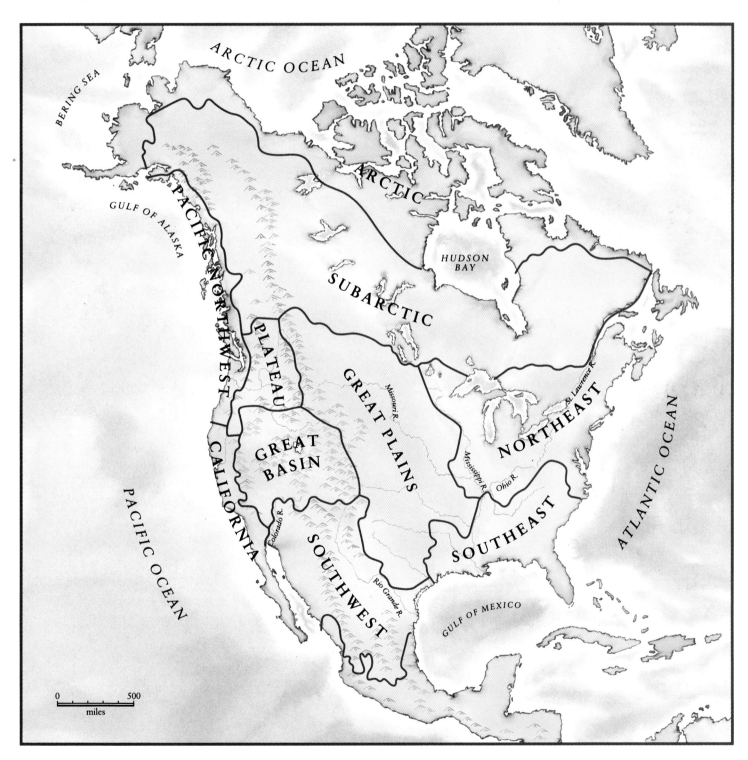

# BIBLIOGRAPHY

Archuleta, Margaret, and Dr. Rennard Strickland. *Shared Visions: Native American Painters and Sculptors in the Twentieth Century*. New York: New Press, 1991.

Armstrong, William H. *Warrior in Two Camps: Ely S. Parker, Union General and Seneca Chief*. Syracuse, N.Y.: Syracuse University Press, 1978.

Axelrod, Alan. *Chronicle of the Indian Wars: From Colonial Times to Wounded Knee*. New York: Prentice Hall, 1993.

Axtell, James. *The European and the Indian: Essays in the Ethnohistory of Colonial North America*. New York: Oxford University Press, 1981.

Bakesless, John. *America as Seen by Its First Explorers*. New York: Dover Publications, 1950.

Battey, Thomas C. *Life and Adventures of a Quaker Among the Indians*. Boston: Lee and Shepard, 1891.

Beck, Warren A., and Ynez D. Haase. *Historical Atlas of the American West*. Norman: University of Oklahoma Press, 1989.

Berger, Justice Thomas R. *Northern Frontier, Northern Homeland: The Report of the Mackenzie Valley Pipeline Inquiry*. Ottawa: Ministry of Supply and Services, 1977.

———. *Village Journey: The Report of the Alaska Native Review Commission*. New York: Hill and Wang, 1985.

Bernal, Ignacio. *The Olmec World*. Berkeley: University of California Press, 1969.

Bernstein, Alison R. *American Indians and World War II: Toward a New Era in Indian Affairs*. Norman: University of Oklahoma Press, 1991.

Beverley, Robert. *The History and Present State of Virginia*. Edited by Louis B. Wright. Chapel Hill: University of North Carolina Press for the Institute of Early American History and Culture, 1947.

Brandt-Sero, John Ojijatekha. "Deganiwideh, the Law-Giver of the Caniengahakas." *Man* (1901): 166–67.

Brown, Dee. *Bury My Heart at Wounded Knee: An Indian History of the American West*. New York: Henry Holt, 1970.

Brown, George W. *Dictionary of Canadian Biography, Volume I: 1000–1700*. Toronto: University of Toronto Press, 1967.

Brown, Joseph Epes. *The Sacred Pipe: Black Elk's Account of the Seven Rites of the Oglala Sioux*. Norman: University of Oklahoma Press, 1953.

Bureau of American Ethnology. *Annual Reports of the Bureau of American Ethnology, Reports 1–38, 1880–1917*. Washington, D.C.: U.S. Government Printing Office.

Calloway, Colin G. *Crown and Calumet: British–Indian Relations, 1783–1815*. Norman: University of Oklahoma Press, 1987.

Churchill, Ward, and Jim Vander Wall. *Agents of Repression: The FBI's Secret Wars Against the Black Panther Party and the American Indian Movement*. Boston: South End Press, 1988.

Clark, Laverne. *They Sang for Horses: The Impact of the Horse on Navajo and Apache Folklore*. Tucson: University of Arizona Press, 1966.

Clifford, James. *The Predicament of Culture: Twentieth-Century Ethnography, Literature, and Art*. Cambridge: Harvard University Press, 1988.

Coe, Michael D. *The Jaguar's Children: Pre-Classic Central Mexico*. New York: The Museum of Primitive Art, 1965.

Coffer, William E. *Spirits of the Sacred Mountains: Creation Stories of the American Indian*. New York: Van Nostrand Reinhold, 1978.

Colden, Cadwallader. *The History of the Five Indian Nations Depending on the Province of New York in America*. Ithaca, N.Y.: Great Seal Books, 1958.

Cole, Douglas, and Ira Chaikin. *An Iron Hand Against the People: The Law Against the Potlatch of the Northwest Coast*. Seattle: University of Washington Press, 1990.

Cordell, Linda S. *Prehistory of the Southwest*. Orlando, Fla.: Academic Press, 1984.

Cowan, C. Wesley, and Patty Jo Watson, eds. *The Origins of Agriculture: An International Perspective*. Washington, D.C.: Smithsonian Institution Press, 1992.

Crow Dog, Mary, with Richard Erdoes. *Lakota Woman*. New York: Harper Perennial, 1990.

Debo, Angie. *And Still the Waters Run: The Betrayal of the Five Civilized Tribes*. Princeton: Princeton University Press, 1940.

Deloria, Vine, Jr. *Custer Died for Your Sins: An Indian Manifesto*. New York: Macmillan, 1969.

Deloria, Vine, Jr., and Clifford Lytle. *The Nations Within: The Past and Future of American Indian Sovereignty*. New York: Pantheon, 1984.

De Sahagun, Bernardino. *Florentine Codex, General History of the Things of New Spain, Book II: The Ceremonies*. Monographs of the School of American Research no. 14, pt. 13. Translated by Arthur J. O. Anderson and Charles E. Dibble. Santa Fe, N.Mex: The School of American Research, 1950–1982.

Dickason, Olive P. *The Myth of the Savage and the Beginnings of French Colonialism in the Americas*. Edmonton: University of Alberta Press, 1984.

———. *Canada's First Nations. A History of Founding Peoples from Earliest Times*. Norman: University of Oklahoma Press, 1992.

Dillehay, Tom D., and David J. Meltzer. *The First Americans: Search and Research*. Boca Raton, Fla.: CRC Press, 1991.

Dippie, Brian. *The Vanishing American: White Attitudes and U.S. Indian Policy*. Middletown, Conn.: Wesleyan University Press, 1982.

Dockstader, Frederick J. *Great North American Indians*. New York: Van Nostrand Reinhold, 1977.

Duffy, R. Quinn. *The Road to Nunavut: the Progress of the Eastern Arctic Inuit Since the Second World War*. Montreal: McGill-Queen's University Press, 1988.

Ellis, Florence Hawley. *San Gabriel del Yunque. As Seen by an Archaeologist*. Santa Fe, N.Mex.: Sunstone Press, 1989.

Erdoes, Richard, and Alfonso Ortiz, eds. *American Indian Myths and Legends*. Pantheon Fairy Tale and Folklore Library. New York: Pantheon, 1984.

Fagan, Brian M. *Ancient North America: The Archaeology of a Continent*. London: Thames and Hudson, 1991.

Fane, Diana, Ira Jacknis, and Lise M. Breen. *Objects of Myth and Memory: American Indian Art at the Brooklyn Museum*. New York: The Brooklyn Museum in association with the University of Washington Press, 1991.

Ferguson, William M., and Arthur H. Rohn. *Anasazi Ruins of the Southwest in Color*. Albuquerque: University of New Mexico Press, 1986.

Ferrell, Robert H., and Richard Natkiel. *Atlas of American History*. New York: Facts on File Publications, 1987.

Fitzhugh, William A. *Cultures in Contact: The European Impact on Native Cultural Institutions in Eastern North America, A.D. 1000–1800*. Washington, D.C.: Smithsonian Institution Press, 1985.

Fixico, Donald A. *Termination and Relocation: Federal Indian Policy, 1945–1960*. Albuquerque: University of New Mexico Press, 1986.

Fletcher, Alice. *The Hako–A Pawnee Ceremony*. 22nd Annual Report of the Bureau of American Ethnology. Washington D.C.: Smithsonian, 1904.

Fussel, Betty. *The Story of Corn*. New York: Alfred A. Knopf, 1992.

Gabriel, Kathryn. *Road to Center Place: A Cultural Atlas of Chaco Canyon and the Anasazi*. Boulder, Colo.: Johnson Books, 1993.

Gardner, Joseph L., ed. *Mysteries of the Ancient Americas*. Pleasantville, N.Y.: The Reader's Digest Association, 1986.

Gehring, Charles T., and William A. Starna. *A Journey into Mohawk and Oneida Country, 1634–1635: The Journal of Harmen Meyndertsz van den Bogaert*. Syracuse, N.Y.: Syracuse University Press, 1988.

Gleach, Frederic. "Indian–White Relations in Early Colonial Virginia: A Joint History of Interaction from Mutual Exploitation to War and Removal." Ph.D. dissertation. Chicago: University of Chicago, 1992.

Goetzmann, William H. *The First Americans: Photographs from the Library of Congress*. Washington, D.C.: Starwood Publishing, 1991.

Gooderham, Kent, ed. *I Am an Indian*. Toronto: J. M. Dent & Sons, 1969.

Gruzinski, Serge. *The Aztecs: Rise and Fall of an Empire*. Discoveries Series. New York: Harry N. Abrams, 1992.

Harris, R. Cole, ed. *Historical Atlas of Canada, Volume I: From the Beginning to 1800*. Toronto: University of Toronto Press, 1987.

Hassrick, Peter H. *Treasures of the Old West. Paintings and Sculptures from the Thomas Gilcrease Institute of American History and Art*. New York: Harry N. Abrams, 1984.

Hausman, Gerald. *Meditations with Animals: A Native American Bestiary*. Santa Fe, N.Mex.: Bear & Co., 1986.

Hertzberg, Hazel. *The Search for an American Indian Identity: Modern Pan-Indian Movements*. Syracuse, N.Y.: Syracuse University Press, 1971.

Hoxie, Frederick E. *A Final Promise: The Campaign to Assimilate the Indians, 1880–1920*. Lincoln: University of Nebraska Press, 1984.

Hudson, Travis, Thomas Blackburn, Rosario Curletti, and Janice Timbrook. *The Eye of the Flute: Chumash Traditional History and Ritual as Told by Fernando Librado Kitsepawit*. Santa Barbara, Calif.: Santa Barbara Museum of Natural History, 1977.

Jameson, Anna. *Winter Studies and Summer Rambles in Canada*. Toronto: Coles Canadiana, 1970.

John, Elizabeth A. H. *Storms Brewed in Other Men's Worlds: The Confrontation of Indians, Spanish, and French in the Southwest, 1540–1795*. Lincoln: University of Nebraska Press, 1976.

Jonaitis, Aldona, ed. *Chiefly Feasts: The Enduring Kwakiutl Potlatch*. New York: American Museum of Natural History, 1991.

Josephy, Alvin M., Jr., ed. *America in 1492*. New York: Alfred A. Knopf, 1992.

———. *The American Heritage Book of Indians*. New York: American Heritage Publishing, 1961.

———. *The Civil War in the American West*. New York: Alfred A. Knopf, 1991.

———. *The Indian Heritage of America*. Boston: Houghton Mifflin Company, 1991.

———. *Now That the Buffalo's Gone: A Study of Today's American Indians*. New York: Alfred A. Knopf, 1982.

Katz, Jane B., ed. *I Am the Fire of Time: The Voices of Native American Women*. New York: Dutton, 1977.

Kehoe, Alice Beck. *The Ghost Dance: Ethnohistory and Revitalization*. New York: Holt, Rinehart and Winston, 1989.

Kent, Donald H., and Merle H. Deardorff. "John Adlum on the Allegheny: Memoirs for the Year 1794." *Pennsylvania Magazine of History and Biography* (1960): 3–4.

Klein, Barry T. *Reference Encyclopedia of the American Indian*, 6th Ed. New York: Todd Publications, 1993.

Kopper, Philip. *The Smithsonian Book of North American Indians: Before the Coming of the Europeans*. Washington, D.C.: Smithsonian Books, 1986.

La Farge, Oliver. *A Pictorial History of the American Indian*. New York: Crown Publishers, 1956.

Lemert, Edwin M. "The Use of Alcohol in Three Salish Indian Tribes." *Quarterly Journal of Studies on Alcohol* 19 (1958): 90–107.

Léon-Portilla, Miguel, and Grace Lobanov. *Pre-Columbian Literatures of Mexico*. Norman: University of Oklahoma Press, 1969.

Liberty, Margot, ed. *American Indian Intellectuals: 1976 Proceedings of The American Ethnological Society*. St. Paul, Minn.: West Publishing, 1978.

Lister, Robert H., and Florence C. Lister. *Chaco Canyon: Archaeology and Archaeologists*. Albuquerque: University of New Mexico Press, 1981.

Lorant, Stefan. *The New World: First Pictures of America*. New York: Duell, Sloan and Pearce, 1965.

Lyman, Stanley David. *Wounded Knee 1973*. Lincoln: University of Nebraska Press, 1991.

Lyons, Oren, John Mohawk, Vine Deloria, Jr., Laurence Hauptman, Howard Berman, Donald Grinde, Jr., Curtis Berkey, and Robert Venables. *Exiled in the Land of the Free: Democracy, Indian Nations, and the U.S. Constitution*. Santa Fe, N.Mex.: Clear Light, 1992.

McDonnell, Janet A. *The Dispossession of the American Indian, 1887–1934*. Bloomington: Indiana University Press, 1991.

McLoughlin, William G. *Cherokee Renascence in the New Republic*. Princeton: Princeton University Press, 1986.

McNickle, D'Arcy. *Wind from an Enemy*. Albuquerque: University of New Mexico Press, 1988.

Mardock, Robert Winston. *The Reformers and the American Indian*. Columbia: University of Missouri Press, 1971.

Matthiessen, Peter. *In the Spirit of Crazy Horse*. New York: Viking Press, 1983.

Maxwell, James A., ed. *America's Fascinating Indian Heritage*. Pleasantville, N.Y.: The Reader's Digest Association, 1978.

Merrell, James. *The Indians' New World: Catawbas and Their Neighbors from European Contact Through the Era of Removal*. Chapel Hill: University of North Carolina Press, 1989.

Milanich, Jerald T., and Charles Hudson. *Hernando de Soto and the Indians of Florida*. Gainesville: University of Florida Press, 1993.

Milanich, Jerald T., and Susan Milbrath. *First Encounters: Spanish Explorations in the Caribbean and the United States, 1492–1570*. Gainesville: Florida Museum of Natural History, 1989.

Miller, Jay, and Carol Eastman, eds. *Shamanic Odyssey: The Lushootseed Salish Journey to the Land of the Dead*. Menlo Park, Calif.: Ballena Press, 1988.

——. *The Tsimshian and Their Neighbors of the North Pacific Coast*. Seattle: University of Washington Press, 1984.

Momaday, N. Scott. *House Made of Dawn*. New York: Harper and Row, 1969.

Mooney, James. "The Ghost-Dance Religion and the Sioux Outbreak of 1890." *Fourteenth Annual Report of the United States Bureau of Ethnology, 1892–93*. Washington, D.C.: U.S. Government Printing Office, 1896.

Nabakov, Peter, ed. *Native American Testimony: A Chronicle of Indian–White Relations from Prophecy to the Present, 1492–1992*. New York: Viking-Penguin, 1991.

——. *Two Leggings: The Making of a Crow Warrior*. New York: Thomas Y. Crowell, 1967.

National Geographic Society. *The World of the American Indian*. Washington, D.C.: National Geographic Society, 1974.

Neihardt, John G., ed. *Black Elk Speaks*. Lincoln: University of Nebraska Press, 1932.

O'Brien, Jean Maria. "Community Dynamics in the Indian-English Town of Natick, Massachusetts, 1650–1790." Ph.D. dissertation. Chicago: University of Chicago, 1990.

O'Connell, Barry. *On Our Own Ground: The Complete Writings of William Apess, a Pequot*. Amherst: University of Massachusetts Press, 1992.

Peckham, Howard, and Charles Gibson, eds. *Attitudes of Colonial Powers Toward the American Indian*. Salt Lake City: University of Utah Press, 1969.

Powell, Father Peter John., ed. *Issiwun: Sacred Buffalo Hat of the Northern Cheyenne*. Billings: Montana Indian Publications & the Cheyenne Educational Committee, ca. 1960.

——. *Sweet Medicine*. Norman: University of Oklahoma Press, 1969.

Proud, Robert. *The History of Pennsylvania in North America (1798)*. Vol. 2. Spartanburg, S.C.: The Reprint Company, 1967.

Prucha, Francis Paul. *Atlas of American Indian Affairs*. Lincoln: University of Nebraska Press, 1990.

Rainer, Howard. *Proud Moments: Generation to Generation*. Wilsonville, Oreg.: Beautiful America Publishing, 1988.

Ridge, Martin. *Rand McNally Atlas of American Frontiers*. Chicago: Rand McNally, 1993.

Rollings, Willard. *The Osage: An Ethnohistorical Study of Hegemony on the Prairie-Plains*. Columbia: University of Missouri Press, 1992.

Ronda, James. *Lewis and Clark Among the Indians*. Lincoln: University of Nebraska Press, 1984.

Rosen, Kenneth, ed. *The Man to Send Rain Clouds*. New York: Viking, 1974.

Rosenstiel, Annette. *Red and White: Indian Views of the White Man, 1492–1962*. New York: Universe Books, 1983.

Rossi, Paul A., and David C. Hunt. *The Art of the Old West: From the Collection of the Gilcrease Institute*. New York: Promontory Press, 1985.

Sabloff, Jeremy A. *The Cities of Ancient Mexico: Reconstructing a Lost World*. London: Thames and Hudson, 1989.

Sagard, Gabriel. *The Long Journey to the Country of the Hurons*. Toronto: Champlain Society, 1935.

Seaver, James E. *A Narrative of the Life of Mrs. Mary Jemison*. Edited by June Namais. Norman: University of Oklahoma Press, 1992.

Silko, Leslie Marmon. *Ceremony*. New York: Viking-Penguin, 1977.

Simmons, William S. *Spirit of the New England Tribes: Indian History and Folklore, 1620–1984*. Hanover, N.H.: University Press of New England, 1986.

Smith, Bruce D., ed. *The Mississippian Emergence*. Washington, D.C.: Smithsonian Institution Press, 1990.

——. *Rivers of Change: Essays on Early Agriculture*. Washington D.C.: Smithsonian Institution Press, 1992.

Smith, Jane F., and Robert M. Kvasnicka. *Indian–White Relations: A Persistent Paradox*. Washington, D.C.: Howard University Press, 1981.

Speck, Frank. *The Naskapi*. Norman: University of Oklahoma Press, 1935.

Spicer, Edward H. *Cycles of Conquest: The Impact of Spain, Mexico, and the United States on the Indians of the Southwest, 1533–1960*. Tucson: University of Arizona Press, 1974.

Stock, Eugene. *Metlakhtla and the North Pacific Mission of the Church Missionary Society*. London: Church Missionary House, 1880.

Sturtevant, William C., gen. ed. *Handbook of North American Indians, Volume IV: History of Indian–White Relations*. Vol. edited by Wilcomb E. Washburn. Washington, D.C.: Smithsonian Institution Press, 1988.

Thomas, David Hurst. *Archaeology*. 2d ed. Fort Worth, Tex.: Holt, Rinehart and Winston, 1989.

Thompson, David. *Narrative: 1784–1812*. Toronto: Champlain Society, 1962.

Thornton, Russell. *American Indian Holocaust and Survival: A Population History Since 1492*. Norman: University of Oklahoma Press, 1987.

Trigger, Bruce G. *Natives and New Comers: Canada's "Heroic Age" Reconsidered*. Montreal: McGill-Queen's University Press, 1986.

Usner, Daniel H. *Indians, Settlers, and Slaves in a Frontier Exchange Economy: The Lower Mississippi Valley Before 1783*. Chapel Hill: University of North Carolina Press, 1992.

Utley, Robert M., and Wilcomb E. Washburn. *History of the Indian Wars*. Edited by Ann Moffat and Richard F. Snow. New York: American Heritage Books, 1977.

Vega, Gacilaso de la. *The Florida of the Inca*. Translated by John Varner and Jeannette Varner. Austin: University of Texas Press, 1980.

Viola, Herman J. *After Columbus: The Smithsonian Chronicle of the North American Indians*. Washington, D.C.: Smithsonian Books, 1990.

Viola, Herman J., and Carolyn Margolis, eds. *Seeds of Change: A Quincentennial Commemoration*. Washington, D.C.: Smithsonian Institution Press, 1991.

Vizenor, Gerald. *Crossbloods: Bone Courts, Bingo, and Other Reports*. Minneapolis: University of Minnesota Press, 1990.

Wade, Edwin L. *The Arts of the North American Indian: Native Traditions in Evolution*. New York: Hudson Hills Press in association with The Philbrook Art Center, Tulsa, 1986.

Waldman, Carl. *Atlas of the North American Indian*. New York: Facts on File Publications, 1985.

Wallace, Anthony. *The Death and Rebirth of the Seneca*. New York: Alfred A. Knopf, 1970.

Weber, David J. *The Spanish Frontier in North America*. New Haven: Yale University Press, 1992.

White, Richard. *The Middle Ground: Indians, Empires and Republics in the Great Lakes Region, 1659–1815*. New York: Cambridge University Press, 1991.

White, Robert H. *Tribal Assets: The Rebirth of Native America*. New York: Henry Holt, 1990.

Woodhead, Henry, ed. *The Buffalo Hunters: The American Indians*. Alexandria, Va.: Time-Life Books, 1993.

——. *The European Challenge: The American Indians*. Alexandria, Va.: Time-Life Books, 1992.

——. *The First Americans: The American Indians*. Alexandria, Va.: Time-Life Books, 1992.

Wright, J. Leitch. *Creeks and Seminoles: Destruction and Regeneration of the Muscogulge People*. Lincoln: University of Nebraska Press, 1986.

Yenne, Bill. *The Encyclopedia of North American Indian Tribes: A Comprehensive Study of Tribes from the Abitibi to the Zuñi*. New York: Crescent Books, 1986.

# INDEX

Page numbers in italic refer to captions and illustrations.

# PICTURE CREDITS

ABBREVIATIONS

**AMNH**: courtesy the Department of Library Services, American Museum of Natural History, New York; **BA**: The Bettman Archive; **GIL**: from the collection of the Thomas Gilcrease Institute of American History and Art, Tulsa, Oklahoma; **GSU**: courtesy Georgia State University Foundation, Archives Preservation Fund; **GW**: courtesy The Greenwich Workshop, Inc.,Trumbull, Connecticut; **HP/SM**: Historical Pictures/Stock Montage; **LOC**: Library of Congress; **NEW**: The Newberry Library, Chicago, Illinois; **NMAI**: courtesy The National Museum of the American Indian, Smithsonian Institution; **NYPL**: Rare Books and Manuscripts Division, The New York Public Library, Astor, Lenox, and Tilden Foundations; **SI**: Smithsonian Institution; **PHIL**: courtesy The Philbrook Museum of Art, Tulsa, Oklahoma.

**Jacket Front**: Portrait of man, NMAI Photo No. 34383; Badlands, North Dakota, photo by Willard Clay. **Jacket Back**: Portrait of Louise Laruse, AMNH neg. #317187, photo by Rodman Wanamaker. **1**: Jeffrey Chapman. **2-3**: Dan V. Lomahaftewa. **4-5**: PHIL. **6-7**: Mike Larsen. **8**: (clockwise from top left, middle image last) NEW; LOC (LC-USZ62-33680); NMAI Photo No. 31777; NMAI Photo No. 31714; NMAI Photo No. 13741; NMAI Photo No. 21584; NMAI Photo No. 46736-c; photo by John H. Fouch, courtesy Dr. James Brust; LOC (LC-USZ62-101151); NMAI Photo No. 31760; NMAI Photo No. 2662; NMAI Photo No. 38009; NMAI Photo No. 34383. **9**: (clockwise from top left, middle image last) AMNH neg. #31716; NMAI Photo No. 34327; NMAI Photo No. 56039; NMAI Photo No. 36332; NMAI Photo No. 2742; photo by Richard D'Amore; SI Photo No. 1746-A-6; NMAI Photo No. 2609; 1937 Oklahoma Publishing Co. from the January 15, 1937, edition of *The Daily Oklahoman*; LOC (LC-USZ62-86438); NMAI Photo No. 36419; photo by John H. Fouch, courtesy Dr. James Brust; AMNH neg. #317187. **10-11**: NMAI Photo No. 41393. **12**: LOC (LC-USZ62-101262). **14-15**: PHIL. **16**: PHIL. **17**: PHIL. **18**: Arthur Amiotte. **19**: PHIL. **20**: courtesy Bentley•Tomlinson Gallery. **21**: PHIL. **22-23**: AMNH neg. #31640. **24-25**: photo by David Muench. **25**: Dan V. Lomahaftewa. **27**: illustration by Greg Harlin/Wood Ronsaville Harlin, Inc. **29**: (top) AMNH trans. #2168; (bottom) GW. **31**: Valjean McCarty Hessing. **33**: illustration by Narda Lebo. **35**: AMNH trans. #2168. **36**: photo by Rosamond Purcell. **36-37**: Arnold Jacobs/photo by D.H.S Photography. **38**: (top and bottom) illustrations by Narda Lebo. **39**: (left, top right, and bottom right) illustrations by Carol Inouye. **41**: illustration by Greg Harlin/Wood Ronsaville Harlin, Inc. **42**: photo by Rosamond Purcell. **43**: illustration by Lloyd Townsend/Wood Ronsaville Harlin, Inc. **45**: LOC (LC-USZ62-47017). **47**: photo by Rosamond Purcell. **48-49**: courtesy G. Dagli-Orti, Paris. **49**: photo by Jeffrey Jay Foxx. **51**: (left) AMNH trans. #1389; (right) AMNH trans. #1262. **52-53**: courtesy G. Dagli-Orti, Paris. **55**: AMNH trans. #1655. **56**: AMNH trans. #1903. **58-59**: NYPL. **59**: Fernando Padilla, Jr. **60**: (left and right) illustrations by Carol Inouye. **61**: PHIL. **62**: illustration by Carol Inouye. **64**: illustration by Narda Lebo. **65**: photo by Rosamond Purcell. **66-67**: photo by Sheldon Preston. **68**: photo by Monty Roessel. **70**: (top) NMAI Photo No. 7/1615; (bottom) photo by Jeffrey Jay Foxx. **71**: (top and bottom) photos by Jeffrey Jay Foxx. **72-73**: photo by David Muench. **75**: illustration by Richard Schlecht. **76**: AMNH neg. #411889. **77**: AMNH neg. #411967. **78**: illustration by Merlin Little Thunder. **79**: Detroit Institute of Arts, Dirk Bakker, photographer, National Parks Service, Chillicothe, Ohio. **80** (left and right) and **81**: illustrations by Carol Inouye. **84**: photo by Rosamond Purcell. **85**: courtesy Ohio State Historical Society. **86**: Georg Gerster/Comstock. **86-87**: illustration by Greg Harlin/Wood Ronsaville Harlin, Inc. **89**: illustration by Mike Larsen. **90**: Lauros-Giraudon. **91**: Greg Beecham. **92-93**: GW. **94**: courtesy Stansbury Ronsaville Wood Inc. **95**: SI Photo No. 77-2861. **96-97**: Colleen Cutschall. **97**: NMAI Photo No. 2190. **99**: Valjean McCarty Hessing. **100**: NMAI Photo No. 2925. **103**: NMAI Photo No. 1502. **104**: courtesy Museum of New Mexico, Santa Fe, cat. #51400/13, photo by Blair Clark. **106**: PHIL. **108-109**: Valjean McCarty Hessing. **110-11**: courtesy Lauros-Giraudon. **112-13**: illustration by Lloyd Townsend. **113**: photo by Rosamond Purcell. **115**: GW. **117**: Arnold Jacobs/photo by D.H.S. Photography. **118**: AMNH neg. #33549. **119**: photo by Rosamond Purcell. **122**: GW. **123**: K. Henderson. **124-25**: NYPL. **125**: LOC (LC-USZ268-45093). **126-27**: Architect of the Capitol. **128**: NEW. **129**: NYPL. **131**: NEW. **133**: HP/SM, Inc. **135**: illustration by Greg Harlin/Wood Ronsaville Harlin, Inc. **136**: PHIL. **137**: The Biblioteca Medicea Laurenziana, Florence, Italy. **138**: GIL. **139**: Roger Perkins. **140-41**: NMAI Photo No. 22/8612. **141**: NMAI Photo No. 38065. **142**: courtesy the collection of Millicent Rogers

Museum. **143**: NYPL. **144-45**: courtesy Santa Barbara Mission Archive Library. **146**: (top) PHIL; (bottom) painting by Cliff Bahnimptewa (Hopi), courtesy collection of The Heard Museum, Phoenix, Arizona. **147** and **148**: (top, center, and bottom) paintings by Cliff Bahnimptewa, courtesy collection of The Heard Museum, Phoenix, Arizona. **149**: courtesy Museum of New Mexico, Santa Fe, cat. #53564/13, photo by Blair Clark. **151**: courtesy Elisabeth Waldo Dentzel Collection, Multicultural Arts Studio, Northridge, California. **152-53**: NMAI Photo No. 23/3791. **153**: photo by Rosamond Purcell. **154-55**: illustration by Greg Harlin/Wood Ronsaville Harlin, Inc. **157** and **160**: illustrations by Narda Lebo. **162**: courtesy National Museum of American Art, Washington D.C./Art Resource, NY #1909.7.9. **163**: SI Photo No. 56827. **164**: (top and bottom) photos by Rosamond Purcell. **167**: neg. #C-5750 National Archives of Canada, Ottawa, Ontario. **168-69**: illustration by Lloyd Townsend. **170** and **171**: HP/SM, Inc. **172-73**: acc. #M1905, McCord Museum of Canadian History. **175**: Liftuguj Micmac First Nation. **176**: courtesy the Mission St. Francis Xavier, Kahnawake, Canada. **179**: photo by Rosamond Purcell. **180**: Architect of the Capitol. **180-81**: LOC (LC-USZ62-17880). **183**: (top) GSU; (bottom) LOC (LC-USZ62-5242). **184-85**: Architect of the Capitol. **187**: HP/SM, Inc. **188**: LOC (LC-USZ62-55237)). **189**: (top and bottom) HP/SM, Inc. **190**: LOC (LC-USZ62-14141). **192** and **193**: HP/SM, Inc. **194-95**: Courtesy of Abell-Hanger Foundation and of the Permian Basin Petroleum Museum, Midland, Texas. **195**: photo by Rosamond Purcell. **196**: (top) from the collection of Debra Jameson; (bottom) photo by Richard Erdoes. **197**: #25/1183 NMAI Photo No. 25/1183. **199**: AMNH neg. #3345548. **200-201**: illustration by Richard Schlecht. **202**: photo by Steve Wilson/Entheos. **203** and **205**: photos by Rosamond Purcell. **206**: LOC (LC-USZ62-101243). **207**: photo by Rosamond Purcell. **208**: PHIL. **210-11**: LOC (LC-USZ62-48427). **212**: PHIL. **213**: Valjean McCarty Hessing. **215** and **216**: The Joslyn Art Museum. **217**: LOC. **218-19**: illustration by Mike Larsen. **220**: PHIL. **221**: NMAI Photo No. 21543. **222**: New-York Historical Society neg. #69873. **223**: (left and right) PHIL. **224**: LOC. **224-25**: GIL. **226-27**: photo by Rosamond Purcell. **228**: illustration by Fernando Padilla, Jr. **230**: GIL. **232**: photo by Rosamond Purcell. **233**: GIL. **234**: (left and right) GSU. **235**: (left and right) GSU. **236**: Field Museum of Natural History, neg. #A106310c, Chicago. **237**: LOC (LC-USZ62-101170-306482). **239**: GIL. **241**: illustration by Fernando Padilla, Jr. **242-43**: LOC. **243**: (top to bottom) illustrations by Greg Harlin/Wood Ronsaville Harlin, Inc. **244**: LOC (LC-USZ62-53602). **245**: GIL. **246**: LOC (LC-USZ62-37832). **247**: The Joslyn Art Museum, Omaha, Nebraska. **248** and **249**: illustrations by Narda Lebo. **250**: from the collection of Nina L. Smith. **251**: LOC (LC-USZ62-69900). **252**: LOC (LC-USZ62-86450). **254**: (top and bottom) GSU. **255**: (top and bottom) GSU. **257**: courtesy Amon Carter Museum, #1961.195, Fort Worth, Texas. **258**: LOC. **259**: The West Point Museum, United States Military Academy, West Point, New York. **260**: (top) Florida State Archives, Tallahassee, Florida; (bottom) LOC. **262-63**: GIL. **263**: PHIL. **266**: GIL. **268**: (top) neg. #C92418; National Archives of Canada; (bottom) neg. #C92414; National Archives of Canada. **270**: (top) LOC (LCUSZ62-3933); (bottom) GSU. **272**: GW. **273**: PHIL. **275**: The New York State Museum, The University of the State of New York, Albany, New York. **278-79**, **280-81**, and **282-83**: GW. **283**: photo by Rosamond Purcell. **285**: LOC (LC-USZ62-42285). **286**: illustration by Greg Harlin. **288** and **290**: GSU. **291**: (top) LOC (LC-USZ62-310572); (bottom) GSU. **292**: BA. **293**: Troy Anderson. **294-95**: courtesy Wollaroc Museum, Bartlesville, Oklahoma. **297**: courtesy Cherokee National Historical Society. **300-301**: Western History Collections, University of Oklahoma Library. **302-303**: illustration by Lloyd Townsend. **303**: LOC (LC-USZ62-55600). **304-305**: courtesy Scotts Bluff National Monument–National

Park Service, Gering, Nebraska. **306-307**: GW. **309**: NMAI Photo No. 20234. **310**: Colorado Historical Society. **311 and 312**: courtesy Scotts Bluff National Monument–National Park Service, Gering, Nebraska. **313**: GIL. **315**: (top) LOC; (center and bottom) Washington State Historical Society, Tacoma, Washington. **317**: (top) Florida State Archives, Tallahassee, Florida; (bottom) PHIL. **318**: (top) The National Archives, neg. #127-G-10H-306073A; (bottom) Florida State Archives, Tallahassee, Florida. **319**: LOC (LC-USZ62-7747). **320**: Wadsworth Atheneum, Hartford, Connecticut. **321**: LOC (LC-USZ62-48287). **322**: photo by Rosamond Purcell. **322-23**: GIL. **324**: NMAI Photo No. 17163. **325**: Oklahoma Historical Society, Archives and Manuscripts Division, Photo No. 12398. **326**: GIL. **327**: (top) GSU; (bottom) courtesy Colorado Historical Society, Denver, Colorado. **329 and 330**: PHIL. **331**: LOC (LC-USZ62-86461). **333**: courtesy Colorado Historical Society, Denver, Colorado. **334-35**: GIL. **335**: LOC (LC-USZ62-56003). **336**: (top) BA; (bottom) NEW (Ayer 290 J 43 1950). **337**: illustration by Narda Lebo. **338**: PHIL. **339**: (left) NMAI Photo No. 34777; (right) NMAI Photo No. 34776. **341**: LOC (LC-USZ62-104561). **342**: SI Photo No. 15339. **343**: (top) NMAI Photo No. 20414. (bottom) photo by Rosamond Purcell. **344**: (top) SI Photo No. 43132; (bottom) NMAI Photo No. 6979. **345**: LOC (LC-USZ62-19837). **346-47**: (left) courtesy Southwest Museum, Los Angeles, California. **347** (right) and **348**: photos by John H. Fouch, courtesy Dr. James Brust. **350-51**: GW. **353**: photo by John H. Fouch, courtesy Dr. James Brust. **354 and 355** (left and right): Cumberland County Historical Society, Carlisle, Pennsylvania. **356**: LOC (LC-USZ62-100543). **357**: Nevada Historical Society. **358 and 359**: PHIL. **360**: Arthur Amiotte. **361**: PHIL. **362**: LOC (LC-USZ62-75779). **363**: AMNH neg. #335475. **364**: The Anschutz Collection, Denver Colorado. **365**: NMAI Photo No. 39356. **366**: SI. **367**: (top) SI Photo No. 47685-B; (bottom) LOC (LC-USZ62-312806). **368**: LOC (LC-USZ62-801). **370-71**: The West Point Museum, United States Military Academy, West Point, New York. **371**: Gina Gray. **373**: NYPL. **375**: (left) Phoebe Hearst Museum of Anthropology, University of California, Berkeley, (right) SI Photo No. 2852-A. **376-77**: PHIL. **377**: Fernando Padilla, Jr. **378**: LOC (LC-USZ62-101166). **379**: NEW (AP 3922). **380 and 381**: Roger Perkins. **383**: Gina Gray. **384-85**: photo by Alan Berner. **386**: courtesy American Indian Contemporary Arts, San Francisco, California. **387**: Kevin Warren Smith. **388**: Peter S. Mecca/Black Star. **389**: courtesy Woodland Cultural Center, Brantford, Ontario. **390**: GIL. **391**: Sid

Richardson Collection of Western Art, Fort Worth, Texas. **392**: (left) LOC; (right) courtesy Bentley•Tomlinson Gallery. **393**: (left) LOC; (right) courtesy Bentley•Tomlinson Gallery. **394 and 395**: PHIL. **396**: courtesy Mr. and Mrs. Gerald Peters, Santa Fe, New Mexico. **397**: The Beinecke Rare Book and Manuscript Library, Yale University, New Haven, Connecticut. **398**: LOC. **399**: (top left) LOC (LC-USZ62-55136); (bottom left) courtesy Mt. Holyoke College; (right) Cherokee North Carolina Travel. **400**: (top) photo by Peter Grimes; (bottom) photo by Monty Roessel. **401**: photo by Jeffrey Jay Foxx. **403**: (top) courtesy Marc Wanamaker/Bison Archives; (bottom left and bottom center) courtesy Turner Entertainment Co.; (bottom right) courtesy the Academy of Motion Picture Arts and Sciences. **404**: PHIL. **405**: (top left) Cumberland County Historical Society, Carlisle, Pennsylvania; (top right) BA; (bottom) photo by Eric Hasse/Contact Press. **406-407**: The Franklin D. Roosevelt Library/BA, Hyde Park, New York. **407**: Roger Perkins. **408**: Arthur Amiotte. **409**: courtesy Steinbaum Krauss Gallery. **410-11**: PHIL. **412**: Associated Press/Wide World. **416**: National Archives. **417**: PHIL. **418**: (top) photo by Monty Roessel; (bottom) photo by Steve Wilson/Entheos. **419**: PHIL. **420-21**: Jesse Cooday. **421**: John Balloue. **422**: LOC (LC-USZ62-306484). **423**: photo by Kenji Kawano. **424**: (left and right) BA. **425**: (top) photo by Sheldon Preston; (bottom) photo by Kenji Kawano. **426**: National Archives. **429**: Associated Press/Wide World. **430**: photo by Don Doll, S.J. **431**: Mike Larsen/photo by Artography. **432**: (top) photo by Steve Wilson/Entheos; (bottom) photo by John Running. **435**: Associated Press/Wide World. **436**: photo by Michael Reagan. **437**: (left and right) photos by Monty Roessel. **439**: BA. **440**: Magnum Photos. **441**: BA. **442**: (top) photo by Don Doll, S.J.; (bottom) courtesy Dan Littlefield/American Native Press Archives, Little Rock, Arkansas. **443**: photo by Howard Rainier. **445**: photo by Don Doll, S.J. **446 and 447**: PHIL. **448-49**: photo by Don Doll, S.J. **450**: The Brooklyn Museum, acc. #30821, Estate of Stewart Culin, Museum Purchase. **451**: (top) photo by Rosamond Purcell; (bottom) PHIL. **452**: PHIL. **454**: (top left and bottom left) photos by Kenny Blackbird; (right) photo by John Running. **455**: photo by Kenny Blackbird. **456**: photo by Jeffrey Jay Foxx. **457**: photo by Kenny Blackbird. **458-59**: Mike Larsen. **459**: Jesse Cooday. **460**: photo by Eric Hasse/Contact Press. **463**: Arthur Amiotte. **464-65**: courtesy Steinbaum Krauss Gallery. **480**: Roger Perkins.

# ACKNOWLEDGMENTS

Turner Publishing and the editorial directors thank the many experts in their respective fields, and the many more interested friends, Indian and non-Indian, who have helped materially, or by sage advice, in the creation of this illustrated history. In particular, the following institutions and individuals are acknowledged for their generous support: Woolsey Ackerman • American Museum of Natural History: Barbara Mathe, Carmen Collazo • Amon Carter Museum: Julie Causey • The Anschutz Collection: Elizabeth Cunningham • The Architect of the Capitol: Dana Strickland • Diana Beach • The Beinecke Rare Book and Manuscript Library: Al Mueller, Patricia Middleton • Kenny Blackbird • The Brooklyn Museum • Dr. James Brust • Buffalo Bill Historical Center: Elizabeth Holmes • Cherokee National Historical Society: Tom Mooney • Colorado Historical Society: Margaret Walsh • Nicole Cordani • Cumberland County Historical Society: Richard Tritt, Barb Landis • The Detroit Institute of Arts: Marianne Letasi • Feathers Gallery, Oklahoma: Karen Miller • Antonella Ferruzzi • Field Museum of Natural History: Nina Cummings • Thomas Fields • Florida State Archives: Joan Morris • Jeffrey Jay Foxx • G. Dagli Orti, Paris: Patricia Samuel • Georgia State University Special Collections: Laurel Bowen, Annie Tilden • Gilcrease Museum: Sandra Hildebrand, Ann Moran • Giraudon Agency, Paris: Anne Hubrecht • Graphics International: David Allen, Nancy Williams, J. C. Poole • Gina Gray • The Greenwich Workshop: Scott Usher, Maureen Intelisano • Barbara Griffin • The Heard Museum: Mary Brennan, Mario Klimiades, Jim Reynolds • Valjean McCarty Hessing • Hopewell Culture National Historic Park: Bill Gibson • Huntington Art Gallery at the University of Texas: Meredith Sutton • Huntington Free Library: Mary B. Davis • IAIA (Institute of American Indian Art): Lynn Hutton • Richard Inglis • Tim Johnson • The Joslyn Art Museum: Larry Mensching • Diane Joy • Jean Snodgrass King • Mary Lapegna • The Library of Congress: Jennifer Brathrove, Evelyn Overmiller, Mary Ison • Oren Lyons • The Multi-Cultural Music and Art Foundation of Northridge: Elizabeth Waldo • Museum of New Mexico: Willow Powers, Louise Stiver • National Museum of the American Indian: Susannah Kellems, John Colonghi, Sharon Dean, Laura Nash, Janine Jones, Maryjane Lenz, Duane King, Mark Clark • The Newberry Library: Rebecca Wiesz • The New-York Historical Society: Jim Francis • The New York Public Library: Ted Teodoro, Rocko Lombardo, Miriam Mandelbaum, Julia Van Haaften • NIIPA (Native Indian/Inuit Photographers Association) • Nancy Fields O'Conner • Ohio Historical Society: Stan Byers • Ohio State Museum: Vernon Will • Roger Perkins • The Philbrook Museum of Art: Chris Kallenberger, Tom Young, Dr. Lydia Wycoff • Rosamond Purcell • Barbara Pyle • Restigouche Band Council: Romy Labillois • Monty Roessel • Margaret Rogers • Scotts Bluff National Monument: Dean Knudsen, Mark Hartig • Seneca-Iroquois Museum: Judy Greene • The Smithsonian Institution: Rick Hill, Rick West, Gaye Brown • The Smithsonian Institution, The National Anthropological Archives: James Harwood • The Smithsonian Institution, Office of Printing and Photographic Services: David Burgevin • Southwest Museum: Ligia Perez • St. Francis Xavier Mission: Francoise Bruyer • J. Stoll • Michael Tomlinson • Bob Venables • Helen Victor • The West Point Museum: David Meschutt.

*Red Jacket* by Roger Perkins (Mohawk), 1992.